Making the Foreign Serve China

1999.
222
238.

Asia/Pacific/Perspectives
Series Editor: Mark Selden

Making the Foreign Serve China

Managing Foreigners in the People's Republic

ANNE-MARIE BRADY

ROWMAN & LITTLEFIELD PUBLISHERS, INC.
Lanham • Boulder • New York • Toronto • Oxford

ROWMAN & LITTLEFIELD PUBLISHERS, INC.

Published in the United States of America
by Rowman & Littlefield Publishers, Inc.
A Member of the Rowman & Littlefield Publishing Group
4501 Forbes Boulevard, Suite 200, Lanham, Maryland 20706
www.rowmanlittlefield.com

P.O. Box 317, Oxford OX2 9RU, United Kingdom

British Library Cataloguing in Publication Information Available

Library of Congress Cataloging-in-Publication Data

Brady, Anne-Marie.
  Making the foreign serve China : managing foreigners in the People's Republic / Anne-Marie Brady.
    p. cm. — (Asia/Pacific/Perspectives)
  Includes bibliographical references and index.
  ISBN 0-7425-1861-2 (alk. paper) — ISBN 0-7425-1862-0 (pbk. : alk. paper)
    1. China--Foreign relations--20th century. I. Title: Managing foreigners in the People's Republic. II. Title. III. Series.

DS775.8.B73 2003
327.51—dc22

2003015562

Printed in the United States of America

♾™ The paper used in this publication meets the minimum requirements of American National Standard for Information Sciences—Permanence of Paper for Printed Library Materials, ANSI/NISO Z39.48-1992.

Be certain to develop extremely close relations with your enemy,
as if you were brothers.

—Guanzi[1]

Contents

Abbreviations

CWIHP	Cold War International History Project
DDXC	Dang de xuanchuan gongzuo wenjian xuanbian
DWBDCK	Duiwai baodao cankao
DWXCCK	Duiwai xuanchuan cankao
HFSP, BYU	Helen Foster Snow Papers, Brigham Young University
MFAT	New Zealand Ministry of Foreign Affairs and Trade Archives
MRP	Maud Russell Papers
NYPL	New York Public Library
SCMP	*South China Morning Post*
UA-UMKC	University Archives, University of Missouri, Kansas City
ZMZ	Zhu Muzhi lun duiwai xuanchuan
ZYWJ	Zhonggong zhongyang wenjian xuanji

Cover of a 1993 *waishi* handbook.

Preface

Chinese former diplomat turned journalist Lu Ning once likened Western analysis of the People's Republic of China's (PRC) foreign affairs to the story of five blind men trying to understand an elephant by each only feeling a different part of it, *mangren mo xiang*.[2] His point was that foreign researchers usually only get one piece of the truth, never the whole answer. The reason for this, is not, as Lu implies, that foreigners are incapable of understanding China's foreign affairs system, *waishi xitong*, rather it is that the Chinese government deliberately withholds information about what has always been, and remains, a highly sensitive subject. In restricted circulation documents, Chinese officials acknowledge that the foreign affairs system is one of the most "crucial" and "secret" aspects of the Chinese government.[3]

This book covers an understanding of foreign affairs which has a much wider meaning here than the usual English definition, concerning state-to-state contact. For this reason, I have chosen to adopt the Chinese term for foreign affairs, *waishi*. *Waishi* is an abbreviation of the full term *waijiao shiwu* (diplomatic matters), which has become a term in its own right. *Waishi* describes the full spectrum of the PRC's external policies, *duiwai zhengce*, to influence and at times control foreigners, as well as Chinese citizens' contact and perception of them and of foreign culture and technology within and outside China. It also includes China's external relations *duiwai guanxi*, meaning both official state-to-state and so-called unofficial or "people-to-people" diplomacy. In effect, *waishi* activities encompass all matters related to foreigners and foreign things in China and abroad, not merely diplomacy.[4] Although the diplomacy of the PRC is a well-researched topic and a number of studies have looked at Chinese perceptions of various nations, China's policy on foreigners and the range of *waishi* activities within China and beyond, *waishi gongzuo*, have not previously been considered in any detail. Though scores of autobiographies and biographies have been written by those the Chinese Communist Party (CCP) calls foreign friends, these accounts have tended to be somewhat uncritical.[5] Writers David Caute, Paul Hollander, and Herbert Passin have discussed the cultural diplomacy of China and other socialist countries.[6] Others such as Jacques Marcuse, Pierre Ryckmans, and Ross Terrill have touched on their personal experiences of it in their writing.[7] Beverley Hooper's *China Stands Up* described the experiences of foreigners in China in the years from 1948-1950.[8] However, none of these studies have considered the policy documents that underlay the phenomena they described. Nor has any study considered what *waishi* means *per se*, an overriding approach to the "foreign," which links state-to-state diplomacy with the management of the foreign presence in China. This study attempts to detail the untold history of the CCP's system of "making foreign things serve China." Since the state-to-state relations of China are such a familiar topic, I have chosen to focus on certain key aspects of *waishi*, which though less researched, may be quite familiar to those who have had contact with the CCP's China–the management of the foreign presence. As I have discovered in my research, this is the most fundamental element in the Chinese Communist Party's attempt to stay in control of China's contact with the outside world, inspiring an extraordinary genre of detailed instructions on Sino-foreign interaction. The book concentrates in particular on *waishi* directed at the West, since China's relations with the Western world, especially the United States, have been particularly important in shaping the CCP's foreign affairs policies throughout the history of the party. I also touch on the role of the Soviet Union in shaping CCP foreign policies, since much of the structures and approaches of China's *waishi* system were initially copied from the Russians, and the Sino-Soviet split in the 1960s had a massive impact on Chinese foreign policy in the 1960s and up until the 1980s.

The book has a particular focus on China's friends, admirers, and agents of influence in the Western world. In this study, I have not covered in any detail China's *waishi* policies with regard to overseas Chinese, the Third World, or Japan. Nor have I attempted to cover in detail every single group of foreigners resident or visiting China. All of these are topics worthy of further study. (Nevertheless, as numerous *waishi* manuals attest, the basic principles and practices are the same, despite who the target group is.) My concern here is with the broader meaning of the *waishi* system in CCP ideology and its significance as a reflection of the party's foreign policy behavior from the 1920s to the present day. If this too is yet one more attempt by a blind observer to describe the elephant, my hope is that the part of the "elephant" I describe may lead the way to further research on this subject of such importance to our future understanding of China.

My fascination with China's foreign affairs system grew out of an earlier research project on one of the CCP's best-known foreign helpers, the New Zealander, Rewi Alley. In my book on Alley I wrote a revisionist account of his life and work, contrasting it with the political myth that he and others wove about his activities in China and earlier, in New Zealand. An essential element of the Alley myth was his long-standing role as a "friend of China." As I conducted my research on this project I began to be aware that the language of "friendship" and "foreign friends" came up again and again in the rhetoric that the Chinese government and many of its citizens used to address foreigners, even permeating the vocabulary of foreigners and foreign governments dealing with China. I was sure that there was a policy behind this rhetoric, and my obsession to find it first took the form of my doctoral research at the Australian National University, and finally has led to this book. This book combines the work I did on my doctoral thesis with research that has been published in *China Information*, *China Quarterly*, *China Review International*, *Revue Bibliographique de Sinologie*, and the *New Zealand Journal of History*.

Early on in the process of conducting this research, I was asked by a senior scholar what my "archive" for the project would be. Due to the restrictions the Chinese government places on social science research, as most researchers in the politics and history of contemporary China will know, one does not usually have access to archives in the usual meaning of that term. Rather, as Gregor Benton so eloquently points out in the preface to his history of the CCP's three-year war in the former Soviet areas, *Mountain Fires*, the researcher of Chinese politics and contemporary history is frequently forced to draw on a much wider interpretation of the understanding of the word "archive" than most political historians would allow.[9] It took some time to establish the "archive" for this topic, for if such a thing as an "archive of *waishi*" exists in China; it is certainly not accessible to foreigners, or even the majority of Chinese scholars. In the period from 1949-1979, when access to China and to Chinese people and Chinese-language materials was strictly controlled, foreign writers could only speculate on the topic of China's *waishi*, based on anecdotal evidence and the contents of a few archives outside the Chinese mainland. Fortunately for my research, the period of reform and opening up in China since the late 1970s led to an enormous expansion of *waishi* activities, with a corresponding need for creating written materials to educate the expanding numbers of the Chinese workforce engaged in *waishi*-related work. Moreover, in the late 1990s, the "marketization" of the Chinese economy meant that many libraries were more accessible than before and many more Chinese people were willing to discuss this still-sensitive topic. Once I knew what to look for, and where to look, I eventually found a whole genre of writing on the topic of *waishi* and illuminating the role of "friendship" and "foreign friends" in China's foreign affairs. Virtually all of these materials are still classified, *neibu*, and some of the most interesting are not widely available, but they are not unobtainable.

The eventual "archive" for this research evolved out of a vast quantity of sources that has overlapped and informed my picture of the *waishi* system and its development throughout the history of the CCP. I gathered materials from a variety of libraries and other locations in China and the Western world, including: the Australian National University; the Alexander Turnbull Library in Wellington, New Zealand; Cambridge University; the Centre Chine in Paris; Cheng-chih University in Taipei; the Chinese People's Association for Friendship with Foreign Countries in Beijing; the Imperial War Museum in

London; the Library of Congress in Washington, D.C.; the Macmillan Brown Library at the University of Canterbury, Christchurch, New Zealand; the Ministry of Foreign Affairs and Trade, New Zealand; the University of Melbourne Library, Melbourne, Australia; the National Library of Australia; the New York Public Library; New York University Library; the National Library, Beijing, China; Beijing University; People's University Library, Beijing; the Edgar Snow Archives in the University Archives of the University of Missouri, Kansas City; and the U.S. National Archives in Maryland. Some of my most useful sources have been the result of serendipitous finds from scouring both new and secondhand bookshops in China in recent years.

I have been fortunate during my research to be able to locate a number of *waishi* handbooks (normally not meant for public circulation) that have detailed the system and its implications.[10] I have also drawn on the numerous *waishi* journals that have appeared in China since 1979. These are useful for understanding both the *waishi* system in the Deng/Jiang era, as well as its history and norms. The collections of party documents available in a number of series published in recent years have also been extremely useful to my work.[11] The massive volume of translations of hitherto unavailable materials, *The Rise to Power of the Chinese Communist Party: Documents and Analysis*, edited by Tony Saich has also been helpful, and the accompanying commentaries have helped me to put documents into their historical context.[12] As the progenitors of much basic *waishi* policy and technique, the collected writings of Mao Zedong, Zhou Enlai, and, for the contemporary period, Deng Xiaoping have been important, as was the massive output of party documents, both historical and more recent, which appeared during the Cultural Revolution years.

Another essential source has been interviews with Chinese *waishi* cadres, both those currently involved in *waishi* activities and others who were active in the 1950s, 1960s, 1970s, 1980s, the 1990s, and up until the year 2001. These interviews have provided crucial knowledge and insights that were not available in written materials, as well as assisting in interpreting published information. Equally important have been interviews I conducted with past and present friends of China and others, not so designated, who have spent time living in or visiting the People's Republic. As targets, unwitting or not, of China's *waishi* system, their experiences have been useful and informative.

As I have described elsewhere,[13] there is a well-developed literature of writing on China's foreign friends, what I have chosen to call FriendLit. These memoirs and biographies have been a further important "archive" for my work, as were the memoirs of a number of former officials involved in *waishi* work. I have also drawn on secondary sources as diverse as linguistic analysis of Chinese language and literary criticism as a resource for my analysis of the *waishi* system and its cultural, political, and social origins. Finally, my own experiences as a foreigner in China, as well as the experiences of my colleagues, have proved instructive, even, indeed particularly, when they were stressful.

Each of these sources has its own value and bias and I have tried to balance and crosscheck them as much as possible.

None of us works in a vacuum, and there are many people to whom I am extremely indebted for their help and support during my research. This project could not have been completed without the support and encouragement of my joint doctoral supervisors, Geremie R. Barmé and W. J. F. Jenner, both of whom, in their own unique ways, have constantly challenged and inspired me. I was most fortunate in being able to conduct my doctoral research in the stimulating atmosphere of Australian National University, with its community of scholars who believe so strongly in the ideals of collegiality and intellectual exchange. In this environment, I was able to draw in particular on the talents and advice of Mark Elvin, Tessa Morris-Suzuki, Jonathan Unger, and Ian Wilson. Thanks must also go to Greg Benton, Tom Grunfeld, Robyn Hamilton, Thomas Kampen, Mark Selden, Warren Sun, and Monica Wehner for their assistance and encouragement at various stages of this project. I would also like to thank Duncan Campbell, who has long been a mentor and friend. I am grateful to Australian National University, the Beijing University-Australian National University Exchange Program, the New Zealand Federation of University Women, the Republic of China's Ministry of Education, and University House at Australian National University for awarding me the scholarships and study trips that made my research possible. A one-year postdoc position at the Centre for East and Southeast Asian Studies at Lund University in Sweden enabled me to begin revisions to turn my doctoral thesis into a book. And the convivial company of my colleagues at the Department of Political Science at the University of Canterbury has made the intense pressures of combining the final months of editing the book with a busy teaching schedule less stressful than it might have been. During my research trips to the United States and United Kingdom I was kindly hosted by Leslie McDowall and family in Washington, D.C., Phallon Vaughter-Hossain and family in New York, Gail Jagoda and family in Kansas City, Neil Radford in London, and Huang Tao-tao in Cambridge. I would also like to thank my brother Konrad Aron for his constant support, both practical and metaphysical. For reasons of political safety, I choose not to name the many Chinese interviewees who have helped me to understand the *waishi* system and its implications and I give only an approximate date for the interview times, but they have my thanks. Those foreigners whose experiences in China have informed this project are listed in the bibliography and I am most grateful to them. For all mistakes, errors, and matters of opinion in this work, I alone am responsible. All translations of Chinese language material, except where indicated, are my own. I have adopted the pinyin system for romanizing Chinese characters, except where the original source used was in a foreign language; in this case I have followed the romanization of the original material, that is, Pékin, Peking. This book is dedicated with love to my dear husband, Z. J., with thanks for his constant faith and support, and to my little daughter Francesca, who has brought such joy into our lives.

Notes

1.   *Guanzi: Political, Economic, and Philosophical Essays from Early China*, translated by W. Allyn Rickett, vol. 2 (Princeton, New Jersey: Princeton University Press, 1998), 225.

2.   See Lu Ning, *The Dynamics of Foreign-Policy Decisionmaking in China* (Boulder, Colorado: Westview Press, 1997), 177.

3.   See Zhan Yincai, *Shewai mishuxue* (Hangzhou: Hangzhou daxue chubanshe, 1993), 316.

4.   Zhao Pitao, *Waishi gaishuo* (Shanghai: Shanghai shehui kexue chubanshe, 1995), 2.

5.   Stuart and Roma Gelder's, *Memories for a Chinese Granddaughter* (London: Hutchinson, 1967) is a rare early exception to this rule. Jan Wong's *Red China Blues: My Long March from Mao to Now* (Sydney: Anchor, 1997) is another rare example of a former "friend of China" who publicly changed her mind about the PRC and its policies.

6.   David Caute, *The Fellow Travelers: A Postscript to the Enlightenment* (London: Wiedenfeld and Nicholson, 1974); Paul Hollander, *Political Pilgrims: Travels of Western Intellectuals to the Soviet Union, China, and Cuba* (New York: Oxford University Press, 1981); Herbert Passin, *China's Cultural Diplomacy* (New York: Frederick A. Praeger, 1963).

7.   Simon Leys, *Chinese Shadows* (Middlesex, England: Penguin, 1974); Jacques Marcuse, *The Peking Papers* (London: Arthur Baker Ltd., 1968); Ross Terrill, *China In Our Time: The Epic Saga of the People's Republic of China from the Communist Victory to Tiananmen Square and Beyond* (New York: Simon and Schuster, 1993).

8.   Beverley Hooper, *China Stands Up: Ending the Western Presence 1948-1950* (Sydney: Allen and Unwin, 1986).

9.   See Gregor Benton, *Mountain Fires, The Red Army's Three-Year War in South China, 1934-1938* (Berkeley: University of California Press, 1992), preface.

10.   Zhao Pitao, *Waishi gaishuo* (Shanghai: Shanghai shehui kexue chubanshe, 1995) was one of the most useful of these sources for my research, providing a comprehensive outline of the *waishi* system, its goals and methods.

11.   Mao Zedong, *Jianguo yilai Mao Zedong wengao*, 13 vols. (Beijing: Zhongyang wenxian chubanshe, 1993); Zhongyang dang'anguan, ed., *Zhongyang zhongyang wenjian xuanji*, 18 vols. (Beijing: Zhonggong zhongyang dangxiao, 1989-1992); Zhonggong zhongyang xuanchuanbu bangongting, Zhongyang dang'anguan bianyanbu, eds., *Zhongguo gongchandang xuanchuan gongzuo wenxian xuanbian 1915-1992*, 4 vols., (Beijing: Xuexi chubanshe, 1996); Zhongyang xuanchuanbu bangongting, *Dang de xuanchuan gongzuo wenjian pian 1949-1993*, 4 vols. (Beijing: Zhonggong zhongyang dangxiao chubanshe, 1994).

12.   Tony Saich, ed., *The Rise to Power of the Chinese Communist Party: Documents and Analysis* (New York: M. E. Sharpe, 1996).

13.   Anne-Marie Brady, "FriendLit, or How to Become a Friend of China," *Revue Bibliographique de Sinologie* (1998): 389-397.

Chapter 1

Introduction

Gu wei jin yong, yang wei Zhong yong—"use the past to serve the present, make the foreign serve China"—the slogan coined by Mao Zedong in 1956,[1] symbolizes the Chinese Communist Party's policy on the suspect past and the corrupting foreign. It is a concept that echoes the cry of reformers of the late-Qing period *Zhongxue wei ti, Xixue wei yong*—"Chinese knowledge as the essence, Western learning for practical use." A further set of phrases is also instructive: *nei wai you bie, nei jin wai song* "treat insiders and outsiders differently, be strict internally relaxed to the outside world." For historical and nationalistic reasons, foreigners occupy an extremely sensitive position in China today. In their public pronouncements, China's leaders talk of friendship, *youhao guanxi*, and trumpet foreign friends, *waiguo pengyou*. Yet in their internal documents, these catchphrases are but the tropes of a deliberate strategy to manage and, where possible, control foreigners' presence and activities both in China and beyond.

From early on, the CCP developed a network of organizations and offices designed to deal with and control foreigners.[2] Partly because of its Marxist-Leninist revolutionary ideology, and partly due to the necessity of dealing with what Mao described as China's "semifeudal, semicolonial" status in the modern era, managing foreigners and establishing people-to-people contacts have long been a priority in CCP foreign affairs. In CCP terms, from an administrative point of view "foreigners" also includes overseas Chinese, Hong Kong, Macau and Taiwan "compatriots" regardless of whether they are foreign nationals, as well as non-Chinese.[3] In the revolutionary years and up until the late 1970s, outsiders were categorized by their political sympathies rather than by their race or nationality (i.e., comrades, progressives, bourgeoisie, imperialists, and later on, "revisionists"). From the late 1970s on, foreigners' ideological beliefs became irrelevant as China engaged in a policy of a (managed) opening up to the outside world.

All matters to do with foreigners and foreign things are encompassed by the term *waishi*. *Waishi* is the opposite of the term *neishi*, "internal matters."[4] China's *waishi*, or foreign affairs, system includes state-to-state and people's diplomacy, laws and guidelines regulating where and how foreigners are allowed to live, do business, marry, give birth, and go to school, as well as covering foreign propaganda, tourism, and the promotion of old and new foreign friends.[5] Such a broad ambit does not fit easily within the realms of standard categorizations of foreign relations activities, which usually focus on state-to-state relations alone. *Waishi* is not controlled by one bureaucracy alone; it consists of a wide range of organizations and subdepartments both publicly known and officially secret, *neibu*, operating in both a vertical and horizontal chain of command, known as a *xitong*, system.[6] Within the *waishi* system different elements of *waishi* policy are enacted in ways appropriate to their target group (i.e., United Front work on overseas Chinese being quite different from the work of the International Liaison Bureau), but all are ultimately covered by the blanket term "*waishi*" and all are part of the *waishi* sector, *kou*, in the Chinese bureaucratic structure. In recent years, *waishi* policy has been coordinated by the State Council Foreign Affairs Office/CCP Central Committee Foreign Affairs Office—the two foreign affairs offices maintain separate name plates, but are one and the same body[7]—on behalf of the CCP Central Committee Foreign Affairs Leading Small Group, which has final decision-making power.[8] This small group is headed by a member of the Politburo Standing Committee; in 2003 Hu Jintao filled this role.

Resolving the issue of how to deal with foreigners both within and outside China has long been a preoccupation of the CCP. After the party came to power in 1949, the foreign presence in China was strictly controlled. In the period from 1949-1952, most foreigners then living in China were forced, either directly or indirectly, to leave the country (after undergoing a process of ascertaining whether they were liable for criminal charges or for notional debts under the laws of the People's Republic). In the first few years after 1949, a comparatively tiny number of foreigners were invited by the party to come to live in the PRC or allowed to stay on; this group were known and trusted by senior CCP leaders before 1949 or had been recommended by their native Communist Party to come and help build new China. From the 1950s to the 1970s, the number of foreigners living in China—whether as students, diplomats, journalists, or foreign employees (the so-called "foreign experts")[9] of the Chinese government—was small. Tourist numbers were also low and most travelers were restricted to visiting China as part of a delegation, engaging in what China called "people's diplomacy." Business people were also restricted, the annual Guangdong Trade Fair being their main means of doing business in China during this period.

The numbers of foreign experts employed by the Chinese government in the period from 1949 to the current era are a useful indicator of changes in *waishi* policy over time. From 1949 to 1960, 16,000 Soviet and East European technological advisers went to China to work, as well as a handful of other foreigners, mostly from the West, who were almost all engaged in teaching foreign languages, translation, and propaganda work. In the following period from 1961 to 1978, only 6,400 foreigners worked in China. However, from 1979 to 1993, the Foreign Experts' Bureau records that 350,000 foreign employees were invited to China. In 1994, China hosted approximately 50,000 foreign experts.[10] By 1997, the number had increased to more than 80,000.[11] The growth in the numbers of foreigners coming to work in China has been matched by a similarly exponential growth in the numbers of foreign tourists, students, business people, journalists, and diplomats visiting the country or staying for a longer period.

The rising foreign presence since the late 1970s has been part of a state strategy, an important component of economic reforms, which aim to utilize foreign technology and foreign investment to modernize China and to help the country establish a prominent position on the world stage. China's modernization policies had a hesitant start in the early 1970s, beginning with the Sino-U.S. rapprochement and China's entry into the UN. Once Deng Xiaoping formally instituted the reform and opening up policy in 1978-79, the economy became the central focus of government activity. In the last twenty years, China's international contacts have increased dramatically. China requires foreign technology and investment to speed up its economic development. To this end, since 1979, China's leaders have conducted an ongoing campaign to change both national and international perceptions about the nation and encourage foreign assistance. The role and scope of *waishi* work has also expanded to cope with these changes. More than ever before, *waishi* is playing a deliberate part in the nation's development.

Since 1949, the management of foreigners within China has been controlled by official *waishi* bureaus and regulated by foreign affairs regulations, *waishi jilü*, which guide Chinese citizens on how to interact with non-Chinese.[12] Theoretically, even ordinary Chinese citizens will have been educated on how to interact with foreigners, but in most cases, rather than direct instruction, it is common sense and an awareness of the hyperpolitical status of foreigners in China that guide most people on how to treat them. In a section on contact between ordinary Chinese citizens and foreigners, a 1993 handbook on *waishi* delineates the extraordinary distance that, even in the era of "reform and opening up," Chinese people are supposed to keep between themselves and the "corrosive influence" of foreigners:

> Chinese citizens who have contact with foreigners must conscientiously observe our nation's laws, decrees and relevant foreign affairs policies and regulations. They must consciously guard against the corrosive influence of capitalist thinking and way of living. They must not voluntarily discuss our nation's internal matters, or divulge party or State secrets to a foreigner. They should not seek out goods from a foreigner, ask foreigners to illegally purchase goods which are temporarily in short supply on the Chinese market, or ask foreigners to pass on letters of appeal or other materials. It is prohibited to intercept foreigners or their vehicles. It is forbidden to engage in immoral behavior with

foreigners, and it is forbidden to collude with foreigners to engage in illicit re-selling of State products. Unless the permission of Foreign Affairs offices has been given, it is forbidden to visit foreign embassies, consulates, apartments and other foreigners' residential quarters. It is forbidden to disseminate to foreigners expressions of discontent, or reactionary views that attack our party or socialist system.[13]

How did China's *waishi* system develop and why? What does it tell us about the way the Chinese government perceives the outside world and the underlying nature of its foreign policy? And what is the role of the foreigner and foreign things in China's modernization process? In this study of *waishi* I have attempted a number of interrelated inquiries. My aim is to discuss the origins of the *waishi* system and its role in Chinese politics and society. I focus mostly on the core aspects of *waishi*, concerning the management and control of foreigners within China from the 1920s up to the present day. The work forms both a political history and an inquiry into official Chinese constructions of the Other, that is, the "foreign" or "*waiguo*." Examining the CCP's *waishi* provides a window on what Ann Anagnost has called "the national narrative" of China in the modern era, a narrative which as Anagnost notes is "constituted always in relation to an 'outside.'"[14] By deepening our understanding of official Chinese constructions of the Other, we are also able to gain a deeper understanding of constructions of the Chinese Self or "Chineseness" in various eras.

The cultural context of CCP *waishi* activities set the scene for the work as a whole. I have examined the cultural dimensions of *waishi* activities both in terms of the culturo-political continuities—whether conscious or unconscious—among party policymakers with late imperial (Manchu-Qing) diplomatic practices. I have also examined *waishi* within the structure of anthropologists' findings regarding interpersonal relationships; the use of nomenclature and a range of cultural practices such as banqueting, gift giving, and so on to invoke, define, and contain various forms of exchange. I have considered how these "cultural dimensions" have merged with Soviet and Western approaches to foreign relations. While doing this I have attempted to avoid simplistic cultural and essentialist assumptions about what is "Chinese" and tried, instead, to discuss *waishi* and its evolution in terms of how "Chineseness" has been invoked and reformulated by CCP leaders, policy theorists and practitioners over a particular historical period. In practice, *waishi* consists of a complex series of structures, practices, and policies that have evolved in a specific historical context, often contingent, always changing. Yet it is also part of a body of knowledge and mechanisms that is presented by the CCP—in internal documents, policy directives, and handbooks—as a pragmatic but at the same time quintessential, universal, and eternal Chinese cultural essence in contrast with the foreign Other.

While institutional development and policy implementation are important activities of *waishi*, the personal dimension is crucial. Throughout the book I have continually focused on the lives and activities of the CCP's foreign friends and how they have coped with the policies of each changing era. Foreigners who have willingly embraced the title of foreign friend and the expectations that no-menclature demands have been the most visible and symbolic examples of the meaning of *waishi* throughout different periods of CCP history. And charismatic figures at the center of party power have not only carried out the policies—always inventing, developing, and transforming them during that implementa-tion—they have also acted as models of *waishi* behavior for the cadres whose task it is to regulate the foreign in China and the outside world.

The book is organized chronologically; following the introduction, the sec-ond chapter discusses thematic issues and the historical background to China's *waishi* system. Chapters 3 through 8 comprise an examination of *waishi* in suc-cessive periods. I have categorized CCP *waishi* activities into a number of dis-tinct phases: the earliest years of the CCP covering the period up to the end of the civil war in 1949; the 1950s; the 1960s; the Cultural Revolution era (1966-1969); 1970 to 1989; and the 1990s, up to the early years of the twenty-first cen-tury. Trends and developments in *waishi* are analyzed in each chronological pe-riod, elucidating differing issues in the CCP's policies on managing foreigners and foreign things: the need for a broad united front in international relations in the 1930s versus the desire to control the foreign presence in China; the Sino-Soviet alliance of the late 1940s to the late 1950s and ridding China of the traces of the "semicolonial" past in the same period; the Sino-Soviet split and the birth of the true friend of China; the claim that China was the center of world revolu-tion in the 1960s; and the ongoing quest to create a modern and strong nation-state which has been the focus of the policies of the last twenty years or more of reform and opening up to the outside world. The concluding chapter, chapter 9, summarizes major findings of this study and discusses the implications of the *waishi* system in the CCP's national and international strategy.

Notes

1.   See Mao's "Tong yinyue gongzuozhe de tanhua" 24 August 1956, excerpted in Zhonggong zhongyang xuanchuanbu bangongting, Zhongyang dang'anguan bianyanbu, eds., *Zhongguo gongchandang xuanchuan gongzuo wenxian xuanbian 1915-1992*, 4 vols. (Beijing: Xuexi chubanshe, 1996), vol. 3, 1168-1174.

2.   One of the primary duties of the CCP's earliest formal Foreign Ministry, established in 1934, was to manage relations with foreigners in the Chinese Soviet Republic. See Michael Hunt, *The Genesis of Chinese Communist Foreign Policy* (New York: Columbia University Press, 1996), 227.

3.   See Shao Zhixiang, ed., *Shewai gongan zhishi wenda* (Beijing: Zhongguo fangzheng chubanshe, 1994), 28-29; Zhonggong Guangzhou shiwei duiwai xuanchuan xiaozu bangongshi, *Shewai renyuan shouce* (Guangzhou: Xinhua shudian, 1985), 67-69.

4.   Liu Luxiang, *Shewai gonggong guanxi* (Dalian: Dalian chubanshe, 1996), 25.

5. Zhao Pitao, *Waishi gaishuo*, 1-2. The term *shewai* is sometimes used interchangeably with *waishi*. According to Zhao Pitao, *shewai* is both a synonym for *waishi*, and a subcategory of *waishi* activities, usually focusing on administrative matters such as Sino-foreign births, deaths, and marriages, Customs, and the police force.

6. For an understanding of how the *waishi xitong* or *kou* fits into the Chinese bureaucracy, see Lu Ning, *The Dynamics of Foreign-Policy Decisionmaking in China* (Boulder, Colo.: Westview, 1997), 7-17. For information on the role of the *xitong* in general, see Kenneth G. Lieberthal, *Governing China: From Revolution to Reform* (New York: W. W. Norton, 1995), 192-208.

7. Zhao Pitao, *Waishi gaishuo*, 5.

8. *Liaowang*, ed., *Guowuyuan jigou gaige gailan* (Beijing: Xinhua chubanshe, 1998), 262.

9. Foreign expert is a polite term used by the Chinese to describe foreign technicians and workers. It has both a general and specific meaning. In its specific sense, it is the highest grade of the sliding pay scale for foreigners who work for the Chinese government.

10. "Tan yinjin zhili," *Duiwai xuanchuan cankao*, hereafter *DWXCCK*, no. 12 (1994): 6-8.

11. "Foreign Experts Awarded," *China Daily*, 30 September 1997.

12. See appendix, for an example of *waishi jilü*.

13. Wang Rihua, ed., *Shiyong shewai changshi shouce* (Beijing: Renmin Zhongguo chubanshe, 1993), 100.

14. Ann Anagnost, *National Past-Times: Narrative, Representation, and Power in Modern China* (Durham and London: Duke University Press, 1997), 3.

Chapter 2

Friendship

Who are our enemies? Who are our friends? This is a question of the first importance for the revolution. . . . . A revolutionary party is the guide of the masses and no revolution ever succeeds when the revolutionary party leads them astray. To ensure that we will definitely achieve success in our revolution and will not lead the masses astray, we must pay attention to uniting with our real friends in order to attack our real enemies.[1]

"Who are our enemies? Who are our friends?" the question posed by Mao in his "Analysis of the Classes in Chinese Society" frames one of the essential points of consideration in CCP ideology. In the language of the Chinese Communist Party, friendship is political. "Friends" may be either "fundamental" or "temporary" depending on political needs and interests.[2] Friendship, *youyi*, is a term that has come to be closely associated with foreigners and the CCP's system of structures and strategies for dealing with them, *waishi*. In Chinese political language, friendship has the meaning of a strategic relationship; it does not have the meaning of good or intimate personal relations. According to a standard handbook on *waishi* activities, "Friendship includes political struggle, while in the midst of political struggle we develop friendship. This is the pattern of our *waishi* work."[3] If it is true, as *waishi* theorist Zhao Pitao claims, that "a state's diplomacy reflects the interests of its ruling class,"[4] then the PRC's foreign affairs system—characterized by friends and enemies, insiders and outsiders—reflects a deep mistrust of, and discomfort with, the outside world.

The political meaning of friendship originally came from the translation of the Soviet Union's term for official friendship, the Russian word *druzhba*. Friendship terminology is a means to neutralize opposition psychologically and to reorder reality. Beijing likes to describe positive diplomatic relations between itself and other countries in "friendship" terms. Foreign politicians who visit China more than once are described as "old friends of the Chinese people" (George Bush Sr., Jacques Chirac, Richard Nixon, and Tanaka Kakuei, are all members of this select group). Foreigners of influence and/or power who assist China's interests are known as "foreign friends," as are those who stay on to work for the Chinese government. The PRC's officially "non-unofficial," *fei guanfang*, diplomacy is conducted by organizations such as the Chinese People's Association for Friendship with Foreign Countries and the Chinese People's Association for Friendly Contact. In the past China has constructed Friendship Bridges for its poorer neighbors, and even today some border points are still known as Friendship Passes. Foreigners can shop in the Friendship Store and stay in the Friendship Hotel. Chinese citizens can buy Friendship brand cigarettes (symbolically decorated with twin Ping-Pong bats to represent the new era of Sino-U.S. relations that began in 1971-1972), or soothe their skin with Friendship brand moisturizer. Significantly, unlike other countries in the world, China calls its sister-city relations, "friendship cities" (reputedly at the suggestion of Zhou Enlai).[5] A 1988 article in the Friendship Association's magazine, *Voice of Friendship*, explains: "To fully reflect equality between the two partners, they were called friendship cities instead of sister cities."[6] In contrast, foreign leaders or prominent individuals who dare to criticize China are classed as "unfriendly," and nations that act against China's interests are lambasted as hegemonist, imperialists, "revisionists," and even, "the enemy."

The Soviet Influence

The origins of many of the methods and much of the terminology of China's *waishi* system lie in the practices formulated by the Soviet Union from the early 1920s. Until 1943, when the Comintern closed down its operations, the Chinese Communist Party was officially a branch of the international communist movement, which was dominated and controlled by the Soviet Union. As in all processes of cultural exchange, the Chinese communists did not adopt Soviet approaches to foreign relations wholesale. What they did, whether consciously or not, was to apply them and interpret them in terms that were culturally appropriate to Chinese norms and traditions. In the present era, *waishi* cadres claim that "Confucian" notions of friendship, including the concept that one should cherish old friends, *bu yao wangji lao pengyou* inform Chinese communist-style friendship diplomacy.[7] It became possible to make such statements from the 1980s on, when the CCP asserted the "Chineseness" of its political system, and claimed to find origins for its policies in China's ancient past; twenty years before this connection would not have been articulated. The irony of such claims becomes deeper if we consider the role of the Jesuits in China in "manufacturing" contemporary ideas of Kongzi (Confucius) in China and the West.[8] Nevertheless, that government officials profess their "Confucian" heritage now does not mean it was not a part of what went before. Many of China's senior leaders have been proud to admit that they only knew the "ABCs of Communism."[9] Their Marxist theoretical knowledge was limited, both by the demands of the revolution and the availability of materials in Chinese in the early years of the Chinese revolution. As we shall see, the Soviet foreign affairs system clearly provided the basic structure for the setting up of China's *waishi* bureaucracy. Yet it is also true that, rather than simply copying verbatim from Soviet models, Chinese cultural norms and the traditions of Chinese realist statecraft are an important influence in China's *waishi* nomenclature and style. Whether they accepted these norms or chose to reject them as revolutionaries, China's communist leaders could not help but be influenced by them. This unusual blend of Marxist-Leninist-Maoist-Statist-Confucian foreign relations is what makes PRC diplomacy and the *waishi* system in total so distinctive and, perhaps, so effective.

The manipulation of public opinion and the use of noncommunist supporters to promote its cause had long been a tactic of the European communist movement.[10] After the success of the 1917 Russian Revolution, such tactics became an essential aspect of Soviet foreign policy. The new government set up what were essentially noncommunist mass organizations over which the Comintern and local parties exercised control through holding key positions within the leadership. The first international "front" organization was International Workers' Aid, also known as Red Aid, created to support starving Russian workers. The organization, directed by a German revolutionary comrade of Lenin's, Willi Münzenberg, combined propaganda work with fund-raising and proved extremely successful. Following that success, Münzenberg was authorized to set up a host of other such front organizations throughout Europe and the United States. Most of the participants were not Communist Party members.[11] For some, the front organizations were an entrée to the world of Soviet espionage.

Over time, the Soviet government devised a set formula for its external propaganda activities: first, a cause which ordinary people could identify with; second, the public support of well-known and respected individuals to give the cause respectability; and third, a hard core of communist activists working behind the scenes to coordinate activities.[12] These efforts aimed to project to the world an image of the Soviet way of life in line with Soviet foreign policy objectives. At the same time, it was paralleled by a massive effort to shield Soviet citizens from harmful "'alien" influences.[13] The systematic utilization of information, artistic, scientific, and other cultural materials as instruments of foreign policy were central to Soviet-style foreign affairs.[14]

The Comintern initially controlled Soviet foreign affairs structures; then after 1943, responsibilities were shared between the Central Committee-controlled Propaganda Department and the International Department.[15] The primary body involved in people-to-people relations, VOKS (the All-Union Society for Cultural Relations with Foreign Countries) was established in 1925. In 1958, it was renamed the Union of Soviet Societies for Friendship and Cultural Relations with Foreign Countries.[16] This organization aimed for a more representative membership, with the goal of coexistence with foreign countries, whereas VOKS had been closely associated with foreign communist parties. Until 1934, when the Soviet Union adopted the "popular front" foreign policy, VOKS and its foreign affiliates had acted openly as auxiliary agencies of the world communist movement.[17] VOKS claimed to be a "voluntary public organization" similar to Western nongovernmental organizations (NGOs).[18] It had sections for law, literature, natural science, agriculture, theater, music, and so on. It was organized geographically, with different sections specializing in certain areas. VOKS' task was to establish links with "individual progressive leaders of culture in foreign countries" as well as inviting larger scale delegations. It had an extensive publications program.[19]

In addition to the organizations set up to influence foreigners outside the Soviet Union, Moscow set up bureaucracies responsible for managing foreigners living in or visiting the country. In the mid-1920s when the Soviet Union sought to attract foreign technicians and overseas Russians to help with the modernization and rebuilding of the new nation, it created a state bureaucracy especially to deal with their needs. In order to retain foreign experts in the Soviet Union, since living standards at that time were low, it was considered necessary to give them privileges not available to ordinary citizens.[20] Foreign workers were given higher wages and better living conditions. They were allowed to buy their necessities at special shops, better stocked than those for ordinary citizens. They were also granted traveling privileges, and private sleeping and dining cars were made available to them.[21] The commissar of foreign affairs in the 1920s even admitted in an interview that foreigners in Soviet Russia enjoyed extraterritorial rights.[22]

The Soviet government tried to convince foreign visitors that they were free to go wherever they desired, giving some favored guests access to closed areas but subjecting them to subtle surveillance.[23] A two-tier currency system was in operation, which forced travelers to go to locations that accepted foreign currency. This situation changed later, but the official exchange rate gave foreigners little money for their foreign currency. Independent travel was extremely expensive in comparison to traveling with a group on an Intourist program.[24] Soviet citizens were carefully briefed on what to say to foreign visitors. At times government authorities even went to the length of replacing whole communities with government propagandists when foreigners visited sensitive areas,[25] similar in concept to the Potemkin villages during the era of Catherine the Great.

Foreign diplomats, journalists, travelers, as well as those enthusiasts who had come to help the Russian Revolution or simply to get a paid job during the depression years, found themselves under constant surveillance by the Soviet authorities. They could only go to places and meet people as arranged for them. All foreign visitors, whether they spoke Russian or not, were provided with official interpreters who were in fact officers of the Soviet police or the Comintern.[26] Those who spoke Russian and were familiar with conditions in the country found themselves more restricted than those who knew nothing at all and were first-time visitors. Soviet citizens who were required to have contact with foreigners because of their occupation, were closely watched.[27] Some locals

cals were especially assigned to befriend foreigners, probably for surveillance purposes.[28] Normal relations between Soviet citizens and foreigners were restricted. Foreigners were kept under surveillance and locals could be arrested for having more than casual contact with them. Foreign radio broadcasts were jammed and professional correspondence between Soviet scientists and their foreign colleagues could only be conducted with the approval of supervisors. Foreign journalists were considered the agents of the ruling classes of their countries. While they were useful for propagating Soviet propaganda, their relations with Soviet people were carefully restricted.[29]

When the Stalinist purges began in the 1930s, accusations of foreign espionage were one of the means Stalin used to bring down his rivals. Ordinary foreigners became caught up in the hysteria and many who had come to work or study in the Soviet Union at this time died in Soviet prison camps. Robert Robinson, a black American engineer who arrived in the Soviet Union in the 1930s and stayed on until the 1970s, wrote in his memoir, "Every single black I knew in the early 1930s who became a Soviet citizen disappeared from Moscow within seven years. The fortunate ones were exiled to Siberian labor camps. Those less fortunate were shot."[30] Unlike the handful of other black Americans living in the Soviet Union at this time and many other foreigners who had come to help out the Russian Revolution, Robinson was careful not to formally give up his foreign citizenship and become a Soviet citizen. According to Robinson this was the main reason for his survival while many others were sentenced to the gulag. Of the other foreign experts he worked with, he wrote, "By mid-July 1941, the number of foreigners working in my factory had been reduced drastically. When I began in 1932 there were 362 of us. Now a Hungarian and I were the only ones left."[31]

The Soviet Union maintained a few resident foreign friends who were given luxurious apartments, which they used to play host to selected foreign delegations. Robert Ross, also a black American, served in this role for more than thirty years, as well as traveling around the Soviet Union giving talks on social conditions in the United States.[32] He was a loyal servant, but in his last years, when he was suffering from cancer, Robert Robinson records that Ross was "reduced to a pauper, he was rejected by his Russian wife of twenty-six years and his Russian friends. He had let himself be used to the fullest. When they had done with him, they threw him away like a piece of garbage."[33]

While the government was both intimidating and cocooning foreign residents in the 1930s and after, the many foreign visitors to the Soviet Union who came as "delegates" seemed oblivious to the abuses of the society they came to report on. Hans Magnus Enzensberger has outlined the *delegatsiya* (delegation) system invented by the Soviet Union in the 1920s and afterwards adopted all over the socialist world. The system had the following basic elements: the visit was highly planned and closely supervised, delegates were invited and usually did not pay their own expenses; they were dependent on their hosts for access to the country and the ability to travel around; they were hosted with a high degree of luxury relative to the resident population; and all their needs were supervised by an organization which mediated the delegates' contact with ordinary citizens. The foreign delegates were pampered with gifts, banquets, receptions, honorary awards, and much publicity. Enzensberger writes, "No cheaper and more effective means for influencing the outside world has ever been devised than the *delegatsiya* system."[34] Most delegates returned to their home countries praising the Soviet Utopia. Those who held a less than favorable impression usually kept silent out of obligation for the hospitality they had been given or, in some cases, out of fear of intimidation from communist true believers. The writings of the Soviet Union's foreign friends were extremely popular in their day, lending the country much-needed international support and prestige.

Other socialist countries also adopted the Soviet foreign affairs approach, all the more so after unity within the Communist bloc deteriorated in the 1960s. Albania, Cuba, North Vietnam, and North Korea all had their particular foreign friends.[35] Since the collapse of communism in Eastern Europe and the Soviet Union, the remaining communist states continue to follow Soviet-style foreign affairs to varying degrees, but none to the extent (or success) of China.

Although the Soviets invented this distinctive foreign affairs system, they were never quite as successful at using it to create loyal foreign friends and admirers as the CCP has been. Those who have had contact with both tend to talk admiringly of the Chinese communists' "loyalty" to their old friends in contrast with Soviet practices. (In the PRC this is officially sanctioned in a deliberate policy, summed up by the saying "when you drink from the well, remember the well-digger."[36]) The Soviets tried to integrate foreign experts into life in Russia, involving them in social clubs and other activities. Those who were long-term residents were put under considerable pressure to give up their foreign passports and the special privileges that went with their foreign status. Rather than isolating them and using privilege to keep them separate from ordinary people, they encouraged them to give up their foreign citizenship and join Soviet trade unions and the Soviet Communist Party. Those foreigners who chose to do so thus came under Soviet control, losing any rights to protection from their home countries.

Max Granich, who worked first in the USSR in the early 1930s, then in China in the late 1930s, says that Moscow "had a contempt for foreigners."[37] Many Americans went to work in the USSR during the depression years. Granich contrasted the harshness of the Soviet Union towards the foreigners who joined their revolution with the friendliness of the Chinese communists:

> The Chinese, the nation of youngsters are a nation of very very naïve people. And they have this quality which I had, not reason to test, but reason to learn that when they say they're you're [*sic*] their friend, when they say that to you, it's like an old, like an Indian in America rubbing bloods together . . . till death do us part. And that was the difference, that *is* some of the difference.[38]

Chinese communist leaders in the 1930s and 1940s were extremely grateful to the few foreigners among the many residents in China at this time who supported their cause. The CCP in the 1930s and 1940s was a guerrilla force, acting in an extremely hostile environment. They had few allies and multiple enemies. Before the Soviet Union's influence began to change China significantly in the period 1949 to 1959, the CCP had already forged links with a number of sympathetic Westerners. These connections would become more important over time, especially after 1970-1972 when China would draw on some of these old contacts to improve trade and diplomatic relations with Western nations. Both in the 1930s and 1940s, then again in the 1970s and up to the present era, China has among other differences, out of necessity, focused much more strongly on individual "foreign friends" than the Soviet Union ever did. Beginning from the 1930s, perhaps because of the dissimilarity in its geopolitical environment, or perhaps because of nationalistic pride and the inescapable effect of tradition, in addition to the Soviet approach to foreign affairs, China's Communist Party developed its own unique version of the foreign affairs system. It was informed and deeply influenced by traditional Chinese notions of relationships and foreign contact.

The Cultural Origins of China's Political Friendship

If a foreigner could be found today who, though admitted to the Chinese banquet, would not hesitate to rant in our name against the present state of China, him I would call a truly honest man, a truly admirable man.[39]

In the contemporary era, the CCP recognizes itself as inheriting a long historical and cultural tradition. Even in the 1950s, China's communist leaders stated that China's tradition and history would set it apart from other socialist countries. Though in his 1940 essay "On New Democracy" Mao Zedong rejected "the worship of Confucius, the study of the Confucian canon, the old ethical code and the old ideas,"[40] the conditioning of education and culture would prove hard to overcome. Only two years before Mao had stated that the assimilation of the Chinese heritage "becomes a method that aids considerably in guiding the present great movement."[41] The domain where Mao seemed to see the influence of Chinese heritage benefiting most was the art of statecraft.[42] Ultimately over time, despite the iconoclasm of the early years of communist rule, China's own traditions came to be recognized as valuable and useful in their own right. China's experience in first discarding and then reclaiming its "tradition" is not unique, the invention of "tradition," the rediscovery of "custom," and the objectification of "culture" have been a common phenomena in other societies, especially those that experienced colonialism, in the nineteenth and twentieth centuries.

   Language is one of the most obvious indicators of the impact of tradition and culture on the CCP foreign affairs system. Linguistically, Chinese is a "positive" and "hearer-based" language and native speakers tend to talk about matters in a positive way in order to avoid conflict.[43] Attempts to bring the addressee closer underlie many of the positive politeness strategies of Chinese speakers. Hence, often people will say things because they are pleasing, rather than sincere and will focus on finding common points. In contrast, in a "speaker-based" language such as English, "communication . . . is ideally direct and to the point."[44] Chinese society maintains a strong awareness of insiders and outsiders: insiders are to be trusted; outsiders are to be feared. Such a mentality can be summed up by the phrase, *nei wai you bie*, "treat insiders and outsiders differently," a concept common in China long before the CCP took it on as a political principle.[45] "Finding things in common," *qiu tong*, is one way in which many Chinese people develop relations, *guanxi*, with nonfamily members and other "outsiders."[46] One can be *tongxiang,* of the same place, *tongxue*, schoolmates, *tongshi*, of the same workplace, or even *tongzhi*, literally "of one will" and in modern terms a "comrade." In their interaction with foreigners, China's *waishi* officials stress finding common ground as a means of building *ganqing* or "mutual sentiment."[47] However, cadres are warned, "Some issues the more you talk about them, the more confusing they become. In the end it is best not to talk about them."[48] In particular, in the 1980s and 1990s the violence of the Cultural Revolution became a topic to be avoided at all costs, as it was thought to create a negative impression of China.[49] The advice reflects Chinese cultural norms, which discourage discussing unpleasant matters openly. In another time, many foreign observers half admiringly, half in fear described such norms as "Oriental inscrutability."

   The language used to describe foreign activities in China is an important indicator of attitudes and strategies in *waishi*. Traditional Chinese society placed a Confucian stress on the rectification of names to maintain social order. Interestingly, the concept of the rectification of names, *zheng ming*, is one point of Confucianism that Mao Zedong explicitly embraced.[50] According to the *Analects,* "If names are not rectified, then language will not be in accord with truth. If language is not in accord with truth, then things cannot be accomplished."[51] Hence if one accepts a name as appropriate it involves a disposition to act.[52] The frequent use of the word "friendship" to symbolize positive relations in China's *waishi* is thus significant. Chinese relationships are usually divided into hierarchies of older and younger such as elder brother and younger brother, uncle and nephew, elder sister and younger sister. Seniority demands the respect of the junior partner in the relationship. However "friend" is a neutral term in this sense: friends can be equal; they can share certain common points of view but hold different views on some matters. In official communist Chinese language, virtually everyone has the potential to be described as a friend (in Chinese *pengyou*): *xiao pengyou* (literally "little friends," children), *guanzhong pengyou* (audience friends), *nongmin pengyou* (farmer friends), even *yumin pengyou* (fishermen friends). From early on in CCP history, foreigners were judged either as "imperialists" or "friends," "friendly" or "nonfriendly." In the contemporary era, those designated as China's "friends" have an unspoken moral obligation to act in a "friendly" way, meaning not to harm China's interests. Not to do so is to risk being cast out into the category of enemy or nonfriend. Here we can see the intrinsically binary nature of the CCP's construction of the Other, symbolized by Mao Zedong's rhetorical questioning as to who are China's friends, who are its enemies.[53]

Chinese cultural notions of *ganqing* (feeling) and *guanxi* (relationship) are important concepts to understand when interpreting the conduct and methods of *waishi*.[54] In Chinese terms, one cannot have *guanxi* without also creating *ganqing*. At the same time, one can develop a relationship by means of building *ganqing* between people. According to these rules of friendship, *guanxi* implies mutual obligation, willingness on the part of both sides to accept or request assistance. Maintaining and developing one's *guanxi* is an essential survival tactic in Chinese society.[55] Though the language and practices of friendship diplomacy may often seem hypocritical to Western observers, these practices have a culturally sound basis in Chinese traditions of negotiation and conflict avoidance. The norms of Western-style negotiation and diplomacy are quite different, focusing on problem solving, showing less concern with personal relationships, and preferring plain talk to symbolic acts. The model of negotiation of many non-Western societies is a nonverbal, implicit, and dense style of communication. Unlike the dominant lawyer-derived American style of diplomatic negotiation, which tends to focus on isolated issues, this model emphasizes long-term goals and is concerned with considerations of status, symbolism, and face; it draws on highly developed communication strategies for evading confrontation.[56]

In Chinese culture, *ganqing* must have a discernible form. The means of materializing *ganqing* in the normal Chinese context include hosting banquets, toasting, giving gifts, and the use of honorary or affectionate titles.[57] *Ganqing* can also be embodied via the exchange of favors, and ritual behavior at occasions such as a funeral. A *waishi* cadre describing how to create foreign friends in the 1990s comments, "*Ganqing* is the response of people to objective events. It is an important motivation for human activity. In order to work on people [i.e., foreigners] we first of all need to establish *ganqing*."[58] One of the most important methods the CCP government has used to establish *ganqing* with foreigners who visit the PRC is official hospitality. In *waishi* terms, "hospitality is political."[59] Hospitality to guests, *jiedai keren*, is seen as a necessary skill in Chinese society.

Official hospitality fits within the long tradition in Chinese statecraft of guest ritual, or *binli*, an important aspect of dynastic China's historical foreign relations praxis. Since the 1990s, the "connection" between contemporary *waishi* and embedded tradition has constantly, and emphatically, been stressed.[60] Under the strategic principle known as *huai rou yuanren*,[61] "treating strangers well in order to win their hearts," by means of the etiquette of guest ritual the imperial court was able to utilize nonmilitary means to maintain its preeminent strategic position.[62] The Beijing-published 1979 Commercial Press *Chinese-English Dictionary* translates *huairou zhengce* pejoratively as "policies of control through conciliation," the techniques of "feudal" rulers who "make a show of conciliation in order to bring other nationalities under control."[63] In the imperial court, "guest" had a different meaning from the usual sense in English. The guest was not invited, but was graciously allowed to visit the Chinese Empire. The guest was not equal with the emperor, nor was the emperor a "host."[64] The requirements of guest ritual demanded a kind of moral behavior rather than etiquette or manners, and its goal was to elicit "feelings of gratitude and humility" from the recipient.[65] The traditions of guest ritual concerned not only interactions between the emperor and his guests, but were a means for regulating and harmonizing visiting in all levels of society, including those between equals.[66]

Historical Chinese notions of foreign relations were hierarchical, in contrast to the seventheeth century Westphalian notion of the equality of sovereign states. The British Macartney mission to China in 1793 is significant as being the first diplomatic contact between imperial China and a leading state of an expansive and self-confident West that expected to be treated as an equal, not a tributary. The Qianlong emperor instructed his officials to deal with the British visit in terms of *huairou* principles:

> In dealing with matters concerning outsiders (*waiyi*), you must find the middle course between extravagance and meagreness (*fengjian shi zhong*), so that you correctly accord with Our imperial order (*tizhi*) . . . the ambassador has sailed far to visit Us for the first time; this cannot be compared to Burma, Annam, or others who have come for many years to present gifts. Liang Kentang and Zhengrui must judiciously care for them and avoid too mean a reception, because that would make these distant travelers to take us too lightly (*qing*).[67]

In contrast to the Chinese approach, the English king, George III, wrote to Qianlong that he hoped the Macartney mission would cement a "firm and lasting friendship."[68] Friendship under these terms implied equality and alliance. The Qianlong emperor's implicit refusal to acknowledge equal relations between the Heavenly Empire and Great Britain was one of the reasons for the failure of the mission. Within a hundred years of that unsuccessful visit however, China had been forced to accept European notions of national sovereignty and (at least in principle) the formal equality of states.

Official hospitality to foreign visitors to the PRC has a similar function to guest ritual. Rather than being an example of Chinese good manners and warmth, as many unwitting recipients often interpret it, it is both deliberate and planned. According to the government's rules on interacting with foreigners, *waishi jilü*, Chinese people are (in theory) only permitted to form friendly relations with foreigners in the interests of the specific political and economic goals of the state. Beginning in the 1980s, as Chinese society has become more open, it has been more acceptable for Chinese people to form other relationships with foreigners, and many people do. However, this is still almost always outside the workplace, and, importantly, "having illicit contact with foreign countries," *litong waiguo*, is still used as an excuse to harass or detain those whom the CCP considers as political irritants or dissidents. Official hospitality, in contrast, is well regulated and officially approved. Official hospitality includes meeting and greeting guests at the airport or train station, giving farewell gifts, enticements of free travel, accommodation, and other special treatment and, the most important ritual of Chinese social intercourse, the banquet. The Chinese banquet or dinner party is particularly significant because of the role of food in Chinese society; offering food to someone implies the consolidation of a relationship and all the obligation and mutual *ganqing* that entails. As one cadre told me, "Eating together is also a form of people's diplomacy." Yet another told me (here it was a complaint about the attempt of Taiwan to attract its own foreign friends), "After you've eaten with someone two or three times, how can you not become friends?"

Hospitality is carefully organized, although *waishi* personnel are informed they must act in a "natural" manner. A 1989 handbook on *waishi* states, "Hospitality towards foreign guests is an important task which is an expression of our nation's foreign policy. Do not be slapdash or under-estimate this kind of work as just functional duties."[69] Instructions are given on every detail of the foreign guest's visit, down to the appropriate response of Chinese waiters if the foreigner wishes to toast them at a banquet in appreciation of their work. (Staff are instructed to "thank the foreigner warmly and depending on the circumstances, have a drink with them.")[70] When foreign guests visit a factory or school, their minders are instructed that workers or students should carry on as usual, "but if the foreign guest takes the initiative to shake hands and chat with our people, then they may enthusiastically make the appropriate responses."[71]

Finally, a further concept of traditional Chinese society stressed in *waishi* publications is the adage of China's most famous military strategist Sunzi, to "know the enemy and know yourself," *zhi yi zhi ji*. The full quote is as follows:

> If you know the enemy and know yourself, you need not fear the result of a hundred battles. If you know yourself but not the enemy, for every victory gained you will also suffer a defeat. If you know neither the enemy nor yourself, you will succumb in every battle.

> Commentary: "Knowing the enemy enables you to take the offensive, knowing yourself enables you to stand on the defensive. Attack is the secret of defense; defense is the planning of an attack."[72]

"Know the enemy and know yourself" is a phrase that appears repeatedly in Chinese *waishi* texts. Until recently, virtually all of China's senior *waishi* officials had personal experience of the "Western mentality" through their education in missionary schools or in the West.[73] The preeminent example of this elite group is Zhou Enlai, who studied at missionary schools in Tianjin and had study and work experience in Japan, France, and Germany as well as brief periods in England and the Soviet Union. As biographical accounts stress, at the same time as having a familiarity with Western ways, Zhou had a strong grounding in Chinese culture and norms—thereby both knowing the "enemy" and knowing the "Self." The idealized qualities of Zhou epitomize what many commentators, both Chinese and foreign, look back on as a golden era of *waishi*, from the 1930s to the 1940s. *Waishi* personnel were certainly adept at combining the strategies of both Western plain speaking and Chinese-style hospitality in these early years, communicating with sympathetic foreigners in a way that was extremely appealing to them. In marked contrast to the Nationalist government, in the 1930s and 1940s CCP cadres appeared to speak the truth and accept criticism in good faith and they won a number of important supporters to their cause because of this. It is significant that the head of the Friendship Association has always been a retired diplomat who had been responsible for dealing with the United States, with pre-1949 experience of dealing with foreigners, among them Wang Bingnan, Huang Hua, Zhang Wenjin, and Han Xu. It is the same for most of China's other people's organizations. More so than their Soviet comrades, CCP *waishi* cadres have been privileged in having a close understanding of their main target, the West, and in their policy documents they continually stress the advantage and necessity of this.

The Foreign Friends

> To make friends with foreigners is the effective way to strive for international sympathy and support. It is an important task of foreign affairs work and its most basic method.[74]

China's foreign affairs system, and in particular the friendship policies, could not have been created without the active cooperation of several generations of foreign friends. The efforts of China and other socialist countries to conduct people's diplomacy drew on a deep sense of alienation and utopianism among certain Western intellectuals. Particularly in the pre- and post-World War II era, those whom Paul Hollander called "political pilgrims" seem to have embraced the title of foreign friend willingly.[75] As visitors, they identified with the power of the victimized, underdeveloped communist world while maintaining their privilege as guests.

After the CCP seized power in 1949, the role of foreigners in friendship activities was complex; many were sympathetic to communist ideals, while desire for access and to be an insider may have attracted others. In the 1920s, 1930s, and 1940s, the foreign leftist community in China and beyond formed an ideological community. They were able to assist the CCP with cover for their illegal activities, passing on money, technology, weapons, and information. The foreign progressives were outsiders in the foreign community within China. Their support for the Chinese nationalist movement signaled an implicit rejection of the privilege foreigners enjoyed in China. Yet, ironically, if they had not had such privileges their assistance could have not been as effective.

For thirty years, from the 1950s to the 1970s, foreign access to China was severely limited. Only those foreigners who were willing to show themselves to be "friends" of China were welcome, and even they sometimes had difficulties obtaining visas. In this period, to be a friend entailed adherence to whatever the current political line was in Beijing, or at least for that part of it for which their cooperation was needed. Old friends who publicly questioned the party line were cast out and even in the liberal 1980s and 1990s, their assistance to the CCP in its early years was noticeably absent or considerably downplayed in official accounts.[76] Those unwilling, wittingly or not, to take on the friend label were restricted to observing China from afar. Tourists were few, and mostly limited to friendship tours where they were carefully guided through designated sites. Diplomats and journalists were even more confined. However, a select group of foreigners was allowed to live in China and work for the Chinese government. They were known as the foreign experts, *waiguo zhuanjia* or, more generally, foreign friends, *waiguo pengyou*. In addition to their technical assistance, these foreigners had an important symbolic role, one of which they were very conscious. They were nominated foreign friends as a mark of their special status differentiating them from diplomats and other foreigners in China. Unlike the imperialists of the past, the friends symbolized the new era in China's foreign relations, whereby Beijing would set the terms on which foreigners visited or lived in the country. The China-based friends worked as scientists, military advisers, propagandists, translators, teachers, medical personnel, researchers, and technicians. In the 1950s the foreigners were mostly from the Soviet Union and Eastern Europe, after 1960 their makeup was more diverse. Despite the economic and political changes of the post-Cultural Revolution era, foreign experts working in China continue to have a symbolic role.

Among the many generations of foreign friends, whether living in China or just visiting, it is noticeable that those who were writers or journalists received particular attention and favor. Following the methods of the Soviet Union, in addition to the propaganda work of its own writers, the CCP has long had a policy of encouraging foreign authors to write about the territory under its control. This is what is known as "using foreign strength to do propaganda work for China," *liyong waili wei wo xuanchuan*.[77] Foreign journalists such as Edgar Snow and Anna Louise Strong are among the earliest and best-known examples of this policy. *Waishi* historians frequently cite Snow's *Red Star over China* as the first of many foreign works that promoted CCP aims. The efforts of senior leaders Mao Zedong, Zhou Enlai, and others to host Snow on his first and later visits to CCP-controlled China are used as a model to later generations of *waishi* cadres as an example of successful hospitality work. Immense goodwill was built up towards the CCP in the Western world as a result of Snow's book and later writings of other foreigners. In the reform era, some of the most useful "friend" propagandists are deemed to be those pushing investment opportunities in China, but the principles and practices of hosting them and winning their support are little changed.

Apart from the efficacious method of propagandizing the "foreign strength" policy provides, the Chinese authorities believe it also has the benefit of encouraging influential foreigners to help China. CCP propagandists argue that because they are foreigners writing about China, other foreigners are likely to regard foreign friends as their own people, *ziji ren*, making them feel more accepting of their writing. Foreign journalists, foreign experts, and diplomats are regarded as particularly good candidates for propagandizing on China's behalf. But potentially the authorities believe any foreigner who lives, works in, or visits China can be a propagandist. Sometimes, a foreigner who is clearly not an admirer of Chinese communism can do the best propaganda work. The first step is for *waishi* cadres to do effective hospitality and propaganda work on them. If this is done well, foreigners will return home with a good impression. Getting foreigners to promote China makes economic sense, saving the government the cost of opening up public relations offices all over the world.

Making foreign friends has long been one of the most basic tasks of *waishi* cadres. One of the methods by which foreigners are encouraged to become friendly to the goals of the Chinese government is the promotion of a few prominent individuals as official "friends of China." There are a number of distinct ranks for China's "friends": the most basic is "foreign friend," sometimes used interchangeably with "international friend," *guoji youren*; next in rank is the title "old friend of the Chinese people," *Zhongguo renmin de lao pengyou*; and the highest accolades are "internationalist/internationalist fighter," *guojizhuyizhe/guojizhuyi zhanshi*; and "friendship envoy," *youhao waijiao shizhe*. These higher titles are reserved for those who have given long service to the Chinese revolution. Nevertheless, since the 1980s, highest status and its rewards are given to those who already have high standing, and more importantly, influence, in their own right, such as latter-day "old friends" Henry Kissinger, George Bush, Jacques Chirac, Sir Percy Cradock, and Australia's former prime minister Robert J. Hawke.

Less prominent foreigners can still become friends if they meet the needs of the government. A handbook on *waishi* written in 1995 advises:

> The more friends we have the better, yet we also have to be selective. We especially want to make friends with such foreigners who are friendly to us, have some social prestige, have economic power, or academic achievements, or have political influence; this will be most advantageous for the achievement of a peaceful international environment and to support our nation's economic construction.[78]

Friendship is not just from the Chinese side; many foreigners have enjoyed being described as a friend of China. Friendship appeals to foreigners who feel China is misunderstood; who are ashamed, or disapprove of the way the West treats China. To be a friend has implications of moral superiority over other foreigners in China. The desire to be seen as a friend of China, to participate in an alternative entity to Western society has been appealing to many in the past. China's friends are banqueted and praised; they are made to feel their input is useful and valuable.

The rewards for those who have conformed to such controls are high, both in terms of status, access to information, and in the current era, for many of China's high-profile former politician friends, monetary, in the form of consulting fees paid to them by firms who hope to use their connections to do business in China. If one resists the pressure to be seen to be friendly, the warm treatment from the Chinese side will suddenly cease. People will refuse to speak with you, and access will be denied. In more politically sensitive periods, there is an unspoken threat of excommunication, and loss of access to China, in some cases, possible imprisonment, or expulsion from the country. The pressure to conform is subtle, but pervasive. Sometimes it is nothing more than the deprivation of VIP status. In contrast, useful foreigners who are obedient and loyal will be banqueted and fêted, and given access that nonfriends are denied.

Commentators in the West have often portrayed China's foreign friends as politically naïve. But as we shall see, many of those who have maintained long-term relationships with the Chinese communists have a startlingly clear understanding of their role and its limitations. One longtime supporter, Max Granich, who was quoted earlier comparing the Soviets unfavorably with the Chinese communists, when asked if he would like to live in China full time told an interviewer, "That's a question mark. Not unless, not unless we can live in an environment that we feel free to talk easily. To develop Chinese friends and not the casual friend that comes and with a long session and finish, and it's through" [sic].[79] Granich's comments are apt and to the point: as we have seen, the CCP's political friendship is a deliberate strategy, an integral part of the PRC foreign affairs system. It is very different from the genuine friendships formed from ordinary human interaction. China's political friendship is clearly an application of united front principles to divide the enemy by focusing on contradictions and uniting all forces that can be united around a common goal.

The United Front and CCP Foreign Policy

> Can a communist, who is an internationalist, at the same time be a patriot? We hold that not only can he be but must be . . . patriotism is applied internationalism.[80]

Palmerston's well-known adage in international relations "there are no permanent friends, only permanent interests" fits CCP-style *waishi* well. Significantly, an important handbook on *waishi* written in the 1990s makes a point of quoting this maxim when discussing the nature and task of *waishi*.[81] CCP strategists have taken Lenin's tactic of forging temporary alliances with various groups against common enemies and exploiting rifts among enemy ranks, *liyong maodun*, and made it their own. Lenin wrote in *"Left-Wing" Communism: An Infantile Disorder*,

> The more powerful enemy can be vanquished only by exerting the utmost effort, and *without fail*, most thoroughly, carefully, attentively and skillfully using every, even the smallest, "rift" among the enemies, of every antagonism of interest among the bourgeoisie of the various countries and among the various groups or types of bourgeoisie within the various countries, and also by taking advantage of every, even the smallest, opportunity of gaining a mass ally, even though this ally be temporary, vacillating, unstable, unreliable and conditional. Those who fail to understand this, fail to understand even a particle of Marxism, or of scientific, modern Socialism *in general*.[82] (Italics in the original)

From the mid-1930s the CCP began to put the Comintern/Soviet strategy of using friendly "personages" to influence public opinion to wider use. The CCP's united front divided society into left (friends), right (enemies) and middle (neither for nor against). It was an adaptable strategy far more flexible than the Soviet Communist Party's concept of a united front between parties or armies.[83] The CCP united front could be used both against and with foreign groups, depending on the particular circumstances. It could be used to manipulate feelings both of patriotism, *aiguozhuyi* (the preferred CCP word for Chinese nationalism) and internationalism, *guojizhuyi*. Both elements have been alternating aspects of CCP foreign policy throughout the last eighty years though nationalism has tended to dominate, justified in Mao's terms as "applied internationalism."[84]

The CCP's united front implied ideological laxness and tolerance of difference; the means to offset the dangers of this was party discipline. Discipline united the will of *waishi* cadres, creating a uniform approach whatever the foreign policy tactic or activities were. The strength of CCP discipline was one of the key points setting the party apart from the Nationalist government, which both before and after 1949, also made efforts to create foreign friends favorable to its interests. Even in the current period, CCP discipline is supposed to be maintained by regular "rectification" campaigns and thorough training. In his influential study on the CCP's united front tactics, Lyman Van Slyke commented that the CCP's rectification campaigns aimed to create "a hard core immune to the impurities of united front allies, unable to be swayed from ultimate goals yet able to defer them for a prolonged period."[85]

United front alliances are inherently transient and end once they have achieved their goal. Van Slyke analyzed the united front within China as the CCP's long-term strategy for "neutralizing, isolating, and ultimately displacing and destroying" the power of Chinese society's middle and upper levels. This same strategy was used against the authority of foreigners in China in the pre- and post-1949 eras. In the period when it was still fighting to gain power before 1949, the CCP used foreign support for its activities to strengthen its position. After 1949, the CCP manipulated already existent antiforeign feeling within

China, polarizing foreigners into either friends or enemies. Diplomats, missionaries, aid workers, foreign business people, foreign things and ideas, all were scrutinized. CCP propaganda emphasized national self-sufficiency, partly out of necessity, partly out of nationalism, thereby forming a new united front within China, against U.S. imperialism. As a state founded on revolutionary struggle, China's leaders had to become astute in forming strategic allegiances.

As well as forming united fronts against foreign threats such as the Japanese or the United States, the CCP used the methodology of the united front to conduct its foreign relations. Theoretically "on behalf of the Chinese people," from the 1930s to the present day, CCP officials have met with those whom they call "foreign friends" and attempted to use relations with them to subvert and bypass the policies of unfavorable foreign governments. This strategy is known as "using the people to bring the governments closer together," *yi min cu guan*.[86] The tactic proved as useful in the Cold War era as it did in 1989. During times of political conflict with other nations, Chinese leaders stress that they are opposed to foreign governments and their policies, not to the "people" of those countries. In Marxist terms, this form of diplomacy is a form of class struggle, uniting the people of the world against a common enemy or for common goals. *Waishi* theorists in the 1990s claimed Mao Zedong and Zhou Enlai invented people's diplomacy, with other antecedents going back as far as the Zhou dynasty.[87] As we have seen, however, people's diplomacy was very much a creation of the Soviet Union long before the People's Republic of China came into being. The objectives of China's people's diplomacy are "to make as many friends as possible," *guangjiao pengyou*; "expose enemies," *jielu diren*; and "promote China," *xuanchuan ziji*.[88] Despite its name, people's diplomacy does not mean ordinary Chinese citizens can become diplomats, rather that the government makes use of a wide range of officially nonofficial contacts with other countries to expand its influence. People's diplomacy was an important means for conducting the CCP's foreign relations in the days when most countries recognized the Republic of China (ROC), rather than the People's Republic. Nowadays it is one of the most important means of conducting diplomacy for the ROC.[89]

In the years since 1949, China's people's or "friendship" diplomacy has focused on such goals as the diplomatic recognition of the PRC; attempts to influence public opinion in the West, and ultimately, to split blocs of power of countries opposed to the PRC; symbolic solidarity with the people of the world (meanwhile reordering the status of foreigners in China); and affirmation of China's global influence and status. In the era of reform and opening new issues have come to the fore, such as attracting foreign investment and technology; undermining attempts to sanction Beijing over its actions after June 4 and other human rights abuses since then; the diplomatic isolation of Taiwan; and affirmation of Beijing's right to control Tibet. China's friendship diplomacy is neither merely "cultural diplomacy" as it is usually defined, nor a naïve name for standard international diplomatic practices. It is a remarkably effective approach for dealing with the outside world. As a fundamental element of the *waishi* system, it symbolizes China's unique perspective on international relations and the means it adopts to achieve its objectives, as well as including some of the standard aspects of cultural diplomacy: publications, cultural exchanges, and so on. From the founding of the PRC in 1949 to the present day, Mao Zedong, Zhou Enlai, Deng Xiaoping, Jiang Zemin, and other senior leaders have all made statements describing China's external relations in terms of "half state-to-state diplomacy and half people's diplomacy." Although since the 1970s the PRC has established diplomatic relations with most nations, rather than declining, people's diplomacy activities have actually increased in the reform era.

China and the West

> Imperialist aggression shattered the fond dreams of the Chinese learning from the West. It was very odd—why were the teachers always committing aggression against their pupil? The Chinese learnt a great deal from the West, but they could not make it work and were never able to realize their ideals.[90]

In order to understand modern China's foreign policy and policy on foreigners it is useful to review some of the events of recent history from the perspective of CCP historiography. There are clear historical and political reasons for why foreigners occupy such an unusually sensitive position in the People's Republic of China, and these reasons have become part of the canon of CCP-guided history writing and are part of the litany of wrongs incurred by the West against China which inform the contemporary Chinese notion of the Other. The definitive CCP summary of the Opium War period and its outcome can be found in the *Selected Works of Mao Tse-tung* in essays such as "On the People's Democratic Dictatorship" and "On New Democracy."[91] Even in recent times, few mainland Chinese historians deviate significantly from Mao's analysis. Mao's thinking was a product of what Michael Hunt calls an "international affairs orthodoxy" which developed among the political Left in China between 1920-1934. This orthodoxy consisted of anti-imperialism, approval of the Soviet Union as a potential model for China, solidarity with other colonized peoples, and a desire to reform the international system.[92] According to this view, the *waishi* system and modern China's deeply suspicious attitude toward foreigners and the outside world are a logical and justifiable outcome of China's experiences. In the following paragraphs I will briefly cover some of the main points of this, to use David Apter's word "mytho-logical,"[93] understanding of Chinese history.

Mao Zedong dates China's modern history as beginning in 1840 after China's defeat in the Opium War.[94] According to this viewpoint, from this period on the traditional Chinese world order, which posited Chinese civilization at the center of a host of satellite states, was irrevocably destroyed. China's contact with the West in the nineteenth century challenged the entire state and social system in a way no other foreign incursion had ever been able to. As a result,

Mao notes, several generations of Chinese scholars, including himself "looked to the West for truth" for answers to the problems of China.[95] Qing-era reformers advocated a strategy known as self-strengthening, *zi qiang*. The term has its origins in the Song dynasty and meant implicitly both not yielding control to foreigners in China's foreign relations and the introduction of Western technology in China so that it could stand up to the Western powers.[96] Late-Qing reformers such as Li Hongzhang identified Western power as stemming from technological superiority. Li advocated what he referred to as "changing Chinese ways through barbarian methods," *yong yi bian Xia*.[97] Qing official Zhang Zhidong proposed the concept of "Chinese learning for fundamental principles, Western learning for practical applications," *Zhongxue wei ti, Xixue wei yong*. The objective was to make selective use of Western technology, not Western values or social structures. Both these approaches failed. During the Hundred Days of Reform (11 June-21 September 1898), scholars Kang Youwei and Liang Qichao proposed wide-scale reforms within the imperial structure, this too was thwarted by intransigence and intrigue within the Qing court.

After the 1911 revolution, the two-thousand-year-old imperial system finally collapsed. This had a strong antiforeign element, set off by the 1911 railway protection movement, which opposed foreign control of China's rail networks. Revolutionary leader Sun Yat-sen envisaged a modern China influenced by Western models. Yet according to Maoist historiography, the failure of this model due to corruption, warlordism, and foreign intervention led to widespread disillusionment in China with the Western system.

To Chinese radicals like Mao Zedong, the October 1917 revolution in Russia provided inspiration for China's struggle, and the Soviet leaders soon after provoked further admiration in China by being the first Western country to abolish their extraterritorial rights there. The success of the Bolshevik revolution gave Chinese intellectuals new tools to critique the Western system and offered an alternative model for China's development.[98] The Marxist concept of "feudalism" was used to describe the imperial system and China's collapse into warlordism, while "imperialism" explained the weakness of the Chinese state and the presence of foreign enclaves on her shores. China's national humiliation was linked to international forces; salvation was to come from uniting with the international working class.[99]

The Chinese Communist Party was founded in 1921 under the direction and guidance of the Comintern, and it continued to be discreetly funded and supported by it for many years afterwards. Foreign assistance and involvement in China's communist revolution was crucial to its success, but both for practical reasons of secrecy during the years of struggle before 1949 and even after,[100] and even more so because of nationalism, this influence and support was downplayed, denied, and discredited. Despite the internationalist ideals of its Marxist-Leninist ideology, China's communist revolution was to be primarily a movement of nationalist liberation. From its earliest origins, the CCP presented the revolution as totally Chinese, nationalistic, and patriotic, opposed to the foreign aggression that had weakened China so severely. Hence, the foreign ideology on which the party was based, the vital assistance of foreigners in the early years of setting up the party and supporting its development had to be downplayed. Over time, the CCP would even devise its own versions of communism, first Maoism, then Dengism, now even Jiangism. In China in the 1980s, capitalism was rediscovered as "socialism with Chinese characteristics," a semantic gloss necessary for China's psychological resurgence as a unique, independent state with its own culture and traditions.

For thirty years after the CCP victory in 1949, China's leaders rejected the Western capitalist system as a model for China and set to removing the traces of the colonialist past. Yet China needed technical assistance, trade, and knowledge from the West in order to modernize and strengthen itself. It had to operate in an international system dominated by Western structures and culture. The dilemma of China's new leaders was to both wean the Chinese people from the idea of the superiority of the West, while making use of the achievements which had helped make those countries rich and powerful. This would require both practical measures such as nationalizing foreign industries in China after 1949 and a massive, ongoing reeducation program, teaching Chinese people how to behave around foreigners.

From the earliest days of its formation, influenced by China's recent history and guided by Marxist-Leninism, the CCP stressed the importance of resolving the foreign presence in China, eradicating the harmful, taking what was useful and bringing it under Chinese control. The challenge for the CCP was to devise both a new foreign policy and a new policy towards foreigners. The *waishi* or foreign affairs system was set up to this end. *Waishi* symbolizes China's reconciliation with the outside world; it is a defensive tactic to control the threat of the impact of foreign society on the government's political power. China's *waishi* policies are a means to cope with the pressures of Westernization and modernization. They are part of the cultural crisis, a conflicting inferiority/superiority crisis that Chinese society has faced since its earliest contacts with the technologically superior Western world in the nineteenth century.

The sense of cultural crisis which *waishi* is a response to is symbolized by the handbooks on *waishi* etiquette that first circulated among the relatively small corps of foreign affairs workers in the 1950s and 1960s, but in the era of expanded Sino-foreign contact beginning in the 1980s, have virtually become a genre in themselves, targeted at any Chinese citizen who is likely to come into contact with a foreigner. Typically in such works, Chinese citizens are warned on points of etiquette such as "stand up straight," "keep your nose hair clipped," "don't pick your nose," and so on when in the company of foreigners. These lists of potential faux pas echo the concerns of Sun Yat-sen in his important 1924 speeches on the Three Principles of the People when he criticized the Chinese people's lack of concern about personal grooming and manners, thereby earning the disdain of foreigners. According to Sun, reclaiming the respect of foreigners would be a prerequisite for reclaiming the right to govern China.[101]

Similarly the Nationalist government's 1934 New Life Movement promulgated ninety-six regulations on matters such as daily hygiene and observing traffic regulations.[102] How one behaved in front of foreigners and how one behaved in front of Chinese people were matters for particular attention for many of those who have been concerned with reforming the Chinese body politic. In 1967 Jiang Qing lambasted Red Guards for engaging in violent struggle "*in front of foreigners*" (presumably if they did it when foreigners were not around, it was not so bad).[103] In recent years handbooks on the appropriate etiquette to be followed when in the company of foreigners have become widespread.

Because *waishi* is a reflection of China's response to modernization, I would argue that its main target is the West (which I assume to include the United States, Western Europe, Japan, and the British Commonwealth countries of Canada, Australia, and New Zealand). This has been especially so since the period of "reform and opening" began in 1978-1979.[104] Though countries of the developing world are also affected by *waishi* policies such as friendship diplomacy, they are not currently the primary targets. China's championing of Africa, Asia, and Latin America in the first thirty years of its existence was an attempt to realign international forces, marshaling the power of the weak, underdeveloped, colonized countries to form a moral united front against the West. CCP rhetoric notwithstanding, China's leaders do not identify with the developing world. China's mirror, the model it aspires to, is the Western world. In the Chinese psyche, the globe is divided between East (represented by China) and West (the European and Europeanized countries), the rest of the world is peripheral to the fundamental goal of achieving China's preeminence in international affairs. China's leaders see their country through the eyes of the Western world; all achievements and failures are measured against that mirror.

China's senior leaders have long been obsessed with the belief that one of the most important goals of the Chinese revolution was to catch up with, and eventually exceed, the development of the Western countries. From the call of Mao Zedong in 1958 that China would exceed Great Britain's industrialization in fifteen years,[105] to Jiang Zemin's desire to make China into a superpower,[106] it is clear that China's modern leaders aspire to challenge the prevailing world order. This desire stems from a historical sense of China being at the center of world events and consciousness. A national sense of pride towards imperial China's history and culture demands that modern China too should be acknowledged as a major power. Ultimately, the long-term objectives of the CCP's *waishi* strategies, from the 1930s to the present day, are not aimed at developing solidarity with the underdeveloped world. The CCP's long-term goal has been to regain what many Chinese believe is China's rightful place in the world as a leading power, if not *the* leading power.

China's foreign policy in the last 150 years has focused, whether directly or indirectly, primarily on relations with the developed countries of the West. Since 1949, the CCP-led government has sought not only to become equal with, and even surpass, the West on a material level, it has also sought to destroy the psychological power of Western might and the authority that comes with that might. The careful reconstruction of the past, in particular constantly invoking the wrongs committed by the Western powers in China, is one of the means by which the CCP legitimates its power. The communist authorities have constructed a notion of the ancestral land, *zuguo*, which legitimates their rule. To oppose this rule is to be unpatriotic, even unfilial. The slogan which sums up this concept "Without the communist party there would be no new China," *mei you gongchandang, jiu mei you xin Zhongguo,* is a phrase drummed into the consciousness of all Chinese people. In CCP ideology, the party *is* new China, the spiritual and actual embodiment of the resurgence of an ancient civilization. The foundation mythology of the PRC posits the horror of the oppressor Western countries against the innocence of the Chinese people, using victimhood as a weapon. In its historical accounts the CCP depicts itself as the savior that rescued the Chinese people from the brutality of Western oppression.

Since 1949, for ideological as well as strategic reasons, the foreign presence in China has been strictly controlled. The imperialist past is continually stressed; it is used to chasten foreigners and remind them of their guilt. It is also used to unite Chinese people against a common foreign enemy. Hence, China's relationship with the West, both in the past and in the present day, is also an important tool in government control, part of its claim to legitimacy. This is what Chen Xiaomei describes as "official Occidentalism": whereby the Chinese government uses its essentialization of the West to create a form of state-controlled nationalism that ultimately effects the internal suppression of the Chinese people.[107] Chen's analysis concerns the 1980s and early 1990s, but as my research demonstrates, her theory is apt for describing the policies of the CCP from its earliest days. Arthur Waldron has described similarly the "internal dimension" to PRC foreign policy, which utilizes the history of imperialist aggression against China to unite the population.[108] Victimism has been a powerful and useful narrative to China's communist leaders. Government propaganda focuses on the harm caused to China by the foreign presence, while downplaying the violence of Chinese against Chinese in the turbulent history of the last 150 years— the Taiping Rebellion, the Nationalist government and assorted warlords, and the actions of the Chinese Communist Party itself in its struggle to gain power and then maintain it.

Antiforeignism is not only engendered by the CCP government.[109] In fact, at times the government has had trouble containing the intense xenophobia and antiforeign feelings in China. Chinese who are overly interested in Western society and culture are scorned by their critics with the term *chong yang mei wai* (to fawn over and idolize all things foreign),[110] cursed as foreign "running dogs" (*zougou*), and satirized with the earthy *waiguoren de pi dou shi xiang de* (even foreign farts are fragrant).[111] Those who choose to leave China and live elsewhere are often accused of being insufficiently *aiguo* (patriotic). Chinese leaders risk being called "traitors" (*han jian*) for appearing to be too conciliatory to Western interests. Such epithets embody a deep-seated cultural antagonism to the outside world. Many Chinese people regard evincing a more than superficial or pragmatic interest in Western societies and culture as a form of national betrayal. Even those Chinese who have spent all their lives or several generations outside China, are considered to be Chinese both by the government and Chinese people, and they are expected to consider themselves as such. As the government is well aware, nationalism is a powerful force for unity in Chinese society.

Notes

1. Mao Tse-tung, "Analysis of the Classes in Chinese Society," *Selected Works of Mao Tse-tung*, vol. 1 (Peking: Foreign Languages Press, 1961), 13.
2. Zhou Enlai, speech to Chinese diplomats, 30 April 1952, Zhou Enlai, *Selected Works*, vol. 2 (Beijing: Foreign Languages Press, 1984), 98.
3. Zhao Pitao, *Waishi gaishuo*, 30.
4. Zhao Pitao, *Waishi gaishuo*, 3.
5. "Friendship Cities Bear Fruits," *Voice of Friendship* (February 1988): 16.
6. "Friendship Cities Bear Fruits," 16.
7. Interview with *waishi* cadres, December 1997.
8. See Lionel M. Jensen, *Manufacturing Confucianism: Chinese Traditions and Universal Civilization* (Durham and London: Duke University Press, 1997).
9. This is, in fact, the name of a book that was part of the study program for CCP cadres in the 1930s, N. Bukharin and E. Preobrazhensky, *The ABC of Communism*, edited by E. H. Carr (London: Penguin Books, 1969).
10. See Stephen Koch, *Double Lives: Spies and Writers in the Secret Soviet War of Ideas against the West* (New York: The Free Press, Macmillan Inc., 1994).
11. Clive Rose, *The Soviet Propaganda Network: A Directory of Organizations Serving Soviet Foreign Policy* (London: Pinter Publishers, 1988), 30-32.
12. Rose, *The Soviet Propaganda Network*, 37.
13. Frederick C. Barghoorn, *The Soviet Cultural Offensive: The Role of Cultural Diplomacy in Soviet Foreign Policy* (Princeton: Princeton University Press, 1960), v.
14. Barghoorn, *The Soviet Cultural Offensive*, 11.
15. Rose, *The Soviet Propaganda Network*, 25.
16. Barghoorn, *The Soviet Cultural Offensive*, 17.
17. Barghoorn, *The Soviet Cultural Offensive*, 162.
18. Barghoorn, *The Soviet Cultural Offensive*, 162.
19. Barghoorn, *The Soviet Cultural Offensive*, 162.
20. Sylvia R. Margulies, *The Pilgrimage to Russia: The Soviet Union and the Treatment of Foreigners, 1924-1937* (Madison, Milwaukee, and London: The University of Washington Press, 1968), 91.
21. Margulies, *The Pilgrimage to Russia*, 94.
22. Margulies, *The Pilgrimage to Russia*, 95.
23. Margulies, *The Pilgrimage to Russia*, 115.
24. Margulies, *The Pilgrimage to Russia*, 121.
25. Margulies, *The Pilgrimage to Russia*, 125-126.

26.   J. Bernard Hutton, *The Great Illusion* (London: David Bruce and Watson Ltd., 1970), 31.

27.   Margulies, *The Pilgrimage to Russia*, 127.

28.   Margulies, *The Pilgrimage to Russia*, 135.

29.   Barghoorn, *The Soviet Cultural Offensive*, 103.

30.   Robert Robinson with Jonathan Slevin, *Black on Red: My 44 Years inside the Soviet Union* (Washington, D.C.: Acropilis Books, 1988), 13.

31.   Robinson, *Black on Red*, 141.

32.   Robinson and Ross both owed their place and role in the Soviet Union to their skin color and nationality. In the internal and external propaganda war against the United States, it was useful for the Soviets to maintain a number of high-profile black Americans who could talk about racial discrimination in the Western world and promote the racial harmony of the Soviet system in contrast.

33.   Robinson, *Black on Red*, 308.

34.   Hans Magnus Enzensberger, "Tourists of the Revolution," in *Raids and Reconstructions* (London: Pluto Press, 1976), 231.

35.   See Paul Hollander, "Durable Significance of Political Pilgrimage," *Society* 34, no. 5 (July-August 1997): 45-55.

36.   *Yin shui bu wang jue jing ren*, Zhao Pitao, *Waishi gaishuo*, 80.

37.   Max Granich, interview transcript, 8, Granich papers, New York University Library.

38.   Max Granich, interview transcript, 79.

39.   Lu Xun, *Lu Xun quanji*, vol. 1 (Beijing, 1963), 314, quoted in Simon Leys, *Chinese Shadows* (Harmondsworth, Middlesex: Penguin, 1978), ii.

40.   Mao Tse-tung, "On New Democracy," *Selected Works of Mao Tse-tung*, vol. 2 (Peking: Foreign Languages Press, 1975), 369.

41.   See Schram, *The Thought of Mao Tse-tung* (Cambridge: Cambridge University Press, 1989), 72.

42.   Schram, *The Thought of Mao Tse-tung*, 72-73.

43.   Robin Lakoff in the preface to Zhan Kaidi, *The Strategies of Politeness in the Chinese Language* (Berkeley: Institute of East Asian Studies, UCLA at Berkeley, 1992), x.

44.   Lakoff in the preface to Zhan Kaidi, *The Strategies of Politeness*, x.

45.   It should be noted that the *nei wai you bie* policy does not only concern foreigners, the concept of insiders and outsiders is also used for circumscribing relations between party members and nonparty members, and contact between overseas Chinese and native born Chinese.

46.   See Zhao Pitao, *Waishi gaishuo*, 17.

47.   "Duiwai bianji jiagong de ABC," *DWBDCK*, no. 2 (1983): 29.

48.   "Duiwai bianji jiagong de ABC," 29.

49.   See for example, Zhu Muzhi, "Guanyu duiwai xuanchuan de jige wenti," 10 September 1981, *ZMZ*, 26; "Dali jiaqiang guoji yulun douzheng," 5 July 1989, *ZMZ*, 233.

50.   See Stuart Schram, *The Thought of Mao Tse-tung*, 73.

51.   Analects Book 13.3, Wing-Tsit Chan, *A Source Book in Chinese Philosophy* (Princeton, N. J.: Princeton University Press, 1963), 40.

52.   See David L. Hall and Roger T. Ames, *Thinking through Confucius* (Albany: State University of New York, 1987), 299.

53.   Mao Tse-tung, "Analysis of the Classes in Chinese Society," *Selected Works*, vol. 1, 27.

54.   On the subject of the importance of *guanxi* and *ganqing* in Chinese society see Mayfair Mei-hui Yang, *Gifts, Favors, and Banquets: The Art of Social Relationships in China* (Ithaca and London: Cornell University Press, 1994), and Andrew Kipnis, *Producing Guanxi: Sentiment, Self, and Subculture in a Northern China Village* (Durham, N.C.: Duke University Press, 1997). Here I draw both on my understanding of Yang and Kipnis's work and on instructional material for *waishi* cadres.

55.   According to Mayfair Mei-hui Yang, *guanxixue* "the exchange of gifts, favors and banquets; the cultivation of personal relationships and networks of mutual dependence; and the manufacturing of obligation and indebtedness" (Yang, 6) is "oppositional to state power" (Yang, 174). Yang formulates a chronology of popular *guanxixue* that began to develop after the end of the Cultural Revolution. In the context of CCP foreign relations, however, *guanxixue* has been an important element in the CCP repertoire for building alliances and defeating enemies. For the CCP, *guanxixue* is a diplomatic guerrilla tactic using *guanxi* to get access or gain support through nonofficial channels.

56.   Raymond Cohen, *Negotiating across Cultures: Communication Obstacles in International Diplomacy* (Washington, D.C.: United States Institute of Peace Press, 1991), 154.

57.   Kipnis, *Producing Guanxi*, 27.

58.   Wang Yonghua, "Zhou Enlai de waijiao yishu," *DWXCCK*, 7 (1994): 5-8.

59.   "Jin yi bu gaige waishi baodao," *DWBDCK*, 20 (1983): n.p.

60.   See for example, Duiwai maoyi jingji hezuobu jiaojishi, ed., *Shewai liyi ABC* (Beijing: Zhongguo renmin chubanshe, 1997); Li Guosheng, Wang Enhong, eds., *Waishi zhishi gailan* (Shenyang: Baishan chubanshe, 1993), 30; Liu Renmin, Li Qun, eds., *Xiandai shewai liyi* (Beijing: Zhongguo huanjing kexue chubanshe, 1997), 4; Pei Xiannong, *Zhou Enlai de waijiaoxue*, 222-224, 226-227.

61.   This principle is sometimes referred to as *rou yuanren* and *rouyuan*.

62.   The traditional term for this practice was "using guest etiquette to bring other states close," *yi binli qin bangguo*, James L. Hevia, *Cherishing Men from Afar: Qing Guest Ritual and the Macartney Embassy* (Durham, N.C.: Duke University Press, 1995), 120.

63.   The *Cihai* (1989 edition) dictionary locates the earliest reference to *huai rou* in the Book of Odes, "to appease the spirits," *huai rou bai shen*, and in the *History of the Three Kingdoms*, we find "the superior man sets the style, gracious to strangers he overcomes all things," *jun xuan dao ti feng, huai rou bai yue*. The term *huai yuan* can also be found in *Huai Nanzi*, "Magnanimous so as to contain the masses, virtuous so as to pacify those who come from afar," *da zu yi rong zhong, de zu yi huai yuan*. In the *Mao zhuan* we find "When guests come from afar, treat them graciously and there will be peace," *huai, lai, rou, an*.

64.   Hevia, *Cherishing Men from Afar*, 117.

65.   Hevia, *Cherishing Men from Afar*, 145.

66.   Hevia, *Cherishing Men from Afar*, 118.

67.   Hevia, *Cherishing Men from Afar*, 143.

68.   Hevia, *Cherishing Men from Afar*, 61.

69.   Chen Benlin, *Shewai zhishi daquan* (Shanghai: Shanghai renmin chubanshe, 1989), 774.

70.   Chen Benlin, *Shewai zhishi daquan*, 771.

71.   Chen Benlin, *Shewai zhishi daquan*, 756.
72.   Sun Tzu, *The Art of War*, translated by Lionel Giles (London: Hodder and Stoughton, 1995): 26-27.
73.   See Lu Ding, *The Dynamics of Foreign Policy Decisionmaking in China* (Boulder, Colo.: Westview, 1997): 42-43.
74.   Zhao Pitao, *Waishi gaishuo*, 166.
75.   Paul Hollander, *Political Pilgrims: Travels of Western Intellectuals to the Soviet Union, China, and Cuba* (New York: Oxford University Press, 1981).
76.   For example Otto Braun (mentioned in chapter 3) sent by the Comintern to help the CCP in the early 1930s and the only foreigner to go on the Long March ended up on bad terms with the CCP leadership and his contribution is always derided in official histories. "Asiaticus" (Heinz Schippe) an Austrian communist who died fighting the Japanese alongside CCP forces in 1942, criticized both Edgar Snow and Mao and is barely mentioned in official histories. Foreigners sent by the Comintern generally receive a bad write-up (if they receive any mention at all) in official histories, as do Soviet advisers. British academic Michael Lindsay (mentioned in chapter 3) was excommunicated after he criticized the PRC's foreign policy after 1949. Contemporary accounts of his work in Yan'an with Xinhuashe are very unfavorable to him. Journalists Wilfred Burchett and Alan Winnington (mentioned in chapter 4) who were both very useful to China in promoting propaganda about the UN Command's alleged use of germ warfare in the Korean War, fell foul of the Chinese government after they expressed different views from the official line. Winnington fell out over the Sino-Soviet split and what he regarded as China's increasing belligerence, while Burchett chose to take the Vietnamese side in the Sino-Vietnam war. If one did not know the reasons why, it would seem particularly curious that Burchett is not commemorated by China or his native Australia as a "friend of China" for his work as a journalist both before and after 1949. In Australia, Burchett is still regarded as a "traitor" for reporting for the other side during the Korean War, while in China his support for the Vietnamese put him beyond the pale.
77.   Information for the following two paragraphs is based on the article "Guanyu liyong waili wei wo xuanchuan," *DWXCCK*, no. 23 (1985): 4.
78.   Zhao Pitao, *Waishi gaishuo*, 166-167.
79.   Granich, interview transcript, 431.
80.   Mao Tse-tung, "The Role of the Chinese Communist Party in the National War," *Selected Works of Mao Tse-tung*, vol. 2 (Peking: Foreign Languages Press, 1961), 196.
81.   Zhao Pitao, *Waishi gaishuo*, 2.
82.   V. I. Lenin, *"Left-Wing" Communism, an Infantile Disorder* (Moscow: Foreign Languages Publishing House, 1950), 91. Stalin quotes this in an article written after the end of the first united front between the CCP and the Nationalists. See, "Notes on Contemporary Themes: China," in *The Essential Stalin, Major Theoretical Writings 1905-52*, ed. B. Franklin (London: C. Helm, 1973), 207-208.
83.   Gregor Benton, *New Fourth Army: Communist Resistance along the Yangtze and the Huai, 1938-1941* (Richmond, Surrey: Curzon, 1999), 171.
84.   There is no one term in modern Chinese that fully translates all the shaded meanings of "nationalism" as it is understood in English. It can be translated as "*guojiazhuyi*" a literal translation that could also mean "statism," other translations of the term are "*minzuzhuyi*," which has implications of ethnic-based nationalism, similarly "*mincuizhuyi*;" "*daguozhuyi*," which implies chauvinism, and finally Mao's preferred term "*ai-*

guozhuyi," literally "love of the nation." As Mao rationalized in his speech "The Role of the Chinese Communist Party in the National War," *Selected Works of Mao Tse-tung*, vol. 2, 196, for Chinese communists, love of China, to the point of defending its borders and national interests was a form of internationalism.

85.   Lyman P. Van Slyke, *Enemies and Friends: The United Front in Chinese Communist History* (Stanford: Stanford University Press, 1967), 115-116.

86.   Pei Xiannong, *Zhou Enlai de waijiaoxue*, 272; interview with *waishi* cadres, December 1997.

87.   See for example, Zhao Pitao, *Waishi gaishuo*, 72.

88.   Interview with *waishi* cadres, December 1997.

89.   See Chen Jie, "Beyond Diplomacy," *Free China Review* 49, no. 4 (April 1999): 36-41; and Maysing Yang, ed., *Taiwan's Expanding Role in the International Arena* (Armonk, New York: M. E. Sharpe, 1997).

90.   "On the People's Democratic Dictatorship," *Selected Works of Mao Tse-tung*, vol. 4 (Peking: Foreign Languages Press, 1961), 413.

91.   *Selected Works of Mao Tse-tung*, vols. 2 and 4 (Peking: Foreign Languages Press, 1961).

92.   Hunt, *The Genesis of Chinese Communist Foreign Policy*, 83-84.

93.   See David E. Apter, "Yan'an and the Narrative Reconstruction of Reality," *Daedalus*, 122, no. 2 (Spring 1993): 207-253.

94.   "The People's Democratic Dictatorship," *Selected Works of Mao Tse-tung*, vol. 4, 412.

95.   "The People's Democratic Dictatorship," *Selected Works of Mao Tse-tung*, 413.

96.   Kwang-ching Liu, "The Beginnings of Modernization," in *Li Hungchang and China's Early Modernization*, ed. Samuel C. Chu and Kwang-Ching Liu (New York: M. E. Sharpe, 1994), 6.

97.   Kwang-ching Liu, "The Beginnings of Modernization," 11.

98.   Schram, *The Thought of Mao Tse-tung*, 131.

99.   Saich, *The Rise to Power of the CCP*, xiiv.

100.   See "Zhongyang xuanchuanbu guanyu bianji chuban huiyi dixia douzheng duiwu yingdang zhuyi wenti de tongzhi," 29 April 1982, *DDXC*, vol. 2, 1020-1022; "Zhongyang xuanchuanbu zhuanfa renmin chubanshe 'Guanyu chuban huiyilu zhong yixie wenti de chuli banfa' de tongzhi," 30 November 1982, *DDXC*, vol. 2, 1035-1040; "Zhongyang xuanchuanbu bangongting guanyu sheji waiguo zhuanjia de jishixing baogao wenxue zuopin yingzhuyi de wenti de tongzhi," 27 March 1990, *DDXC*, vol. 4, 1981.

101.   John Fitzgerald, *Awakening China: Politics, Culture, and Class in the Nationalist Revolution* (Stanford: Stanford University Press, 1996), 9-12.

102.   Jean Chesneaux, Françoise le Barbier, Marie-Claire Bergère, *China: From the 1911 Revolution to Liberation* (New York: Pantheon Books, 1977), 205-206.

103.   "Tan waishikou wuchanjieji wenhua dageming," *Waishi zhanbao*, 18 September 1967, 1.

104.   See Zhu Muzhi's comments in "Geng hao fahui duiwai he dui Tai xuanchuan de zuoyong," 16 May 1987, *ZMZ*, 164.

105.   Maurice Meisner, *Mao's China and After: A History of the People's Republic* (New York: The Free Press, 1986), 211.

106.   Quoted in "Jiang Wants Foreign Policy Role Immortalized," *South China Morning Post*, (hereafter *SCMP*), 16 July 1998.

107.   Chen Xiaomei, *Occidentalism: A Theory of Counter-Discourse in Post-Mao China* (New York: Oxford University Press, 1995), 5.

108.   Arthur Waldron, "Friendship Reconsidered," *Free China Review* (April 1993): 56.

109.   For a detailed study on this topic, see Liao Kiang-Sheng, *Anti-foreignism and Modernization in China 1860-1980* (Hong Kong: The Chinese University Press, 1984).

110.   See for example *Shewai renyuan shouce* (Guangzhou: Xinhua shudian, 1985), 19-20.

111.   The late Qing novelist Wu Chien-jun complained "To the comprador, even the foreigner's fart is fragrant," Lynn Pan, *Tracing It Home: Journeys around a Chinese Family* (London: Secker and Warburg, 1992), 68. In 1956 Mao indicated his concern at a potential psychological dependence on the Soviet Union with the comment, "some people are so indiscriminating that they say a Russian fart is fragrant." Mao Tse-tung, *Selected Works*, vol. 5, 317; Peter Vladimirov, *The Vladimirov Diaries: Yenan, China: 1942-1945* (New York: Doubleday and Co., 1975), 72.

Chapter 3

Internationalists

The Soviet Union didn't have the drawing power that China had. You could always sense that there was a difference there. . . . The Yan'an Spirit was exhilarating. Material life was difficult . . . we were not all that demanding of material comforts . . . the life there was tough, but if you got used to it, it was like camping out.

—Joan Hinton[1]

The years when the CCP based itself in Yan'an are remembered as a golden age by many of China's best-known foreign Maoists, only a handful of whom spent more than a few months there, where they lived in relative comfort, high up the cadre ranking scale.[2] For Joan Hinton, as for many foreign and Chinese Maoists alike, Yan'an was less a place, than a state of mind—site of the "Yan'an spirit." For the CCP's foreign admirers, the CCP's years at Yan'an, coinciding with some of the worst years of the Stalinist purges in the Soviet Union, are symbolic of what they see as the difference between Maoist and Stalinist communism. In *waishi* terms, the Yan'an era is important as marking the time when the CCP began to develop its foreign support network and worked on expanding its contacts with foreign embassies based in China. Foreign supporters of the CCP in the late 1930s and 1940s garnered foreign sympathy, assistance, and legitimacy for the party and strengthened the international united front. The Yan'an era was certainly the time when many of what would become the trademark features of CCP-style foreign affairs were tried out and perfected. Yet, I would argue that many of these policies were a development of trends that had been apparent from the CCP's earliest days. To claim that CCP foreign policy or policies on foreigners developed solely from this period, as most scholars in China do,[3] is a reflection of the Maoist stranglehold on CCP history, whereby virtually every achievement is attributed to Mao's leadership and every mistake to his enemies. Because anti-imperialism was such a fundamental element of Chinese communist rhetoric foreigners always had a sensitive role within the CCP, even supportive ones such as the Comintern advisers and foreign admirers like Joan Hinton.

China's *Lafayettes*: Foreigners and the Chinese Revolution

The task of distinguishing between the useful and harmful consequences of China's contact with the West was a particular concern for China's reformers in the late-Qing and early Republican period. The founding of the CCP in 1921 was a result of both these and other indigenous political trends and the Soviet Union's early efforts to export revolution. In early 1920, foreign revolutionaries from all over the world traveled to the Soviet Union to attend the Second Congress of the Third International (more commonly known as the Comintern). Soviet leaders believed their government had a twofold task: both to make the Soviet system work and to facilitate the spread of communism all over the world.[4] Not long after the May 4th movement of 1919, a tiny number of study groups formed in a few of China's major cities to discuss Marxist philosophy. In the spring of 1920, the Comintern dispatched two agents, Gregory Voitinsky and Yang Mingzhai, to assist in setting up a Chinese Communist Party. Voitinsky set up headquarters in Shanghai and assembled a group of leftists who formed the nucleus of the new party.[5] In 1921 the Comintern sent Maring (Henk Sneevliet) to attend the First Congress of the CCP. Maring's influence was quite strong at that time; as a result of his advice the Third Congress of the CCP decided in 1923 that the Chinese communists should forge an alliance with the Nationalists and make use of their administrative structures for the CCP's own revolutionary purposes.[6] It was also in 1923 that Michael Borodin came to China as a representative of the Soviet government and adviser to Sun Yat-sen. Soon after his arrival in Canton, Borodin and his Russian colleagues began reorganizing the Nationalist government and armies along Soviet lines.[7] Under the terms of the first united front between the Nationalist government and the tiny Communist Party, CCP members were merged into the Nationalist military and bureaucracy.

Sun Yat-sen sought out and welcomed foreign assistance to his cause: he often said that the Chinese revolution "should have its Lafayettes no less than the American."[8] Sun Yat-sen also attempted to manage and manipulate foreigners, and had his own troupe of foreign supporters. Sun wanted a united and strong China that could "regulate and police foreign enterprise."[9] He argued that the "former imperialists could be made to serve China's economic development, while earning a reasonable profit for themselves."[10] Sun hoped to attract foreign investment and make use of foreign technology. In the 1920s, there was optimism and desire for a new style of Chinese-foreign relations based on equality and "friendship." The Soviet Union's relations with the Nationalist government in Canton were a model for such optimism. However, enthusiasm would eventually sour following the actions of influential Comintern officials such as Maring, Borodin, and M. N. Roy.

While the Soviet government sent advisers to help the Nationalists, the Soviet-dominated Comintern sent advisers to guide and observe the CCP's development. It provided most of the fledgling party's funds in its earliest years, and paid for cadres to undergo training in Moscow. Although the Chinese revolutionaries were grateful for the assistance they received, much tension was felt at the dictatorial behavior of those sent to guide the party in the 1920s. The Chinese revolutionaries' traditional term for foreigners, especially foreign communists, was Maozi (the Hairy Ones).[11] Wang Fanxi, onetime CCP cadre who later became a Trotskyist, wrote in his memoirs of the hostility of senior party activists toward cadres who had undertaken "foreign study"—such as studying at Sun Yat-sen University in Moscow—which he says reflected their general contempt for theory.[12]

From 1921 to the mid-1930s, all foreign powers except Soviet Russia were described as "imperialist" in party documents. Anti-imperialist education was an important part of CCP indoctrination. During the period of the first united front between the Nationalists and the CCP (and particularly after 1924) the Nationalist government also adopted a strident tone against the foreign presence in China, demanding an end to the unequal treaties. In 1926 the Nationalist forces, led by Chiang Kai-shek (who had taken over the leadership of the party after the death of Sun Yat-sen in 1925), launched the Northern Expedition aimed at reuniting the rest of China. After a succession of rapid victories, a Joint Council composed of communists and leftist Nationalists formed in Wuhan, in preparation for the arrival of the full Nationalist government from the south, which was to make Wuhan its new capital.[13] Maud Russell, later to become an outspoken supporter of Mao's China in the United States during the McCarthy era, was a missionary working for the YWCA and living in Wuhan at the time of the revolutionary government there of 1926-1927. She recorded what she saw in regular letters home:

> One of the most significant things that happened on Sun Wen's[14] birthday was a letter issued by the Kuomintang (Revolutionary Party) [the Nationalists] to their "foreign friends": it appeared in the foreign newspapers and thousands of copies were distributed in the foreign concessions. It expressed cordial and friendly sentiments to foreigners in general in this country. After all the denunciation of everything foreign by the more radical groups in China it comes as a surprise to have the party admitting that everything in China is not yet perfect, that the West has helped China in spirit and in material; it expresses the hope that "our dear friends of various nations will cooperate for the maintenance of the peace of the world, the improvement of human welfare, and the development of the worldly civilization." Here one sees proof that the Revolutionary Government wants to cooperate with rather than antagonize outside powers.[15]

Russell reported that the trade union headquarters in Wuhan made a distinction between missionary foreigners and "community foreigners," meaning those who were there to do business in China. Only those Chinese who worked for "community foreigners" had to go on strike, those who worked for missionaries did not.[16]

Russell collected the handbills of the revolutionary government during its brief few months of existence. One she found heralding the arrival of the Soviet adviser Borodin to the revolutionary capital is a model of *waishi* education. The notice is entitled "The Welcome to the Nationalist Official and Adviser Borodin":

> Adviser Borodin is our dearly loved friend. He is a comrade who links us in strength to the Soviet; he is a leader of the World Revolution. He has put forth great effort in helping China's Revolutionary Movement. On all sides is the sound of military victory. The leaders of the World Revolution have all come to Wuhan which was held by the Northern militarists for so many years. We are almost beside ourselves with joy.[17]

There were a number of other Comintern agents working in Wuhan at this time. Among them were veteran propagandists William and Rayna Prohme, who were part of a network that promoted Soviet foreign policy objectives.[18] The Moscow-based radical American journalist Anna Louise Strong also arrived in the new capital to report on and promote the revolutionary government.

Anti-imperialism was an essential unifying element in the Chinese revolution and it was constantly stressed in party propaganda during the 1920s and early 1930s. Among other handbills Russell found was the following: "The imperialists have used the chloroform of a cultural invasion. In China they have opened not a few schools where this chloroform is sold. The fruit of these schools, other than a few foreign slave graduates are a few patriotic students who have all been driven out."[19] It was an indication of an obsession that would be a feature of Chinese politics in the years to come: fear of the enemy within, of those who had succumbed to foreign dominance and were potentially agents for foreign influence.

1927-1936 Isolation and Anti-imperialism

The first united front between the CCP and the Nationalist government ended violently in April 1927, when Chiang Kai-shek split with the communists and purged the Nationalist Party of leftist influence. The CCP went underground in the cities and began to develop its own armed forces, retreating into remote mountain areas in Jiangxi, Fujian, and elsewhere, far from the foreign enclaves and centers of Nationalist power. CCP foreign policy in this period developed under the guidance of Comintern analysis and priorities, a model that at times conflicted with the realities in China.[20] Though the stage that the Chinese revolutionary process had reached was a topic of debate between Trotskyists and Stalinists, there was no debate on the necessity of anti-imperialism for China's future. Given foreign support for Chiang's crushing of CCP supporters, it is not surprising that in the first few years after the collapse of the united front, the party line on the foreign presence became strident, even violent.[21] Nevertheless, in the long run, the necessities of survival and a pragmatic view of the advantages of creating allies, however temporary, forged the prevalence of a more tolerant attitude toward foreigners in China. At the Third Plenum of the Sixth Central Committee of the CCP in 1930, Zhou Enlai and Li Lisan were among those arguing for this new approach. It was agreed at the plenum that contact with "imperialists" did not constitute capitulation and would not necessarily threaten the anti-imperialist spirit of the Chinese people. It was hoped that taking a more conciliatory attitude would weaken opposition to the CCP and accentuate contradictions. In theory, hostile acts were to be avoided.[22] In reality, however, communist groups in some areas continued attacks on foreign boats and took foreigners, especially missionaries, as hostages. A former employee of the British firm Butterfield and Swire who skippered a ship along the middle part of the Yangzi River recalled He Long's forces as being particularly active in these activities in the early 1930s.[23] In 1932 in Anhui, a Canadian missionary named Ferguson was kidnapped by communist forces and exhibited through the streets in a cage. He died from the ordeal.[24] To try and restrain this sort of behavior, in 1930, 1931, and 1934 detailed instructions were issued on how to deal with foreigners active in areas under communist control. According to these guidelines, foreign businesspeople and missionaries who respected CCP regulations and political authority were to be unharmed, and random firing against foreign ships was prohibited.[25] These milder policies on dealing with foreigners did not mean the CCP had put aside more long-term revolutionary goals. The 1931 Constitution of the Chinese Soviet Republic declared:

> The soviet regime of China shall set itself the goal of freeing China from the yoke of imperialism. It shall declare the complete sovereignty and independence of the Chinese people, shall refuse to recognize any political or economic privileges for the imperialists in China, and shall abolish all unequal treaties and foreign loans contracted by the counter-revolutionary governments. No foreign imperialist troops, whether land, sea, or air shall be allowed to be stationed on any territory of the Chinese soviets. All concessions or territories leased by the imperialists in China shall be unconditionally returned to China. All customs houses, railways, steamship companies, mining enterprises, factories, etc., in the hands of the imperialists shall be confiscated and nationalized. At the present time, it shall be permissible for foreign enterprises to renew their leases (for their various businesses) and to continue production, provided they fully comply with the laws of the soviet government.[26]

At the same time, the constitution offered asylum to Chinese and foreign revolutionaries persecuted for their revolutionary activities; and foreigners living in areas under the jurisdiction of the Soviet regime were to enjoy equal rights as stipulated by Soviet law. The party declared readiness to form a united revolutionary front with the world proletariat and all oppressed peoples, and proclaimed the Soviet Union as its ally.[27]

Continuing that theme, a report by Zhang Guotao to a 1934 CCP conference stressed the necessity of emphasizing anti-imperialist education in the Red Army. He stated, "Revolutionaries must be internationalists. Soldiers must learn about the international situation and why imperialism is the main enemy of the workers and peasants."[28] The report was almost a blueprint for the future behavior of the CCP when it finally came to power in 1949. Zhang Guotao outlined the CCP's ten political programs as follows:

> First, drive the imperialists out of China. Second, confiscate all the imperialists' businesses and banks in China. Third, national self-determination for the Chinese people. Fourth, overthrow [Nationalist] rule. Fifth, establish Soviet power. Sixth, the eight-hour workday . . . Seventh, confiscate the land of the rich and redistribute the land to workers, peasants, and soldiers. Eighth, provide soldiers with a livelihood and land. Ninth, abolish levies, establishing a unified tax law. Tenth, unite with the world proletariat, weak and small nations, and the Soviet Union.[29]

Anti-imperialist education among Red Army soldiers was particularly important at this time because, from the latter half of 1933, the party began to explore the possibilities of a new united front against Japanese aggression in China. This new front would recognize all anti-Japanese elements, whether in China or abroad as "friends of our Chinese nation."[30] Under these circumstances, it was essential that CCP rank and file understood both the short-term strategy of uniting with forces in China and beyond from across the political spectrum, as well as the long-term policy of removing foreign dominance in China.

Still, policies and promises were one thing; the practical realities of survival against the ever-encroaching Nationalist attacks often had a greater impact in deciding outcomes in CCP foreign relations. In the autumn of 1934, the Red Army began its strategic retreat from the Chinese Soviet Republic later known as the Long March. Under these desperate circumstances, notions of a broad united front became irrelevant, and any landlord or foreigner who had the misfortune to be in the path of the retreating army was an easy target for extortion or summary execution. The Reverend Rudolf Alfred Bosshardt was one such victim. He was kidnapped and held for an exorbitant ransom by He Long's Second Front Army in 1934 along with seven other members of the China Inland Mission. Two other missionaries captured nearby were shot as their baby daughter lay in bushes nearby.[31] Most of the others were released, but Bosshardt and another missionary, the Reverend Arnolis Hayman, were forced to accompany their captors. For two years Bosshardt and Hayman marched with the Red Army through Guizhou, Sichuan, Hubei, Hunan, and Yunnan Provinces. Along with Chinese prisoners, the two missionaries were at times beaten, degraded, and threatened with execution. Their guards abused them calling them "Foreign Devil," *yang guizi*, "Imperialist," *diguozhuyizhe*, and "Big nose," *gao bizi*.[32] When they were on good terms with them they called them "Teacher," *laoshi*, and once, even "Foreign comrade," *waiguo tongzhi*.[33] A Red Army judge was appointed to try them. Bosshardt wrote, "He accused us of being spies for an imperialist government. The Communist creed stated that missionaries were spies and government agents, covering up their motives by propaganda and religion."[34]

The pair were frequently used as props for anti-imperialist education in mass meetings along the march. They were forced to sit on chairs in the main street of the villages they passed through and signs were pinned on them: "This is an Englishman," "This is a Swiss."[35] The village crowds abused them, calling them "Big nose, hook nose, foreign devil, deserve-to-die imperialists." Their exhibitor, General Xiao Ke, declared, "There's been a great victory over the foreigners. Their religious society must pay a huge ransom."[36] Such exhibitions went on for several hours.[37] The humiliations the pair experienced, similar to those meted out to landlords and other undesirables, served as a means for a public expulsion of the foreigners from the Chinese communities they had formerly worked with, a deliberate expression of the "insiders and outsiders are different" principle. The frequently stated goal of the CCP's *waishi* policies, particularly in the years before and immediately after 1949, was to stop the Chinese people being in awe or afraid of the power and might of foreigners and foreign things. Hence the deliberate dehumanizing of foreigners, emphasizing their "role" in imperialism, was a necessary task of *waishi* education in this period, as it would be in the years after 1949.

A further public trial was held after the pair attempted to escape. They were tried on three charges:

> We had a camera and had taken pictures of strategic places; we wore Chinese dress and spoke the language of the people even to the extent of learning the tribal languages to conceal our true motives; and we were preaching Christ's doctrine of non-resistance. In addition, we had escaped from prison, a capital crime in itself, so we were doubly deserving of death.[38]

In the end the pair were not killed, their propaganda value and the ransom they were being held for of cash and medical supplies was too useful for He Long's forces to squander. After the ransom was paid, however, the communist leaders allowed only Bosshardt's companion, Hayman, to leave. Bosshardt was forced to stay behind in exchange for more demands.

Soon after Hayman's release, a German priest, Father Heinich Kellner, was captured after a raid on a Catholic mission and he too was held for ransom, though his mission organization refused to pay out any money for him. In early 1936, Bosshardt was finally released, Xiao Ke told him:

> We have decided to differentiate between foreigners in future. You're a Swiss citizen, and Switzerland is not an imperialist country. You have no unequal treaties with China, neither have you any concessions, so we've decided to free you tomorrow.[39]

Kellner was not released, because, Xiao Ke told Bosshardt, "He's from Hitler's country, no friend of communists."[40] Kellner died ten days after Bosshardt was released, weakened by the poor food and harsh treatment he had received from his communist captors. A coffin was confiscated from a rich landlord to bury him and bearers were given money to bury him. But they abandoned the coffin and soon after it was pried open by "bandits" in search of booty. The priest's body was left exposed to the elements and was consumed by wolves that night.[41]

In contrast to Kellner's sorry fate, towards the end of Bosshardt's imprisonment, there had been a dramatic change in the way he was treated. In a tactic that would be familiar to readers of the classic Chinese novel *The Water Margin*,[42] Bosshardt was suddenly transformed from being regarded as an enemy to being seen as a friend and potential ally. His captors urged him, "When you report to the newspapers you must remember we are friends. You've seen how good we are to the poor, how we work on principle, and are not common bandits as we are slanderously reported to be."[43] Bosshardt's release and the change in attitude of his captors toward him were no accident. They were the result of major changes in CCP foreign policy, instigated by a shift in the Comintern's own international line.[44]

A New Era in *Waishi*: The Second United Front

At the Seventh Congress of the Comintern in August 1935, Moscow called for a new united front policy for China and a number of countries.[45] The CCP was instructed to make a strategic move from civil war against the Nationalists to a united front against Japanese aggression in China. In December 1935, a new resolution on party policy was announced, which proposed a united front against Japan, both within China and without, aimed at establishing "close and friendly relations with the nations and countries that show sympathy, assistance and friendly neutrality towards the Chinese national movement."[46]

The first gestures of foreign support for the CCP's new line came from a few sympathetic expatriates already based in China. From around the early 1930s, a small community of leftist foreigners in China who supported the CCP had formed in Shanghai; they were linked with Song Qingling, and indirectly, with the Comintern.[47] Beginning in 1933, a small group took part in a secret Marxist-Leninist study group in Shanghai, reputedly the first such study group for foreigners in China.[48] Unlike the Comintern agents posted to China to spy and work with the underground CCP, this group of foreigners were all China-based and committed to China first, rather than to worldwide revolution. The group became involved in helping the CCP underground, providing safe houses, writing for the Comintern-sponsored English-language journal *Voice of China*, and other activities. As a proportion of foreigners in China in the 1920s and 1930s, those who were sympathetic to the Chinese revolution were few. Yet the extraterritoriality of the foreign-controlled areas created a safe zone in China, which enabled communist activity to flourish.

The American journalist Edgar Snow was on the fringes of that circle although he had moved to live in Beijing (then known as Beiping) in 1932. Snow was involved in getting Chinese left-wing writers published in the West, and he worked with Song Qingling to gather information on the political situation in China and get it published overseas. He and his wife, Helen Foster Snow, were both active in supporting the 1935 student protest activities in Beijing that later became known as the December 9th movement. Snow also collected money for Chinese trade unions and the CCP. By 1936, Edgar Snow's writing on China was highly partisan, critical of Chiang Kai-shek, curious about Chinese communism, and very anti-Japanese. In letters to friends he mentioned reading some works on communism, such as John Strachey's *The Coming Struggle for Power*.[49] He was not a member of a Communist Party, but definitely sympathetic to the Chinese revolution.

Edgar Snow's trip to the communist-controlled areas in the northwest came about after the party leadership contacted Song Qingling in Shanghai, asking her to arrange for a foreign journalist who was not associated with the Comintern and a doctor to visit the Soviet areas.[50] The Chinese Red Army forces had established a new base in Shaanxi, far from the reach of Nationalist troops. In order to increase contact with foreigners and strengthen foreign propaganda activities, an International Liaison Bureau had been established in January 1936, under the charge of Qin Bangxian.[51] Edgar Snow was a perfect choice to promote the CCP: not only was he the textbook "progressive" and influential writer communist propagandists aimed to attract for united front activities; he had also been trying to get an interview with CCP leaders for some time. He later informed a friend that the idea to write what became the book *Red Star over China*, occurred when his publisher, Harrison Smith, offered him "a contract with an advance royalty of US$750 to write a book about the communist movement in China."[52] On June 1, 1936, Snow wrote to the editor of the pro-Labor London *Daily Herald*, L. M. MacBride, telling him of his plans to visit the "scene of warfare between Chinese Reds and the government troops" (Zhang Xueliang's soldiers). It was rumored a truce had been agreed between them based on a united front against Japan. Snow told MacBride that he planned to interview Zhang Xueliang, the northern warlord, as well as CCP senior leaders:

> In all the years that the Reds have been in action no foreign newspaperman has penetrated a Red-controlled region. This is a remarkable fact. There are no first-hand accounts of conditions in the Soviet areas. No interviews with any of the famous Red leaders—Mao Tse-tung, Chu Teh, Hsu Hsiang-ch'ien, Liu Tse-tau [*sic*] and others have been published. If I succeed in seeing them as I may, it will be a world scoop on a situation about which millions of words have been written, based only on hearsay and highly colored government reports. What are these men made of that they can stand so much punishment? How do they live? What kind of administration do they give the peasants? How Communist are they? These and many other questions are subjects of wide controversy, but no one has been able to answer them with first-hand in-

formation.[53]

Before Snow's planned trip could come about, it was necessary for him to get advance approval from the CCP. Song Qingling was asked for her opinion of him, as were Max and Grace Granich (U.S. Communist Party members then working in Shanghai for the Comintern-funded *Voice of China*). Liu Shaoqi, then the leading CCP official in northern China, signed a passport for Snow to travel to the communist zone.[54] Snow was accepted as a nonrevolutionary, non-communist news reporter, a "bourgeois journalist," as Mao later called him.

George Hatem, a Lebanese American doctor working in Shanghai, accom-panied Snow on his trip. Hatem's many biographers tend to cite a linear and logical process of Hatem's admiration for the Chinese communist movement leading to his response to the party's call for a doctor to join them. By the mid-1930s, Hatem was certainly interested in Marxism and in helping the worldwide revolution in some way, but personal factors were clearly an important compo-nent of his involvement in the Chinese revolution. Max Granich gives an alter-native and more credible reason for Hatem's trip. Hatem's own letter to a close friend, written in 1935, corroborates this version of events.[55] According to Granich,

> The thing was that [George] was starving in Shanghai as a doctor. The Chinese had no use for him whatever. He worked as a reporter for TOSP [*sic*] for a pe-riod, that kind of thing. So one day, talking with him, he used to come up to the house 3, 4 times a week because he was short of food and he used to go straight to our Frigidaire and open it up and says [*sic*], "Thanks?" that kind of thing (laughs). So we said, "My God (in talking to him) you're a doctor, the Red Army needs doctors, you'd be a goldmine for them." And he said, "I'd give my right arm to go." And I said, "All right, we'll see if we can arrange it." So through Suzie, Madame Sung [Song Qingling], we arranged that he go. And actually, at that period, the question of Ed Snow's going too came up. So, the two of them linked up together in Mongolia.[56]

It was in fact not Mongolia, but in Xi'an, Shaanxi Province that Snow and Hatem met up. After an arduous and dangerous journey, the two Americans en-tered CCP headquarters in Bao'an (though this would soon move to the better-known location at Yan'an). Despite his political sympathies, Snow had been skeptical before the journey of what he might find and he was scared he might be killed. The experiences of Bosshardt, Hayman, and other foreigners under the Red Army were well known in China at the time. However, he was impressed, even overwhelmed, by the welcome he received in the communist base area. In his unpublished diary, he wrote:

> Reaching the main road leading to the gate we were met by most of the offi-cials of the government; Liu Pei-chu,[57] Lo Fu,[58] Po Ku,[59] Wu Liang-p'ing, Lo Man,[60] Lin P'iao[61] and others. The cadets from the military academy were lined up, and the band blared a welcome as we marched between the lines of spectators. The bands and troops fell behind us and marched up the main street,

to the accompaniment of slogans shouted, "Huan-yin, chei [Mei]-kuo tong-shih! Chung-kuo tung-shih Wan Sui! Shih-chieh ke-ming, Wan Sui!"[62] etc., posters and banners of welcome decorated the walls of the town, some written in English, some in Latin-hua [sic], many in Chinese. It was the first time I had been greeted by the entire cabinet of a government, the first time a whole city had been turned out to welcome me. The effect pronounced on me was highly emotional. Had I been called up to make any kind of speech I would have been unable to do so. I was overcome with emotion at the warmth of the greeting. The incredible experience of receiving it far in the interior of this little city fortified by many ribbed ranges of mountains, and the strange thrill of solemn military music in the stillness and vastness of these mountains. I dared not look at Haiti [George Hatem]. Later he confessed to me that he felt exactly the same.[63]

The two men were treated with a style of political hospitality that would before long become a standard of the CCP repertoire. Much grander and more generous than the Soviet system it had been based on, it was clearly designed to make the visitor feel especially important and valued. Considerable effort had gone into preparing for the visit of the two men, including the preparation of a party directive on how to reply to Snow's interview questions.[64] In Snow's case it worked well: making him feel "highly emotional." After the welcoming ceremony, following Chinese tradition, the two men were given a lavish banquet, of which their Chinese hosts ate little. The men were not only given hospitality treatment for their own benefit, the visit was used to educate the Red Army soldiers on "good" foreigners and about the international united front. When Snow and Hatem were asked to give a speech to the Red Army at a meeting in northwest Shaanxi, large banners proclaimed, in English and Chinese, "WE ARE NOT ISOLATED. WE HAVE THE SUPPORT OF INTERNATIONAL FRIENDS."[65]

Over a period of ten days, Mao met with Edgar Snow daily to discuss CCP policy and, at Snow's request, narrate his autobiography. Snow spent more time with Mao than any of the other leading figures in the base area; most of the other senior leaders were absent during Snow's visit.[66] The high profile given to Mao in Snow's book would later assist in promoting the myth of Mao's predominance in the CCP from the late 1930s.[67] Mao placed a high priority on foreign relations, and at Yan'an all foreign policy, even to the smallest detail, came to be controlled by him.[68] Mao told Snow he was sure an "intimate friendship" could develop between the people in Great Britain and the United States and China, if only those countries would assist in China's war against Japan.[69] At the same time, he boasted,

The Chinese revolution is already the key factor in world revolution and its victory is heartily anticipated by the people of every country, and especially the toiling masses of the colonial countries. When the Chinese revolution comes into full power the masses of many colonial countries will follow the example of China and win a similar victory of their own.[70]

The CCP leaders made an extremely good impression on the visitors. Snow wrote admiringly:

> The Reds had generally discarded all the feudal rubbish of so-called Chinese etiquette, and their psychology and character were quite different from traditional conceptions of Chinese. Alice Tisdale Hobart could never write a book about them, nor could the Chinese author of Lady Precious Stream. They were direct, frank, simple, undevious, and scientific-minded. They rejected nearly all the old Chinese philosophy that was the basis of what was once Chinese civilization, and most important of all, perhaps, they were implacable enemies of the old Chinese familism. Most of the time I felt completely at ease in their company as if I were with some of my countrymen.[71]

On his return to Beijing, Snow wrote up his impressions of the Chinese "Reds" into the book he entitled *Red Star over China*. In a fiction maintained to the end of his career, despite his own dabbling in communism and personal involvement in supporting the left-wing movement in China, Snow deliberately downplayed the ideological aspects of the book to his editor when he got back from Bao'an.

> I wonder if it is the political angle of the story that is perplexing you? If it is, you may safely drop your worries in that direction. It is the human epic in the story of the Red Army that interests me, and the politics only secondary, and I have no intention (in fact am quite incapable) of going into heavy polemics on the pros and cons of communism in China. (The average age of Red "warriors" is 19, and of officers 23, and it gives you the feeling of being with an army of school boys who have suddenly quit playing football and decided to make a revolution—and it's things like that which interest me about the Reds and I think will interest the readers of the Herald).[72]

That Snow's work was a conscious propaganda piece is confirmed by the comment of Snow's close friend James Bertram in his memoirs *Capes of China Slide Away*. Writing of his life and friendships when he was living in Beijing in the 1930s, Bertram described how Helen Foster Snow went off to Yan'an not long after her husband returned from his trip, "determined to do for the women of the Red Army what Ed was doing for Mao and the other communist leaders."[73] Huang Qing (also known as Yu Ch'i-wei), the Snow's CCP contact in Beijing, also described their writing on the CCP and the Beijing student movement as "propaganda work."[74] Snow's book was important and useful to both Mao Zedong personally and the CCP in general at this time, because it established Mao as both a national and an international figure and promoted the Chinese revolutionary cause. In the 1930s, this was a helpful anti-Chiang Kai-shek tactic, and to Chinese readers as well as the Comintern it strengthened Mao's claim to the leadership of the CCP. No other book on the Chinese communists put Mao in such prominence, nor would any other ever be so successful. The book came out in a period when U.S. East Asian specialists had become frustrated and disbelieving of the Nationalist government's propaganda on the CCP, while the onset of the Sino-Japanese war had aroused much sympathy and interest about China in the West.[75] Soon after publication, Snow's book sold over one hundred thousand copies in Great Britain (through the Soviet-subsidized Left Book Club)[76] and approximately fifteen thousand in the United States.[77] Between 1938 and 1966, some 65,000 copies of the book were sold in the U.S. It was translated into half a dozen languages, including Chinese, where it was very influential on the youth of the 1930s and 1940s. As a result of the Nationalist government's restrictions on materials related to the CCP, Snow's book was the first positive account of the party many Chinese readers encountered.[78] Edgar Snow's writing created an image of the Chinese communists that was influential in the West for years to come. He destroyed the notion of them as bandits and stooges of the Soviet Union and promoted the idea that they had their own style of Marxism. Snow interviewed the CCP leaders at a crucial time, on the cusp of the new united front policy.[79]

Although Edgar Snow claimed he had written *Red Star over China* under no constraint or pressure, his work was in fact quite carefully managed to reflect current CCP policy. Mao was very cautious in his interview with Snow, insisting that the transcript of their interview be translated twice, first into English, then back into Chinese to check its accuracy and make any corrections (and probably to show the other senior leaders in Bao'an what was being said). After he returned to his home in Beijing, Snow received a letter in December 1936 from George Hatem, passing on the message from Mao that he wanted him to tone down talk of "class struggle" in the book while emphasizing the anti-Japanese line.[80] Snow received a further letter from Mao himself in March 1937, asking him to make further adjustments to reflect changes in CCP policy.[81] Zhou Enlai also later asked that revisions be made. During his interview with Snow, he had expressed opinions that differed from the Comintern line, declaring that the Chinese revolution would likely come about by means of the anti-Japanese movement. He was also extremely critical of Chiang Kai-shek and the Nationalist government. However after the two parties formed a united front, Zhou asked Snow to remove his comments from the text.[82] Snow acquiesced to all these requests for "adjustment." A further problem was that Snow had been too critical of the Soviet Union's (i.e., Stalin's policy) on China, thus making the book too "Trotskyist." According to former Comintern worker Max Granich, Snow was told that he if didn't change this "we'll denounce it [the book]."[83] Snow later told U.S. Communist Party leader Earl Browder that he had voluntarily edited some sentences from the book that he thought "might be offensive to the party."[84] He did not specify which Communist Party he was trying to avoid offending: the American, Chinese, or Russian. In late 1937, Mao ordered the recall of the CCP Chinese translation (there were several versions even in this period), when his rival for political power, Wang Ming, launched an attack on the founding father of the CCP, Chen Duxiu.[85] In his interview with Snow, Mao had acknowledged Chen's political and personal influence on him in his youth.[86] Despite all the changes he (and others) had made, Snow and his book were still regarded unfavorably by some in the Soviet Union.[87] For reasons of unity however, Moscow's dissatisfaction over the book would not be made public until much later.

George Hatem's journey with Snow to the communist areas was kept secret for the next thirty years. He seems to have wanted to disappear off the face of the earth for a while, apparently to escape his family and their expectations of him.[88] Hatem stayed on to become a medical adviser in the Red Army's Department of Health in Shaanxi. Sidney Shapiro, in his biography of George Hatem, writes that in the late 1930s, the Soviet Union offered only limited assistance to China, and the United States assisted Japan until 1941, hence "international friends" were particularly cherished at this time.[89] Hatem became a symbol of the international support for China's war effort, as well as adding to the limited medical facilities of the CCP base. Hatem was generally well liked, even the Comintern agent based in Yan'an, Otto Braun (who was generally hostile to the CCP's foreign friends), described Hatem favorably, writing of him,

> He possessed qualities which stood him in good stead in every situation: rapid comprehension, great adaptability, and youthful nonchalance. He learned to speak, but not to read or write, Chinese very quickly, joined the Party, established himself as a general practitioner for the people . . . He got along well with everyone, was never in anyone's way, and made himself useful where he could.[90]

However, Hatem's altruism made him an object of suspicion to some. In the 1942 party rectification campaign, Kang Sheng led an attack against Hatem and his Chinese wife, Zhou Sufei. Hatem was asked, "Why should a foreigner give up a comfortable life in America to endure hardships in Yan'an. He might be a spy."[91] The suspicion that Hatem was a spy deepened in 1946 when he flew to Beijing as a medical adviser to the Chinese Liberated Areas Relief Association (CLARA), the first and only internationally supported organization to recognize the CCP's political control of large parts of China prior to 1949.[92] On arrival, the U.S. soldiers who controlled the airport questioned Hatem for a few minutes, and this was recorded in his file as "several hours."[93]

The Chinese communists' foreign friends in the late 1930s were few, but very useful. In December 1936 Chiang Kai-shek was captured by the northern warlords Zhang Xueliang and Yang Hucheng and held on condition that he would agree to a pact with the CCP to fight the Japanese invasion. During what became known as the Xi'an Incident, CCP and Nationalist leaders negotiated China's future, while three foreigners were on hand to broadcast the news to the world. The American writer Agnes Smedley, the New Zealand journalist James Bertram, and the German wife of *waishi* cadre Wang Bingnan, Anna Wang (née Martens), broadcast the CCP viewpoint from the party's own shortwave radio station in Xi'an.

In his book-length account of the Xi'an incident, Bertram described the Red Army soldiers he encountered in the northwest:

> There is something the Red Army does to its young recruits. All who have

come in contact with the Chinese Reds (and this includes, in recent months, a number of American journalists) have noticed at once the change of personality they put on with the red star. There are gaïety, comradeship, a touch of reck-lessness, for the average age in the Red Armies is probably under twenty; but there are also a strength and a self-reliance that are not common among Chi-nese brought up in the old family traditions. With this goes an openness of manner that is curiously Western; the whole personality seems to come to the surface.[94]

Bertram's descriptions are highly romantic and contrast strongly with the views of the missionary Rudolf Alfred Bosshardt (who admittedly met the Red Army under somewhat different circumstances). The following year, Bertram traveled to Yan'an to interview Mao. This had been his original plan, until he was way-laid to help broadcast the outcome of the Xi'an incident. Bertram never received the special attention Snow had received on this visit, nor did he become Mao's "special friend" as Snow had. As an American, and a prominent international journalist, Snow was much more useful to the CCP, and he was given special treatment accordingly.[95] Bertram's interview with Mao was significant however, because it came at a time when the CCP was trying to get publicity for its cause in Great Britain. Unfortunately, none was available at the right moment. Though he was born and bred in New Zealand and spent most of his life there, Bertram was categorized as a *British* journalist, since this suited the CCP's propaganda needs, both at the time and much later in Mao's *Selected Works* and *Quotations from Mao Tse-tung.*[96]

Following the setting up of the second united front, CCP cadres had more freedom to move and operate in the government-controlled areas. At a meeting held in December 1937, the CCP Central Committee decided to set up its offi-cial representative office in Hankou, then the wartime capital of the Nationalist government. Senior leaders Wang Ming, Qin Bangxian, Zhou Enlai, and Ye Ji-anying were given responsibility for activities such as negotiating with the gov-ernment and dealing with the foreign community.[97] A decision was also made to set up the Yangzi Bureau, also known as the Nanfangju, to deal with CCP affairs in southern China. This organization was to share offices with the Hankou Bu-reau, and was initially headed by Wang Ming, with Zhou Enlai second in charge. Eventually the decision was made to merge the two bodies internally, but maintain separate nameplates for external purposes.[98] Staff cultivated rela-tionships with influential foreigners, especially British and American officials and journalists.[99] In 1938 a Foreign Propaganda Small Group was set up within the bureau, its responsibility was to translate CCP materials into English and make them available to foreign opinion-makers in China. The early prominence given to foreign propaganda demonstrates its importance in CCP foreign affairs. Mao stressed the important role of foreign propaganda work in a 1938 speech on Chinese foreign policy that was republished many times in Cultural Revolution texts. The themes in this speech are still an important element of Chinese foreign policy.[100] In 1939 the Nanfangju Foreign Affairs Small Group, *Nanfangju wai-*

shi xiaozu, was formed: Wang Bingnan, Chen Jiakang, and Gong Peng were key members of this group and after 1949 formed the nucleus of the PRC Foreign Ministry. The task of the Foreign Affairs Small Group was to advise the central leadership on international politics, do public relations work among foreigners in China, and continue the work of cultivating foreign reporters, diplomats, soldiers, and scholars.[101]

Snow's visit to the CCP-controlled areas and the ensuing worldwide publicity that resulted encouraged numerous other foreign journalists, writers, and activists to visit.[102] Indeed, visiting the Red Army base areas became so common for a period in the late 1930s, that the procommunist writers W. H. Auden and Christopher Isherwood deliberately avoided a visit there when they traveled to China to research their book *Journey to a War*. At a meeting with Qin Bangxian at the Eighth Route Army Office in Hankou they turned down an offer to tour Yan'an, saying they didn't think it necessary to go since, "so many journalists have been up there already, and written about it so well."[103] Other American journalists visited Yan'an not long after Snow's visit, but they were never promoted in the way Snow later was by the CCP. For example United Press journalist Earl H. Leaf visited in April 1937 and wrote favorably of what he found.[104] But he appears to have offended his Chinese hosts. Helen Foster Snow who was visiting Yan'an at the time wrote to her husband that Leaf was "telling the Chinese leaders what to do."[105] The CCP was in need of foreign assistance in the late 1930s, but it had to be on CCP terms and strictly under CCP control. Mao told Evans Carlson, "We welcome those foreigners who come to help us. But the trouble with so many foreigners is that they soon want to dictate. They must remember this is China, and that while their advice is eagerly received, we are the ones to decide if and how it will be used."[106] Other foreign helpers had offended by making excessive complaints, demanding money for their services, or only being willing to help for short periods of time. There was also a fear that some of the foreigners had a dual purpose of spying on the CCP for other agencies. The obvious answer to this problem was to restrict acceptance of practical offers of assistance to foreign Communist Party members only, as well as a handful of noncommunist foreigners who were closely under party control. In July 1939 Edgar Snow reported that there were "about 50 refugee doctors from Spain, ready to come to China if they can get credentials."[107] However this offer was not taken up because both the Eighth Route and New Fourth Army refused to work with foreigners if it was not satisfied with their "credentials"—in other words, their political trustworthiness. Even old friends like Edgar Snow and Rewi Alley were affected by this attitude, which hampered their efforts to develop the Chinese Industrial Cooperatives in the CCP-controlled areas.[108]

It was in this period that China's foreign affairs system began to develop its own characteristic style. The CCP leaders made a strong impression on their foreign guests; Mao Zedong, Zhu De, and Zhou Enlai were particularly admired. Mao was a correspondent's delight, relaxed and generous with his time, eminently quotable. Polish journalist Ilona Ralf Sues, who worked as a propagandist for the Nationalist government, seems to have fallen under Mao's spell, writing that he had "the most wonderful face I had ever seen . . . the Chinese nation incarnate."[109] She praised Zhu De for his warmth and "frank, simple replies."[110] Both images were quite a contrast to the picture of corruption and lies that was building around the Nationalist government in the 1930s. Zhou Enlai was praised by many as charming and urbane, equally comfortable in a Western or a Chinese environment. Even before he officially took charge of *waishi* activities at the CCP's representative office in Hankou, Zhou was the CCP official who made the strongest impression on foreigners in the wartime capital.[111]

After the Nationalist government moved their capital to Chongqing, Zhou Enlai followed and took full charge of the Yangzi Bureau. A brilliant diplomat, Zhou has been widely credited with being one of the most important influences on establishing China's foreign affairs traditions. One of his methods is known as the "five diligences," *wuqin*: diligent eyes, diligent ears, diligent mouth, diligent hands, and diligent feet. Zhou's "five diligences" were aimed at encouraging *waishi* officials to work actively to build up foreign contacts. A 1988 textbook for *waishi* workers explains:

> Diligent eyes means studying hard and understanding conditions and policies; diligent ears means to listen to all kinds of opinions and views; diligent mouth means explain things to people; diligent hands means work hard, diligent feet means be active, make friends everywhere, don't stay at home waiting for people to come and find you. All *waishi* personnel would do well to remember these requirements.[112]

Zhou was the product both of a traditional Chinese and a contemporary Western-style education. He spoke reasonable English and a smattering of a number of other foreign languages. His experiences in his youth in Japan and Europe gave him a deeper understanding of the world beyond China than most senior CCP leaders.[113] The son of a family of scholar-officials that had fallen on hard times, Zhou seemed to have had a skill for forging alliances with opposing forces from an early age. He told close friends in 1922 that he was "conciliatory in nature."[114]

Clearly one of the primary tasks in Zhou's *waishi* work was to garner support for CCP positions by establishing relationships with influential and useful foreigners.[115] In the 1930s, the CCP was weak in comparison to the Nationalist government and personal contacts were one of the most essential methods of expanding the party's influence. Among Zhou's conquests were such influential figures as the British ambassador Sir Archibald Clarke-Kerr, the Anglican bishop of Hankou, Bishop Logan Roots, U.S. military attaché Joseph Stilwell, U.S. consul general John Davies, and marine colonel Evans Carlson, as well as a host of lesser-known, but useful individuals in Western embassies and other organizations in China at that time. Zhou paid particular attention to cultivating foreign journalists, an effort that would pay off handsomely in the CCP's ongoing propaganda war against the Nationalist government.[116] During the CCP's most difficult eras, Zhou always seemed to be able to find appropriate and influential journalists to "proclaim China's true situation to the world."[117] Zhou's advice for working on foreign journalists went as follows:

> Establish friendly feelings with the foreign media, make friends with every single one of them, and form close friendships. At the same time, he emphasized that doing work on foreign journalists requires thorough research and investigation, one should "know the enemy and know oneself," one must adopt a practical and realistic style of work, do things gradually and make use of every bit of time and space. One should not put pressure on people.[118]

To Zhou Enlai, the work of meeting with foreign journalists was a means to "ingeniously blend together the implementation of our nation's diplomatic policies; using the foreign media to the utmost in order to push forward the development of China's foreign relations."[119] Foreign journalists had ready access to the communists in Hankou throughout 1938, the most cooperative phase of the united front between the CCP and Nationalist government. Anglican bishop Logan H. Roots's residence became an open house for people from all political backgrounds. Zhou Enlai and his staff were regular guests, as were Nationalist officials and Western correspondents. Western journalists could meet with CCP leaders at the headquarters of the Eighth Route Army in Hankou, as well as at the offices of the *New China Daily, Xinhua Ribao*, the CCP newspaper in Nationalist-controlled areas. The American radical Agnes Smedley also acted as a channel for contacts between foreigners and the CCP in the temporary capital, as well as being involved in fund-raising activities to support the Eighth Route Army.[120] CCP officials continued to court Western journalists and officials when the Nationalist government moved to Chongqing, assuring them that they would be given a warm welcome in Yan'an and guaranteeing they would be free to investigate and report on conditions there.[121]

Western journalists who visited Yan'an in this period or had contact with CCP personnel in the Nationalists' capital almost unanimously emphasized that the Chinese Communist Party was different from the Soviet Communist Party and that they had created their own form of communism. Victor Keen, T. A. Bisson, Helen Foster Snow, Agnes Smedley, Philip J. Jaffe, Owen Lattimore, and travel writer Violet Cressy-Marcks were among many foreign visitors to Yan'an in the late 1930s.[122] The writers produced a rich harvest of positive publicity for the CCP in exchange for the hospitality they received. CCP hosts told their foreign guests they were free to write whatever they wanted about what they saw in the "Communist Base Areas," the zone controlled by CCP forces.

It was not really necessary to directly control the writing of foreign visitors to Yan'an in this period; instead they were given "guidance." Guidance consisted of showing them the good things, treating them well, and paying polite attention to their opinions and suggestions.[123] In any case, those who were openly hostile to the CCP were not welcome.[124] Few foreign visitors, then as now, spoke Chinese. In what became a standard tactic of CCP political control, senior leaders focused on finding common points with their foreign visitors. Linking the united front against Japan was a common point on which many diverse and ordinarily antagonistic groups and individuals could agree. In their publicity to foreigners and Chinese alike, the CCP presented itself as the only credible force opposing the encroaching Japanese. Many of those who took the trouble to make the trip to Yan'an were already openly supportive of the Chinese communists, and they were mostly quite willing to protect the movement and hide its flaws.

It should be noted that the policy on foreigners was by no means uniformly positive; a clear distinction was made between "friends" and "enemies." "Progressive" foreign journalists and officials who could be won over to the CCP point of view were friends, most missionaries and anyone who worked for the Nationalists were not. In 1940, for example, CCP forces led by Commander Liu Bocheng tortured to death a Belgian priest who led a rival Catholic-organized anti-Japanese relief network in the northwest of China.[125]

As relations between the two parties deteriorated, access to Yan'an and contact with CCP staff in Chongqing became increasingly difficult. The effective end of the second united front between the government and the CCP was brought about by the New Fourth Army incident in January 1941, when the New Fourth Army headquarters were destroyed by Nationalist troops. But even before this, by early 1940, foreigners were generally not permitted by Nationalist forces to enter the communist-controlled area.[126] This blockade was both a response to the barrage of procommunist reports written by Western journalists and an indication of the deterioration of relations between the two sides. In this period the Nanfangju in Chongqing was virtually the only outlet for the CCP to make external contacts. The public relations work of Zhou and his team was essential. Scattered reports of conditions in the communist-controlled area also came from individuals who entered via Japanese-occupied China.

The Nationalists tried hard—but ineffectively—to suppress such sources of information about the CCP. Hollington K. Tong, the Nationalist government vice-minister for information, told a journalist for the *Christian Science Monitor* in 1941 that anyone who attended a press conference held by the CCP was "an enemy of China." Journalists who chose to ignore Nationalist disapproval and meet with the CCP could lose their cable privileges, were disqualified from getting information from official sources, and suffered many other inconveniences.[127] The Nationalists had their own core of fluent English-speakers who served as guides to visiting foreigners.[128] Foreigners' movements inside Nationalist-controlled China were regulated by a government travel service; special permits were required for visits to certain sensitive areas. Like the CCP, the Nationalists also tried to mould foreign attitudes towards supporting their regime, though they were not nearly as effective at it.[129] Though they had more money to lavish on visitors and vastly more personnel with good foreign language skills and international experience, the Nationalist government's blatant corruption and general indifference to the well-being of the Chinese people failed to convert foreigners to support their regime, other than from a pragmatic point of view.

Internationalism

> What kind of spirit is this that makes a foreigner selflessly adopt the cause of the Chinese people's liberation as his own? It is the spirit of internationalism, the spirit of communism, from which every Chinese communist must learn . . . We must unite with the proletariat of all the capitalist countries, with the proletariat of Japan, Britain, the United States, Germany, Italy and all other capitalist countries, before it is possible to overthrow imperialism, to liberate our nation and people, and to liberate the other nations and peoples of the world. This is our internationalism, the internationalism with which we oppose both narrow nationalism and narrow patriotism.[130]

Internationalists in communist usage are generally defined as the dedicated individuals who devote their energy to other countries' revolutionary struggles.[131] Internationalists in the CCP sense specifically refers to foreigners who dedicate themselves to the *Chinese* revolution. In the context of the PRC's *waishi* system, internationalist is the highest-rank title for foreigners who support CCP rule. Internationalism has long been epitomized in the PRC by the Canadian doctor Norman Bethune, memorialized in Mao's famous speech.[132] Bethune died in 1939 in northern China while working for the Eighth Route Army. Bethune was the first foreigner to be used as a symbol of devoted service to the Chinese revolution and could be said to be the symbol of CCP Occidentalism. By no means a model figure in real life, according to those who knew him well, Bethune was an extremely bad-tempered, autocratic, but thoroughly dedicated doctor.[133] As a prominent member of the Canadian Communist Party, when Bethune arrived in Yan'an, Mao singled him out for prestigious treatment.

When Mao praised Bethune, it was surely not to inspire the Chinese people to imitate his devotion to another country's revolution, but to praise his spirit of "selflessly adopt[ing] the cause of the *Chinese* people's liberation" and encourage them to do the same. In 1939, Mao chose Bethune as a symbol of the commitment to the Chinese revolution he required of CCP cadres, and in the post-1949 period, of the Chinese people. That commitment was characterized by the virtues of self-sacrifice and hard work, serving the party rather than the individual or the family unit. In addition, according to the needs of the united front, promoting the work of a foreigner in CCP forces was a means to encourage other foreigners in China to do the same. It also served the purposes of *waishi* education by letting Chinese people know that it was appropriate to cooperate with some foreigners, that not all foreigners in China were imperialists. The fact that Bethune came from a prosperous Western country was helpful for the CCP's propaganda needs at the time, as it sought Western support for China's struggle against Japan and recognition of CCP status. Comintern agent Otto Braun noted bitterly Mao's close contact and interest in Western visitors to Yan'an: "Mao Tse-tung made shrewd use of these people either to introduce his political views or objectives or to conceal them and portray himself in the most favorable light for Western nations."[134] In contrast, he reported, a group of four or five Indian doctors who came to help the CCP were virtually ignored by Mao. One of the group, Kotnis, died while serving in China. Unlike Bethune however, he was not selected as a model figure.[135] In this era, solidarity with the people of other colonial nations was not a priority for CCP propaganda. Mao Zedong's focus in this period was on getting the assistance and support of Western countries, rather than support for internationalism *per se*.

Mao hoped to use the united front against the Japanese as a means to strengthen relations with the Western world, particularly the United States. Significantly, Mao never wrote an article publicly commemorating the many Soviet comrades who died fighting for China in World War II, promoting a figure from a Western country further served the task of affirming the independence of the Chinese communist struggle.[136] The article commemorating Bethune was especially prominent during the Cultural Revolution, when Mao was concerned with, among other things, renewing the spirit of selfless dedication to the revolution among Chinese youth and purging Soviet influence. Even in the 1990s in China, Norman Bethune was still one of the most famous foreigners in China, symbolizing both dedication to the Chinese revolution and the CCP's gratitude to its foreign friends. Bethune is also well known in the West as a result of a number of books and films based on his life. In the 1950s Bethune's life was dramatized in the fictionalized biography *The Scalpel and the Sword*. In the novel the fictionalized Mao thanked Bethune for his support and that of other foreigners. "Their support," he told him, "was a striking example of the solidarity, of friendship with the Chinese people. He added, "China's fighters would know how to remember their friends, and someday, repay them."[137]

In 1940, the CCP instructed cadres to distinguish between the imperialism of Japan and the other Axis powers on the one hand, and that of the United States and Great Britain who were now opposed to Japan on the other hand.[138] This change in policy led to an even greater focus on united front work, both among Chinese and foreigners. United front tactics to be used on prospective Chinese allies bear a close similarity to the techniques also used on foreigners. Criticizing past policy, a 1940 report on united front work advised:

> In the past, the usual slant was toward political contacts; very rarely was conscientious work done to make friends, to the point of being extremely distant and unable to really work together. Hereafter, we must use all possible social connections (relatives and family, fellow townsmen, classmates, colleagues, etc.) and customs (sending presents, celebrating festivals, sharing adversities, mutual aid, etc.), not only to form political friendships with the subjects, but also to become personal friends with them, so that they will be completely frank and open with us.[139]

As the battle for China intensified, the CCP increased its efforts to expand its friends and allies. Yet although the current propaganda line stressed unity toward the common cause of opposing the Japanese invasion, the long-term goal of communist revolution had not been omitted from internal, party members' eyes only documents. In an article on CCP foreign policy in 1940, Mao Zedong outlined the importance of the anti-imperialist struggle in China. It is significant in that it was remarkably close to the line the party would adopt after 1949:

> In this world all the imperialists regard us as their enemy; if China wants to be independent, it can never be so without the aid of the socialist countries and the international proletariat. This is to say that China cannot be without the support from the Soviet Union, or without the victories of the proletariat in England, America, France, and Germany in their struggles against capitalism in their own countries . . . victory can be won only by including their strength; there is no doubt about it.[140]

Mao described CCP foreign policy in standard united front terms of "exploiting the contradictions . . . in order to win over the majority, oppose the minority, and crush the enemies separately."[141] During World War II, CCP foreign policy made a number of important distinctions. First, was a distinction between the Soviet Union and the capitalist countries; while relations with Britain and the United States were to be treated differently to those with Germany and Italy. A further distinction was to be made between the peoples of Britain and the United States and their governments. And a final important distinction was that made of past actions of foreign powers in relation to China and present policy.

In 1941, Japanese forces bombed Pearl Harbor, the United States formally entered World War II, and the battle for control of the Pacific began. The CCP's 9 December 1941 declaration called for an anti-Japanese and antifascist front in the Pacific region, uniting all the governments and peoples opposing Japan. From this time on the United States and Great Britain were seen as having a particularly important role to play in defeating Japan and bringing about unity in China. Party members were instructed to cooperate with the British and American armed forces in China and "left" deviation was to be avoided.[142] The CCP adopted a softer line on imperialism and Great Britain and the United States were frequently described in party newspapers as the "allies" and "friends" of China.

After 1941, foreigners from Allied countries escaping from the Japanese who ventured through CCP territory were treated especially well by their communist hosts. Following the outbreak of the Pacific war, eight Westerners escaped from Beijing to North China, passing through CCP territory before eventually being sent on to Chongqing. The escapees were a conservative group, by no means communist sympathizers. Among them was a bank manager, several university professors, and a part-time agent for British intelligence, Michael Lindsay.[143] Once they made it safely out of Japanese territory, the escaping foreigners were taken to Yan'an, stopping at every town on their route for a "welcoming" reception that had as much to do with publicizing the Allied forces' support for China as it did about welcoming the fortunate foreigners. This was important propaganda on the united front for the local population. It was a means of demonstrating to them that unlike the past, this time Western nations and the Chinese were fighting on the same side, and that the CCP was in control of this relationship. The evacuees were extremely well looked after, provided with much better conditions than their Chinese traveling companions. Some of them were even given money to continue their journey back to their home countries. Government agents harassed some of the group when they returned to the Nationalist-controlled areas. The government was hoping to prevent any further positive publicity about the communists.[144] Nevertheless the CCP had already asked the foreign refugees to write testimonies of their visit and the good treatment they received. This became the pamphlet *How the 8th Route Army Helped Us to Escape from Peip'ing* published by the CCP Foreign Propaganda Group in September 1942. The frontispiece of the CCP pamphlet republished an editorial from *Xinhua Ribao*, "On the Rescue of Our Foreign Friends and Their Arrival in Yan'an." The piece was aimed both at educating the Chinese population under CCP control and encouraging further contact and support with the Western powers:

> We Communists have frequently expressed our willingness to cooperate with all our foreign friends. In May 1941 the Border Region Government published the following regulations: "Every foreigner is permitted to travel freely in the Border Region and to engage in any kind of anti-Japanese economic or cultural activities, under the condition that the laws and rights of the Chinese Republic are respected." After the outbreak of the Pacific War the Central Committee of our Party has given the following instructions: "Chinese Communists must work together with the British and the Americans in sincere and honest cooperation . . . The fact that these foreign friends have sought the assistance of our army shows that they realize our program of national and international unity, from firm resistance in the areas behind enemy lines and that they regard the Chinese Communists as their sincere friends. In the past few years foreign friends have constantly given us encouragement and help, have shared our fight in the war of resistance and our work for the construction of new China. Here again we take the opportunity to express our deep appreciation and gratitude to them.[145]

Even Japanese soldiers and Chinese pro-Japanese puppet forces could be included in the international united front if they were willing to support CCP objectives. Article 20 of the Democratic Program of the Shaan-Gan-Ning Border Region stated that CCP forces should,

> carry out without exception a program of leniency towards the officers and rank and file of the Japanese and the puppet army who are taken prisoner in the battle, regardless of whatever situation [*sic*]. To accommodate and extend hospitality to any of them who desire to participate in our war of resistance and to release those who do not wish to remain.[146]

Japanese soldiers were reeducated and trained in CCP anti-Japanese propaganda activities, with great success in many cases.[147] Their cooperation was a useful ideological warfare tactic and a core method of the CCP version of the united front. In the years after the CCP victory, the skills developed in these early experiments in turning enemies into friends and allies would be put to good use in the development of Sino-Japanese relations in the Cold War era.[148]

Not all foreigners who had contact with the CCP in this time were treated well. Hospitality to foreigners, as always, was political and deliberate. Foreigners who served no useful political purpose as an enemy-turned-friend or as a living example of the CCP's "link" to the Western alliance were not welcome in the "Liberated" Areas. In 1944 a group of four foreigners (three Russians and a Yugoslavian) attempted to pass through CCP-controlled territories hoping to start a new life in Southeast Asia or Australia. The group was held under detention and eventually executed in early 1947 when the CCP was forced to make a tactical retreat from Yan'an during the civil war.[149]

Apart from their usefulness in propaganda, the role and place of foreigners in China was also both a sensitive topic and a useful weapon in inner-party power struggles. During the party rectification movement of 1942, Mao Zedong criticized foreign (meaning Comintern) influence in the CCP, blaming it for failures in the revolution.[150] Although such views were common among CCP leaders, the criticisms were in fact an implicit attack on Mao's rivals in the party at this time who owed much of their prominence to Moscow's support. Although Mao himself closely followed the Soviet Union's strategic advice once he achieved a leading role, there was a constant tension within the party between the ideals of internationalism (which in the 1940s meant following the Soviet Union's lead regardless of local conditions) and those of "patriotism" which held such an important place in the ideology of the CCP-led revolution.

Diplomatic Breakthrough: The 1944 Dixie Mission and Journalists' Visit

Beginning in 1943 and up until June 1945, the CCP conducted a major propaganda campaign to garner U.S. support for the party and destroy its faith in the Nationalist government.[151] However, the U.S. government did not reciprocate CCP efforts to cooperate until 1944, when the American military observer mission was sent to Yan'an. At the same time, after an interval of several years, when few foreigners and no journalists had been able to visit the communist controlled area, in 1944 the pressure on the Nationalist government became too much to withstand. The government gave permission for a small group of Chinese and foreign journalists, to visit Yan'an.[152] Six foreign journalists, nine Chinese journalists, and four Nationalist government officials undertook the trip. Leaving out the issue of the recognition of communist-controlled areas altogether, the group was officially designated "the press party to the Northwest." CCP leaders regarded this visit very seriously. It was a means both to have CCP views known in the West, as well as to find out the attitude of Great Britain and the United States towards the Nationalists and the CCP and other matters important to the party's bid for power.[153] Of the six foreign journalists, one was from the Soviet Union, the remaining five reported for a number of the major newspapers in Great Britain and the United States. It was these five who were of greatest interest to Mao.[154]

Mao met with the foreign and Chinese journalists both individually and as a group. In private discussions, Mao told the American journalists that China hoped to be a bridge between the United States and the Soviet Union after the war. In contrast, with the Soviet journalist, he discussed China's future revolutionary direction after the war.[155] The journalists' reports on their visit to Yan'an were highly favorable, much to the satisfaction of party leaders.[156] The group's visit was carefully controlled, they were restricted as to what they were allowed to view and they had to submit their reports to the Ministry of Information for censorship.[157] Nonetheless, there seemed to be a strong willingness to *believe* in what they were shown.

While the group of journalists was still visiting Yan'an, the U.S. military observer group known as the Dixie Mission arrived to meet with CCP leaders.[158] The visit was considered to be even more important than that of the journalists. Though far from securing the establishment of official relations between the United States and CCP-controlled China, in CCP eyes, the military observer group's visit was still a form of *de facto* recognition for the party's status. Senior leaders regarded the Dixie Mission as a major development in CCP diplomacy.[159] Propaganda activities were carefully arranged during the group's stay. On the eve of the arrival of the Americans at Yan'an in July 1944, a celebration was organized to commemorate the Fourth of July, U.S. Independence Day. All senior party members, foreigners living in Yan'an, and the visiting journalists attended. Mao wrote an essay published in the *Liberation Daily*, commemorating U.S. Independence Day as a day to remember the "glorious struggle for freedom and democracy."[160] The article gave high praise to the U.S. independence and civil wars and cited Washington, Jefferson, and Lincoln as men of great influence in the worldwide struggle for freedom and democracy. After the observer group arrived at the communist base, Mao published a further article entitled "Welcome to Our Comrades in Arms the American Military Observer Mission."[161] It is significant that Mao chose to use the term "comrades in arms," *zhanyou*, literally "war friends," to describe the U.S. group. Mao hoped that by emphasizing that the CCP and the United States were already united through their common fight against the Japanese, he would be able to strengthen the relationship for the postwar period.

The end of the war was in sight and both sides were thinking about the new strategic balance. Mao told the U.S. advisers what they wanted to hear on the subject of the CCP's view on democracy:

The United States will find us more cooperative than the Kuomintang. We will
not be afraid of democratic influence—we will welcome it. We have no silly
ideas of taking *only* Western mechanical techniques. Also we will not be interested in monopolistic, bureaucratic capitalism that stifles the economic development of the country and only enriches the officials. We will be interested in
the most rapid possible development of the country on constructive and pro-
ductive lines . . . America does not need to fear that we will not be cooperative.
We must cooperate and we must have American help. That is why it is so important to us Communists to know what you Americans are thinking and plan-
ning. We cannot risk crossing you—cannot risk any conflict with you.[162]

Mao's claim to support Western-style democracy was a short-term strategy
aimed at the long-term goal of a one-party Leninist dictatorship. It was true in
the sense of the united front policies of the time, when the CCP wanted political
equality with the Nationalists. In 1944 the CCP was relatively weak in comparison to the Nationalist government, its main strength being its armed forces.
Hence it hoped to gain U.S. support in order to strengthen its position. Mao
minimized CCP-Soviet relations in his discussion with the military mission, at
the same time as subtly hinting that he did have a Soviet option if the United
States refused to assist the CCP.[163]

    Not long after the visit of the two delegations, the CCP Central Committee
issued an important early directive on diplomacy.[164] The directive stated that the
CCP would conduct foreign relations from a firmly nationalistic stance, being
neither antiforeign, nor the "foreign-fearing, foreign-fawning" of the previous
one hundred years.[165] CCP *waishi* personnel were advised when dealing with
foreigners to "focus on people's good points, and become good at cooperating."[166] The directive stated that the visit of the two groups signified the beginning of CCP diplomacy, forming part of the development of a new international
united front. The international united front, it was argued, could bring great
gains, as indeed the domestic united front had. This united front could continue
after the war with Japan had ended; from it would first come military cooperation, then cultural cooperation, and finally political and economic cooperation.
The directive identified the most important nations for China as the United
States, the Soviet Union, and Great Britain.[167] It also advocated that China
should, "on the one hand, strengthen national self-respect and self-confidence;
but this does not mean keeping the foreigners out. On the other hand, we should
learn other people's strengths and be good at cooperating with others; but this is
not xenophobia or foreign worship."[168] The tactics of this new-style diplomacy
were "seeking the initiative in everything and never falling into a passive position." In contrast to the behavior of the Nationalist government when dealing
with foreign powers, CCP *waishi* personnel were told not to ask for aid directly,
but to allow "outsiders" to make the offer first, "this will increase their respect
for us." About public information given to outsiders, cadres were instructed,
"things that we reveal should be true; things that cannot be revealed should be
concealed. . . . Things that are not convenient to answer should be avoided or

evaded." Finally, the words used in the directive to describe how to treat guests were a distinct echo of the Qing emperor's instructions to his courtiers regarding the Macartney mission, "On the one hand, there should be no extravagance; on the other hand we should not be cold."[169]

For a brief period, as a result of the Dixie Mission's successful visit to Yan'an, the American Office of Strategic Services (OSS) and the CCP military cooperated. The CCP asked the OSS to provide it with money and communications technology. At the CCP's request, the OSS officers in the Dixie Mission in 1944 agreed to equip 25,000 guerrillas with guns, but the chief of the U.S. special mission in China, Patrick Hurley, and the Nationalist government opposed this offer. Hurley arrived in Yan'an in November 1944, and negotiated a grand plan for post-World War II CCP-Nationalist relations that was immediately scotched by Chiang Kai-shek. Soon after, Hurley announced complete U.S. support for the Nationalist government and purged the core group of U.S. China experts whom Mao and his colleagues had cultivated.[170] The CCP became suspicious of OSS motives and put a halt to a further plan for military aid. In May and August 1945 CCP forces detained two groups of OSS agents who parachuted into puppet-held areas in north China. They shot and mutilated one OSS officer, John Birch, on 25 August 1945 thereby creating a martyr for the right-wing movement in the United States.[171] In two anonymous editorials in July 1945, written for the Xinhua News Agency, the CCP warned that the policy of the United States towards China as represented by Ambassador Hurley was a "threat to world peace."[172] It was a presage of the emerging realignment of CCP foreign relations, a warning that it seems, only those foreigners who held firmly anticommunist views were willing to heed. Some foreigners in isolated areas under the control of the CCP experienced harsh treatment from PLA forces at this time, but there was clearly a different policy for areas where foreigners were more numerous and foreign journalists had more ready access. Between 1945 and 1946, Italian Jesuit priest Father Carlo Suigo was imprisoned and humiliated by the PLA who used him and the other priests of his mission as props to educate the local Chinese population on anti-imperialism. In contrast, the understandably ardent anti-communist Suigo, with some dismay, described the pro-CCP sentiments of UNRRA workers he encountered in Changde as "full of enthusiasm for the way in which the Reds organize the country," though they were not actually living under CCP control.[173]

Civil War

Not long after the Japanese surrender, the hostility between the CCP and the Nationalist government intensified. In the first two years after the Japanese defeat, negotiations between the two parties continued under the mediation of U.S. general George C. Marshall, the personal envoy of President Truman. The positions between the two sides became more intransigent, rather than less, as a result of the talks. The CCP continued its anti-U.S. propaganda movement, attempting to form a "domestic patriotic front" against the United States and their "running dogs" the Nationalists.[174] In November 1946 the CCP Central Committee Foreign Affairs Group, *Zhongyang waishizu*, was formed to act as a de facto Foreign Ministry. Ye Jianying and Wang Bingnan headed the group, under Zhou Enlai's leadership.[175] Setting up a de facto Foreign Ministry was a sign of CCP confidence in its future role in power and an assertion of CCP equality with the Nationalist government. No one could predict exactly when victory might come, but the indications were clear that CCP power was on the rise.

In early 1947, the talks collapsed and full-scale civil war broke out. During the latter half of the civil war period the number of foreigners willing to help the CCP continued to grow, some of them attracted to CCP-style communism. Theoretically, according to the principles of communist internationalism foreigners had a right to join the Communist Party of whichever country they were in. Significantly, two Americans, George Hatem and Sidney Rittenberg, were allowed to join the CCP in the 1940s; the Indian doctor Kotnis was also allowed to join; as was the German doctor Hans Mueller and an Austrian doctor, Richard Freis, who were both working in the CCP-controlled zone.[176] The CCP had foreign supporters in CLARA, CNRRA, and their parent body UNRRA, the United Nations Relief and Rehabilitation Association; U.S. personnel in the truce teams who attempted to negotiate relations between the Communist and Nationalist forces before the civil war began; as well as in the China-based military and foreign affairs corps of a number of Western countries.[177] The party was able to draw on these contacts for support and information and utilize them to spread disinformation about party policies. Foreign supporters of the CCP were still a tiny minority however, in comparison to the numbers of foreigners in China at this time.

In the early years of the civil war, Mao also hoped to attract interest and support for the CCP cause from foreigners outside China, creating an "international united front for peace" whose implicit enemy was the United States.[178] The American journalist Anna Louise Strong was invited to Yan'an in 1946 and conducted a series of interviews that later formed the basis of her book *The Chinese Conquer China*.[179] The most important of these interviews was an informal chat with Mao over dinner that became the much-publicized "paper tiger" talk, when Mao likened Western imperialism to paper tigers: only superficially frightening. Mao explained his views on communism, differentiating his opinion from that of the Soviet Union. He told Strong to go to the West and publicize his views to both the communist and noncommunist worlds. To communists she was to say that *he* believed he would be in power within two years, to noncommunists she was to give this as her personal opinion rather than Mao's.[180]

Strong wrote up these informal chats into two articles, the aforementioned "paper tiger" article and another introducing Mao Zedong thought, which excited some attention as it was the first time a foreign writer had written about

Mao's theories on revolution. She submitted both articles to Lu Dingyi, head of the Propaganda Department, and a team of senior officials edited and improved on them.[181] However as with Snow's *Red Star over China*, by the time Strong's book was written up, the CCP line had altered somewhat. In mid-1948 the war began to turn in the CCP's favor; it had become less necessary for the party to seek the support of those who it had long identified as the main enemy, the imperialist Western powers. As power seemed to be close within his grasp, Mao could begin to act on his long stated revolutionary desire to alter the international balance of power. From this period on Mao focused on seeking a closer relationship with the Soviet Union.[182] Strong was asked to make a number of important changes to reflect the new CCP policy. Unlike Edgar Snow, however, Anna Louise Strong insisted on keeping in what had originally been said to her in interviews. Strong disagreed with CCP editing on two important points: mention of the "Li Lisan line" and that the "dogmatists" who had followed Moscow's instructions on the Chinese revolution in the 1930s "had studied in Moscow." Strong told her friend Maud Russell that CCP advisers wanted both these cut "in order not to seem to criticize Moscow." Disobeying their wishes, she kept the two points in: "I feel sure that if I had been able to have conference, they would have agreed . . . I also think this is needed to show the independence and Chinese nature of the Chinese communists today."[183] Strong seemed oblivious to the CCP's sensitive relations with Moscow; in 1948 the CCP could not afford to offend its sole ally. Stalin had called Mao a turnip—"red on the outside, white on the inside"—and said he was a "margarine Marxist"—not the real thing.[184] He was suspicious of the foreign friends the CCP cultivated. Stalin was afraid that, like Yugoslavia, the CCP would follow its own path separate from the Soviet Union. In 1948, in order to appease Stalin's anxieties, the CCP cut references to Mao Zedong thought in its propaganda. By late 1948 Anna Louise Strong's writings openly favored the Chinese communists, a position that suited neither the CCP nor Moscow at the time. After the Sino-Soviet split this partisanship was useful; in the late 1940s it was an embarrassment. Soon after the publication of Strong's book during a stopover in Moscow on her way to China in 1949, she was arrested as a spy and briefly detained before being expelled. These trumped-up charges did much to destroy Strong's influence and contacts in the communist world.

The Soviet Union pressed the CCP to cut off its contact with noncommunist foreign supporters, accusing some of them of being U.S. agents.[185] From late 1948, CCP policy hardened against individual foreigners, returning to the hard-line language of the prewar period. Once again all foreigners except Soviet citizens were regarded as in the imperialist camp, with the exception of those who proved themselves useful to CCP interests. Few foreigners made the transition to being considered "comrades." The change in line was not solely at the instigation of the Soviet Union; antiforeignism, or rather antagonism toward Western countries, soon became an important tool in CCP efforts to reunite China, both physically and psychologically.

The new stance on foreigners was a further indication that the CCP was gearing up for victory against the Nationalist government. The rapid advance of People's Liberation Army (PLA) forces on Nationalist positions in late 1948 made it imperative that the CCP develop clearly defined policies on its foreign relations. The invading forces were faced with the pressing issue of how to deal with the many foreign nationals, banks, schools, businesses, newspapers, news services, and consulates in "semicolonial, semifeudal" China. The incidents arising out of the Ward case in November 1948, demonstrate the transitional phase of CCP foreign policy in this period. When the victorious PLA forces arrived in Shenyang, the officials of the U.S. Consulate there, led by Consul Angus Ward, were at first treated as if the CCP were prepared to acknowledge their diplomatic status, and implicitly, that they would recognize the diplomatic relations already established between the Nationalist government and foreign powers. This was in accord with CCP directives on how to deal with foreigners issued on 7 February and 1 November 1948.[186] However, within days of taking the city, at the suggestion of the Soviet representative in Shenyang, the communist authorities suddenly informed all Western diplomatic missions in Shenyang that they were to hand over all radio transmitters within thirty-six hours and they immediately ceased recognizing the official status of the diplomats. Of the foreign representatives in the city, only the U.S. Consulate had a radio transmitter; and when they refused to hand it over, the consular officials were placed under house arrest. It was close to a year before the consular staff was released and given permission to return to the United States. The case contributed to the dramatic worsening in the CCP's relations with the United States.[187]

The bungling of the Ward case was the impetus for a number of new directives on *waishi*. Two important meetings in January and March 1949 would decide the basic principles of CCP foreign policy in the Mao era.[188] In January 1949, a Politburo meeting was held at Xibaipo and a "Directive on Diplomatic Work" was published by the Central Committee, drafted by Zhou Enlai and revised by Mao.[189] The directive affirmed the policy of nonrecognition of the Nationalist government's diplomatic relationships and stated that this policy would release China from the humiliating diplomatic ties of the past, assisting in eradicating imperialist privileges in China as well as aiding the nation to achieve independence. The CCP Central Committee ordered that a Foreign Nationals Management Bureau, *waiguo qiaomin guanli ke*, should be set up in every Chinese city with more than one hundred foreigners in residence.[190] All foreigners in these cities would be required to register with these offices, stating their activities in China and reasons for being there. Officials were instructed to gather information relating to the foreign presence within the areas under their control, report these materials back to the central authorities and act only under strict instruction.[191] A February 1949 directive gave further instructions on the new line that would be followed in foreign trade, policies that were closely related to the overall foreign relations line. This directive stressed that new China would focus on trade with the socialist world, only dealing with capitalist countries when absolutely necessary.[192]

In March 1949 the Second Plenum of the Seventh Party Central Committee was held, also at Xibaipo. At the meeting, Mao advocated the principle of "wiping out the control of the imperialists in China completely and methodically."[193] This was a further affirmation that the CCP would not recognize the legitimacy of the foreign relations and treaties established between the Nationalist government and Western countries. Mao also advocated restricting the activities of Western journalists in China, most of whom Mao suspected of being spies.[194] Foreign trade was to be controlled, foreign businesses brought under government management and the customs system restructured. All these would demonstrate to the "foreign imperialists" that the Chinese people were prepared to stand up to them. Foreign economic and cultural establishments in China were to be permitted to exist for the time being, "subject to our supervision and control, to be dealt with by us after country-wide victory." In theory, the "legitimate interests" of ordinary foreign nationals would be "protected and not encroached upon."[195] The new policy was publicized in a September 30, 1949, report in *People's Daily*. However, an earlier internal policy of "squeezing out," *jizou fangzhen*,[196] foreigners from China had been in effect since mid-November 1948 that negated Mao's public guarantees on the protection of legitimate foreign interests. Under this policy the CCP encouraged the "elimination of imperialist influence" from China, in order to prevent enemies "digging themselves in."[197] Putting the U.S. consular officials in Shenyang under house arrest was part of that policy, as was the gradual raising of taxes on foreign enterprises and the encouragement of numerous lawsuits against foreign employers that would bleed them dry without an official declaration of the nationalizing of foreign-owned industry in China.[198] The contradiction between the two policies was deliberate, the confusion gave the CCP more time to consolidate its power in the last months of the civil war and the first years of the People's Republic. Once CCP control was more assured, open antagonism towards foreigners would increase.

The dramatic change in line shocked diplomats and journalists who had been familiar with the more tolerant policies of the 1940s and it made sympathetic foreign supporters more careful in their behavior in China. Up until 1945, there had been a clear contrast between Chongqing and Yan'an, and the CCP's prestige was high even among many anticommunist foreigners. After 1945, the CCP stepped up its rhetoric against the U.S. government, distinguishing between the government and its people and continuing to favor those foreigners in positions of influence who might be able to help the CCP cause. Under the new policies even pro-CCP Western journalists were made to feel unwelcome. They were not given the right to conduct interviews or report on events and were to be treated in the same way as ordinary foreigners.[199] Senior CCP *waishi* cadres such as Huang Hua and Gong Peng actually went to the length of crossing the street to avoid talking to those foreign journalists they had once courted.[200] The new anti-imperialist line was expressed in numerous such symbolic gestures.

When Lin Biao's PLA forces made their dramatic entry into Beijing in February 1949 after several months siege, the soldiers marched into the city carrying American guns, leading many foreign and Chinese observers to believe that they had captured them in their battles with Nationalist troops. However until just before they entered Beijing, Lin Biao's soldiers had actually been using weapons of Soviet, Czech, and Japanese make that had been given to them by the Soviet command in Manchuria. Mao told the Soviets that the last minute switch of weapons had been done to show that "Chiang Kai-shek equipped the troops of the People's Liberation Army with American weaponry."[201]

From January 1949, foreign news services were banned in China and all media outlets in CCP-controlled areas were instructed to rely on the reports of the New China News Agency, *Xinhuashe*, for their international news. In a circular announcing the new policy, the CCP Central Committee described foreign news services as "one of the most powerful weapons of imperialist reactionary propaganda."[202] The *Peip'ing Digest* reported in March 1949, "Decadent U.S. films are to be ousted by healthy Russian films. Fifty Russian movies are already in circulation in North China and thirteen are to be shown in Peip'ing."[203] In May 1949, the CCP Central Committee began to make urgent plans to radically expand Russian language training in China.[204] It was the outward symptom of the new direction in China's foreign affairs, what Mao Zedong called "leaning to one side." In June 1949, Mao Zedong's article "On the People's Democratic Dictatorship" established the historiographical line on the legitimacy of communist rule based on the failure of the Western model in China. In it he outlined the justifications for China's decision to "lean to one side" and align itself with the Soviet Union. In the summer of 1949, Mao launched an intensified nationwide anti-U.S. propaganda campaign.[205]

Also in June 1949, Liu Shaoqi led a delegation from the CCP Central Committee to the Soviet Union and signed a number of agreements on cooperation between the two countries. In a report presented to Stalin on the nature and form that the new CCP government would take the delegation explained the meaning of the "people's democratic dictatorship" which would underpin its rule, a much more inclusive notion than the Leninist "dictatorship of the proletariat" (the underlining and comments are Stalin's): "The point is that China is a <u>semi-colonial state and that during the revolution and after its victory we shall long need concerted action by all forces in the struggle against imperialism and its agents.</u>" In the margin of the report Stalin wrote in bold letters "<u>Yes!</u>"[206] As Stalin acknowledged, since imperialism would constitute the main contradiction in the new society, the control and management of foreigners and foreign things would be an essential unifying force in the future PRC. Instead of making "foreign friends," as *waishi* officials in the war years had been instructed to do, "concerted action" against the forces of imperialism and its agents would be one of the most important tasks of the various *waishi* organizations in the first years after the founding of the PRC.

A large group of Soviet advisers returned to China with the CCP delegation, some came to advise the Chinese Party on setting up a new system of government, others were involved in economic reconstruction, building up the CCP airforce and navy, and upgrading CCP propaganda facilities.[207] The Soviet Union was to provide the blueprint for major reforms in China's education, arts, military, transportation, and foreign affairs system. New China was to be modeled in the image of the Soviet Union, with Western models discarded and discredited. After the CCP victory in October 1949, China's leaders rejected the Western capitalist system as a model for China and set about removing the traces of the colonialist past. Yet China needed technical assistance, trade, and knowledge from the West in order to modernize and strengthen itself. It had to operate in an international system dominated by Western-created structures and political culture. The dilemma of China's new leaders would be to wean the Chinese people from the idea of the superiority of the West, while making use of the achievements which had helped make it rich and powerful.

Notes

1. Joan Hinton, interview, 22 December 1997.
2. Of course the CCP's foreign detractors, noticeably those in the Soviet camp, don't have fond memories at all. This is not surprising, since unlike foreign friends of the CCP, they had no personal investment in the Yan'an mystique. See Otto Braun, *A Comintern Agent in China 1932-1939*, translated by Jeanne Moore (London: C. Hurst and Co., 1982); and Peter Vladimirov, *The Vladimirov Diaries: Yenan, China: 1942-1945* (New York: Doubleday and Co., 1975).
3. See for example Niu Jun, *Cong Yan'an dao shijie*, 1-28; and Zhang Baijia, "Zhou Enlai," in *Chinese Communist Foreign Relations 1920s-1960s*, ed. Hunt and Niu, 71.
4. Robert North, *Moscow and the Chinese Communists* (Stanford, Calif.: Stanford University Press, 1953), 5.
5. North, *Moscow and the Chinese Communists*, 54; C. Martin Wilbur and Julie Lien-ying How, *Missionaries of Revolution: Soviet Advisers and Nationalist China 1920-1927* (Cambridge, Mass.: Harvard University Press, 1989), 27.
6. Tony Saich, *The Origins of the First United Front in China: The Role of Sneevliet (Alias Maring)*, 2 vol., (Leiden: E. J. Brill, 1991), 64.
7. North, *Moscow and the Chinese Communists*, 75.
8. Israel Epstein, *Woman in World History: Song Qingling (Madame Sun Yat-sen)*, 2d ed. (Beijing: New World Press, 1995), 64. Sun affectionately called Soviet adviser Borodin "Lafayette." Vladilen Vorontsov, "Mikhail Borodin: Life Exploit and Tragedy," *Far Eastern Affairs*, no. 1 (1991): 216.
9. Hunt, *The Genesis of Chinese Communist Foreign Policy*, 91.
10. Hunt, *Genesis*, 91.
11. Wang Fan-hsi, *Memoirs of a Chinese Revolutionary*, translated and with an introduction by Gregor Benton (New York: Columbia University Press, 1991), 174. This

derogatory term had a longer history than the CCP usage, the Boxer term for Chinese Christians was "*er mao*," secondary "hairy ones." Mark Elvin, personal communication.

12. Wang Fan-hsi, *Memoirs of a Chinese Revolutionary*, 116.

13. Sheridan, *China in Disintegration*, 177.

14. Sun Wen = Sun Yat-sen.

15. Maud Russell, letter to Asilomar Division, 16 November 1926, Box 1, Maud Russell papers, New York Public Library (hereafter MRP, NYPL).

16. Maud Russell, letter to Orange, 2 December 1926, Box 1, MRP, NYPL.

17. "Three Months of Handbills in Wuchang, Hupeh," 9, trans. Maud Russell, Box 1, MRP, NYPL.

18. Koch, *Double Lives*, 207.

19. "Three Months of Handbills in Wuchang, Hupeh," 13, trans. Maud Russell, Box 1, MRP, NYPL.

20. Hunt, *The Genesis of Chinese Communist Foreign Policy*, 99.

21. See Frederick B. Hoyt, "Protection Implies Intervention: The U.S. Catholic Mission at Kanchow," *The Historian* 38, no. 4 (August 1976): 709-727, for an account of CCP attacks on Catholic missionary stations in Jiangxi in the late 1920s.

22. Hunt, *The Genesis of Chinese Foreign Policy*, 100-101; *ZYWJ*, vol. 6, 241-242, 370-371.

23. Christopher Cook, *The Lion and the Dragon: British Voices from the China Coast* (London: Elm Tree Books, 1985), 140-142.

24. Orvar Karlbeck, *Treasure Seeker in China*, translated by Naomi Walford (London: Cresset Press, 1957), 173.

25. Karlbeck, *Treasure*, 101; *ZYWJ*, vol. 6, 488-490, 370-371; vol. 7, 284-290, 433, 530-534, 802-803; vol. 10, 248-259.

26. "Outline of the Constitution of the Chinese Soviet Republic" (7 November 1931), in Saich, ed., *The Rise to Power of the Chinese Communist Party*, 554.

27. Saich, *Rise*, 556.

28. Zhang Guotao, "Political Report to the Conference of the Fourth Front Army of the Red Army on Party and Political Work" (2 November 1934), Saich, *Rise*, 569.

29. Saich, *Rise*, 576.

30. Hunt, *The Genesis of Chinese Communist Foreign Policy*, 136; *ZYWJ*, vol. 10, 685.

31. R. A. Bosshardt, *The Guiding Hand* (London: Hodder and Stoughton, 1973), 9.

32. R. A. Bosshardt, *The Restraining Hand: Captivity for Christ in China* (London: Hodder and Stoughton, 1936), 22.

33. Bosshardt, *The Restraining Hand*, 129.

34. Bosshardt, *The Guiding Hand*, 70.

35. Bosshardt, *The Restraining Hand*, 21; and Bosshardt, *The Guiding Hand*, 77.

36. Bosshardt, *The Guiding Hand*, 77.

37. Bosshardt, *The Restraining Hand*, 22-23.

38. Bosshardt, *The Guiding Hand*, 99.

39. Bosshardt, *The Guiding Hand*, 139.

40. Bosshardt, *The Guiding Hand*, 139.

41. Harrison Salisbury, *The Long March: The Untold Story* (New York: Harper and Row, 1985), 309, citing a personal communication from Bosshardt.

42. *The Water Margin* (*Shuihu zhuan*) is one of China's most popular novels. Written in the Ming and set in the Song dynasty, it describes the exploits of a gang of "righteous" bandits, led by a former Confucian scribe Song Jiang.

43. Bosshardt, *The Guiding Hand*, 142.

44. Reflecting another major policy shift in *waishi*, the "opening up to the West" policies of the Deng era, in 1984 CCP officials traced Bosshardt to his home in England. In October 1984, the fiftieth anniversary of the Long March, he was featured in a front-page article in the *People's Daily* as the "second" foreigner to go on the Long March (after Braun). Hayman and Kellner didn't get a mention. Salisbury, *The Long March*, 303.

45. Thomas Kampen, *Mao Zedong, Zhou Enlai and the Evolution of the Chinese Communist Leadership* (Copenhagen: Nordic Institute of Asian Studies, 2000), 82.

46. "Resolution of the Central Committee on the Current Political Situation and the Party's Tasks" (25 December 1935), Saich, *The Rise to Power of the Chinese Communist Party*, 714. See also Mao Zedong, "On Tactics against Japanese Imperialism," *Selected Works of Mao Tse-tung* (Peking: Foreign Languages Press, 1975), 171-172.

47. Song Qingling worked closely with Comintern personnel in China, see Frederick S. Litten, "The Noulens Affair," *China Quarterly*, 138 (June 1994): 494. However she did so as a sympathizer rather than as a member, subject to party discipline.

Many of the group of foreigners met through the Zeitgeist Bookshop in Shanghai, both a propaganda outlet and a front for transmitting espionage information. Run by German Irene Wiedemeyer, the bookshop was a base for Comintern double agent Richard Sorge. See Koch, *Double Lives*, 18. As I discussed in chapter 2, Chinese materials tend to downplay the role of foreigners in the revolution, keeping particularly silent on those with Comintern links. Deng Shengshou, "Xibei geming genjudi de waishi huodong," *Zhongguo geming genjudi shi yanjiu*, ed. Ma Gongwu, (Nanjing: Nanjing daxue chubanshe, 1992), 271, mentions briefly the work of Dr Wunsch, a German dentist who was also a Comintern agent and helped the CCP until he was killed during the Xi'an Incident. Agnes Smedley was also an important figure in bringing this group of foreigners together.

48. Rewi Alley, in his memoirs, lists the Marxist-Leninist study group as consisting of himself, Alec Camplin, George Hatem, Ruth Weiss, Trude Rosenberg, Heinz Schippe, Irene Wiedemeyer, Talitha Gerlach, Maud Russell, Lil Haas, Cora Deng, and Cao Liang (Alley, *At 90: Memoirs of My China Years* [Beijing: New World Press, 1986], 79). However, according to Ruth Weiss (interview, 4 September 1997) only George Hatem, herself, Heinz Shippe, and Trude Rosenberg were participants. Shippe was a Comintern agent who died in Shandong in 1941. Rosenberg was Shippe's de facto wife, she died in 1997. She spent her last years living at the Chinese government's expense in the Beijing Friendship Hotel. Ruth Weiss says that what Rewi Alley and others were involved in was a political discussion group, whose participants were also linked with Song Qingling, but quite separate from the original group. Weiss's claim is backed up by the original diary of Maud Russell, kept during the 1930s, and now held in the New York Public Library. Russell recorded a discussion group whose participants are quite different from those Weiss cites, but similar to those on Alley's list. In the post-1949 years, for long-term residents such as Weiss and Alley, claims to membership of a Marxist-Leninist study group were a means to establish political credentials.

49. John Strachey, *The Coming Struggle for Power* (London: Gollancz, 1933). Strachey was a popular writer on socialism in the 1930s.

50.   Wang Jiliang, *Sinuo zhuanji* (Beijing: Huayi chubanshe, 1995), 155; Peter Rand claims the CCP had been told by Moscow to get a foreign journalist to visit the area, but gives no source for his information; see *The China Hands, the Adventures and Ordeals of the American Journalists Who Joined Forces with the Great Chinese Revolution* (New York: Simon and Schuster, 1995), 157; Rewi Alley says Song Qingling was asked to find "a progressive journalist" and a doctor to go to the Soviet area, but does not mention the Moscow connection, Alley, *At 90*, 89.

51.   Deng Shengshou, "Xibei geming genjudi de waishi huodong," 271; Hunt, *The Genesis of Chinese Communist Foreign Policy*, 227.

52.   Edgar Snow, letter to Nelson Johnson, 6 February 1937, Folder 11, Edgar Snow papers, University Archives, University of Missouri-Kansas City (hereafter UA-UMKC).

53.   Edgar Snow, letter to L. M. MacBride, 1 June 1936, Folder 10, Edgar Snow papers, UA-UMKC.

54.   Edgar A. Porter, *The People's Doctor: George Hatem and China's Revolution* (Honolulu: University of Hawaii Press, 1997), 60.

55.   George Hatem, letter to Lazar Katz, 1 August 1935, KC/19/27, George Hatem Collection, UA-UMKC.

56.   Granich interview, transcript, 94.

57.   Liu Pei-chu=Lin Boqu or Lin Zuhan.

58.   Lo Fu=Zhang Wentian.

59.   Po Ku=Qin Bangxian.

60.   Lo Man=Luo Mai or Li Weihan, later head of the United Front Department.

61.   Lin P'iao=Lin Biao.

62.   *Huanying Meiguo tongzhi! Zhongguo tongzhi wansui! Shijia geming wansui!* (Welcome American comrades! Hurrah for the Chinese comrades! Hurrah for the world revolution!)

63.   Edgar Snow, notes, 8-18 July 1936, Folder 121, Edgar Snow papers, UA-UMKC.

64.   Cheng Zhongyuan, "Zai Sinuo 'xixing' zhi qian," *Dang de wenxian*, no. 1 (1992): 94-95; *Nie Rongzhen huiyilu*, (Beijing: Junshi chubanshe, 1983), 484-486.

65.   Shapiro, *Ma Haide: The Saga of an American Doctor George Hatem in China* (New York: Cypress Press, 1993), 40.

66.   Zhang Guotao and Zhu De were still on the Long March, Chen Yi and Xiang Ying were in the south, Liu Shaoqi was in the north, Wang Ming, Chen Yun and Kang Sheng were in Moscow. See Thomas Kampen, *Mao Zedong, Zhou Enlai and the Evolution of the Chinese Communist Leadership* (Copenhagen: Nordic Institute of Asian Studies, 2000), 126.

67.   Kampen, *Mao Zedong*, 126.

068.   Hu Qiaomu, *Hu Qiaomu huiyi Mao Zedong* (Beijing: Renmin chubanshe, 1994), 331.

69.   Edgar Snow, Diary 15, 2, Folder 124, Edgar Snow papers, UA-UMKC.

70.   Edgar Snow, Diary 15, 21, Folder 124, Edgar Snow papers, UA-UMKC.

71.   Edgar Snow, *Red Star over China* (London: Victor Gollancz, 1937), 381. Alice Tisdale Hobart was a popular writer on China; see for example, Alice Tisdale Hobart, *By the City of the Long Sand: A Tale of New China* (New York: Grosset and Dunlap, 1926). On Lady Precious Stream (Wang Baoquan), see S. I. Hsiung, *Lady Precious*

Stream: An Old Chinese Play Done into English According to Its Traditional Style (London: Methuen, 1934).

72.   Edgar Snow, letter to L. M. MacBride, 29 December 1936, Folder 10, Edgar Snow papers, UA-UMKC.

73.   James Bertram, *Capes of China Slide Away: A Memoir of Peace and War* (Auckland: Auckland University Press, 1993), 123.

74.   Helen Foster Snow, "Notes of David Yu," 9 December 1982, Folder 9, Box 2, Helen Foster Snow papers, L. Tom Perry Special Collections, Harold B. Lee Library, Brigham Young University (hereafter cited as HFSP, BYU).

75.   Kenneth E. Shewmaker, *Americans and Chinese Communists, 1927-1945: A Persuading Encounter* (Ithaca and London: Cornell University Press, 1971), 56.

76.   The Left Book Club was a publishing outlet partly funded by the Soviet Union. Soviet agents in Paris, manufacturing "intellectual chic," influenced book choices. Koch, *Double Lives*, 191.

77.   The American Communist Party banned the book from its bookshops, which hampered sales among the American Left. The party (probably party leader Eric Browder, since he had been closely involved in Comintern China activities) objected to the criticisms of Comintern policy in China in the book; Shewmaker, *Americans and Chinese Communists*, 57-58.

78.   Shewmaker, *Americans,* 57.

79.   Shewmaker, *Americans,* 70.

80.   George Hatem, letter to Edgar Snow, 3 December 1936, Folder 10, Edgar Snow papers, UA-UMKC.

81.   Mao Zedong, letter to Edgar Snow, 10 March 1937, Edgar Snow papers, UA-UMKC. The letter does not identify what the changes were.

82.   Bernard S. Thomas, *Season of High Adventure: Edgar Snow in China* (Berkeley, Calif.: University of California Press, 1996), 136.

83.   Granich, interview transcript, 115-116.

84.   Edgar Snow, letter to Earl Browder, 20 March 1938, Folder 12, Edgar Snow papers, UA-UMKC.

85.   The earliest Chinese version seems to be *Waiguo jizhe xibei yinxiangji* (Shanghai: Dingchou bianyishe, 1937). A partial copy is in the Wang Fu Shih collection, UA-UMKC. *Red Star over China* was also published under the title *Xixing manji* and *Mao Zedong zizhuan.*

86.   Wang Fan-hsi, *Chinese Revolutionary,* 240-241.

87.   See Wang Ming, *Mao's Betrayal* (Moscow: Progress Publishers, 1979), 173.

88.   See Edgar Snow, diary 11, 11 June 1936, Folder 120, Edgar Snow papers, UA-UMKC; Edgar Snow, letter to Lance Zavitz, 24 April 1956, Folder 2, correspondence 1956, Alley papers, UA-UMKC.

89.   Shapiro, *Ma Haide,* 64.

90.   Otto Braun, *A Comintern Agent in China,* 253.

91.   Sidney Shapiro, *Ma Haide,* 76.

92.   CLARA was in charge of the CCP-controlled areas, while CNRRA (China Nationalist Areas Relief and Rehabilitation Administration) was in charge of all other parts of China. Both worked under the aegis of UNRRA (the United Nations Relief and Rehabilitation Administration). Jean Chennaux, interview, 23 March 1998.

93.   Sidney Shapiro, *Ma Haide,* 147.

94.   James Bertram, *First Act in China: The Story of the Sian Mutiny* (reprint of 1937 edition *Crisis in China*) (Westport, Conn.: Hyperion Press, 1973), 241. See also Bertram, *Unconquered: Journal of a Year's Adventures among the Fighting Peasants of North China* (New York: John Day and Co., 1939); and *Return to China* (London: Heineman, 1957).

95.   Former *waishi* cadre, interview, September 1995.

96.   Bertram was a New Zealand-born British subject, not the same as being a Britisher. New Zealand did not issue its own passport until 1948. Bertram returned to China on a number of occasions after 1949, twice as a member of New Zealand "Friendship Delegations." Then and earlier, his hosts could have been in no doubt about his citizenship. As Bosshardt's experience showed, the CCP was extremely sensitive to issues of nationality, both before 1949, and after, when foreign visitors came from countries that did not yet have diplomatic relations with China they were frequently described as "representing" their countries in the form of people's diplomacy.

97.   Lu Ning, *The Dynamics of Foreign-Policy Decisionmaking in China*, 66.

98.   This practice, known as "one institution, one team of staffers but with two name plates," is still common in CCP bureaucracy, noticeably in *waishi*. Lu Ning, *Dynamics*, 66.

99.   Zhao Pitao, *Waishi gaishuo*, 32.

100.   "Yi zili gengsheng wei zhu tongshi bu fangsong zhengqu waiyuan," *Mao Zedong waijiao wenxian* (Beijing: Zhonghua renmin gongheguo waijiaobu, 1994), 15.

101.   Zhang Baijia, "Zhou Enlai," in *Chinese Communist Foreign Relations 1920s-1960s*, ed. Hunt and Niu, 70; Pei Xiannong, *Zhou Enlai de waijiaoxue*, 84.

102.   For some of the numbers involved and their backgrounds see Margaret Stanley, *Foreigners in Areas of China under Communist Jurisdiction before 1949: Bibliographical Notes and a Comprehensive Bibliography of the Yenan Hui* (Reference series no. 3, the Centre for East Asian Studies, University of Kansas, 1987).

103.   W. H. Auden and Christopher Isherwood, *Journey to a War* (London: Faber and Faber, 1939), 51.

104.   Earl H. Leaf, "Chinese Reds in Shensi Work Hard and Play Hard; Soviet Capital Scene of Much Laughter, Fun and Sports," *North China Star*, 26 April 1937, 1; "Persons and Personages: Six Women of China," *Living Age*, CCCLIV (March 1938): 40-42.

105.   Helen Foster Snow correspondence, Edgar Snow papers, UA-UMKC.

106.   Evans Fordyce Carlson, *Twin Stars of China* (reprint) (Westport, Conn.: Hyperion Press, 1975), 169.

107.   Edgar Snow, letter to Helen Foster Snow, 12 July 1939, Folder 18, Box 4, HFSP, BYU.

108.   Edgar Snow, letter to Helen Foster Snow, 12 July 1939.

109.   Ilona Ralf Sues, *Sharks Fins and Millet* (Boston: Little, Brown and Co., 1944), 283. Sues visited Yan'an in 1938.

110.   Sues, *Sharks*, 235.

111.   See Stephen R. MacKinnon and Oris Friesen, *China Reporting: An Oral History of American Journalism in the 1930s and 1940s* (Berkeley: University of California Press, 1987), 80-86.

112.   Duan Liancheng, *Duiwai chuanboxue*, 59.

113.   Zhang Baijia, "Zhou Enlai," in *Chinese Communist Foreign Relations 1920s-1960s*, ed. Hunt and Niu, 68.

114. Zhonggong zhongyang wenxian yanjiushi, ed., *Zhou Enlai shuxin xuanji* (Beijing: Zhongyang wenxian chubanshe, 1988), 41.

115. See Zhang Baijia, "Zhou Enlai," in *Chinese Communist Foreign Relations 1920s-1960s*, ed. Hunt and Niu, 69. Many of these useful contacts were involved in setting up and supporting the Chinese Industrial Cooperative Movement (CIC, sometimes known as Indusco), an anti-Japanese economic effort that made use of refugee labor and untapped resources in the interior. Because C.I.C. worked both in Nationalist and communist-controlled areas and had the support of senior leaders in both parties, it was one means of maintaining the fragile united front. After 1949, critics derided C.I.C. as an attempt to steer a "middle way" between the CCP and the Nationalists.

116. See Paul Gordon Lauren, ed., *The China Hands Legacy, Ethics and Diplomacy* (Boulder: Westview Press, 1987), 151-177; and Shewmaker, *Americans and Chinese Communists*, 86-109.

117. "Zhou Enlai tongzhi zenmeyang zuo waiguo jizhe gongzuo," *DWXCCK*, no. 6, (1994).

118. "How Comrade Zhou Enlai Worked on Foreign Journalists."

119. "How Comrade Zhou Enlai Worked on Foreign Journalists."

120. See Agnes Smedley, *China Correspondent* (previously published as *Battle Hymn of China*) (London: Pandora Press, 1984).

121. Shewmaker, *Americans and Chinese Communists*, 158.

122. Apart from journalistic reports, many of these visitors wrote books describing their contact with the CCP; see T. A. Bisson, *Yenan in June 1937: Talks with Communist Leaders* (Berkeley and Los Angeles: Center for Chinese Studies, University of California, 1973); Violet Cressy-Marcks, *Journey into China* (New York: E. P. Dutton, 1942); Agnes Smedley, *Battle Hymn of China* (London: Victor Gollancz, 1944); *The Great Road: The Life and Times of Chuh Teh* (New York: Monthly Review Press, 1956); Helen Foster Snow, *Red Dust: Autobiographies of Chinese Communists* (Stanford: Stanford University Press, 1952).

123. Even cynics could be converted with skillful guidance and warm hospitality. Joy Homer, whose travel book on China openly supported the Nationalist government and portrayed a high degree of skepticism towards the CCP, described Yan'an in the most positive terms after she visited there in 1939. See Joy Homer, *Dawn Watch in China* (Boston: Houghton Mifflin Company, 1941).

124. For an example of the screening of foreigners who wished to visit the communist-controlled areas see Violet Cressy-Marcks, *Journey into China*, 144.

125. Yu Maochun, *OSS in China: Prelude to Cold War* (New Haven: Yale University Press, 1996), 219.

126. Shewmaker, *Americans and Chinese Communists*, 124.

127. Shewmaker, *Americans*, 126.

128. Carlson, *Twin Stars of China*, 47.

129. See for example the experiences of Auden and Isherwood in *Journey to a War*. See also Lachlan Strachan, *Australia's China: Changing Perceptions from the 1930s to the 1990s* (Cambridge: Cambridge University Press, 1996), 28.

130. Mao Zedong, "In Memory of Norman Bethune," 21 December 1939, *Selected Works of Mao Tse-Tung*, vol. 2 (Peking: Foreign Languages Press, 1965), 337.

131. This section draws on a discussion of Norman Bethune in Brady, *Friend of China: The Myth of Rewi Alley* (Richmond, Surrey: RoutledgeCurzon, 2002), 191-192.

132.   Other foreigners later promoted as Internationalists include the Indian doctor Kotnis, who like Bethune, died in the service of the Chinese people; American journalists Agnes Smedley and Anna Louise Strong; and Dr George Hatem (Ma Haide).

133.   See Jean Ewen, *China Nurse, 1932-1939: A Young Canadian Witness of History* (Toronto: McLelland and Stewart, 1981). Ewen was equally brave and as worthy of praise as Bethune, yet she has been ignored in Chinese propagandists' accounts of foreigners' participation in the Chinese revolution.

134.   Braun, *A Comintern Agent in China*, 251.

135.   However, in the 1980s Kotnis would be promoted (on a much lower scale than prominent Western friends of China) both as a symbol of positive Sino-Indian relations and as a model foreign friend.

136.   Soviet diplomats and other officials in the Chinese wartime capital Chongqing at this time were careful to keep their distance from all representatives of the CCP there, in order not to give ammunition to the Nationalists' charge that the CCP was a "stooge" of the Soviet Union; see S. Tikhvinsky, "China in My Life," *Far Eastern Affairs*, no. 4 (1989): 98.

137.   Ted Allen and Sydney Gordon, *The Scalpel and the Sword: The Story of Dr. Norman Bethune*, rev. ed. (New York: Monthly Review Press, 1971), 191.

138.   "On Policy," Van Slyke, *Enemies and Friends*, 273.

139.   "The Organization and Work of United Front Bureaus" (an internal directive issued by the United Front Work Department of the Central Committee on 2 November 1940), translated by Van Slyke, *Enemies and Friends*, 269.

140.   Mao Zedong, "New Democratic Politics and New Democratic Culture," 15 January 1940, Saich, ed., *The Rise to Power of the Chinese Communist Party*, 917.

141.   "On Policy" (an internal directive issued by the United Front Work Department of the Central Committee on 25 December 1940), translated by Van Slyke, *Enemies and Friends*, 274.

142.   Saich, ed., *The Rise to Power of the Chinese Communist Party*, 864.

143.   Yu Maochun, *OSS in China*, 166. According to his granddaughter, Lindsay's intelligence work was of a voluntary nature, Susan V. Lawrence, personal communication, 5 January 2000.

144.   See for example the account of Claire and William Band, *Two Years with the Chinese Communists* (New Haven: Yale University Press, 1948).

145.   *How the 8th Route Army Helped Us to Escape from Peip'ing* (Chungking: CCP Foreign Propaganda Group, September 1942), 3.

146.   *I Fight against the War-Makers with the 8th Route Army*, pamphlet (Chungking: CCP Foreign Propaganda Group, March 1943), 1.

147.   For a firsthand account of this, see Sues, *Sharks Fins and Millet*, 279-280. John Dower mentions the impact returned Japanese soldiers who had been in CCP POW camps had on postwar Japanese society in *Embracing Defeat: Japan in the Wake of World War II* (New York: Norton, 1999).

148.   On the development of postwar Sino-Japanese ties built on such wartime links see, Masao Shimada, *Wei youyi jiaqiao sishi nian* (Beijing: Xinhua chubanshe, 1992); *Zhou Enlai yu Riben pengyoumen* (Beijing: Zhongyang wenxian chubanshe, 1992).

149.   Shi Zhe, *Feng yu gu: Shi Zhe huiyi lu* (Beijing: Hong Qi chubanshe, 1992), 216-217.

150.   Saich, ed., *The Rise to Power of the Chinese Communist Party*, 1009, and Jane L. Price, *Cadres, Commanders, and Commissars: The Training of the Chinese Communist Leadership, 1920-1945* (Boulder: Westview Press, 1976), 179.

151.   Hunt, *The Genesis of Chinese Communist Foreign Policy*, 154.

152.   Shewmaker, *Americans and Chinese Communists*, 160.

153.   Hu Qiaomu, *Hu Qiaomu huiyi Mao Zedong*, 333.

154.   Hu Qiaomu, *Hu Qiaomu huiyi Mao Zedong*, 332. Four of the group of the foreign journalists wrote books of their experience in the CCP-controlled areas. See Israel Epstein, *I Visit Yenan: Eye Witness Account of the Communist-Led Liberated Areas in North-West China* (Bombay: People's Publishing House, 1945); Harrison Forman, *Report from Red China* (New York: Henry Holt, 1945); Stuart Gelder, *The Chinese Communists* (London: Gollancz, 1946); Guenther Stein, *The Challenge of Red China* (New York: McGraw-Hill, 1945). Father Cormac Shanahan, who was part of the group as correspondent for the *Sign* and the *Catholic Monthly* and editor of the *China Correspondent* was the only one of the Western journalists not to come out writing positive reports on the CCP; Shewmaker, *Americans and Chinese Communists*, 169. Even Maurice Votaw, who worked for the Nationalists' Ministry of Information gave a favorable broadcast on the CCP when he was in Yan'an, though he did not publish any stories of the trip. Shewmaker, 163.

155.   Hu Qiaomu, *Hu Qiaomu huiyi Mao Zedong*, 333.

156.   Hu Qiaomu cites Harrison Forman's book *Report from Red China* and Guenther Stein's *The Challenge of Red China* as being particularly useful in promoting the CCP viewpoint, Hu Qiaomu, *Hu Qiaomu huiyi Mao Zedong*, 334.

157.   Rand, *China Hands, the Adventures and Ordeals of the American Journalists Who Joined Forces with the Great Chinese Revolution* (New York: Simon and Schuster, 1995), 238; Shewmaker, *Americans and Chinese Communists*, 160.

158.   See "Report by Second Secretary of Embassy in China, John S. Service," Yenan, July 28, 1944, in *Foreign Relations of the United States Diplomatic Papers 1944*, 6 (China); David D. Barrett, *Dixie Mission: The United States Army Observer Group in Yenan, 1944*, China Research Monograph no. 6 (Center for Chinese Studies, University of California, Berkeley, 1970).

159.   Hu Qiaomu, *Hu Qiaomu huiyi Mao Zedong*, 331. Pei Xiannong, *Zhou Enlai de waijiaoxue*, 84.

160.   Hu Qiaomu, *Hu Qiaomu huiyi Mao Zedong*, p. 335.

161.   Hu Qiaomu, *Hu Qiaomu huiyi Mao Zedong*, 336; *Mao Zedong waijiao wenxian*, 34-38.

162.   Jack Service, Report no. 15, 27 August 1944, 790 (italics in original), Dixie Mission papers, National Archives, Washington, cited in James Reardon-Anderson, *Yenan and the Great Powers* (New York: Columbia Press, 1980), 43.

163.   John Garver, *Sino-Soviet Relations 1937-1945* (New York: Oxford University Press, 1988), 254-255. The CCP was careful to conceal the extent of the Soviet presence at Yan'an from the Dixie Mission and foreign journalists. CCP links with the Soviet Union in the 1930s and 1940s were via radiotelegraph, an annual air flight, and sometimes, special envoys. A handful of Soviet staff were based at Yan'an, consisting of a couple of doctors, journalists, and telegraph officers. CCP personnel went to the Soviet Union for study or medical treatment. The Soviet Union gave approximately US$40,000 a month in financial aid to the CCP, but little military aid. See Garver, *Sino-Soviet Rela-*

tions. See also Yang Kuisong, "Sulian daguimo yuanzhu Zhongguo hongjun de yici changshi," *Jindaishi yanjiu*, no. 1 (1995): 245-275.

164. Zhang Baijia "Zhou Enlai," in *Chinese Communist Foreign Relations 1920s-1960s*, ed. Hunt and Niu, 71.

165. Hu Qiaomu, *Hu Qiaomu huiyi Mao Zedong*, 338.

166. Hu Qiaomu, *Hu Qiaomu huiyi Mao Zedong*, 339.

167. "Directive of the Central Committee on Diplomatic Work" (18 August 1944), Saich, ed., *The Rise to Power of the Chinese Communist Party*, 1212; *ZYWJ*, 314-320.

168. Saich, ed., *Rise*, 1214.

169. Saich, ed., *Rise*, 1215; on the Macartney mission see Hevia, *Cherishing Men from Afar*, 143.

170. Hunt, *The Genesis of Chinese Communist Foreign Policy*, 154-155.

171. Yu Maochun, *OSS in China*, 237-241. In 1958 the John Birch Society was founded as an "anti-Communist freedom organization" in the United States. The society continues today as a right-wing lobby group. See: www.jbs.org.

172. Stuart Schram, *The Political Thought of Mao Tse-tung* (New York: Praeger, 1969), 400.

173. Carlo Suigo, *In the Land of Mao Tse-tung*, (London: Allen and Unwin, 1953), 310.

174. See Sheng, *Battling Western Imperialism*, 150.

175. Pei Xiannong, *Zhou Enlai de waijiaoxue*, 84, 87.

176. *Guoji shishi cidian* (Dictionary of International Affairs) (Beijing: Shangwu yinshudian, 1984), 493. Sidney Rittenberg, e-mail to author, 15 June 1999.

177. Exact details on foreigners who covertly assisted the CCP at this time are few and often speculative. Hu Qiaomu, *Hu Qiaomu huiyi Mao Zedong*, 334, mentions an American adviser within the Nationalist government who passed on information to the CCP, and other "foreign friends" who had given the CCP information (Hu Qiaomu, 337). At the same time, the CCP seemed to be aware that Michael Lindsay, adviser in Yan'an on signals equipment and English-language publications, was a part-time British intelligence officer and that he passed on information about the CCP to the OSS during his time at Yan'an. Yu Maochun, *The OSS in China*, 166. Edgar Snow was also always suspected by the CCP of being a U.S. agent, as were many of those who became known as the friends of China, foreigners like George Hatem who stayed on after 1949.

178. See Sheng, *Battling Western Imperialism*, 150-153.

179. *The Chinese Conquer China* (Garden City, New York: Doubleday, 1949). In this period Israel Epstein's, *The Unfinished Revolution in China* (Boston: Little, Brown and Company, 1947) appeared, as did Jack Belden's *China Shakes the World* (London: Gollancz, 1950). Epstein's book was a potted history of China's exploitation by colonial powers. The book was an attempt to gain the support of the American public for the CCP cause in the same way Snow's *Red Star over China* had done. Belden's book included a description of his visit to the communist-controlled areas in China's northeast.

180. Tracy B. Strong and Helen Keyser, *Right in Her Soul: The Life of Anna Louise Strong* (New York: Random House, 1983), 229; Harrison Salisbury, *China's New Emperors: China in the Era of Mao and Deng* (Boston: Little, Brown and Company, 1990), 86; *Selected Works of Mao Tse-tung*, vol. 4, 99-101. The Chinese version of Mao's discussion with Strong can be found in *Qunzhong*, 5 June 1947. The CCP began to work on improving its intraparty relations at this time by establishing the United Front

Department in September 1948, assigned responsibility to handle contact with Asian Communist Parties as well as overseas Chinese, Hunt, *The Genesis of Chinese Communist Foreign Policy*, 227.

181. Strong and Keyser, *Right in Her Soul*, 227.

182. Chen Jian, *China's Road to the Korean War: The Making of the Sino-American Confrontation* (New York: Columbia University Press, 1994), 68.

183. Undated letter to Maud Russell, approximately late 1948, Anna Louise Strong correspondence, Box 5, MRP, NYPL.

184. Nikita Khrushchev, "Mao Zedong and the Split," *Far Eastern Affairs*, no. 3 (1990): 92, and Yang Kuisong, personal communication; see also Li Zhisui, *The Private Life of Chairman Mao: The Inside Story of the Man Who Made Modern China*, ed. Anne F. Thurston (New York: Random House, 1994), 116.

185. Yang Kuisong, personal communication. See also Yang Kuisong, "The Soviet Factor and the CCP's Policy towards the United States in the 1940s," *Chinese Historians* 5, no. 1 (Spring 1992), and Document No. 1 First Conversation of N. S. Khrushchev with Mao Zedong, Hall of Huaizhentan [Beijing] 31 July 1958, Vladislav M. Zubok, ed., *The Khrushchev-Mao Conversations*, http://cwihp.si.edu/files/zubok-mao.htm.

186. *ZYWJ*, vol. 17, 35-39; Sheng, *Battling Western Imperialism*, 171.

187. For a firsthand account of the Ward case see Ivan Kovalev, The Stalin-Mao Dialogue," *Far Eastern Affairs*, no. 2 (1992): 102-103; Chen Jian discusses the Ward case in *China's Road to the Korean War*, 33-38 and 55-57, and "The Ward Case and the Emergence of Sino-American Confrontation, 1948-1950," *The Australian Journal of Chinese Affairs*, no. 30 (July 1993): 149-170. See also Sheng, *Battling Western Imperialism*, 171-74. In mid-1949 the CCP escalated the charges against the U.S. diplomats, accusing them of espionage. Ward and his officials were not allowed to leave China until late 1949.

188. Zhang Baijia, "Zhou Enlai," in *Chinese Communist Foreign Relations 1920s-1960s*, ed. Hunt and Niu, 78.

189. Zhang Baijia, "Zhou Enlai," 79.

190. "Zhongyang guanyu waijiao gongzuo de zhishi," 19 January 1949, *ZYWJ*, vol. 18, 48.

191. "Instructions on Diplomatic Work," p. 49.

192. "Zhongyang guanyu duiwai maoyi fangzhen de zhishi," 16 February 1949, *ZYWJ*, vol. 18, 136.

193. Mao Zedong, "Report to the Second Session of the Seventh Central Committee," 5 March 1949, in *Selected Works of Mao Tse-Tung*, vol. 4 (Peking: Foreign Languages Press, 1961), 301.

194. He Di, "Most Respected Enemy," in *Chinese Communist Foreign Relations 1920s-1960s*, ed. Hunt and Niu, 31.

195. "Report to the Second Session of the Seventh Central Committee," *Selected Works of Mao Tse-tung*, vol. 4, 370.

196. Sheng, *Battling Western Imperialism*, 172-173; Yang Kuisong, "The Soviet Factor and the CCP's Policy," *Chinese Historians* 5, no. 1 (Spring 1992): 22-25.

197. See *Zhongyang guanyu waijiao gongzuo de zhishi*, 19 January 1949, *ZYWJ*, vol. 18, 44-49. For a description of this process and its connection to overall foreign policy of the period, see *Zhejiang sheng waishi zhi* (Beijing: Zhonghua shuju, 1996), 223.

198. All Japanese enterprises had been nationalized after World War II. See "Talks with Mao Zedong, December 1949-January 1950, and with Zhou Enlai, August-September 1952," Bulletin of the *CWIHP*, 6-7, 4.

199. "Instructions on Diplomatic Work," *ZYWJ*, vol. 18, 47.

200. Peter Rand, *The China Hands*, 310. The CCP no longer required the propaganda assistance of Western bourgeois journalists at this stage of the civil war, when victory was assured.

201. Andrei Ledovsky, "Mikoyan's Secret Mission to China in January and February 1949," *Far Eastern Affairs*, no. 3 (1995): 78.

202. Zhongyang xuanchuanbu bangongting, "Zhong gong zhongyang dui chuli diguozhuyi tongxunshe dianxun banfa de guiding," *Dang de xuanchuan gongzuo wenjian xuanbian* 1949-1966 (hereafter *DDXC*) (Beijing: Zhonggong zhongyang dangxiao chubanshe, 1994), 2.

203. *Peip'ing Digest*, 2 March 1949, quoted in Derk Bodde, *Peking Diary: A Year of Revolution* (London: Jonathan Cape, 1951), 118.

204. "Zhonggong zhongyang guanyu chengli waiwen fanyi jigou de jueding," *DDXC*, vol. 1, 11.

205. Chen Jian, *China's Road to the Korean War*, 57.

206. Report of the CPC Central Committee Delegation, 4 July 1949, in "The Moscow Visit of a Delegation of the Communist Party of China in June to August 1949," *Far Eastern Affairs*, no. 4 (1996): 75.

207. According to Stalin's personal envoy, Ivan Kovalev, 250 Soviet specialists returned with this delegation, bringing the number of Soviet advisers working in China at this time to more than 600. Most went to China's northeast. Ivan Kovalev, "The Stalin-Mao Dialogue," *Far Eastern Affairs*, no. 2 (1992): 103. On the Soviet advisers on propaganda, see "Zhongyang xuanchuanbu guanyu kefu xinwen gongzuo xitong zhong wu zhengfu wu jilu xianxiang, jianchi qingshi baogao zhidu de zhishi," *DDXC*, vol. 1, 38-39.

Chapter 4

Cleaning the House before Inviting the Guests[1]

> Although we could translate some books on diplomacy from fraternal countries such as the Soviet Union, or translate works on foreign policy from capitalist countries; the former can only come fairly close to being of assistance while the latter, from a Marxist-Leninist viewpoint, is unscientific. Only if it is arranged according to a Marxist-Leninist viewpoint can it be said to be scientific. From the former we can adopt a little, from the latter, we can only use it as a technical reference. We must Sinicise diplomacy.[2]

In November 1949, in a talk to cadres of the newly established Foreign Ministry of the People's Republic of China, Foreign Minister Zhou Enlai set out the new line on Chinese foreign policy. The need to Sinicize Marxism had long been a concern of CCP leaders.[3] But what did it mean to Sinicize diplomacy? And which aspects of "Chineseness" were suitable for inclusion in new China's diplomatic strategies and practices? Above all, what was the relationship between Sinicized diplomacy and Marxist-Leninist diplomacy? Grounded in the principles and practices that had developed in the pre-1949 years, PRC diplomacy would stress its own norms and code of behavior; it would even have its own language and theory.[4] There would be an emphasis on traditional norms of interpersonal Chinese etiquette such as working on building relationships between people and approaches to resolving conflict such as looking for common points. From early on CCP foreign policy had stressed the principle of the equality of all states, no matter how large or small, influential or not, and insisted on a respect for national borders and noninterference in the internal affairs of other countries. All these were a reaction to Western imperialism in China in the last one hundred or so years. Zhou's call to Sinicize diplomacy in 1949 was an early indication that, despite its close alliance with the Soviet Union, China would make up its own mind about matters which affected the national interest.

Sinicizing foreign relations also involved dealing with the issue of the considerable numbers of foreigners living in China in the late 1940s and re-educating the Chinese people on the appropriate stance on foreigners and foreign things in new China. In July 1949 there were 120,000 foreign residents living in "liberated" China, with more than 65,000 of them living in Shanghai alone. Another 54,000 lived in the area of what had been Japanese-controlled Manchukuo.[5] CCP ideology projected China as the victim of a hundred or more years of foreign exploitation and incursion, with a society dominated by imperialist influence, all of which had to be eradicated before anything comparable to the Soviet system could be fully set up. What Mao Zedong described as "cleaning the house" was regarded as one of the primary tasks of the new government, more important even than establishing diplomatic recognition.[6] China's "semi-colonial" state was a problem the CPSU had not had to face in the early years of its formation. The Soviet foreign affairs system had primarily been set up to control foreigners who came to the country as guests of the Soviet government, either as visitors or to work.

The PRC was in a relatively stronger position strategically than the Soviet Union had been in its earliest years, which undoubtedly emboldened CCP leaders to take a hard line on the foreign presence in China. A further important contribution to the Sinicizing of the Chinese foreign affairs system was the influence of the Yan'an years when Soviet support to the CCP was limited and distant. When Moscow initiated people's diplomacy and the fostering of foreign friends it was the only communist power, so that most foreigners attracted to socialism were drawn to consider the Soviet Union. However China already had its own group of foreign supporters, many of whom admired the CCP because they believed it to be different from the Soviet Union.[7] China's new leaders had long made a point (in private) of distinguishing themselves from the Soviet model. At the same time, the CCP had a history of often difficult and ambiguous relations with the internationalist foreign comrades sent to China by the Comintern to advise and assist the Chinese revolution. These two factors would add to the tension in the Sino-Soviet relationship throughout the 1950s.

Resolving the Foreign Presence in China

In early October 1949, Zhou Enlai summoned foreign diplomats in Beijing and presented them with a communiqué inviting their governments to establish diplomatic relations with the CCP government. A similar meeting was held in the former capital of the Nationalist government, Nanjing.[8] In accordance with the foreign policy framework established in early 1949, the CCP made it clear that diplomatic relations were to be made on their terms only. Not long after CCP forces captured Nanjing, the U.S. vice-consul was arrested and imprisoned for not obeying military authorities. He was forced to apologize and admit his "imperialist" actions. Diplomats whose governments did not recognize the CCP government were no longer given diplomatic privileges: they were treated only as distinguished foreigners or "ex-ambassadors." The new government set up its

Foreign Ministry, *waijiaobu*, in the new capital, Beijing. Only a Foreign Affairs Office, *waishibu*, was established in Nanjing. All matters had to be conducted in Chinese. No other language was acceptable, and a written record was kept of all official discussions. The ex-ambassadors were not allowed to use ciphers in or couriers for their dispatches. They were not allowed to go outside the city walls, and restrictions were placed on the number of vehicles they were permitted to have.

All foreign residents in China at this time were required to register at the local foreign residents' office or their local police station after the CCP victory, explaining their purpose for being in China and their personal history. Derk Bodde wrote of this experience,

> The procedure is long and onerous. It involves several visits, the writing of quadruplicate answers in Chinese to a fairly detailed questionnaire (rejection if answers are incomplete or wrong), submission of six photos. The climax is a personal interview, lasting anywhere from fifteen minutes to an hour, at which all answers are carefully recorded.[9]

For a small number of foreigners the registration process led to their arrest on charges ranging from spying to abuse of labor laws. For most it was simply an uncomfortable experience which confirmed fears that foreigners were no longer welcome in China.

Many foreigners initially welcomed the new regime. Nyarene Masson, who worked in the overseas-funded Shandan Bailie School from 1949-1950, says; "The Chinese weren't anti-foreign, just anti-capitalism and what it had done to their country. The foreigners were exploiting the Chinese, taking their art and living it up." A pedicab driver in Beijing in 1950 told her, "This is our China now."[10] Many, like Bill Sewell, a university lecturer in Chengdu who had been interned by the Japanese, were "thankful that the old order had passed."[11] The Nationalist army had killed many political prisoners as they departed; some were buried alive. Corruption was rife and inflation was skyrocketing. The new government had quickly brought inflation under control and corruption was strictly forbidden. However, Sewell believed that the Chinese people had "rejected the old government, rather than wholeheartedly accepting the new."[12] There was some reserve among many in the population, both Chinese and foreign, as they waited to see how the new government would behave.

Foreign teachers at Sewell's university were asked to continue teaching. They were assured that they were welcome in China, yet warned that, "any subversion would be met by immediate strong action."[13] The university, which had been largely supported by foreign aid, "must no longer be foreign in outlook."[14] Before long a senior American professor was detained and imprisoned for several months, because of his "bad attitude" to the new government. According to Sewell, "What Langham had done appeared quite trivial, but it seemed that the authorities welcomed this chance to show to the people that they had power over Westerners, who previously had been regarded as above the law."[15] A Chinese staff member was also detained on suspicion of being a foreign agent or, at least, Sewell says, because he was "too involved in foreign ways, giving lavish entertainments to his Western colleagues and talking too much. His irrepressible extrovert nature seemed in some ways to be more Western than part of new China."[16]

In addition to diplomats, missionaries, aid workers, and journalists were also singled out for special attention. A new system to monitor and manage the activities of foreign journalists in China was established in 1950, the regulations were said to have been personally edited by Zhou Enlai.[17] Missionaries were told that as China would construct its own Christian church, foreign missionaries were no longer welcome.[18] CCP policy held that the majority of foreign religious workers were spies for foreign governments; certainly some of the Westerners who were found to be spying in China at this time were from a missionary background.[19] But accusations of spying were primarily a means of discrediting the missionary movement in China. CCP leaders were hostile to the transformative urge of Western do-gooders in China; after 1949 foreign charity was not wanted. In 1951, the Chinese government forbade aid money from Western organizations from coming into China. From this point on, those missionaries and aid workers who had not already left the country were ordered to leave by their foreign headquarters. China Inland Mission minister Rudolf Alfred Bosshardt noted, "the mission had concluded that the presence of missionaries in China was an embarrassment to local Christians."[20] The missions and all Chinese associated with them were heavily taxed. Departing missionaries were virtually forced to leave behind their most valuable possessions for the new communist rulers. Bosshardt and his wife had their luggage searched fifteen times before they were allowed to leave.[21]

In accordance with the official policy of protecting the "legitimate interests" of foreigners and the internal policy of "squeezing out" foreigners and foreign enterprises, foreign residents were not officially forced to leave China, but their presence there was made increasingly difficult by means of crippling taxes, travel restrictions, and the insubordination of formerly trusted Chinese staff who were encouraged to distance themselves from their foreign employers or colleagues. Most foreigners began to feel harassed and under suspicion. Within the first two years after 1949, many of those who had initially been positive about the communist victory became embittered against the new government and sought to leave.[22]

Departure from new China was no simple process: foreigners were required to have so-called "shop guarantees" from two Chinese business people before leaving the country. This guarantee was meant to cover any future or continuing liabilities of the departing foreigners. Foreigners were investigated to see if they had committed any crimes in China before they were allowed to leave and many found it difficult to take anything but their most basic possessions with them when they did depart. Bill Sewell wrote:

Foreigners required exit permits and the Foreign Office took its time to produce these. Intent to leave the country had to be advertised in the local press: and from old servants and others arose endless claims which had to be investigated and settled, increasing the delay. The cadres had to make sure that no university property was mixed with private possessions, so that all baggage had to be listed and every item repeatedly checked. Some thought that bloody-mindedness was carefully cultivated by many officials. Further to add to the difficulties many foreigners were finding ready money hard to obtain.[23]

A cadre told Sewell it was necessary to "show everyone that the power of the men from across the ocean is broken."[24] Foreigners' houses were searched to see if they were American spies or had any "subversive tendencies likely to harm the new China."[25] Exhibitions displayed articles confiscated from foreigners, which demonstrated alleged spying activities and instances of Western brutalities against Chinese citizens. The accusations of foreign spying in China were part of the nationwide reeducation program to turn Chinese citizens against the West. Robert Ford, arrested in Tibet as a "British imperialist spy" suffered several years of interrogation, solitary confinement, and death threats until he finally confessed to crimes he had not committed in the hope that this would speed his release. His interrogator told him, "You think we're inferior, don't you? You British are the lords of the earth. But it's not like that in new China. It's no good asking your consul to help you now. You haven't any more extraterritoriality rights. This is our own country now. You have to deal with Chinese people and they are strong."[26] In December 1951, the government moved against the Catholic organization Legion of Mary, accusing it of engaging in "counterrevolutionary activities" within China.[27] Chinese and foreign members of the Legion of Mary were arrested and sentenced harshly for their involvement in the organization.

By the end of 1951, most foreigners who could, had departed China. Some had no means or place to go to. A number of elderly nonpolitical foreigners were allowed to stay on. In 1954 visiting French journalist Adelbert de Segonzac reported that there were still around three hundred Europeans, mostly French or English, living in Shanghai. A similar number of White Russians also stayed on there, living in very reduced circumstances. The Chinese authorities did nothing to assist them, in the hope that this would encourage them to apply to return to their place of origin.[28] Large numbers of White Russians had been resettled in a new city near Khabarovsk across the Russian border; the more fortunate were accepted as migrants to the U.S. and Australia. At the insistence of Stalin, the northeast and Xinjiang became a zone of Soviet influence, with only Chinese and Soviet citizens allowed to live there.[29] A relatively small number of foreigners remained in prison, mostly on spying charges. These detentions became a highly politicized issue in relations between the United States and China, as the majority of those detained were from the United States. In 1955, 157 U.S. citizens were still being denied exit visas from China and 13 U.S. citizens were held in Chinese prisons for what the U.S. State Department called "political crimes."[30] When they were released, many foreign prisoners showed some sympathy for their captors and were held to have been "brainwashed."[31]

Oppose America—Support Korea[32]

The outbreak of the Korean War on 25 June 1950 undoubtedly intensified antagonism within China towards foreigners. Soon after the war began a major political mobilization campaign was approved which focused on internationalism and patriotism. The patriotic fervor stirred up by this campaign was used as the impetus for a renewed offensive against former Nationalist government supporters and officials and pro-Western elements within China.[33] On 8 October 1950, Mao Zedong issued an order to send "Chinese People's Volunteers" to Korea to support Kim Il-sung's regime in its fight against the UN forces, which were by then rapidly advancing on the Chinese-Korean border. PLA participation in the Korean conflict was a major boost for patriotic education. Within China, the country's role in the war was generally referred to with the shorthand "Resist America, Support Korea," *Kang Mei yuan Chao*. In December 1950, in response to China's support for North Korea, the U.S. government seized control of Chinese government property in areas under its jurisdiction, embargoed all trade with the PRC, and all U.S.-registered ships and planes were prohibited from stopping at Chinese ports and transporting goods destined for China.[34] Also in December 1950, the CCP Central Committee Department of Propaganda published a secret directive on developing "anti-American patriotic propaganda." The goal of the new campaign was to "eradicate a section of the population's (especially people in the cities) feelings of affection, admiration or fear towards the U.S., and establish a standpoint of hostility towards U.S. imperialism, disdaining and scorning it."[35]

Patriotic education was an essential task in the early years of the PRC.[36] As much as a tangible physical danger, the United States represented a psychological threat to the new regime as the major ideological challenge to the goals of the Chinese revolution.[37] American-style democracy and individualism were articulated as being the very opposite of the system the government was installing. CCP ideologues sought to destroy the power of these ideas through successive political campaigns.[38] It was assumed that those Chinese who had worked with or had contact with foreigners in China had been tainted by imperialism. In a 1951 speech at a major conference on united front work, propaganda chief Lu Dingyi argued that it was necessary to work to bring these people "onto our side."[39] Control of foreign influence within China was seen as an important means to maintain social cohesion and unity. It was an important aspect of the new government's task to create an image of a new China in the minds of Chinese, and ultimately, foreigners too. As Chen Xiaomei has argued, in the CCP's

China, the Western Other was to be used not for the purpose of dominating the West, but rather to discipline and ultimately dominate the Chinese Self.[40] The "Resist America, Support Korea" campaign became a focus for re-educating the population on the proper attitude towards the West, while rooting out "a hundred or more years of national inferiority."[41] It aimed to encourage nationalism and unite the country against the capitalist, imperialist Western world, while instilling a sense of solidarity for China's Asian, particularly communist, neighbors. It was also aimed at reconstructing the image of the West in China. At mass meetings during the campaign at Chengdu University for example, those Chinese staff who had studied in the United States were encouraged to confess how they had been corrupted by Western "contamination."[42] Local propaganda cadres had been instructed to locate either a returned student who could tell mass meetings of their personal experience of the "dark and reactionary atmosphere in the U.S.;" someone who had suffered directly at the hands of U.S. imperialism; or someone who had formerly admired the United States who would "spit out and criticize their [former] confused viewpoint and wrong intentions" at the meeting.[43] In January 1951, local *waishi* offices established organizations to "control and freeze," *guanzhi yu dongjie*, all publicly and privately-controlled U.S. assets and bank deposits in China, as well as U.S.-funded cultural, educational, religious, and charitable organizations.[44] The anti-U.S. propaganda campaign was combined with a three-year party rectification movement; and on a national scale, it was quickly followed by the Three Antis Movement, *sanfan yundong*, and then the Five Antis Movement, *wufan yundong*, both of which were designed to extend the goals of the earlier campaigns.[45] Further propaganda campaigns such as the antidrugs movement in 1952 and propaganda on the Korean Armistice in 1953 were also designed to stress the negative aspects of Sino-foreign contact in the modern era and Western imperialism in general.[46] It should be noted that in a parallel period, both Chinese residents in the United States and non-Chinese U.S. residents thought to be "communist sympathizers" were also experiencing rough treatment and the U.S. media featured reports detailing an extremely antagonistic view of "Red China."

In February 1952 the North Korean and Chinese authorities announced that they had discovered bacterial bombs dropped by U.S. planes in an attempt to spread plague, typhoid, anthrax, and other diseases.[47] The accusations immediately became contested; the United States and its allies denounced the claims as disinformation, while the Soviet Union, China, and its allies attacked germ warfare and other UN-forces atrocities in the Korean War. China's foreign supporters were closely involved in the worldwide campaign to promote the germ warfare charges. Within China, a massive sanitation campaign was begun, under the slogan "to be sanitary is patriotic."[48] Residents of Liaoning, Jilin, Beijing, and Tianjin were vaccinated against various diseases the infected insects were believed to be carrying.[49] Propaganda materials of the period carried cartoons of strapping Chinese scientists killing off insectlike foreigners, a symbolic representation of the process of eliminating the physical and psychological foreign presence in China.[50]

The Chinese and North Korean claims were supported by the confessions of a number of captured U.S. air force personnel who admitted to being involved in dropping the bacterial bombs.[51] After refusing the offer of an International Red Cross investigation into the allegations, the PRC organized its own international panel, which carried out investigations between June and August 1952. The "International Scientific Commission for the Investigation of the Facts Concerning Bacteriological Warfare in Korea and China," headed by prominent leftist British scientist Joseph Needham, accepted the germ warfare allegations as valid.[52] The report's conclusion was highly controversial and has been much contested over the years. While the issues remain contested, recent research suggests that the germ warfare allegations were in fact false.[53]

The repatriation of Korean War POWs became a major issue in the peace talks. The United States refused to return all the Chinese and Korean POWs, claiming that a number did not wish to go back to their home countries.[54] In response, the Chinese and Korean authorities delayed handing back their own captives. As they had done with Japanese POWs in World War II, Chinese cadres spent much time discussing political issues with those prisoners they considered to be receptive, working to persuade some to come over to the communist side. As part of preparations before entering the war, all Chinese military and political officers had received training on the character of American soldiers.[55] Twenty-one U.S. soldiers and one British soldier refused repatriation.[56]

The 1950s ongoing anti-American campaign was combined with a pro-Soviet campaign. This was necessary in order that Chinese citizens learn to distinguish clearly between foreign enemies and those now designated as foreign friends and comrades. When PLA soldiers led by Marshall Liu Bocheng entered Nanjing in April 1949, one of the first columns of troops to arrive in the city shot at a welcoming delegation of Soviet diplomats and cursed them as "*yang guizi!*" (foreign devils).[57] Faux pas such as this underlined the urgent need for careful ideological training on differentiating foreign friends from foreign enemies. In July 1949 Liu Shaoqi made a point of assuring Stalin that special instructions had been drawn up for party organizations to ensure that "no one might do any wrong to them (Soviet advisers and diplomats)."[58] The pro-Soviet propaganda campaign was led by the Society of Sino-Soviet Friendship, which was established in July 1949.[59] For a brief period in the 1950s, the association's efforts permeated every aspect of Chinese life: each region, or main administrative division, had its own regional office, while each province or special municipality, a branch office; and every enterprise, factory, or school was supposed to maintain a suboffice.[60] Chinese citizens were told "The Soviet Union's Today is Our Tomorrow," *Sulian de jintian shi women de mingtian*.[61] Russian quickly became the most common foreign language in Chinese schools and universities in the 1950s. From this point on Esther Holland Jian, a British woman living with her husband at Xiamen University records:

"Learn from the Soviet Union" was the motto in all walks of life. Soviet advisers came with their families. The first thing for the faculty members was to learn Russian. Training camps and training centers were established and Russian became the first foreign language (actually the only foreign language) in all schools at various levels. On the education front, every minute detail was copied from the Russians, without discrimination, even the lunch hour was pushed back to three in the afternoon in order to ensure the practice of having six classes in succession in the mornings.[62]

Soviet culture was utilized as an attempt to imbue Chinese with a sense of trust and friendship toward the Soviet Union. The Sino-Soviet Friendship Association produced a monthly magazine, distributed books, showed films and plays, held photographic exhibitions, organized Russian lessons, and sponsored visits of Russian writers and performers to China and reciprocal visits of Chinese cultural personages to the Soviet Union.[63]

Following the Korean armistice in 1953, a further, much larger, influx of Soviet advisers arrived in China.[64] Most of this new group were based in Beijing. In addition to military specialists, they included advisers on science, education, and the arts. In 1954 the gigantic Hotel Druzhba (*Youyi Binguan*) was constructed to house the new influx. With 1,560 guest rooms it could accommodate 3,100 residents.[65] The hotel was a world to itself. The Soviet advisers had their own theater, dance hall, library, swimming pool, tennis courts, gym, shops, hairdresser, photographic studio, post office, medical clinic, bar, café, six restaurants as well as a special school for their children. Each two advisers had a limousine at their disposal. They were extremely well paid, many earning enough in a two-year stay to buy a car, normally beyond the means of most Soviet citizens. They also had access to luxurious foods not available to Chinese citizens.[66] The Russians seldom mixed with the other foreigners in China at this time. Long-term British resident David Crook recalls that the Soviet advisers' lives were very controlled—by Moscow, not Beijing: "They had their own regimen. They were not allowed to ride in pedicabs. The women were not allowed to wear trousers and the men were not allowed to wear shorts."[67] The Chinese authorities routinely opened the Soviet advisers' letters and kept a close eye on their activities.[68] Apart from those based in Beijing, many other Soviet advisers were scattered around the country, working on special projects such as the construction of the first bridge over the Yangzi River. During the 1950s, the PRC and the Soviet Union exchanged more than 50,000 long-term visitors. Up to 11,000 Soviet scientists and specialists were based in China and an equivalent number of Chinese specialists and students went to the Soviet Union for further training. Some 30,000 Chinese workers received special training in Soviet factories.[69] In addition to technical assistance, in the period from 1950-1957 alone, the Soviet Union gave China credits totaling US$2.25 billion.[70] And between 1950 and 1959 the Soviet Union delivered ten billion rubles' worth of machines and equipment to China and five billion worth of complete industrial plants. By 1956, 80 percent of China's trade was with the Communist bloc, 70 percent of it with the

Soviet Union. By the end of the 1950s, China was in a position of complete economic dependence on the Soviet Union.[71]

Setting Up a New Kitchen: Establishing the *Waishi* System

In addition to "leaning to one side," *yibian dao*, and "cleaning the house before inviting the guests," *ba fangwu dasao ganjing zai qing ke*, the third major policy direction of CCP foreign affairs in the first three years after 1949 was defined by Mao as "setting up a new kitchen," *ling qi luzao*.[72] This meant establishing the PRC's own foreign relations rather than simply inheriting those of the former Nationalist government. It also entailed setting up a *waishi* system loyal to the views of the CCP. Under the guidance of Soviet advisers, the CCP expanded its already existing foreign affairs operation to fit the new needs of the government. PRC foreign affairs learned much from the Soviet Union. CCP delegations studied the Soviet model of government and administration, including specific instruction on Soviet foreign affairs.[73] Chinese diplomats were advised by Soviet foreign minister Molotov on how to conduct diplomatic talks and Soviet texts on diplomacy were translated into Chinese.[74] The Soviet chargé d'affaires in 1950 gave a series of lectures on international law for future diplomats in training at People's University and Chinese students were sent to the Soviet Union to study at Soviet foreign affairs institutions.[75] The PRC set up foreign affairs organizations apparently identical to Soviet ones, with virtually the same structures and outwardly identical methodology.[76]

The PRC's first fifteen ambassadors were virtually all former senior PLA generals, chosen primarily for political loyalty rather than their foreign affairs knowledge or foreign language skills. Mao told the group at a meeting before their departure,

> You have taken off your military uniform and put on plain clothes. Diplomatic work is a political struggle; you don't engage in a war of weapons, you engage in a war of words. We need good cadres, patient cadres. You are all generals, although you can't speak foreign languages, if we send you off, we're not worried, because you won't be able to run away.[77]

Zhou Enlai also emphasized the issue of loyalty when he spoke to the group, telling them the CCP Central Committee had carefully chosen them rather than other candidates, because firstly, "You won't run off, and second, you won't be afraid, and thirdly, your organizational discipline is very strong."[78] A small corps of diplomats from the Nationalist government was retained as advisers while the rest of the personnel were made up of young graduates with a foreign languages background, former PLA staff, and those who had been involved in united front work, or engaged in underground party work in White areas.[79]

The Foreign Ministry was only one of a number of organizations involved in foreign affairs activities. The most important of these was the CCP Central

Committee International Liaison Department, *Zhonggong zhongyang lianluobu*. This organization handled the visits of high-ranking communists or sympathizers in addition to having a crucial policymaking role. Partly for ideological purposes and partly because of the practical reason that for many years after 1949 only a minority of countries recognized the PRC, so-called "peoples" or unofficial diplomacy had an important role in the foreign policy of new China.[80] After 1949 the CCP set up a number of "people's organizations" which were involved in various forms of "unofficial" diplomacy. In 1950, the Conference of Asian and Australian Trade Unions set up a liaison bureau of the World Federation of Trade Unions in Beijing that acted as an offshoot of Cominform (the post-World War II version of the Comintern). The CCP had been assigned the task of taking over responsibility for supporting communist parties, trade unions, and peace activists in the Asia and Pacific region.[81] Established in late 1949, the Chinese People's Committee for Defending World Peace, *Zhongguo renmin baowei shijie heping dahui*, commonly abbreviated as *He da*, had an important role in these early years. The organization's activities were closely linked to its counterparts in the Soviet bloc. In the first three years of its existence it hosted 1,041 visitors from 54 countries and sent 2,096 Chinese delegates to 27 different events.[82] In December 1949 the China People's Institute of Foreign Affairs, *Zhongguo renmin waijiao xuehui*, was established to make contact with senior political leaders of various nations in a semiofficial capacity.[83] It soon became an important channel for China to expand diplomatic contacts.

Participation in world peace activities had been identified as a priority for the countries of the Communist bloc at a November 1949 Cominform meeting in Prague. The final report of the meeting stated that "it was of the utmost importance to unite all genuine supporters on the broadest possible "fight for peace" platform, in order to counter the "imperialist" powers who were "pursuing a policy of aggression and preparation for a new war."[84] Communist support for the worldwide peace movement was essentially an effort to postpone the threat of the Third World War erupting into a reality. From Moscow's point of view, support for the international peace movement was a means to slow down the U.S. atomic program, giving the Soviet Union more time to build up its own program. For the CCP, peace meant an acceptance by the West of the Chinese revolution, an acknowledgment that the Chinese Communist Party was the legitimate government of China, and an end to Western aggression against China. By no means did Chinese peace imply China's demilitarization or disarmament.[85]

Beginning in 1952, in addition to those that came for short-term visits, the Peace Committee was host for a small group of foreigners designated in English as "permanent guests of the Peace Committee," in Chinese *changqi zhu He Da*. These were foreigners who often for political reasons were unable, or chose not, to return to their home countries, who involved themselves in "peace" activities such as writing propaganda and attending international peace conferences. Ostensibly representing their own countries, they inevitably mimicked the Chinese line.[86] A 1952 lecture given to *waishi* cadres explained the PRC's support for the peace movement in the following terms:

> There are now large scale, powerful peace campaigns in capitalist countries. Those participating in these campaigns represent all kinds of people, including petty-bourgeoisie and even capitalist elements. Although such campaigns are not socialistic in nature, they are against imperialism, the deadly enemy of the working class. The development of such campaigns is undoubtedly helpful to the liberation of the working class. Therefore, the CP must participate in and lead such peace campaigns.[87]

Ninteen-fifty-two was significant as the year the Asia Pacific Peace Festival was held in Beijing, attended by several thousand foreign delegates.[88] It was also important in that it was considered that most of the activities to eliminate imperialist influence in China had been completed by this time.[89] People's diplomacy activities went into a higher gear after this year, with the numbers of visitors increasing considerably. Several hotels were hurriedly built in Beijing to cope with the influx of visitors from this time on.

In 1952 the China Council for the Promotion of International Trade, *Zhongguo guoji maoyi cujin weiyuanhui*, was established to enable Beijing to pursue trade relations with those countries with whom diplomatic relations had not yet been set up and to break through the "imperialist economic blockade."[90] All trade between the PRC and foreign countries was to be conducted on the basis of "equality and mutual benefit."[91] In 1954 the Chinese People's Association for Cultural Exchanges, *Zhongguo renmin duiwai wenhua xiehui*, was set up. Its goal was to improve China's international image as well as being a means to facilitate nonofficial contact with other countries. Its purpose was to "expedite the development of international relations."[92] In addition, concomitant, *duikou*, China Friendship Associations were formed with various countries, beginning with the aforementioned Sino-Soviet Friendship Association.[93]

Foreign propaganda work supported the activities of all the various *waishi* organizations. Following the Soviet approach, propaganda was regarded as a "science" in the PRC. Foreign propaganda was targeted at specific groups in an appropriately specialized format. The PRC's shortwave service (in these days known as Peking Radio, or simply Radio, by the foreign experts who worked there) had been broadcasting since 1948. In the early 1950s a number of propaganda magazines were established aimed at a variety of foreign readerships. *China Reconstructs* was one of the earliest and most prominent of these magazines. In 1952, the stateless Israel Epstein, whose application for U.S. citizenship had been rejected due to his known pro-CCP sympathies, was invited back to China to run the magazine, though Song Qingling was the nominal chief editor. The Foreign Languages Press was created in the same period, to translate selected Chinese books into foreign tongues. It also had responsibility for translating politically acceptable foreign books into Chinese. Reporting on all foreign matters was strictly controlled. After 1952, all coverage of international events was administered by Xinhua News Agency and *Renmin Ribao*. Chinese media personnel were instructed that they were only allowed to report international events with the permission of the central authorities. The only discretion in reporting matters related to international affairs was the ruling that if foreign guests visited a given area, local papers could mention the visit without the need to get permission from Beijing. This was seen as in the interests of "international etiquette."[94] In 1954 an organization called the Friendship Alliance, *lianyihui*, was set up specifically to host the visits of foreign journalists to China. The organization existed in name only. If foreign journalists asked to know whom its members were, the Chinese journalists hosting them were instructed to tell them that they themselves were.[95]

Beginning in 1952, further local *waishi* offices were established in areas open to foreign visitors such as Zhejiang Province, location of the tourist city Hangzhou. Administration and *waishi* work was standardized and professionalized according to a system of *waishi* rules and regulations, *waishi guizhang zhidu*.[96] *Waishi* relating to more long-term residents was the responsibility of the *waishi bangongshi* (*waiban*), or Foreign Affairs Office, in the small number of universities and other work units that accepted foreigners in the 1950s era. Overall responsibility for most foreigners employed by the Chinese government was the task of the Foreign Experts Bureau, formed in 1954 to deal with those formally designated as "experts."[97] Foreign experts were paid wages ten times that of the ordinary worker and three to four times that of Chinese professors.

In the early 1950s the party and military leadership dominated *waishi* strategy. The outbreak of the Korean War delayed the shift to a civilian regime in virtually all areas of government. In 1954, a new constitution was established and a civilian government established. Nevertheless, most major policy decisions were still made by senior leaders. *Waishi* matters came under the responsibility of a number of bureaucracies: the Party Secretariat under Deng Xiaoping which was concerned with party and mass work (including fraternal relations with other communist parties and Overseas Chinese Affairs); the Military Commission of which Zhou Enlai was executive vice-chairman; and the State Council under Zhou Enlai, which among other matters made decisions on the economy and noncommunist foreign relations.

In 1955 the *waishi* decision-making structure was changed once more. The CCP set up departments at every level of authority, responsible for each functional subsystem in the government. Under this new structure, *waishi* was controlled by the CCP Central Committee International Activities Guiding Committee, *Zhongyang guoji huodong zhidao weiyuanhui*, which made recommendations on policy and coordinated its implementation through the various party bureaus. The International Liaison Department handled foreign relations and foreign policy research, the Propaganda Department foreign propaganda, the Investigation Department focused on intelligence work, and the Finance and Trade Department dealt with foreign economic relations.[98] A further CCP Central Committee foreign affairs organ was established in 1956 to handle foreign cultural and educational exchanges: the Foreign Culture Department. This was the Chinese equivalent of the Soviet Union's VOKS. As it would be in the years to come, the foreign affairs organizational structure was not a strictly vertical top-down link. Bureaucratic responsibilities and associations reached vertically as well as horizontally, depending on the issue in question.[99]

Establishing the Norms of *Waishi*

Until 1949, *waishi* was dominated by a small group associated with Zhou Enlai. Once the CCP came to power there was an urgent need to expand *waishi* staff and skills.[100] *Waishi* personnel in the first years after 1949 consisted of a mixture of trusted CCP officials and former PLA personnel (who would almost all have been party members), large numbers of nonparty intellectuals with foreign language skills and a small number of officials who had formerly worked in foreign affairs for the Nationalist government. All key positions were held by senior, politically trustworthy CCP members. Periodic training sessions, *peixun ban*, were held and strict discipline, *jilü*, was stressed.[101] The CCP had established its own Foreign Languages School at Yan'an as early as 1941, and after 1949 the core of that institution became the Beijing Foreign Languages Institute, a major source of *waishi* personnel. People's University in Beijing was a further training ground for *waishi* personnel in these early years.[102] In 1955 the Diplomatic School, *Zhongguo waijiao xueyuan*, was opened, as were special courses to train *waishi* personnel at Beijing and Fudan Universities. Other top universities were also encouraged to put forward their best students for future *waishi* work.[103]

Waishi bureaus received the important overseas papers and knew what was being said about China in the international press. *Waishi* cadres were required to be familiar with foreign affairs policies and regulations and the current foreign propaganda line. At regular "report meetings," *baogao hui*, important directives were discussed. Those personnel who were involved in handling foreign visits were given particular instructions on "how to be kind to people" and "how to be caring."[104] They were also given summaries of successful visits to study. Occasionally larger-scale conferences would be held to keep staff up to date with the party's line on foreign policy and *waishi* procedures. Personnel from a wide range of organizations involved in *waishi* work attended.[105] In the early years of *waishi*, the stress was on knowing how to manage and host foreigners; from the 1957 Anti-Rightist Campaign onwards the emphasis would be on not making a political mistake.[106]

Those involved in *waishi* work were discouraged from having overseas contacts or nonofficial relationships with foreigners. They even had to be careful about contact with some Chinese. Any contacts outside the work unit had to be notified to senior staff. Most of the lower level and middle-ranked *waishi* staff in the early 1950s had overseas links and came from what were now regarded as "bourgeois" backgrounds. They were familiar with Western society and customs. After 1955, a new policy began to train those from a "proletarian" class background to engage in *waishi*. The goal was that these "proletarian" cadres would eventually take over from those with a bourgeois background.[107] The assumption was that this new generation of *waishi* personnel, untainted by contact with the corrupting West and of good proletarian or peasant stock, were of a higher quality, *suzhi*, than those of bad class origins. Such an assumption was a logical follow-on from the CCP's obsession with purging China of the stain of the imperialist past.

The personnel of Chinese organizations involved in people's diplomacy prepared for a typical visit from a foreign delegation by attempting to find out as much as they could about the group and the opinions of its members. They tried to find a common point on which they could all agree on and thereby strengthen the relationship. Common points included children, sports, gardening, and other topics, not only politics. Cadres were required to report all conversations with their foreign charges; in particular they were required to extract foreigners' opinions on various political questions. Even nonofficial conversations with foreigners had to be reported back.[108] All Chinese personnel who had contact with foreigners were required to follow *waishi* regulations on how to interact with them. For example, Chinese interpreters were not supposed to sit next to foreigners in a car.[109] If *waishi* staff received a gift from a foreigner, this had to be handed in to the work unit. Chinese who visited their foreign friends had to give a précis of what they had discussed after each visit.[110] During officially arranged meetings, it was necessary for Chinese citizens to speak with foreigners through an interpreter, even if they were fluent in the language of their foreign guest. New Zealand visitor Courtney Archer recalled a visit to his old friend Song Qingling during a trip to China in 1956,

> when I visited Madame Sun [Song Qingling] in 1952 with a group of New Zealanders, she spoke through a translator although her English was perfect as I knew from previous, pre-1949 visits. She did speak a few words of English on that occasion—as the group left Madame Sun took my arm and whispered in my ear, in English, "This is fun, isn't it." It was widespread in the early years for people with good English to have to use interpreters in all contacts with foreigners, often to the exasperation of people being interviewed while the translator struggled especially with technical words or subjects. I suspect this device was used so that the speakers could always claim that they were mistranslated if there was unfavorable comment in foreign publications.[111]

The foreign visitors' contact with ordinary Chinese was carefully scripted and controlled. Those with responsibilities for hosting foreign visitors or who had contact with foreigners outside of China such as Chinese diplomats, students, and officials traveling on business were given detailed instructions on the line they were to take on sensitive issues of interest to foreigners such as the nationalization of Chinese industry and the Hundred Flowers campaign of 1956-1957.[112] One of the important tasks of *waishi* officials assigned to manage these visits was to persuade the foreigners in their charge to accept the current line.[113] Chinese researchers were instructed that if their work brought them into contact with foreign experts or visitors, all interactions were to be conducted in the presence of another staff member.[114] Foreign visitors in the 1950s were often given expensive gifts such as handmade suits, and according to one former minder for the Asian-Australian Liaison Office of the World Federation of Trade Union, "even the rightists liked this."[115] In addition to senior leaders, a number of Chinese figures with international reputations were selected to be on hand to meet with foreign guests. In the 1950s writer Guo Moruo and the widow of Sun Yat-sen, Song Qingling, were among the most prominent. Song Qingling had a special budget to invite foreign heads of state and prominent foreign friends for "intimate" dinners at her official mansions in Beijing and Shanghai—Ho Chi-minh, Nehru, Sukarno, and Edgar Snow were among those invited there.[116] In all its people's diplomacy activities, CCP *waishi* experts advised that each visitor should be put in touch with contacts appropriate to their occupation, "Soldier to soldier, general to general, each profession should be put together."[117] This meant that a much wider range than those officially employed in foreign affairs work could take on a foreign affairs role, depending on the circumstances.

Political Tourism

The only persecution I saw in China was of the fly.

—Australian Labor Party MP, Leslie Haylen,
1959[118]

Foreign guests in the 1950s were relatively few, but each was regarded as a symbolic blow to the U.S.-led policy of isolation and blockade of the PRC. Visitors were selected for their credibility and their favorable attitude toward Beijing. Those who were invited and did not accept the views of their Chinese hosts were met with strong hostility and a refusal to conduct further discussions. They were not likely to be invited to return.[119] A visit to see new China was not meant to be an exchange of ideas: the visitors' role was to learn and admire, and if possible write favorable reports which could be used in China and the West. Many delegations came to China as part of a tour to a number of communist countries, one of many Soviet-led efforts to weaken opposition towards communist countries in the West. For China such delegations and visitors also supported a goal relevant to its own national interests, diplomatic recognition of the People's Republic. This approach was summed up by the policy, "First engage in people's diplomacy, then use people's diplomacy to establish official relations."[120]

Simone de Beauvoir and Jean-Paul Sartre made a high-profile two-month visit to China in 1955. De Beauvoir described the trip in her book *The Long March*, but her letters to her former lover Nelson Algren are a more reliable gauge of her views on China at the time. She knew that she was expected to write a book on the trip; de Beauvoir told Algren that it would be "filled with lies about the things I did not see, and so I must do some heavy research."[121] She certainly did a lot of research for the book, filling 501 pages with notes taken from information sessions after numerous visits to newly constructed dams, bridges, and other symbols of new China. De Beauvoir and Sartre were unhappy that they were never free to wander at will. Guides were constantly with them, effectively insulating them from any informal contact. De Beauvoir suspected many of her conversations with the Chinese she visited were censored in the course of translation[122]—though it is questionable that even if she had spoken Chinese herself that she would have fared any better at getting close to Chinese people in this period. Yet in the published book of her trip she emphasized that she was free to meet whoever she wanted, that her interpreter "is not under any instruction to erect fences around me or to sieve the remarks made by people I meet."[123] Praising the Chinese author Chen Xuezhao who accompanied the two French philosophers on a tour from Shenyang to Canton, de Beauvoir wrote,

> Never a word of nonsense or propaganda from her lips; she is so firmly convinced of the benefits conferred by the regime and its necessity that she has no need to tell fibs to herself or anyone else; independent, sponta-neous, fond of laughing and fonder yet of talking, she knows nothing of self-censorship: witty, tranquil, her frankness in great measure made up for the inflexibility of most of the cadres I had dealings with.[124]

Chen Xuezhao's 1990 memoirs show another side to the account of the two phi-losophers' China travels. In the brief description she gives of her tour guide du-ties, Chen mentions her embarrassment when de Beauvoir and Sartre encour-aged her to return to France for a visit. In reply, in line with the CCP policy of encouraging overseas Chinese to return to serve the motherland, she asked them to tell an old acquaintance, the writer Cai Boling, that *he* should leave *France* and return to China. What de Beauvoir described as Chen's "frankness" and "spontaneity" was officially sanctioned by "the leadership," who allowed her to speak directly to the philosophers, rather than through the interpreter who ac-companied them at all times.[125] As planned, this resulted in the pair finding her more "believable" than others they spoke to.

Simone de Beauvoir and Jean-Paul Sartre were based in Beijing for a month, attending the National Day celebrations on the Tiananmen podium with Mao Zedong; they also visited Shenyang, Shanghai, Hangzhou, and Guangzhou. Everything about the trip was "official" and thus, as de Beauvoir wrote to Al-gren, "drab and boring, nothing memorable except some of the scenery."[126] Years later de Beauvoir called the book, "hasty journalism" and admitted it was "written to get money."[127]

Michael Croft, writing in 1958, had an equally cynical view of the delega-tion experience, though unlike de Beauvoir, he did not feel obliged to hide this from his foreign readers:

The delegation was housed in the Peace Hotel, a name which it shared, together with the insignia of the Picasso dove, with hundreds of other hotels from
Prague to Peking at any point on the Red circuit where a delegation might stop
off for the night. These hotels have an atmosphere of their own, for nobody is
ever seen to pay a bill and, while everybody is being looked after by somebody
else, nobody seems to know who anybody else is. There is no animation; nobody seems either glad or sorry to be there. People talk in little groups at their
own tables, are provided with their wants, retire to their rooms, disappear in
government coaches and cars, but what they have been doing and where they
are going are questions which nobody cares to ask. This is not to suggest that
there is anything furtive about their movements, only to indicate the air of un-
reality which seems to permeate the delegation traffic on this particular
route.[128]

Croft participated in a "youth" delegation (of whom only three members could
properly be described as youthful), which visited Czechoslovakia, the USSR,
and China with all expenses paid. The delegation was supposed to be a representative group of "all shades of religious and political opinion."[129] It was rumored
that there were fourteen hotels in Beijing which served the delegation traffic in
the 1950s. During Croft's brief visit there were the following delegations:

> Japan had sent a Trade Union delegation, a Youth and Women's Delegation, a
> Scholars' Mission, a Writers' Mission and a Fertilizers' Delegation; from Paki-
> stan came a Medical Mission, a Scientific Delegation and the Prime Minister
> from India, a Parliamentary Mission and a Goodwill Military Mission. There
> was a Burmese Women's Delegation, a Norwegian Students' Delegation, a
> French Film Delegation, a Singapore Trade Mission, an Italian Socialist Party
> Agricultural Mission, a Hong Kong Industrial Delegation, a Finnish Trade Un-
> ion Mission and a Delegation of Syrian MPs.[130]

Nevertheless, for many foreign visitors to China in the 1950s (often those who
were least familiar with communism, or knew the least about China), the chance
to be a participant in "people's diplomacy" was exhilarating. In his book of one
such trip, R. M. Fox, invited to China as part of an Irish cultural group in 1959
enthused:

> After Chou En-lai's speech the rostrum was thrown open to the visitors, mainly
> from the Asiatic countries. Listening to them I felt that I was present at a great
> uprising of the Eastern peoples, filled and exalted with a sense of irresistible
> power. Like soldiers marching to battle, they followed one another at the mi-
> crophone—yellow, brown and black—speaking sometimes for barely ten
> minutes but in tones that rung and vibrated through the hall. They gave me the
> feeling that the days of Western domination were definitely over and it would
> be wiser for all to recognize this fact.[131]

Most visits were timed to coincide with Chinese national festivals, such as National Day and May Day. The Chinese authorities worked hard to create an impression of strength and unity on such occasions. The presence of the foreign

visitors at such major events validated the government's claim to legitimacy to Chinese and foreign observers alike.

The PRC's efforts to court prominent foreigners were closely watched by the Western powers.[132] Some Western governments acted to thwart the participation of their citizens in China's people's diplomacy activities. The British government's policy was to ensure that people's diplomacy activities such as the Afro-Asian Solidarity Conference in Cairo, of which China was a major supporter and organizer, were poorly attended and received the "maximum adverse publicity." In particular any "delegates" not entitled to speak for their respective peoples were to be disowned, whether by the government or the media of the countries concerned.[133]

Sinicizing Diplomacy: Zhou Enlai's Influence

The highlight of a visit to new China for many foreign visitors was the chance to meet with Zhou Enlai. On paper, Zhou Enlai only served as minister of foreign affairs from 1949-1958, but he closely supervised China's foreign relations from the 1930s until his death in 1976. Although other senior Chinese leaders were involved in *waishi* activities to varying degrees, none did so with such finesse and élan as Zhou Enlai. In the 1990s, many Chinese people view Zhou as a secular saint, a model for present day *waishi* cadres. His admirers describe Zhou as being extremely good at "handling people, *shanyu zuo ren de gongzuo* . . . he knew what to admire and what to hate. He was rich in Eastern human heartedness and many foreign friends were overwhelmed with admiration for him."[134] In the 1950s, Zhou told *waishi* cadres, "you have to get out and about and make lots of friends. You can't live a secluded life, only opening the door when guests arrive."[135] Certainly Zhou Enlai had what amounted to a highly successful formula for acquiring foreign supporters:

> Zhou Enlai spared no effort to find every opportunity to talk with foreign friends, sometimes even talking as long as seven or eight hours. Not only was he good at listening to different opinions, he also worked hard to create an atmosphere to make the guests feel they could express their own opinions. He said, "Only when you have different opinions can you have a united opinion, only with contradictions can one sort out differences." In discussions he was good at finding common points . . .[136]

Zhou constantly stressed the principle of finding common points to unite with foreigners. In 1955 he told a group of representatives from the Chinese Women's International Democratic League, "There are many political systems in the world and various ideologies; it is difficult for them to join together. We have to find points in common. For example, women want peace; this is a point in common, *gongtong dian*."[137] Emphasizing common points became an important principle of Chinese foreign policy, even to the extent of appointing ambassadors. In the early 1950s, Chinese Muslims were sent to make contact with Muslim North African states, virtually the only independent states in the African continent at the time.[138]

Zhou Enlai had excellent public relations technique. He would frequently ask foreign visitors if they had any comments or criticisms. Australian doctor Ces English, who was a guest of the Chinese government from 1956-1958, recalls that when Zhou asked him this question, he replied, "No, everything is wonderful." Zhou told him, "You obviously haven't been here long enough."[139] To English and many other foreign visitors this was an example of Zhou's disarming frankness. Zhou demonstrated his care for and interest in foreign visitors by being concerned about their daily lives, sometimes to the minutest detail. He was a micromanager when it came to *waishi*, setting the code of behavior for *waishi* personnel—*waishi jilü*—himself, based on his own experiences and skills.[140]

In 1954, Zhou Enlai established five principles for *waishi* personnel who dealt with foreign journalists accredited in the PRC or on short visits there:

1. Do not reject those who come, but be discriminating in how you treat them.

2. Be prudent, but not overcautious; maintain secrecy but do not be mysterious; take the initiative but do not act rashly.

3. Reply to reporters' questions; do not overuse "No comment."

4. As for provocations, rebut them in a principled manner, but do not get aggressive.

5. Hospitality towards foreign reporters should include questions and answers, it should lead us to a greater awareness of the situation, and [through it] we should selectively and deliberately make friends.[141]

Zhou advised officials to check into reporters' backgrounds, and find out what they had written about China in the past. In the 1950s, those who had written unfavorably on the CCP in the past were not welcome to visit. When foreign journalists toured China, their local hosts were instructed to "carry out factual education [on them] and strive to get them to make impartial reports that will serve China."[142] Usually fellow journalists in the areas they were visiting would be instructed to host foreign journalists since they would have more in common with each other, though the method of handling the particular visit was guided by the Information Department of the Foreign Ministry.[143]

Zhou Enlai-style *waishi* can be summed up by his advice to cadres, "Make as many friends as possible, talk frankly about our opinions, talk about weaknesses as well as talking about good points."[144] This advice, though useful, in Zhou's day and after, would have been difficult to follow because of the nature of the Chinese cadre system which makes it risky for personnel to do things on their own initiative. Only someone with Zhou's authority could get away with "talking frankly about our opinions." Zhou told his staff that the goal of foreign affairs activities, *duiwai huodong*, was to "Establish good will, understand the situation, propagandize, influence one's opponent, win friends and win hearts."[145] This was the case whether in terms of people-to-people or state-to-state diplomacy.

International Friends

A tiny number of foreigners were allowed to stay on in China after 1949 because of their political sympathies with the new regime and their personal connections within the CCP. Gerry Tannenbaum, who was working with Song Qingling in the China Welfare League in Shanghai, found it easy to get permission to stay on.[146] Sid Engst and Joan Hinton, who were working as agricultural consultants on a CCP-run farm near Xi'an, similarly had few problems after 1949. Rewi Alley, later to become one of China's most prolific foreign propagandists, had more difficulty in getting accepted into the new society, due to his previous connection with foreign aid organizations.[147] A few other trusted foreigners living outside China who had worked with the CCP in the past were invited to return, mostly to work as language polishers for CCP foreign propaganda organs. Still others were sent by their respective communist parties to help the new government in various fields. These chosen few foreigners were known initially as international friends, *guoji youren*,[148] to distinguish them from the foreign detritus of assorted imperialists, missionaries, and the like who were being cleaned out of new China. They were a separate group from the Soviet advisers.

Despite occasional objections, even in the hardest times in China CCP functionaries treated the international friends with particular privilege. "Privilege" in the worst of times meant that they got more to eat and better food than all but the highest of Chinese leaders, in better times it meant that they were given high salaries and comfortable accommodation far superior to ordinary Chinese. As the international friends were acutely aware, privilege was one of the means with which foreigners were reminded of their outsider status. In the first few years of the People's Republic, international friends, like Chinese cadres, were on the higher ranks of the "supply system" receiving "food, clothing, shelter, toilet articles, etc., and a little pocket money."[149] Their status was still considerably lower than the Soviet experts, however, indicated by their title of "advisers." Russian-language teacher Sam Ginsberg applied to "be admitted to the ranks of the revolutionary cadres," that is, not to receive special treatment. This was approved, but he still got better rations than his Chinese comrades.[150] It was a useful tactic for the CCP to remind even long-term foreign residents of China that they were still outsiders and "guests" in new China. The underlying message was that foreigners were only allowed to live in China at the will of the government. China was to be run by the Chinese and they would only use foreigners as and when it suited them.

For the foreigner in new China, as for the Chinese, it was important to belong to a work unit, *danwei*. The *danwei* provided housing and health care and much more. Non-Soviet foreigners in China after 1949 worked as translators, language polishers, university teachers, broadcasters, doctors, and technicians. Unlike the pre-1949 era, they were always in secondary roles, under the authority of Chinese staff. After the CCP came to power it was impossible for foreigners to work in China outside the government system, unless they were among the tiny number of diplomats and accredited journalists. Some foreigners were never assigned jobs at all: particularly foreign women married to Chinese men, former White Russians, and other Europeans who served no useful propaganda or other purpose. There was a strong sense of hierarchy among the foreign residents. In the 1950s, foreigners usually had to be approved by the Communist Party of their home country to be allowed to teach at a Chinese university, or to work as a foreign expert.[151] After finally being granted a job at the Foreign Languages Press, Sonia Su, originally from Germany with a Chinese husband, wrote of how her living standards improved with her new status:

> Material conditions were easier. We now had a two room apartment to ourselves with a private kitchen, toilet and bathroom. I also enjoyed some of the privileges associated with foreigners, although at the time I had become a Chinese citizen. Thus I would go on yearly educational trips to various parts of the country.[152]

Due to his long association with the party, and most probably also because of his U.S. citizenship,[153] George Hatem was one of the elite among the foreign residents. He and his family were given accommodation in the former residence of a Manchu aristocrat beside the Houhai Lake in central Beijing. When General Ye Jianying was made mayor of Beijing he ordered the place renovated to a standard suitable for receiving foreign visitors.[154] Along with his friend Rewi Alley (who from 1958 was given spacious accommodation in the former Italian Legation in Beijing), one of Hatem's activities was to host foreign delegations to China.

Nevertheless, even those with designated roles were not fully trusted. Despite, or perhaps because of, his political credentials, party insiders regarded George Hatem as politically unreliable. According to longtime resident Sidney Rittenberg, Hatem was considered undisciplined because he would "rub shoulders with anybody," which aroused doubts about his loyalty. This affected the way he was treated in his work unit, the Ministry of Health.[155] The communist takeover in 1949 marked for Hatem the "beginning of a long period in which he was the victim of discrimination and mistreatment."[156] He was given very lowly positions, despite his qualifications and experience, and China's desperate shortage of doctors. His colleagues proposed him as the head of the Institute of Dermatology and Venereology at the Ministry of Health. His appointment was blocked because of spying accusations against him on his personal file.[157] The high-profile Rewi Alley was also always under heavy suspicion because of his pre-1949 work with the Nationalist government and before that in the International Settlement in Shanghai.[158]

As a mark of their solidarity with the regime and commitment to living in new China, many of the long-term resident foreign friends applied for Chinese citizenship. American George Hatem was the first to be granted this in 1950.[159] Some foreigners who worked as foreign experts were pressured to change their citizenship.[160] This would be to their disadvantage in the Cultural Revolution years, when those who maintained their foreign citizenship would be treated better than those who held Chinese citizenship. Historically, taking a Chinese wife, adopting Chinese dress and customs, and having a Chinese name were regarded as the traditional signs of barbarian submission.[161] Thus it is notable that Hatem, generally regarded as the most Sinicized of the foreign friends, who lived in a Chinese residence with his Chinese wife, spoke Chinese fluently, and lived a life close to that of many ordinary Chinese people, became widely known by both foreigners and Chinese alike, according to his Chinese name, Ma Haide. In contrast, Rewi Alley, in keeping with his official role as a "permanent guest" in China always maintained his foreignness, his foreign lifestyle in a foreign-style apartment, his foreign name and citizenship.

In addition to specific duties in their respective work units, resident friends were encouraged to write about new China for foreign audiences. One regular outlet for their writing was American Maud Russell's broadsheet *Far East Reporter*. An active member of the tiny group of "progressive" Westerners living in China in the 1930s, Russell had returned to the United States in 1942 and after 1949, became involved in a one-woman campaign to increase awareness of new China in her home country. Her efforts were individual by necessity: to form a nationwide pro-PRC group would have been too controversial during the anti-communist McCarthyist hysteria of the 1950s. Foreign residents such as Nan Green, David Crook, Elsie Fairfax-Cholmeley, Israel Epstein, Talitha Gerlach, Rewi Alley, and, after 1958, Anna Louise Strong were Russell's regular correspondents, reporting on political developments in the PRC. To avoid political trouble, rather than writing articles, the foreigners sent long letters to Russell on political and economic developments that were mostly virtually verbatim reports from *Xinhua*. Under considerable pressure in the right-wing climate of the United States in the 1950s, Russell found her work quite stressful. In 1956 she wrote to her old friend from YWCA days, Talitha Gerlach, "You and Cora [Deng] must revel in this opportunity to maintain world-wide contacts—that [sic] you do not live in an iron-clad era such as the USA in these days . . ."[162]

In fact, the foreign friends were much less free to move around and express their opinions publicly than Russell. Foreigners were required to carry registration booklets with them at all times and needed to apply for a travel permit to go outside their designated area of residence. In 1954, American Sid Engst, then working with his wife Joan Hinton as an agricultural adviser on a farm in

Shaanxi Province on the outskirts of Xi'an, went on a business trip with some of the other staff from his work unit to Qingdao, in Shandong Province. When he arrived at the Qingdao train station, the police asked for his foreign registration booklet. After he told them he did not have one, they put him under house arrest until they were able to contact his work unit and get them to vouch for him. On his return to Xi'an, Engst went to his local police station to register. Engst recalled that the staff were very "low-key" about it. Engst and his family were the only foreigners living in their area at this time; they were well known to the local authorities as "progressives" who had formally worked in Yan'an.[163] Cities with a large concentration of foreigners were much stricter about controlling their movements. The only time most resident foreigners left their residence and workplace was if they were granted the privilege of participating in an organized group tour for foreign residents. Foreigners who were traveling outside their area of residence were required to carry a travel pass, in addition to their passports, which listed in detail the places where they were allowed to visit. When foreigners arrived and departed at each destination security personnel had to stamp the card.[164]

In the 1950s most resident foreigners were assigned minders who would spy on them and find out their views on various issues. Morris Wills, an American Korean War, defector described such individuals as the "baby-sitter."[165] In the mid-1970s when the practice continued, Pierre Ryckmans called such individuals "professional friends."[166] Informers, *gaomizhe*, would be asked by the Ministry of State Security to "keep an eye on" someone.[167] *Waishi* personnel such as translators or guides were frequently asked to spy on foreign guests and experts in their charge. In the case of foreign students, their Chinese classmates would be assigned this task. Sometimes Chinese people who were previously unknown to a foreign resident would be assigned to meet them accidentally and become their "friend."[168] In addition, Chinese colleagues were encouraged to report on the views of their foreign workmates to senior staff. Some foreigners also became notorious for informing on other foreign residents.[169]

Foreign residents knew that their overseas mail was being read both by the Chinese authorities and officials outside China, so they tended to be very guarded about what they said in letters.[170] Those designated as "foreign friends" were discouraged from mixing with "bourgeois" foreigners from the diplomatic community or noncommunist journalists and they were expected to live a relatively spartan lifestyle. The few who indulged in decadent pleasures such as listening to rock and roll music and drinking excessive amounts of alcohol were criticized. British Communist Party member and journalist Alan Winnington was warned by his boss at *Xinhua* that he "should not have parties at which Chinese and foreigners met or in which 'reactionary' journalists and diplomats mixed, danced, ate and drank and made noise. Come to that, I should have less to do with bourgeois journalists anyway, owing to the confidential nature of my work for *Xinhua*."[171]

For many pro-CCP foreigners living in Beijing from 1952-1959 the focal point of social life was political study groups. Foreigners in the capital were not permitted to attend the study groups for Chinese personnel held at their work units. Their study groups were divided along language and national lines. Unlike Chinese citizens, attendance at a political study group was not compulsory for foreigners, but there was a certain amount of peer pressure and most attended. The groups read translations of Marxist-Leninist thought, selected articles of Mao Zedong thought and discussed contemporary political issues.

On the whole, resident friends of China were as much linked by displacement from their own societies as they were by a strong ideological commitment to Chinese communism. A run through the background of some of the more prominent members of this community illustrates the thread of exile which most shared as a common point. Sidney Rittenberg was a radical union organizer and American Communist Party member who joined the Chinese cause after a spell in the U.S. army. Israel Epstein, Sam Ginsberg, and Ruth Weiss were Jewish escapees from the chaos of Europe in the early twentieth century. Epstein and Ginsberg were stateless, while most of Weiss's family died in the Holocaust. Other China-based friends were also outsiders in their own societies. In 1951, Talitha Gerlach was dismissed from the YWCA for her political views on China after twenty-seven years of working for the organization. Song Qingling invited her to return to China and help with the China Welfare Institute in Shanghai.[172] Japanese aristocrat Saionji was an anomaly within his own society, a "Red aristocrat" as he called himself. New Zealander Rewi Alley and American Bob Winter were both gay men who had moved to China in the 1920s where they found more sexual freedom than in their own countries. In the 1950s, many other non-Soviet foreign residents were escapees from McCarthyism in their home countries; as victims of the Cold War; they had little to go back to. A significant number of China's "international friends" who stayed on after the Soviet split had Chinese partners and families. For many, leaving China would have been too much of an upheaval for those who had never had any great commitment to the Soviet-led international communist movement. Certainly those foreigners living in China at this time supported the nation's development into a strong and united country, but those who were truly committed to the communist parties of their home countries left China after the Sino-Soviet split began. Those who remained often stayed because they had nowhere else to go.

Nevertheless, among foreign friends and Chinese alike, the 1950s were generally a time of great idealism and enthusiasm for the new government. There was a strong sense that things were getting better and better, and that life had improved dramatically since 1949. In contrast, the Western world seemed fascist and aggressive. Foreign supporters of the PRC were disturbed by the spread of McCarthyite attitudes in the Western world and United States support for former war criminals in Germany and Japan. Those who had been associated with the CCP before 1949 and returned to the United States often suffered for their associations.[173]

In addition to those based in China as foreign experts, the CCP adopted the Soviet practice of cultivating certain foreigners it hoped would be influential in their own societies to promote pro-China policies. Ces English lived in the PRC from 1956-1958 where he was treated for arthritis with Chinese medicine at the Chinese government's expense. He originally came to China for three weeks as a guest of the Peace Committee after the 1955 Helsinki Peace Conference. All delegates to this conference were invited to the People's Republic for a three-week "study tour," as well as to the Soviet Union. English was a member of the Australian Communist Party as well as the Australian Peace Committee at the time. During his two years in China, English stayed at the Xinqiao Hotel in Beijing with all expenses paid. He had his own masseur, and his arthritis was treated at a Chinese hospital, also free of charge. English had trained as a doctor in Australia and he was interested in links between Chinese and Western medicine, though he had little chance to explore that while he was there. English says he and his friend Rewi Alley spent most of their time traveling to antique markets and visiting temples. He did some editing for a medical journal and helped with subtitles for films.[174] On his return from China, Ces English became one of the leading figures in the Australia-China Society, until he was ousted in the late 1970s in a factional struggle.[175]

Beginning in 1951, China hosted groups of foreign communists from Australia, Vietnam, Thailand, Malaya, Burma, Indonesia, Singapore, Japan, and later New Zealand to study Marxist-Leninism and Mao Zedong thought on three-year courses at an institute in the western suburbs of Beijing.[176] The students were thoroughly isolated from Chinese life as well as from other foreigners in China, only leaving their quarters on supervised excursions. As early as 1951, China also offered scholarships to small numbers of students from Asian countries to study in the PRC. By the mid-1950s, several hundred students from Eastern bloc countries were also studying there as exchange students. A further effort to foster relations between China and the Third World was the Asian and African Student Sanatorium, which mostly treated tuberculosis, set up in 1953 in the Western Hills of Beijing. In 1959, a secret school for training in guerrilla warfare was established near Beijing for foreign revolutionaries, mostly from Latin America and Africa.[177]

Shifting Allegiances: Foreign Policy Trends in the 1950s

By the mid-1950s, after the antagonistically anti-imperialist foreign policy line of the years immediately after 1949, the CCP began to adopt a more conciliatory approach. In April 1954 the PRC and India signed an agreement on Tibet that included the Five Principles of Peaceful Coexistence. These principles were mutual respect for territorial integrity and sovereignty, nonaggression, noninterference in each other's internal affairs, equality and mutual benefit, and peaceful coexistence. The PRC soon after signed a similar agreement with

Burma. It was a sign that China was breaking out of diplomatic isolation with a new and peaceful foreign policy approach. This approach would be characterized by opposition to great power dominance and full equality and reciprocity when dealing with other nations.[178] Both India and Burma agreed that they would pursue a policy of neutrality in the Cold War and would maintain peaceful relations with Beijing.

The next step in this new approach to international relations was the convening of the 1955 Bandung Conference for African and Asian nations to discuss the question of neutrality. Zhou Enlai's speech to this conference added on to the Five Principles the concept of recognition of racial equality and respect for the rights of all peoples to choose their own way of life and political and economic system. Out of this meeting the nonaligned movement was formed; Beijing saw itself as a natural leader of this group.[179] In late 1956-1957 Zhou Enlai attempted to expand China's influence in south and southeast Asia by visiting a number of countries in the region and offering aid. Previously China's foreign aid had been restricted to communist allies on its borders, Korea, Mongolia, and the North Vietnamese.[180] It gradually became evident that this formed part of the Sino-Soviet rivalry for political influence in the region.[181] At the same time China stepped up its foreign propaganda efforts, creating a standardized system of organizing the writing of materials for foreign audiences to be published in the foreign media, rather than relying solely on China's own propaganda organs.[182]

The more conciliatory line adopted from the mid-1950s on allowed the PRC to expand its foreign relations beyond the Soviet orbit. In 1956 Soviet leader Khrushchev openly criticized Stalin (who died in 1953) and demanded that the Soviet Union (and implicitly Khrushchev) be recognized as the undisputed leader of the Communist bloc. The Chinese leadership objected to this dictatorial approach. Mao was particularly concerned about the Sino-Soviet relationship, in particular the threat of psychological dependence, the importation of harmful ideas, and Soviet influence on Chinese politics.[183] In his 1956 speech, "On the Ten Great Relationships," Mao sounded the alarm for the first time on the threat of overdependence on the Soviet Union. He told senior leaders "we had been slaves far too long and felt inferior to others in every respect—too much so. We could not hold up our heads in the presence of foreigners . . . some real effort is needed on this problem, to raise the self-confidence of our people."[184] Mao called for an independent China, strong and reliant on no one. At a series of meetings in Chengdu in March 1958, he outlined his plan for what became the Great Leap Forward. Concerned at the unquestioning borrowing of the Soviet experience to construct new China he complained, "Chinese people have got so used to being slaves that they seem to want to go on."[185] An even more serious blow to Sino-Soviet relations occurred in 1958, when the Soviet Union demanded the right to establish a radar station and a jointly commanded submarine fleet in China. To Beijing this implied that for the Soviets the relationship

was that of a strategic dependency.[186]
Soon after the Chengdu meetings, the Great Leap Forward began in earnest. The Leap Forward was a political movement aimed at speeding up the process of China's economic development by using mass labor to work long hours on massive infrastructure projects, as well as the infamous attempt to expand China's steel production by making pig iron in backyard furnaces at every work unit. It was a deliberate challenge to Soviet economic ideas and as such was a none too subtle notice of China's independence. Friction started among the foreign experts at this and other obvious displays of Chinese nationalism.

In June 1958, during the Leap Forward, *waishi* policymaking was centralized, taking virtually all decision-making authority away from state *waishi* bureaucracies such as the Foreign Ministry. The CCP Central Committee Foreign Affairs Leading Small Group, *waishi lingdao xiaozu*, was set up at this time, supervised by Zhou Enlai and the new foreign minister, Chen Yi. This body coordinated all policy on *waishi* matters, delegating its implementation to the relevant party bureaus.[187] Influence in *waishi* policymaking shifted towards Mao, Zhou, and Chen Yi, working through the *waishi* small group, and away from senior leaders who had been active in the Sino-Soviet alliance structure run through the Party Secretariat, including Liu Shaoqi, Deng Xiaoping, Peng Zhen, and Wang Jiaxiang. The change in leadership structure corresponded with a change in focus toward the Afro-Asian-Latin American world, and away from the Soviet camp.[188] Beginning in 1959, CCP propaganda began to stress Mao Zedong thought once more, an indication that China was prepared to follow its own path to socialism. In 1960, Mao denounced Soviet leader Khrushchev with the first open salvo of the bitter split that would cause disunity in the Communist bloc for many years to come.

Notes

1.   *Ba fangwu dasao ganjing zai qing ke*. This is one of the slogans used by Mao to describe the period from 1949-1952 when the CCP focused on resolving the foreign presence in China and foreign visitors were few.

2.   Zhou Enlai, "Xin Zhongguo waijiao," 8 November 1949, Zhonghua renmin gongheguo waijiaobu, Zhonggong zhongyang wenxian yanjiushe, *Zhou Enlai de waijiao wenxian* (Beijing: Zhongyang wenxian chubanshe, 1990), 1.

3.   Mao Zedong had spoken of the need to Sinicize Marxism in an important speech in 1938. See Schram, *The Thought of Mao Tse-tung*, 70.

4.   See Pei Xiannong, *Zhou Enlai de waijiaoxue*, 270-272.

5.   Andrei Ledovsky, "Moscow Visit of a Chinese Communist Delegation," *Far Eastern Affairs*, no. 4 (1996): 81.

6.   In February 1949 Mao told Anastas Mikoyan, Stalin's special envoy to the CCP, "The later the U.S. and other Western countries recognize us the better, because our house is still very dirty, only after we have cleaned the house can we properly host

guests." See "Shi Zhe tongzhi tanhua jilu," *Zhonggong dangshi jiaoxue cankao ziliao,* vol. 77, cited in Pei Xiannong, *Zhou Enlai de waijiaoxue,* 110.

7. See for example the comments of Michael Lindsay, *China and the Cold War* (Melbourne: Melbourne University Press, 1955), 22.

8. K. M. Panikkar, *In Two Chinas* (London: n.p., 1955), 51-61. See also John Leighton Stuart, *Fifty Years in China: The Memoirs of John Leighton Stuart, Missionary and Ambassador* (New York: Random House, 1954), 241-259; Chester Ronning, *A Memoir of China in Revolution: From the Boxer Rebellion to the People's Republic* (New York: Pantheon Books, 1974), 131-166; and Seymour Topping, *Journey between Two Chinas* (New York: Harper and Row, 1972), 49-95.

9. Derk Bodde, *Peking Diary: A Year of Revolution* (London: Jonathan Cape, 1951), 220.

10. Nyarene Masson, interview, 26 January 1996.

11. William G. Sewell, *I Stayed in China* (New York: A. S. Barnes and Co., 1966), 62. See also Michael Lindsay, "Report of a Visit," *International Affairs* 26, no. 1 (January 1950): 22-31; and Ralph and Nancy Lapwood, *Through the Chinese Revolution* (London: Spalding and Levy, 1954).

12. Sewell, *I Stayed in China,* 72.

13. Sewell, *I Stayed in China,* 70.

14. Sewell, *I Stayed in China,* 70.

15. Sewell, *I Stayed in China,* 70.

16. Sewell, *I Stayed in China,* 114.

17. Pei Xiannong, *Zhou Enlai de waijiaoxue,* 378.

18. Hooper, *China Stands Up,* 121.

19. Pei Jianzhang, ed., *Zhonghua renmin gongheguo waijiaoshi* (1949-1956) (Beijing: Shijie zhishi chubanshe, 1994), 257.

20. Bosshardt, *The Guiding Hand,* 174.

21. Bosshardt, *The Guiding Hand,* 174.

22. Bodde, *Peking Diary,* 264.

23. Sewell, *I Stayed in China,* 126.

24. Sewell, *I Stayed in China,* 127.

25. Sewell, *I Stayed in China,* 128.

26. Ford, *Captured in Tibet,* 150.

27. Li Yun, ed., *Nanchang waishi zhi* (Nanchang: Jiangxi renmin chubanshe, 1994), 253-255; *Zhejiang sheng waishi zhi* (Beijing: Zhonghua shuju, 1996), 223-225.

28. A. de Segonzac, *Visa for Peking,* trans. Marion Barwick (Kingswood, Surrey: Windmill Press, 1956), 150.

29. "Mao Zedong on the Comintern's and Stalin's China Policy," *Far Eastern Affairs,* no. 4-5 (1994): 139.

30. 5 May 1965, Confidential Report, U.S. State Department, R59/250/49/07/01 Box 1, National Archives. Kenneth T. Young describes the negotiations to release these prisoners, in exchange for Chinese living in the U.S. in *Negotiating with the Chinese Communists: The United States Experience, 1953-1967* (New York: McGraw-Hill, 1968), 63-90.

31. William Sargant, *Battle for the Mind: A Physiology of Conversion and Brainwashing* (London: Pan Books, 1957), 144. See also Robert Jay Lifton, *Thought Reform and the Psychology of Totalism: A Study of Brainwashing in China* (London: Gollancz, 1961). For an account of some of the experiences of foreigners in CCP prisons, see

Bao Ruo-wang (Jean Pasqualini) and Rudolph Chelminski, *Prisoner of Mao* (New York: Coward, McCann and Geoghan, 1973); Geoffrey Bull, *When Iron Gates Yield* (London: Hodden and Stoughton, 1955); John F. Donovan, *The Pagoda and the Cross* (New York: Scribner's, 1967); Robert Ford, *Captured in Tibet* (London: George Harrap and Co., 1957); Isobel Kuhn, *Green Leaf in Drought: The Story of the Escape of the Last C.I.M. Missionaries* (London: China Inland Mission, 1958); Allyn and Adele Rickett, *Prisoners of Liberation: Four Years in a Chinese Communist Prison* (New York: Anchor Press, 1973); and Harold Rigney, *Four Years in a Red Hell: The Story of Father Rigney* (Chicago: Regnery Press, 1956).

32.   *Kang Mei yuan Chao*, the political campaign to arouse support for the Korean War and resistance to the United States.

33.   Zhonggong zhongyang xuanchuanbu bangongting, Zhongyang dang'anguan bianyanbu, eds., *Zhongguo gongchandang xuanchuan gongzuo wenxian xuanbian 1915-1992*, 4 vols. (Beijing: Xuexi chubanshe, 1996), vol. 3, 91-98.

34.   See Aron Shai, *The Fate of British and French Firms in China, 1949-1954: Imperialism Imprisoned* (London: Macmillan, 1996), 10.

35.   "Zhonggong zhongyang guanyu jixu kaizhan kang Mei yuan Chao xuanchuan de zhishi," *DDXC*, vol. 1, 54-56.

36.   "Zhonggong zhongyang guanyu jixu kaizhan kang Mei yuan Chao xuanchuan de zhishi," and "Zhonggong zhongyang guanyu puji xuanchuan kang Mei yuan Chao he zhunbei 'wu yi' quanguo shiwei de zhishi." March 1951, *DDXC*, vol. 1, 81-83.

37.   He Di discusses Mao's perceptions of the U.S. threat to China in "Most Respected Enemy," *Chinese Communist Foreign Relations 1920s-1960s*, ed. Hunt and Niu, 27-65. See also Chen Jian, *China's Road to the Korean War*, 15-16.

38.   See Zhongyang xuanchuanbu, Xinhuashe, "Guanyu 'minzhu de gerenzhuyizhe' de wenti, gei Huadongju, Shanghai shiwei de zhishi," 1 September 1949, *DDXC*, vol. 1, 32.

39.   Lu Dingyi, "Zhengqu he tuanjie guangda jiaotu, suqing diguozhuyi zai Zhongguo de wenhua qinlüe de yinxiang," 19 January 1951, Zhonggong zhongyang tongzhanbu yanjiushi, *Lici quanguo tongzhan gongzuo huiyi gaikuang he wenxian* (Beijing: Dang'an chubanshe, 1988), 45.

40.   Chen Xiaomei, *Occidentalism: A Theory of Counter-Discourse in Post-Mao China*, 5.

41.   "Zhonggong zhongyang guanyu jixu kaizhan kang Mei yuan Chao xuanchuan de zhishi," *DDXC*, vol. 1, 54.

42.   Sewell, *I Stayed in China*, 122.

43.   "Zhonggong zhongyang guanyu jixu kaizhan kang Mei yuan Chao xuanchuan de zhishi," *DDXC*, vol. 1, 55.

44.   *Nanchang waishi zhi*, 30-31.

45.   See "Zhonggong zhongyang guanyu 'san fan' yundong he 'wu fan' yundong dui guowai xuanchuan de zhishi," March 1952, *DDXC*, vol. 1, 94-95.

46.   "Zhongyang xuanchuanbu zhongyang gonganbu guanyu jin du xuanchuan de zhishi," July 1952, *DDXC*, vol. 1, 116-118; "Zhongyang xuanchuanbu guanyu Chaoxian tingzhan tanpan wenti de xuanchuan de tongzhi," April 1953, *DDXC*, vol. 1, 151-155.

47.   Gavan McCormack, *Hot War, Cold War: An Australian Perspective on the Korean War* (Sydney: Hale and Iremonger, 1983), 147.

48.   See "Dui Nie Rongzhen, Su Yu guanyu di ji zai Dongbei diqu sa xijun he wo fang cuoshi de baogao de piyu," 5 March 1952, *JGYL*, vol. 3, 318; "Dui xinhuashe zi-

yuanjun zongfenshe shangbao de fangyi gongzuo ziliao de piyu," 16 March 1952, *JGYL*, vol. 3, 339, "Dui Hua bei yibing fangzhi qingkuang baogao de piyu," 17 March 1952, *JGYL*, vol. 3, 341.

49.   "Guanyu Fushun shijiao faxian dapi kunchong deng de piyu," 4 March 1952, *JGYL*, vol. 3, 303; "Zai Nie Rongzhen guanyu guonei fangyi gongzuo baogao shang de piyu," 9 March 1952, *JGYL*, vol. 3, 328; interview with former *waishi* cadres, March 1999.

50.   *Fensui Meiguo xijun zhan* (Dongbei yixueyuan chubanshe, 1952). Harold Rigney also mentions this, see *Four Years in a Red Hell*, 145.

51.   "US Germ Warfare in Korea is Undeniable: A Report of Interrogation of Two American POWs, Flight Lieutenants Kenneth L. Enoch and John S. Quinn, by a group of 24 Korean and Chinese specialists, news correspondents and cameramen, between May 1 and 8, 1952, broadcast by Peking Radio in its Kuo-yu program overseas on May 17, and released by Hsinhua in its English and Chinese Morse Casts from Peking on the same day," 69/3072, Department of External Affairs, National Archives of Australia. In the standard work on the foreign relations of the People's Republic of China, the main evidence given as proof of germ warfare in the Korean War are the airmen's confessions. See Xie Yixian, ed., *Zhongguo waijiao shi 1949-1979* (Kaifeng: Henan sheng xinhua shudian, 1988), 99. The POWs later denied the veracity of their confessions.

52.   *Report of the International Scientific Commission for the Investigation of the Facts Concerning Biological Warfare in Korea and China* (Peking, 1952).

53.   See "Deceiving the Deceivers: Moscow, Beijing, Pyongyang, and the Allegations of Bacteriological Weapons in Korea," *CWHP*, Bulletin 11—Cold War Flashpoints, no. 3 (1999); Milton Leitenberg, *The Korean War Biological Warfare Allegations Resolved*, Occasional Paper 36 (May 1998) (Center for Pacific Asia Studies at Stockholm University). For an example of scholarship supporting the germ warfare allegations see Stephen L. Endicott, "Germ Warfare and 'Plausible Denial,'" *Modern China* 5, no. 1 (January 1979): 79-104; and Endicott and Edward Hagerman, *The United States and Biological Warfare: Secrets from the Early Cold War and Korea* (Bloomington: Indiana University Press, 1999).

54.   There were 96,600 Korean, 20,000 Chinese POWs. The United States had agreed to return 83,000 POWs, mostly Korean. "Talks with Mao Zedong, December 1949-January 1950, and with Zhou Enlai, August-September 1952," Bulletin of the *CWIHP*, 6-7, 13. For a contemporary view supporting the communist point of view on this issue, see Wilfred Burchett and Alan Winnington, *Koje Unscreened* (published by the authors, Peking, 1953). For a contemporary viewpoint from the UN perspective, see "Atrocities in Korea against POWs," 22 November 1953, R59/250/49/06/03 Box 1, U.S. State Department, National Archives.

55.   Chen Jian, *China's Road to the Korean War*, 146, quoting Du Ping, *Zai zhiyuanjun zongbu: Du Ping huiyi lu* (Beijing: Jiefangjun chubanshe, 1988), 24-25, and 29. 56.   A. de Segonzac, *Visa for Peking*, describes meeting some of the men in 1954 and says they seemed in good spirits, 199-200. However, before long, most of the soldiers found life in China difficult. Within a few years most of them requested repatriation. For a long time the Chinese authorities refused, imprisoning some of the men for their insubordination. Finally, in 1963, all those who wished to were allowed to leave. Before their departure, the Chinese Red Cross sent them on a six-week, all-expenses-paid trip around China, with "red-carpet treatment." J. Robert Moskins and Morris Wills, *Turncoat, an American's 12 Years in Communist China* (New Jersey: Prentice-Hall,

1967), 143. See also Adam J. Zweiback, "The 21 'Turncoat GIs': Nonrepatriations and the Political Culture of the Korean War," *The Historian* 60, no. 2 (Winter 1998): 345-362; and Robin Moyer, "Yanks in China," *Life*, 11, no. 14 (December 1988): 101-104.

57.   "Reminiscences of Veterans," *Far Eastern Affairs*, no. 5 (1989): 26. In another well-publicized breach of discipline, PLA soldiers broke into the bedroom of the U.S. ambassador Leighton Stuart in the early hours of the morning shortly after communist forces arrived in the city. They were ushered out without incident, stating that they were simply "looking around." The soldiers were reportedly later detained and given political reeducation. Topping, *Journey between Two Chinas*, 75.

58.   "The Moscow Visit of a Delegation of the Communist Party of China in June to August 1949," *Far Eastern Affairs*, no. 4 (1996): 69.

59.   S. Tikhvinsky, "China in My Life," *Far Eastern Affairs*, no. 4 (1989): 124. Liu Shaoqi, then secretary of the CCP Central Committee was its first chairman, 127.

60.   K. E. Priestley, "The Sino-Soviet Friendship Association," *Pacific Affairs* XXV, no. 3 (September 1952): 287. *Nanchang waishi zhi*, 29, mentions the beginning of intensive Russian classes in April 1950 in Nanchang, organized by the local Sino-Soviet Friendship Association.

61.   Steven M. Goldstein, "Sino-Soviet Relations," in *Chinese Foreign Policy*, ed. Robinson and Shambaugh, 235.

62.   Esther Holland Jian, *British Girl, Chinese Wife* (Beijing: New World Press, 1985), 133. Holland Jian's claim that Russian was the only foreign language taught in China at this time is an exaggeration.

63.   Hooper, *China Stands Up*, 159; and *Nanchang waishi zhi*, 32.

64.   See V. Zhuravlyov, "Mission in China: Memoirs of a Movie Director," *Far Eastern Affairs*, no. 2 (1987): 77-90, 107.

65.   *The Foreign Experts' Handbook—A Guide to Living and Working in China* (Beijing: New World Press, 1988): 89.

66.   Stalin had demanded that Soviet specialists be given superior pay and conditions when negotiating the exchanges with Liu Shaoqi in 1949, see "The Moscow Visit of a Delegation of the Communist Party of China in June to August 1949," *Far Eastern Affairs*, no. 4 (1996): 68. In contrast, Chinese scientists visiting the Soviet Union were not treated well, they were offered inferior accommodation and meals. See Mikhail A. Klochko, *Soviet Scientist in China* (English translation) (New York: Frederick A. Praeger, 1964), 126.

67.   David Crook, interview, 23 April 1996.

68.   Klochko, *Soviet Scientist in China*, 163.

69.   Harry Harding, "China's Co-operative Behavior," in *Chinese Foreign Policy*, ed. Robinson and Shambaugh, 378. See also Lowell Dittmer, *Sino-Soviet Normalization and Its International Implications, 1945-1990* (Seattle and London: University of Washington Press, 1992), 21-23.

70.   Harry Hamm, *China: Empire of the 700 Million*, trans. Victor Anderson (New York: Doubleday, 1966), 125, citing an announcement in 1957 by Chinese Finance Minister Li Xiannian.

71.   Hamm, *China*, 126.

72.   Lu Ning, *The Dynamics of Foreign-Policy Decisionmaking in China*, 69.

73.   Andrei Ledovsky, "The Moscow Visit of a Delegation of the Communist Party of China in June to August 1949," *Far Eastern Affairs*, no. 5 (1996): 85, 92-95.

74. As were English texts, which came via the Soviet Union with a Soviet foreign affairs specialist's preface, see Rt. Hon. Sir Ernest Satow, *A Guide to Diplomatic Practice* (London: Longmans Green and Co., 1957), which was translated into Chinese in 1957 and published by the New World Press.

75. Ledovsky, "The Moscow Visit of a Delegation of the Communist Party of China in June to August 1949," no. 4, 155 and no. 5, 84.

76. See David Shambaugh, "The Soviet Influence on China's Worldview," *The Australian Journal of Chinese Affairs*, no. 27 (January 1992); Ronald C. Keith, *The Diplomacy of Zhou Enlai* (London: Macmillan, 1989), 35-36. On the setting up of the new administration in China after 1949, see Ma Yongshun, *Zhou Enlai zujian yu guanli zhengfu shilu* (Beijing: Zhongyang wenxian chubanshe, 1995).

77. Waijiaobu waijiaoshi yanjiushi, *Dangdai Zhongguo shijie waijiao shengya*, (Beijing: Shijie zhishi chubanshe, 1995), 158-159.Wang Jiaxiang, fluent in English and Russian, the PRC's first ambassador to the Soviet Union was a noticeable exception.

78. *Dangdai Zhongguo shijie waijiao shengya*, 159.

79. Zhao Pitao, *Waishi gaishuo*, 183; Pei Xiannong, *Zhou Enlai de waijiaoxue*, 86-88.

80. Han Xu, "Mao Zedong de minjian waijiao sixiang he zhongyao juece," *Mao Zedong waijiao sixiang yanjiu*, ed. Pei Jianzhang (Beijing: Shijie zhishi chubanshe, 1994), 50.

81. Chen Jian, *China's Road to the Korean War*, 74. This had earlier been proposed during Liu Shaoqi's meetings with Stalin in the summer of 1949, see Ivan Kovalev, "The Stalin-Mao Dialogue," *Far Eastern Affairs*, no. 2 (1992): 97.

82. Han Xu, "Mao Zedong de minjian waijiao sixiang he zhongyao juece," in *Mao Zedong waijiao sixiang yanjiu*, ed. Pei Jianzhang, 51.

83. Han Xu, "Mao Zedong," 53. See also *Guoji shishi cidian* (Dictionary of International Affairs) (Beijing: Shangwu yinshudian, 1984), 93-94.

84. Roland Perry, *The Exile: Burchett, Reporter of Conflict* (Richmond, Australia: William Heineman, 1988), 101.

85. It is interesting to note however, that in 1955 and as late as 1966, *He Da* organized meetings throughout China to oppose the use of nuclear weapons, *Nanchang waishi zhi*, 34 and 42.

86. Some of the most well-known of such foreigners were Chilean artist Jose Venturelli, Sudanese "freedom fighter" Ahmed Kheir, New Zealand "peace worker" Rewi Alley, and the Japanese aristocrat Saionji Kinkazu. For a detailed list of those who "propagandized and introduced new China" through peace activities, see Han Xu, "Mao Zedong de minjian waijiao sixiang he zhongyao juece" in *Mao Zedong waijiao sixiang yanjiu*, ed. Pei Jianzhang, 52.

87. Hu Sheng, Yu Kuansheng, Yu Kuanyuan, and Wang Huide, "Strategies and Tactics of the Communist Party," Series no. 27 of Lectures on the Fundamental Knowledge of the Social Sciences, *Xuexi*, no. 1 (1952): 41, cited in Frederick T. C. Yu, *Mass Persuasion in Communist China* (London: Pall Mall Press, 1964), 24.

88. For a description of the activities of the peace conference see Margaret Garland, *Journey to New China* (Christchurch, N.Z.: The Caxton Press, 1954), 114-118.

89. *Zhejiang sheng waishi zhi*, 223.

90. *Zhejiang sheng waishi zhi*, 223; see also *Guoji shishi cidian*, 98.

91. Zhang Hanfu, deputy minister for foreign affairs, 19 July 1952, cited in Arai, *British and French Firms in China*, 47.

92.   Zhonggong zhongyang tongzhanbu yanjiushi, *Tongyi zhanxian gongzuo shouce* (Nanjing: Nanjing daxue chubanshe, 1986), 288. See also Wenhuabu dangshi ziliao zhengji gongzuo weiyuanhui, Duiwai wenhua lianluoju dangshi ziliao zhengji gongzuo lingdao xiaozu, ed., *Dangdai Zhong wai wenhua jiaoliu shiliao* (Beijing: 1990).

93.   Han Xu, "Mao Zedong de minjian waijiao sixiang he zhongyao juece" in *Mao Zedong waijiao sixiang yanjiu*, ed. Pei Jianzhang, 52.

94.   "Zhonggong zhongyang guanyu guoji shishi xuanchuan de guiding," August 1952, *DDXC*, vol. 1, 96.

95.   "Zhongyang xuanchuanbu guanyu waiguo jizhe dao gedi caifang ying zhuyi shiqing de tongzhi," October 1954, *DDXC*, vol. 1, 241.

96.   *Zhejiang sheng waishi zhi*, 233.

97.   Foreign experts had previously been the responsibility of the Experts' Employment Office (*Zhengwuyuan zhuanjia gongzuo banggongshi*) and Experts' Affairs Management Office (*Zhengwuyuan zhuanjia shiwu guanliju*) of the Government Administration Council and State Bureau of Foreign Experts respectively. *The Foreign Experts' Handbook*, 85.

98.   Carol Lee Hamrin, "Elite Politics and the Development of China's Foreign Relations," in *Chinese Foreign Policy*, ed. Robinson and Shambaugh, 85-87. See also, "Zhonggong zhongyang pifa zhongyang xuanchuanbu 'guanyu xiang guowai gongying gaoqian gongzuo de qingkuang he gaijin yijian xiang zhongyang de baogao,'" 5 May 1956, *DDXC*, vol. 1, 300.

99.   Interview with *waishi* cadres, December 1997.

100.   By the late 1940s *waishi* work was divided between a number of bureaus and offices. Regional bureaus in areas with high concentrations of foreigners such as the Nanfangju in Chongqing and the Dongbeiju in Harbin provided important information on local *waishi* matters as well as representing party interests and implementing party policy in their respective regions. As they would continue to do after 1949, *Xinhua* journalists stationed in locations such as Hong Kong were also the eyes and ears of the party abroad. The military had earlier on had its own *waishi* office in Lanzhou between 1937-1939 to handle Sino-Soviet military cooperation. Up until the dissolution of the Comintern in 1943, party representatives in Moscow also played a role in foreign policymaking. Hunt, *The Genesis of Chinese Foreign Policy*, 227-228.

101.   Ji Pengfei, "Chu shi Minzhu Deguo jishi," Waijiaobu waijiaoshi yanjiushi, *Dangdai Zhongguo shijie waijiao shengya*, 158.

102.   Pei Xiannong, *Zhou Enlai de waijiaoxue*, 87.

103.   Pei Xiannong, *Zhou Enlai de waijiaoxue*, 87

104.   Former *waishi* official, interview, December 1998.

105.   *Zhejiang sheng waishi zhi*, 254.

106.   The Anti-Rightist Campaign was launched in June 1957 to attack those who had criticized the party during the 1956-1957 Hundred Flowers Campaign. Mao believed that "certain people made use of the party's rectification movement to unfold an acute class struggle." *Renmin Ribao*, 8 June 1957.

107.   Former *waishi* official, interview, December 1998.

108.   Former *waishi* official, interview, December 1998. Alex Yang, interview, 5 November 1990.

109.   Klochko, *Soviet Scientist in China*, 126.

110.   Ces English, interview, 2 February 1997.

111.   Courtney Archer, letter to author, 11 May 1994.

112. "Zhonggong xuanchuanbu guanyu dui guo wai xuanchuan zibenzhuyi gong-shangye gaizao wenti de tongzhi," May 1956, *DDXC*, vol. 1, 318-320; "Zhonggong zhongyang guanyu 'bai hua qi fang, bai jia zheng ming' deng zhengce zai guo wai xuan-chuan zhong ying zhuyi shiqiang de tongzhi," 12 June 1957, *DDXC*, vol. 1, 342-343.

113. Former *waishi* official, interview, December 1998.

114. "Guowuyuan pizhuan guojia kewei, Zhongguo kexueyuan, waijiaobu guanyu banfa kexue jishu renyuan duiwai tongxun lianxi he jiaohuan shukan ziliao liang ge guid-ing de qingshi," 1 February 1979, *DDXC*, vol. 2, 648.

115. Former *waishi* official, interview, December 1998.

116. Israel Epstein, *Woman in World History Song Qingling (Madame Sun Yat-sen)*, 520.

117. Han Xu, "Mao Zedong de minjian waijiao sixiang he zhongyao juece" in *Mao Zedong waijiao sixiang yanjiu*, ed. Pei Jianzhang, 54.

118. Leslie Haylen, *Chinese Journey: The Republic Revisited* (Sydney: Angus and Robertson, 1959), 13.

119. See Michael Lindsay's description of the experiences of some dissenting guests in the 1950s, *China and the Cold War*, 62.

120. Zhao Pitao, *Waishi gaishuo*, 76.

121. Deidre Bair, *Simone de Beauvoir: A Biography* (London: Vintage, 1991), 455.

122. Bair, *Simone de Beauvoir*, 456.

123. Simone de Beauvoir, *The Long March* (London: Andre Deutsch, 1958), 19.

124. De Beauvoir, *The Long March*, 26.

125. Chen Xuezhao, *Surviving the Storm: A Memoir*, edited with an introduction by Jeffrey Kinkley, trans. Ti Hua and Caroline Greene (New York: M. E. Sharpe, 1990), 43.

126. Bair, *Simone de Beauvoir*, 456.

127. Bair, *Simone de Beauvoir*, 456.

128. Michael Croft, *Red Carpet to China* (London: The Traveling Book Club, 1958), 7.

129. Croft, *Red Carpet*, 8.

130. Croft, *Red Carpet*, 39.

131. R. M. Fox, *China Diary* (London: Robert Hale Ltd., 1959), 174.

132. See for example the detailed analysis of the PRC's people's diplomacy in "Travel to Communist Countries," SEATO Security and Anti-Subversion Measures, Agenda Item 4 (c), PM 120/7/18 part 1, 23 September-27 October 1960, National Ar-chives, New Zealand.

133. "Afro-Asian Solidarity Conference in Cairo," T. D. O'Leary, Office of the High Commission for the UK letter to J. P. Marshall, New Zealand Department of Exter-nal Affairs, 30 December 1957, PM 440/1/5, MFAT.

134. Wang Yonghua, "Zhou Enlai de waijiao yishu," *DWXCCK*, no. 7 (1994): 5.

135. Zhao Pitao, *Waishi gaishuo*, 166.

136. Zhao Pitao, *Waishi gaishuo*, 166.

137. Zhou Enlai, "Duo zuo heping youhao gongzuo," 22 May 1955, Discussion with representatives from the Women's International Democratic League, Zhonghua renmin gongheguo waijiaobu, Zhonggong zhongyang wenxian yanjiushe, *Zhou Enlai de waijiao wenxian* (Beijing: Zhongyang wenxian chubanshe, 1990), 145.

138.   Philip Snow, "China and Africa," in *Chinese Foreign Policy*, ed. Robinson and Shambaugh, 285.

139.   Ces English, interview, 2 February 1997.

140.   Former *waishi* cadre, interview, December 1998.

141.   "Zhou Enlai tongzhi zenmeyang zuo waiguo jizhe de gongzuo," *DWXCCK*, no. 6 (1994): n.p.

142.   "Zhongyang xuanchuanbu guanyu waiguo jizhe dao gedi caifang ying zhuyi shiqing de tongzhi," October 1954, *DDXC*, vol. 1, 241. On the restrictions foreign journalists faced under the new regime, see *France-Soir* journalist A. de Segonzac's account of a visit to China in 1954, *Visa for Peking*, trans. Marion Barwick (Kingswood, Surrey: Windmill Press, 1956).

143.   "Zhongyang xuanchuanbu guanyu waiguo jizhe dao gedi caifang ying zhuyi shiqing de tongzhi."

144.   "Guangjiao pengyou, tanshuai de taolun ziji de guandian, shuo quedian, shuo youdian", *waishi* cadres, interview, December 1997.

145.   "Zhou Enlai de waijiao yishu," *DWXCCK*, 1994, no. 7, p. 5.

146.   Gerry Tannenbaum, interview, 11 April 1997.

147.   Brady, *Friend of China*, 74-86.

148.   Mao Zedong, "Zai Zhongguo renmin zhengzhi xieshang huiyi di yi jie quanti huiyi shang de kaimuci," 21 September 1949, in *Mao Zedong sixiang wansui*, 284; Rewi Alley, *Yo Banfa!* (Shanghai: China Monthly Review, 1952), 83.

149.   David Crook, "The Treatment of Foreigners Working in China and the Cultural Revolution," Correspondence January-March 1973, Box 9, MRP, NYPL.

150.   Ginsberg, *Living in China: By Twenty Authors from Abroad* (Beijing: New World Press, 1979), 8.

151.   Sidney Rittenberg, interview, 29 April 1998.

152.   Sonia Su, *Living in China*, 218.

153.   Although the PRC does not recognize dual citizenship, in the case of George Hatem who had a propaganda role, it was useful for Hatem to maintain his foreign status when meeting with foreign guests. Hatem's U.S. passport lapsed in the early 1950s, but he was issued a new one in the early 1980s.

154.   Shapiro, *Ma Haide: The Saga of an American Doctor George Hatem in China*, (New York: Cypress Press, 1993), 107. Hatem lied about this when questioned by Edgar Snow in 1960, showing him his U.S. passport issued in Beijing in 1947. See Snow, *Red China Today*, 269.

155.   Sidney Rittenberg, interview, 29 April 1998.

156.   Shapiro, *Ma Haide*, 147.

157.   Edgar A. Porter, *The People's Doctor: George Hatem and China's Revolution* (Honolulu: University of Hawaii Press, 1997), 215.

158.   See Brady, *Friend of China*, 82.

159.   Sid Shapiro, *Ma Haide*, 107.

160.   Esther Holland Jian, *British Girl, Chinese Wife*, 201. Some of the foreign residents, such as Rewi Alley and Gladys Yang were actually denied permission to take up Chinese citizenship. Others preferred to keep their foreign passports as an insurance policy in case things went wrong in China.

161.   Richard J. Smith, "Li's Use of Foreign Military Talent," *Li Hongchang and China's Early Modernization*, 128.

162. Maud Russell, letter to Talitha Gerlach, 29 May 1956, Correspondence 1956, Box 5, MRP, NYPL.

163. Sid Engst, interview, 19 December 1997.

164. This system still persists in 2003, although the locations where foreigners are allowed to travel freely have increased enormously since 1979. Edgar Snow described how the system operated in the 1960s, see *Red China Today: The Other Side of the River* (Harmonsworth, Middlesex: Penguin, 1971), 55.

165. Moskin and Wills, *Turncoat*, 116.

166. See Simon Leys, *Chinese Shadows*, 5.

167. Former *waishi* cadre, interview, December 1999. Other expressions for informers in Chinese are *ermu*, "ears and eyes" and *tanzi*, spy. The most infamous story of a relationship between a Chinese minder and a foreign contact is that of "M. Butterfly," the romance between a French Embassy officer in Peking and his Chinese lover, who the Frenchman believed to be a woman. See Joyce Wadler Readers, "For the first time, the real-life models for Broadway's M. Butterfly tell of their very strange romance (Shi Peipu, Bernard Boursicot), *People Weekly*, 30, no. 6 (8 August 1988): 88-95. A more recent saga of spying and Sino-foreign romance is Meihong Xu and Larry Engelman's, *Daughter of China: A True Story of Love and Betrayal* (John Wiley and Sons, 1999).

168. Moskin and Wills, *Turncoat*, 116-117.

169. Former *waishi* cadre, interview, March 1999.

170. Ces English, interview, 2 February 1997.

171. Alan Winnington, *Breakfast with Mao: Memoirs of a Foreign Correspondent* (London: Lawrence and Wishart, 1986), 195.

172. Talitha Gerlach, letter to Maud Russell, 9 June 1951, Correspondence 1951, Box 5, MRP, NYPL.

173. See Paul Gordon Lauren, ed., *The China Hands Legacy, Ethics and Diplomacy* (Boulder: Westview Press, 1987), 28-31, 139-150, for an account of the experiences of William and Sylvia Powell who had edited the *China Weekly Review*, in the late 1940s and early 1950s in Shanghai. When the Powells returned to the United States in 1953, they were accused of treason for their support of the CCP line on issues such as germ warfare in the Korean War. Julian Schuman, a journalist for the *China Weekly Review*, was also accused of these charges, see *China: An Uncensored Look* (New York: Second Chance Press, 1979). Writer Bill Hinton, who wrote an account of land reform under the CCP, had his research notes confiscated for ten years by the U.S. State Department when he returned to the United States from his time in China. See William Hinton, *Fanshen: A Documentary of Revolution in a Chinese Village* (New York: Penguin, 1966).

174. Ces English, interview, 2 February 1997.

175. Ces English, interview.

176. Eric Aarons, *What's Left? Memoirs of an Australian Communist* (Sydney: Penguin Books Australia, 1993), 92.

177. The school was located in the vicinity of Changping, a small town north of Beijing. Even today the former school is off limits to nonmilitary personnel. Anonymous source.

178. Hunt, *The Genesis of Chinese Communist Foreign Policy*, 26.

179. Mark Mancall, *China at the Center: 300 Years of Foreign Policy* (New York: The Free Press, 1984), 421-422.

180.   On China's aid in this period, see Wolfgang Bartke, *The Economic Aid of the PR China to Developing and Countries*, 2nd and rev. ed. (München: K.G. Saur, 1989); John Franklin Copper, *China's Foreign Aid* (Lexington, Mass.: Lexington Books, 1976).

181.   Mancall, *China at the Center*, 423.

182.   "Zhonggong zhongyang pifa zhongyang xuanchuanbu 'guanyu xiang guowai gongying gaojian gongzuo de qingkuang he gaijin yijian xiang zhongyang de baogao,'" 5 May 1956, *DDXC*, vol. 1, 299-302.

183.   Steven M. Goldstein, "Sino-Soviet Relations," in *Chinese Foreign Policy*, ed. Robinson and Shambaugh, 240.

184.   Stuart Schram, *Chairman Mao Talks to the People* (New York: Pantheon Books, 1974), 82. Since Sino-Soviet relations at this time were outwardly relatively amicable, it would be some time before Mao's speech would be made public.

185.   Schram, *Chairman Mao Talks to the People*, 99.

186.   Li Jie, *Mao and Sino-Soviet Relations, 1949-69* (paper presented at the AACPCS/ANZSA International Conference of Communist and Post-Communist Societies, Melbourne, July 1998), 3.

187.   Waishi xiaozu, "Guanyu tiaozheng he jiaqiang duiwai xuanchuan gongzuo lingdao de baogao," *DDXC*, vol. 1, 371-373. See also Lu Ning, *The Dynamics of Foreign-Policy Decisionmaking in China*, 107.

188.   Hamrin, "Elite Politics and the Development of China's Foreign Relations," in *Chinese Foreign Policy*, ed. Robinson and Shambaugh, 87.

Chapter 5

Beijing's Friends, Moscow's Enemies

How does one get weight down? I am 200 and should be 170. Only one way I suppose. That strong push away from the table!![1]

—Rewi Alley, 1961

Beginning in late 1958, the Western media began reporting signs of famine in China.[2] These reports were strongly refuted by China's foreign admirers. Claims that the PRC was suffering a severe famine were a challenge to new China's image. It was not that China had not experienced famine and natural disasters before, but the new government had promised that such problems would be a thing of the past. For Western governments, to be able to demonstrate that China's famine was due to government mismanagement would constitute an important blow in the propaganda war against communism. In the post-Mao era, even Chinese officials now admit that millions died in what is officially called "Three Years of Natural Disasters," *sannian ziran zaihai* (1958-1961). Credible estimates of the number of deaths caused by starvation or severe malnutrition in this period range from fifteen million to thirty million. Many more who survived suffered permanent damage from the famine conditions. It was one of the worst man-made disasters in history,[3] a direct result of the misguided policies and practices of the Great Leap Forward.

In the early 1960s, China's foreign friends loyally denied that there was any famine in the People's Republic (in interviews I conducted in 1997, some even continued to deny it). They wrote letters to Western newspapers and contacts abroad describing conditions of abundance and prosperity; and denounced reports of famine as exaggerated and politically motivated.[4] For those who accepted the label as friends of China, to have done otherwise would have been seen as an act of great disloyalty. Some may have been unaware of the extent of the famine. Foreigners were not free to travel at will and most of them lived very separate lives from Chinese citizens. None would have been allowed to visit the from traveling to other locations. Even those who were married to Chinese citizens may have been protected from knowing the worst of what was going on.

Nevertheless, the misery of people's lives at this time was still obvious to those who spent more than a few weeks on a guided tour. According to one foreign student based in China from 1960-1962, ordinary Chinese people were not afraid to tell foreigners they felt they could trust of the "merciless hunger" they suffered.[5] Foreigners who were not part of the privileged foreign expert system survived on minimal rations along with Chinese people.[6] Rather than actual ignorance of the famine conditions, it seems clear that the foreign friends chose to keep what they knew of it to themselves. In 1961 Elsie Fairfax-Cholmeley wrote to Maud Russell, "Not a single person died from starvation, not even any serious malnourishment."[7] However, the following year when conditions were a little better, Fairfax-Cholmeley admitted that the previous years had been tough and that things had improved.[8] Both in his public pronouncements and letters to friends and family, Rewi Alley continually insisted that all was well in this crisis period. He told Russell:

> The people of New China have parceled out the grain shortage caused by the other two bad droughts, and no one will die though often the older folk give more to the young ones than they should perhaps. It has been superbly managed and the city folk made to feel that they are part and parcel of the whole land—not something that is exempt as in the old day. Actually many of the young folk look better now than they did before the anti-waste campaign started.[9]

In 1960 Alley wrote to his brother Pip in New Zealand, "Mike [his adopted son living in Beijing] sends you a card. He is well, and the kids are better than they have been. More vitamins in the coarse grain they are having now than in the polished rice of before."[10] According to Jasper Becker, the author of a book on the famine, the greatest numbers of people died from starvation in 1960.[11] A year later Alley wrote, "Yes of course people who do not want to struggle run to Hong Kong—that is the same in all revolutions. The magnificent thing about present day's China is the way she has gotten over three years of fantastically bad weather and kept on going."[12] Pip was still not convinced, so that Alley was forced to assure him still further, "Don't worry about HK. The $3^{1}/_{2}$ million there all have relatives in Guangdong, and they come and go. . . . In the off season many people like to go there to stay with friends and relatives, and so on. Don't worry. No one is starving."[13]

The claim that China was experiencing worse than usual natural disasters was part of the disinformation campaign the CCP undertook in its propaganda directed at both foreigners and Chinese citizens alike to reject the rumors of famine. In fact, according to data published by China's own meteorological office, in the three-year period weather conditions were better than usual.[14] As the Sino-Soviet verbal war intensified, the Chinese government also claimed that the economic difficulties were caused by the Soviet Union's recent demands to have all its loans paid back at once. Another line pushed by the government at this time was that China was engaging in an "antiwaste campaign" and stressing frugality out of idealism, rather than necessity. Foreign students at the Beijing Medical College were told that the metabolism of Chinese people was such that they did not require fats and proteins.[15] When the crisis had passed, the Chinese government and their foreign supporters presented the disaster as a victorious triumph over natural forces, rather than the result of human error.

Foreign experts, students, diplomats, journalists, short-term, and "permanent guests" like Alley were given extra food rations during this period. Along with senior party cadres, they had access to special shops which provided goods unavailable to ordinary Chinese people. Their salaries and scholarships were also at least double that of their Chinese counterparts, enabling them to purchase nonrationed goods.[16] The extra rations were a source of embarrassment for some. In 1979, when it was politically acceptable for China's foreign friends to talk more frankly about this period, Denise Lebreton, a French teacher with a Chinese husband wrote of how she would never forget,

> the memories of the "difficult years" from 1959 to 1961, the search for food, the food tickets more precious than money and our embarrassment, we foreigners, at being privileged for the essentials of life. We saw very clearly that our colleagues were poorly housed, that no new living quarters were built and buildings of economic interest had priority. In short, the life of the people was not improving fast enough. But the greatest blows came from abroad: the changed policies of the Soviet Union, the breaking of its contracts with China, the withdrawal of its experts. The people lost confidence in "foreign friends" and instinctively withdrew from us too.[17]

Still, even this more frank account of the "difficult years" omits to mention the famine and puts much of the blame for the hardship on the Russians. Also in 1979, Sonia Su wrote of the period,

> I could see the comrades getting thinner or even suffering from oedema. I was spared some of these hardships as I could buy food in a special shop set up for foreigners—a thoughtful but also realistic policy of the government and party. But never did my comrades complain, nor did any of them allow me to buy them anything.[18]

Foreigners who did not have expert status did not receive extra rations. Jane Su, an American living in Xi'an with her Chinese doctor husband and three children, suffered from extreme hair loss and her teeth fell out due to lack of nutrition during the famine years. Although she did not receive special rations, her husband, as an army doctor, did. When her friend, fellow American Joan Hinton, came to visit her, she brought her own food, as there was none to spare for guests.[19] Esther Holland Jian was in a similar position to Jane Su; not having any special status she was not eligible for extra rations. Luckily for her, her family in England sent her food parcels.[20] Numbers of foreigners such as White Russians who had been seeking out a living in China post-1949 without becoming part of the new system were repatriated in this period; reports of these evacuees described them as looking "bony, desperate, ill" obviously as a result of near starvation.[21]

It was hard for foreign journalists in China to give accurate details about the famine, although they did report food shortages and repeat the rumors of famine. Their main source of information on what was going in the worst-affected areas was restricted to reports from refugees who managed to escape through Macau and Hong Kong. At the time the export of all Chinese papers except *Renmin Ribao* was forbidden, as the other newspapers were filled with advice on "where to find edible herbs, leaves, grasses and roots."[22] Foreign journalists had little opportunity to observe the situation at firsthand or, in many cases, the ability to accurately interpret what they were observing. In this period only journalists representing communist newspapers were given long-term visas, Western journalists were only given visas lasting a few months.[23] Communist journalists were under the control of party discipline and could be trusted to report along party lines (whatever they might think in private). Few of the noncommunist journalists spoke Chinese and virtually none had been posted to China in the pre-1949 period. This was the result of a deliberate policy by the Chinese government, whereby old China hands were the least likely to be allowed to visit China. All foreign journalists (along with diplomats) were confined to a ten-mile radius surrounding the main cities and could only travel outside these areas after applying for a travel permit for each place they wished to visit. In most cases they were only allowed to travel outside the big cities in a group of other foreign journalists; if they were permitted to travel "alone" they were still accompanied by translators, local officials, or simply "under the surveillance of the masses," *qunzhong jiandu*.[24] Even their reporting on the life they observed from their bases in Beijing was extremely restricted, their main contact with Chinese citizens being restricted to interactions with the various "minders" and translators assigned to them. Those who spoke fluent Chinese were no better off, according to Frederick Nossal, foreign reporters who spoke Chinese found that people they spoke to in the street "either smiled politely and say nothing or would simply walk away." Even shop assistants kept their distance, so that "most of the time you were confined to taking wordless strolls through Peking, or you could sit in your hotel room reading translations of the Communist Press."[25]

As a result of the severe hardship experienced within China in the three famine years, in 1961 the International Liaison Department under Wang Jiaxiang recommended a change in foreign policy, including a reduction in tensions with the West, the Soviet Union, and India, as well as a reduction in aid to Third World nations to speed economic recovery. Mao rejected these suggestions, choosing to increase emphasis on political struggle at home and abroad. Mao's influence over *waishi* became stronger as a result of this disagreement, with a corresponding decline in the role of the CCP Central Committee Foreign Affairs Small Group.[26] At Mao's suggestion, research centers focusing on Africa, Asia, and Latin America were set up in 1961, reflecting the new shift in

PRC foreign policy. At the same time, the already existing International Relations Research Institute was instructed to focus on researching Western capitalist countries' (especially U.S.) politics, economy, and way of thinking.[27] This research was for the purpose of fueling the Sino-Soviet polemics. Researchers were instructed to draft theoretical articles predicting the imminent collapse of imperialism; this was in line with the PRC's uncompromising position on monopoly capitalism compared to the Soviet Union's relatively flexible stance at this time.[28]

"Old Friends": Edgar Snow returns to China

Just as the Sino-Soviet split was becoming public knowledge and reports of the Chinese famine were still dominating the news, in June 1960, the American journalist Edgar Snow was allowed to return to China. Snow had attempted to return on a number of occasions before, but had been prevented by the intransigence both of the U.S. and Chinese governments. As a U.S. citizen Snow was prohibited from visiting the PRC, while the PRC refused to allow him to visit in his capacity as a journalist. Finally, in 1960, Beijing accepted him as a writer, guest of his old acquaintance Rewi Alley and officially under the care of the Chinese Writers' Association. Meanwhile, Washington gave him permission to visit the PRC as a journalist. Snow's difficulties in returning to China may also have had to do with Soviet opposition. Snow and his book *Red Star over China* were regarded unfavorably by Moscow. Critics there considered the book to be anti-Soviet, and guilty of spreading pro-Maoist heresy in the United States.[29] After the Sino-Soviet split, Snow critics in the Soviet Union asserted that *Red Star* was "the originating source and principal propagator of the Maoist line in American historical writing and political thought."[30]

The timing of Snow's visit was obviously politically motivated—at least from the Chinese side. His Chinese hosts clearly hoped that he would write a book supporting China's claims that there was no trace of famine and that all was well in China. Moreover, as it had been when Snow came to Yan'an in 1936, the CCP was moving towards a new international united front in 1960 and wanted a trusted "friend" like Snow to be on hand to begin promoting it. Snow's trip was carefully managed and controlled, he was personally escorted on his five-month-long travels around the country by Rewi Alley and George Hatem. Edgar Snow wrote in his diary how he felt about the new China, his first visit since leaving in 1942:

> I realized what it is that is strange about these meetings and interviews thus far. I am cordially received and given every co-operation technically correct. But no intimacy is established no spark of human warmth established. It is as if you knew that you were never going to see a person again and it cannot be the beginning of a friendship. Rewi Alley keeps telling me "not to be expecting any-

thing to be done on a personal basis" I wanted to combine renewal of ~~friend-ship~~ [*sic*] acquaintance with interviews and business but Rewi Alley said that's the last thing to ask for. They'll do everything to avoid that.[31]

Not only were the Chinese cool to Snow, he noticed the foreign friends, including Alley and Hatem, were rather distant. They were no doubt afraid that Snow would attempt to get information from them about what was really happening in China. As Anna Louise Strong told senior diplomat Liao Chengzhi (then chairman of the Overseas Chinese Commission and director of the China Peace Committee), "[Snow] is not discreet with facts that seem to him to make a good story."[32] Strong was particularly anxious that Edgar Snow should not find out the extent to which she was dependent on the Chinese government for her livelihood.

Snow found the extreme anti-imperialist rhetoric of the new government tiresome. He recorded in his personal diary during the visit:

"American imperialism wants to colonize Asia and Africa" says everybody. It is not open to debate. It is a simple historical fact. Every worker learns such facts in political study from 2 to 4 hours a week after work. Who am I, one American, to suggest that many Americans (many millions) resent U.S. policy and help to keep war and imperialism from leading to another world war. That there is good will and good humanity behind all this "restraint" too?[33]

Not surprisingly, given the political climate of the time, though Snow was privately critical, the book he published of this visit, *The Other Side of the River: Red China Today*, did not air his doubts too obviously. As his CCP hosts had no doubt hoped he would, Snow actually publicly rejected claims of the famine in his book:

I assert that I saw no starving people in China, nothing that looked like old-time famine (and only one beggar, among flood refugees in Shenyang) and that the best Western intelligence on China was well aware of this. Isolated instances of starvation due to neglect or failure of the rationing system were possible. Considerable malnutrition undoubtedly existed. Mass starvation? No.[34]

Snow knew he had to be careful, or he would not be invited back. His whole career had been defined by his connections in China, and it seems, that was a connection he was unwilling to break. To have criticized new China would be regarded as an unfriendly act, not what was expected of an "old friend of the Chinese people."

Sino-Soviet Split

Edgar Snow noted in the account of his visit how few Soviets or Eastern Europeans he saw. He had arrived just as all Soviet advisers were ordered to return home by Moscow; regardless of when their contracts were to expire they left almost immediately, taking their blueprints with them. In the summer of 1960, a total of 1,390 Soviet specialists returned to the Soviet Union along with their families.[35] Moscow explained the decision in terms of its concern at Beijing's public criticism of the Soviet advisers and their work in China, the government's spying on the advisers' activities and attitudes, and forcing them to support their views in the Sino-Soviet ideological debate.[36] From Beijing's point of view, Moscow's action revealed the lengths the Soviets would go to undermine China's sovereignty and national development. Now not only had the Soviets shown themselves to be "revisionist" (not true revolutionaries), they were imperialists (social imperialists) too. Moscow's decision to remove its foreign specialists from China was a crucial step towards the complete breakdown of the Sino-Soviet alliance.

Even more so than the famine, the Sino-Soviet split was a test of the loyalty, or in some cases an indication of the lack of other options, for China's foreign supporters. At this point, as in other periods of Sino-foreign tension under CCP rule, the authorities expected foreigners to take a clear stand as to whether they were friends or enemies. The hard-line position of both the Soviets and the Chinese forced a major upheaval in both the communist and left-wing world, as comrades and admirers of communism were compelled to choose sides. Communist parties split within a number of countries and various front organizations such as the Friends of the Soviet Union and the peace movement were affected. Over time parallel rival organizations would be set up funded either by the Chinese or the Soviets, thereby maintaining the ideological battle through their foreign supporters.

Those foreign residents who took the Chinese side made a point of making their position obvious very early on. U.S. cinematographer Jay Leyda, an old friend of the Soviet Union then living in the PRC as a foreign expert for the Chinese film industry, wrote of "undignified doings" at celebrations in Beijing to commemorate the forty-fourth anniversary of the Russian Revolution in 1961:

During the Soviet ambassador's speech noses were picked, heads were stroked and the ceiling was studied—even before our little (Albanian) champions huffed out, followed by well-prepared "spear-carrier" students, brought in for the staging. Rewi [Alley] a hulk of theatrical indignation during the same speech (he gets his cues fast). X more Chinese than the Chinese in intermission. There were only two who sounded as sad as we felt.[37]

The split was not discussed openly by the foreign friends in their writings for overseas audiences, although its effects were obvious among their own ranks. During the 1950s, most of the foreign experts were members of foreign communist parties. Many foreign experts did not approve of Mao's policies after the Great Leap Forward, so they left China. Still others were ordered to return by their home communist parties. Those foreigners who chose to stay on had to accept the Maoist line in the Sino-Soviet split. The foreigners' political study group became totally pro-Mao, those who did not accept this stopped coming.[38] Those foreigners who supported the Chinese line were excluded from Soviet-organized activities such as the annual Moscow Peace Conference. Anna Louise Strong, who regularly attended such activities, explained her absence from the 1962 conference to Maud Russell by saying she needed to finish her book on Laos.[39] Also in 1962, "peace worker" and high-profile pro-China propagandist Rewi Alley was snubbed at an international peace conference based in Cuba, which had taken the Soviet side in the dispute.[40]

The foreigners who remained in China after the Sino-Soviet split were known by their detractors as the "Sunshiners" (a scatological reference to their extreme admiration for Chairman Mao) or the "Three Hundred Percenters" (because of their three-hundred-percent support for the Chinese line). From a propaganda point of view, the support of the friends of China, both China-based and abroad, was used as if it were significant evidence of the correctness of Mao's line in the ideological battle against the Soviet "revisionists." Following the break with the Soviet Union, more than ever before, the foreign friends' symbolic role became important in Chinese domestic politics, even when they counted for little in their own countries.

China worked hard to gain support for its line among the international communist movement and its sympathizers, inviting leaders from various communist parties on high-profile visits. During the 1960s a number of parties split into pro-Soviet and pro-Chinese factions as a result of China and the Soviet Union's machinations. Those factions who followed the Chinese lead found themselves boosted up to high status in PRC propaganda. The New Zealand Communist Party (NZCP), led by Victor Wilcox, was the only national Communist Party (outside Albania which had been the proxy for the Sino-Soviet polemics in 1960) to follow the Chinese line. Wilcox visited China frequently and he was greeted as if he was the statesman of a major country, instead of being the chairman of an obscure and politically irrelevant Communist Party in a South Pacific nation. Senior Chinese leaders turned out to greet him at the airport, behaving as if a world leader had arrived.[41] *Renmin Ribao* featured front-page articles on his arrival and departures. All his important speeches were translated and made widely available in China, as was the party newspaper, *People's Voice*, a useful way of disguising a subsidy to the tiny party. In the 1960s, Wilcox was one of the most well-known foreigners in China.

Uniting against Common Enemies: Support for Asia, Africa, and Latin America

As relations between China and the Soviet Union worsened and the United States maintained its hostile stance, Beijing focused on strengthening relations with the countries of Latin America, Africa, and Asia and lent its support to national liberation movements around the globe. Mao's talks with various friendship delegations from 1960 on, were published widely in political study texts of the period.[42] In May 1960, Mao spoke to a group of delegates from fourteen countries in Latin America and Africa. The editors of a pamphlet that was produced on these and other "important talks" with similar groups recorded:

> Chairman Mao had a cordial talk with these friends, expressed to them the firm support of the 650 million Chinese people for the national and democratic movements now being carried on by the peoples of Cuba and the whole of Asia, Africa and Latin America. He thanked them for their support and help to New China and pointed out that: Our common enemy is U.S. imperialism, we all stand on the same front and need to unite with and support each other. The people of the whole world, including the people of the United States, Chairman Mao Tse-tung said, are our friends.[43]

The pamphlet was translated into numerous foreign languages and widely distributed internationally, via Xinhua news bureaus and the Chinese government-controlled China Books and China Friendship Societies. All forms of propaganda directed at the countries of Latin America, Africa, and Asia dramatically increased throughout the 1960s.[44] Mao's meetings with the visitors were publicized to strengthen China's claim to leadership of the underdeveloped, decolonized world, indeed, now that the Soviets had shown themselves to be "revisionists" of the world revolution itself. The stress on relations with these countries and the leaders of obscure political groups in the Western world served to emphasize to Chinese and foreigners alike that despite worsening Sino-Soviet relations, China was not alone, that the people of the world were on China's side, especially those who had suffered the effects of Western imperialism. Jay Leyda, whose occupation gave him a unique perspective on CCP propaganda noted, "by 1963 and even more by 1964 . . . the 'white world' was depicted as China's antagonist. Even China's one European ally, Albania, was mystically linked to the Asian and African and Latin American worlds where China still had hopes of influence."[45] The new line on Chinese foreign policy was "oppose revisionism, oppose imperialism," *fan xiu, fan di*: opposition both to the United States and the Soviet Union.[46] Not only were "revisionism" and "imperialism" code words for China's primary foreign enemies, they also hinted at factional struggles between Mao and opponents of his Great Leap Forward policies that had lead to such famine and hardship throughout China. These ruptures in party unity would not become obvious to outsiders until much later.

In a talk with the general secretary of the NZCP, Victor Wilcox, Mao described the new foreign policy line as "The Three Struggles, One Increase," *san dou yi duo*, the struggle against imperialism, revisionism, and the reactionaries of all countries, and increase in aid to anti-imperialist, Marxist-Leninist revolutionary parties and factions.[47] Beijing kept a close watch on protest movements overseas, as evidence of Mao's claim that the end was nigh for the twin tigers of revisionism and imperialism.[48] Protest movements in the capitalist world and liberation struggles in Latin America, Africa, and Asia were regarded as signs of a new phase in the world revolution.[49] Particular attention was focused on the black civil rights movement and protests against the Vietnam War in the United States, and the peace movement in various Western countries, as evidence of the proletarian struggle against imperialism. Student demonstrations and union struggles were regarded as proof that the intensity of class struggle in the developed world was increasing. Certainly the 1960s was an era of popular protest in the West. However, despite Chinese claims at the time, it is unlikely that these protests had anything more than a remote connection with a "Chinese-led" world revolution.

Not only did the CCP observe the protest movements, it actually provided assistance to some, from giving financial aid to offering China as a safe haven when foreign activists faced arrest. In 1963 Mao stated that he considered "supporting all oppressed people and nations in their revolutionary struggle" as one of the basic principles of a socialist country's foreign policy.[50] National liberation movements and radical groups were given money and high status in the news. Writers and senior foreign leaders were flattered with requests to translate their published works into Chinese. The cultivation of left-wing forces was very pragmatic;[51] apart from "patriotic" overseas Chinese, these groups were virtually the only source of international support China had at this time. By the early 1960s, not only had China been cut off by the United States from both international recognition and trade for more than a decade, now it was moving to alienate its only major international alliance, with the Soviet Union and its allies.

Reflecting China's isolation, in this period activists from Latin America, Africa, and Asia were given the highest priority for official invitations to party conferences and National Day. After the 1964 National Day celebrations Talitha Gerlach informed Maud Russell, "over 3,000 visitors were invited from just about every part of the globe. Asia, Africa and Latin America were most liberally represented."[52] In contrast, few visitors from Western countries received invitations. From 1959-1960 more than 200 separate delegations from Latin American countries alone were invited to China, while 24 Chinese delegations were sent to the region. From 1961-1962, 90 Latin American delegations were received while 50 were dispatched, while from 1963-1964, 115 delegations were received and 16 delegations were sent. In 1965, 47 delegations were received and only 4 sent.[53]

Funds for left-wing and rebel groups around the world were funneled through the CCP Central Committee International Liaison Department, which after 1962, was dominated by Kang Sheng, also China's chief of public security. Resident foreigners trusted by the International Liaison Department—and there were not many—would be asked to have dinner with visiting groups and evaluate them.[54] Black American civil rights leader Robert Williams was invited to China and, according to longtime foreign resident, Gerry Tannenbaum, "treated as if he was Chairman Mao." Tannenbaum says Williams's visit served as political education for the Chinese populace, Beijing needed to prove it was not internationally isolated: "This demonstrated that China was not alone in its struggle and that it was leading a whole array of revolutionary people worldwide."[55]

Chinese leaders asserted that the CCP's revolutionary experience could show the way for other societies. In 1963 Mao told a group of visiting Africans, "the people who have triumphed in their own revolution should help those still struggling for liberation. This is our internationalist duty."[56] This was not an example of idealism in international relations. There were good rational reasons for such a policy. It was advantageous both for China's domestic propaganda and foreign image. Thousands of technicians, engineers, and medical staff were sent to Africa and Asia to assist in PRC-funded aid projects. China's aid workers were carefully instructed on how to behave in the country where they would be working. They were required to live at much the same standard as the local residents, make efforts to learn the local language and spread CCP doctrine where they could.[57] China also practiced "benevolent trade" in this period: buying up large quantities of products from countries in Africa, Asia, and Latin America— often for goods for which there was little demand—selling much-needed commodities at bargain prices.[58] Even during the famine years, the PRC channeled thousands of tons of grain to African states such as Guinea and the Sudan, grain which China sorely needed itself.[59]

The CCP tended to support those countries or liberation movements who were not on friendly terms with the USSR or the United States. China in the 1960s was known as a haven for foreign revolutionaries. French Sinologist Marianne Bastid-Bruguière was a student in Beijing in the mid-1960s. She remembers that at the time "there were remnants of every single revolutionary movement in the world."[60] Foreign revolutionaries would contact the Chinese through the embassy in Switzerland. To outsiders, it appeared that "China aimed to establish another Comintern with the Third World opposing Russia."[61] Clandestine guerrilla warfare schools for foreigners were established in the early 1960s at the Nanjing and Wuhan Military Academies,[62] in addition to the previously established school in Beijing. The PLA trained insurgent groups from Algeria, Angola, Botswana, the Cameroons, the two Congos, Guinea, Indonesia, Kenya, Malawi, Malaysia, Niger, Nigeria, South Africa, and Thailand among other countries. Students were trained in how to make and use explosives, how to blow up bridges, houses, railways, tanks and trucks; how to conduct sabotage and set ambushes; how to deal with unsympathetic locals, infiltrate organizations and deal with traitors.[63] Not all students from Third World countries at this time studied guerrilla warfare; others enrolled in more pedestrian courses.

Revolutionary rhetoric aside, Third World students still experienced much racism in China. One African student, Emmanuel Hevi, felt so strongly about the discrimination he experienced in the PRC that he wrote a book as a "warning" to other Africans about the true situation in China.[64] According to Hevi, Chinese girls who were caught dating African students (who were mostly male) were sent to prison camps for their immoral behavior.[65] In 1962, in a dispute over the sale of cigarettes, a Zanzibari student was beaten by Beijing hotel staff.

African students protested with sit-ins and hunger strikes and many returned home.[66] As Sven Lindqvist, a Swedish student studying at Beijing University in the early 1960s observed, "the people in Peking whose friendship the Chinese tried most strenuously to win, were precisely those who were most alien and incomprehensible to them."[67]

During the early to mid-1960s, people's diplomacy took on even greater prominence in China's foreign policy. Since China's relations with both the governments of the United States and its allies and the Soviet Union and its allies were not amicable, according to this strategy, it would appeal to the citizens of those countries through propaganda and popular-level contacts to influence their societies. Foreign delegations to the PRC soon became pawns in the Sino-Soviet struggle. They were given special briefings to explain the Chinese point of view, and *waishi* cadres who accompanied them on their visit were instructed to find out their opinions and do ideological work on them. Not all cadres did this with the same level of enthusiasm. One former *waishi* cadre who worked as a translator/guide in this era says she suspects many of her colleagues made up what they reported back to their managers on the opinions of their foreign charges. Most foreigners visiting in this period were as cautious as their Chinese minders were of saying what they really thought to outsiders.[68]

From the early 1960s, the title "friend of the Chinese people," *Zhongguo renmin de pengyou,* became official and legitimate, previously foreign supporters of China had been described in terms of their support for common causes of the worldwide communist movement or known as "international friends," *guoji youren.* The resident "friends of China" were directly involved in people's diplomacy, both on a personal and on a professional level. Some acted as unofficial envoys of Chinese foreign policy at international forums. They acted as interlocutors for "new" China when foreign delegations visited. They participated in propaganda activities aimed at both the Chinese population and foreigners outside China. Many of them wrote articles praising Chinese-style communist revolution which were published in their home countries and in the Chinese media. And they assisted in the mammoth task of translating and broadcasting Mao Zedong thought worldwide, an activity that dramatically increased as the Sino-Soviet war of words worsened and the struggle between Mao and his opponents within the party intensified.

Despite the polemics and international antagonism, China was not completely isolated or dependent on people's diplomacy alone. By the end of the 1950s, thirty-three countries had established diplomatic relations with the PRC. Between 1960 and 1965 the number increased to fifty, most of the countries being from the newly independent African states. France recognized the PRC in 1964, the first major Western power to do so (the United Kingdom had still not established full diplomatic relations at an ambassadorial level). *Waishi* staff numbers had to increase rapidly to cope with these new developments. By 1960, the Foreign Ministry was ten times its size in 1949.[69] In 1965 the College of International Relations, *Guoji guanxi xueyuan,* was founded to meet the need for more *waishi* personnel.[70] In the antiforeign climate of the 1960s, rather than choosing personnel with appropriate language and professional skills, only those whose loyalty to the party was assured were acceptable. Ambassadors for China's newly established embassies were selected from among senior party officials, the military, and local government.[71]

Tightening Controls on Foreigners: 1960-1966

Despite the rhetoric about solidarity with Asia, Africa, and Latin America and the increased stress on friends of China, following the Sino-Soviet split, antiforeign feeling increased and was even encouraged by government policies designed to keep foreigners and Chinese apart.[72] When Sino-Soviet relations deteriorated, the Soviets had accused China of "indoctrinating foreigners."[73] The government responded, long-term foreign resident David Crook recorded, by "push[ing] foreign personnel further and further out of Chinese social and political life, allowing only specially designated individuals to have contact with them."[74] Mao's growing fear of "Soviet agents" within the Chinese government and throughout the party resulted in a restrengthening of controls on foreigners and of Chinese people's relations with them. The increased separation between foreigners and Chinese was probably also a result of stepped up security due to the famine. Resident foreigners became even more isolated from Chinese life; in particular excluded from participating in political activities or activism.[75]

Esther Holland Jian had never been part of the foreign experts system. She was ostracized and suspected of being a spy in this new era, after she returned home to England to visit her family and came back earlier than expected.[76] She and her Chinese family were ordered to move from their home at Xiamen University because it was considered too close to the sensitive Nationalist base at Jinmen Island (Quemoy), just off the Fujian coast. The antiforeignism of the 1960s was not just directed at individual foreigners, foreign culture was also a target. Holland Jian recalled:

> It seemed at that time that anything foreign was deemed conducive to revisionism. Music by masters like Beethoven, Mozart and Chopin were no longer heard on the radio and the works of famous writers like Shakespeare, Goethe and Dickens were removed from libraries.[77]

Whether cocooned by privilege or shunned by antiforeignism, foreigners' lives in the PRC became increasingly remote from those of ordinary Chinese. The activities of the small number of foreign students in China at this time were particularly tightly controlled. Sven Lindqvist reported that not only were the students segregated from their Chinese classmates, they were also isolated from those of their own countries:

> The Chinese try to make their control of the environment as complete as possi-

ble. They use various means to intimidate a student and prevent him from keeping in touch with his embassy and people of his nationality. He lives in a room where nothing audible is secret, often with a companion he cannot fully rely on. The exits to the dormitory are either guarded or closed. The Chinese staff, his Chinese companions, and some of the foreigners are obliged to report continually on his social activities, his habits, and his conversations. People read his letters and poke around his room when he is out. There are signs that the Chinese get a hold over some students in this way, with a view to using them as tools of the Chinese government.[78]

There was some tension among the group of students from Western countries between those whose countries were considered "capitalist" and those who were "socialist." Major political disputes were generated by matters as small as the quality of the food in the students' dining hall. Lindqvist noted, "In a socialist society nothing is apolitical. Even food is political food, and criticism of food is political criticism."[79]

From 1964, new regulations controlling foreigners' movements and activities were introduced, much stricter than those that had been implemented after 1949. In Xi'an, the local Foreign Affairs Office contacted Joan Hinton, Sid Engst, and Jane Su, the only three foreign adults living in the Xi'an area at the time and told them which sections of the city and surrounding countryside they were restricted to. To her distress, Joan Hinton's then twelve-year-old son, Fred, was called into the office separately and asked by officials, "Why are you living in China?" From this time on, foreign children were not allowed to wear young pioneer scarfs—a serious disappointment to children who had all their lives grown up among Chinese children. The decision set them apart, making them feel different.[80] At the same time, beginning in May of that year, a national campaign was initiated to increase propaganda on China's "friendship with foreign peoples." It was an effort to avert racist incidents, which were becoming increasingly common as China opposed both Western capitalist countries and the Soviet Union and resentment grew at the privileges of foreigners in China in comparison to the lives of ordinary Chinese.[81]

In early 1966, Sid Engst, Joan Hinton, and their three children were forced to move to Beijing from the Shaanxi farm where they had lived and worked since 1949. The couple were told they were needed to help polish English for China's foreign propaganda machine. Hinton worked for the Committee for Cultural Relations with Foreign Countries, while Engst polished English for Chinese films. They were shocked by the treatment of foreigners they found in Beijing, so much more confined than the life they had led in Shaanxi. Living in the Chinese capital, they were given what Joan Hinton called a "keeper," the person "who controlled all our activities." They had to get permission from this "keeper" to go anywhere outside their usual schedule. Unlike in the early years after 1949, Engst and Hinton were disappointed to find they were not allowed to participate in political meetings with Chinese people. Alienated from what was going on around them, they say they felt that they were treated as "living typewriters," rather than revolutionary comrades. Now that the Soviet experts had left, most foreigners lived in what the couple derisively called, the "Golden Ghetto"—the renamed Friendship Hotel (former home of the Soviet experts)— in luxury, and far removed from Chinese people's lives. This made managing the foreigners more convenient, and kept them out of sight from ordinary Chinese, whose lives were much harsher. To internationalists like Sid Engst and Joan Hinton, this was anathema, a contradiction of all they had struggled for.[82]

Expert and Red: Inviting Noncommunist Foreign Experts to China

At the same time that the political role of China's foreign friends took on a new form, China altered its policy on hiring foreign helpers. Since the CCP could no longer rely on the fraternal support of other national communist parties (other than Albania and New Zealand), it had to seek assistance from other sources. In 1962, the PRC let it be known through its foreign contacts that it needed foreign language teachers. Applicants were asked to write brief autobiographies outlining their work experience and political sympathies and were interviewed by Chinese embassy staff in those countries where the PRC had diplomatic relations.[83] From this period on, a new group of foreign experts was invited to China: people chosen primarily for their professional qualifications rather than their political credentials.[84] They were, in Maoist terms, more "expert" than "red."[85] However, although most of them were not Communist Party members, the majority of them were basically sympathetic to the aims of the Chinese revolution. Only those who were viewed as friendly to the PRC would be given employment and they were carefully vetted before being selected. In the political climate of the 1960s, to be willing to live and work in communist China was in itself a political statement.

In August 1964, David Crook wrote to Maud Russell that there was to be a still further increase in foreign language experts as well as foreign translators.[86] Campuses such as Wuhan, Canton, and even the small coastal city of Qinhuangdao in Hebei, were to have foreign teachers. Foreign Minister Chen Yi told a meeting of foreign friends at a gathering in Beijing, "China already has 48,000 specialists and technicians in foreign countries, and . . . next year the number will rise to between 50 and 60,000." Crook told Russell, "This helps explain the expansion in foreign language teaching and translation. It also shows how high China's prestige stands abroad, especially in Asia and Africa, and makes nonsense of talk about her being 'isolated.'"[87]

The foreigners were met on their arrival at Beijing Airport with a reception in their honor, bouquets of flowers and warm greetings from the leaders of their Chinese work units.[88] Once they were settled in, only a very limited attempt, if any, was made to increase their revolutionary consciousness. Some were invited to attend the remaining foreigners' political study groups, although this was not compulsory, and asked to participate in revolutionary public demonstrations and meetings.[89] The foreigners living in Beijing tended to be much more politicized (and were much more numerous in number) than in other cities. The English communist journalist Eric Gordon, who lived in the Friendship Hotel in Beijing and was part of a group that arrived in 1965, complained, "The Chinese made no overt moves whatsoever to interest their foreign colleagues in politics, not even the left-wingers or communists . . . The Chinese went out of their way, however, to keep foreigners entertained."[90] This was not the revolutionary China he had imagined he was coming to work for. The newly arrived foreigners tended to form two distinct groups: those who were interested in Chinese politics and those who were not. Instead of political activism, foreigners in Beijing were kept amused by regular excursions to the Great Wall, Summer Palace, Ming Tombs, weekly dances, twice-weekly films, and Beijing opera visits. Foreign experts in other cities were similarly entertained. Gordon was very disappointed that foreigners were left out of Chinese political discussions, "As a communist, I thought the Chinese would be only too glad to proselytize the 'cause,' instead they appeared to want to foster a sort of mercenary relationship—what we thought of as employees, was of no consequence to them."[91] Gordon and his wife joined the foreigners-only English-speaking political discussion group. After they stopped going to the group, other foreigners reported this to the authorities as an indication of their political unreliability.[92] There were tensions among foreign friends in Beijing in this period, with people spying and reporting on each other. Whether voluntary or encouraged, such activities resulted in a climate of mistrust among the foreigners. The Gordons were also disturbed that relations between Chinese and foreigners were strictly controlled. Their Chinese colleagues had to get permission from their work-unit political instructor simply to invite them to their homes for dinner.[93]

There was a role for foreign activism in this period, however, it was kept apart from Chinese activities following the "insiders and outsiders" principle. The introduction to the Chinese political scene was facilitated for many of the new residents based in Beijing by Sidney (Sid) Rittenberg, a former GI who had elected to stay on in China after 1945.[94] Rittenberg had learned Chinese in the U.S. Army and was renowned for his extraordinary Chinese language skills. Rittenberg joined the CCP in 1948, but in early 1949, he was arrested by CCP security forces. He was held in prison for six years on accusations of being an American spy. Rittenberg had been fingered by Stalin, who was suspicious of the CCP's overly close relations with Westerners of dubious political origins.[95] Rittenberg underwent a conversion-type experience during his incarceration. His reaction was similar to other foreign prisoners in China in the early 1950s, many of whom on their release, after undergoing "ideological remolding" showed a similar sympathy for their captors. Rittenberg's experiences in this period set him apart from other "international friends" in China after 1949 and help to explain his extreme zeal and ultraorthodox political views in the 1950s and 1960s.

After his release Rittenberg took up a senior position at Radio, on the lowest tier of the high-ranking cadres in his work unit the Ministry of Broadcasting. The post was helpful for his activities among the community of foreigners in Beijing as many of them also worked within the same bureaucratic system or *xitong* as did Rittenberg. According to Rittenberg, he was authorized by Liao Chengzhi (then vice-foreign minister and, because of his pre-1949 experiences, an important liaison figure for China's foreign supporters) to expand as widely as possible CCP influence among the foreign community in Beijing, and through them, "to influence the world-wide contest between the Chinese and the Russians for the loyalty of revolutionaries everywhere."[96] Rittenberg acted as one of the go-betweens for the Chinese in managing this disparate group of foreigners. Each language group and in some cases national group, had an unofficial representative who the Chinese authorities would deal with for supervising the various foreign experts.[97]

As in the era of the Soviet advisers, the foreign residents of the Friendship Hotel led a completely separate life from Chinese people. The hotel had two large restaurants to cope with the ethnic diversity of its experts: one with Western and one with African-Asian cuisine. There were shops for all the foreigners' needs: a tailor, grocer, butcher, chemist, post office, shoe repairs, bank, laundry, photographer, hairdresser, even a secondhand shop, a billiard room, cinema, dance hall, cards and Ping-Pong room, roof garden for summer drinks and dances, open-air swimming pool, gymnasium, tennis courts, football pitch, winter skating rink, fish ponds, gardens, and a miniature zoo.[98] Cars and coaches took the foreigners to their jobs or out to the sights. In those days the Friendship Hotel was surrounded by dusty countryside and a few institutes, five miles from downtown Beijing. A twice-daily bus was available to take the foreigners into town. Ordinary Chinese were not allowed into the hotel. The foreign experts were still paid considerably more than their Chinese counterparts. Language polishers were paid 500 yuan, while foreign language teachers received 380. They were also given free accommodation and transportation to their work unit if required. In comparison, salaries for most Chinese staff were much lower: high school teachers were paid around 55 yuan, while workers got 70 yuan and soldiers received a mere 6 yuan.[99]

Hierarchical differences became even more pronounced among the foreigners living in China at this time. At the top were those who had given political support to the CCP before 1949. Significantly, despite China's pro-Afro-Asia-Latin America rhetoric of this time, they were all from English-speaking Western countries. This reflected the continuing importance of the Western English-speaking world as a target of PRC propaganda of this era. The American journalist Anna Louise Strong had been invited to come and live in the PRC in 1958 by senior leaders, and she arrived "ready to denounce the Soviet CP after the way she had been treated by Stalin in 1949."[100] It was easy for Strong to take a pro-CCP stance after the split, since she believed (rightly) that the reason for her detention on spying charges in the Soviet Union in 1949 was her pro-CCP writing. By the early 1960s she had become the most important figure in the English-speaking community of China's foreign friends. British journalist Alan Winnington wrote of her:

> Anna Louise Strong held court—it is scarcely an exaggeration—in a magnificent flat not far from the Peking Hotel. From the time I first met her until her death she reflected every twist of official policy and was given flattering opportunities to do so. Her international reputation was built up by Mao and Zhou Enlai and she paid with hypocrisy for the dubious honor of becoming their trusted mouthpiece.[101]

Strong's high status in China was both because of her loyalty and long-standing support of the Chinese revolution—she had been in Wuhan in 1927 with Borodin and first came to China in 1922 to report the Canton Uprising—but also because she was such an experienced propagandist. Her news sheet *Letters from China* was used by senior leaders to give their version of events to the outside world. It had begun at the suggestion of Zhou Enlai, and topics for articles were proposed by senior officials who were closely involved in editing drafts to ensure they followed the correct party line.[102] Strong saw herself as "China's mouth-piece to English-speaking countries" and she had very close contacts to the CCP leadership.[103] Through the work of Strong and other pro-CCP writers, the party had connections to many major Western newspapers, even if their own materials were not published directly, the information and views they expressed were.[104] Anna Louise Strong sent Maud Russell commentary on the Sino-Indian border dispute based on her interviews with Zhou Enlai and other senior officials. She asked not to be quoted, but that it be used for Maud Russell's editorial in *Far East Quarterly*.[105] *Letters from China* was translated into almost every major language group, forming part of a network that according to Sid Rittenberg, "helped nurture anti-Soviet splinter communist and left-wing nationalist groups in many countries."[106]

In addition to Strong, Rewi Alley, who also had a high-level propaganda role, and Sid Rittenberg, there were two other foreigners singled out for high status in this period. The two men were the closest thing that China ever had to defectors from the West. Both were senior former U.S. government economists. Frank Coe and Sol Adler arrived to settle in China in the early 1960s, forced to leave the United States because the FBI was investigating them as suspected members of a Soviet espionage ring.[107] Both Coe and Adler had been underground communist sympathizers. Coe had participated in the Bretton Woods economic negotiations after World War II and was the first secretary of the International Monetary Fund. Adler had been a senior Treasury Department economist. The two men already had links with China before they came: Frank Coe through his brother Bob Coe, a "progressive" who was in contact with Song Qingling; Adler from his days at the U.S. Embassy in Chongqing in the 1940s. Though the Chinese government recognized the two economists' high status by giving them better treatment than other foreigners, their economic expertise was not fully utilized. Both were advisers to the Research Center for Economic, Technological and Social Development under the State Council, the Ministry of Foreign Trade and Economic Cooperation, and the Institute of World Economy and Politics under the Chinese Academy of Social Sciences. Their main job was to read the Western press and produce a digest of major political and economic trends. They were also involved in the high-prestige task of assisting with the translation of Mao's *Selected Works* into English, rather a waste of energy for two such high-flying academics.[108] Every year the pair was asked to write reports on U.S. society, in which they inevitably predicted the end of capitalism. According to Gerry Tannenbaum, the reports seemed to be treated with some significance by some in the CCP, at least, when giving his annual speech to the foreign residents in Beijing, Foreign Minister Chen Yi would always emphasize that "the end of capitalism is nigh."[109]

A select few of the other foreign residents were also chosen as advisers on the West. French Sinologist Viviane Alleton was close to American Bob Winter who taught English and French at Beijing University. She was surprised how well-informed he was about internal Chinese politics when she first met him in 1965. When she asked him why, she says, "He laughed a big American laugh and said he was a 'guinea pig' for the Chinese." Winter's spare-time job in this period was to give an American reaction to Chinese political moves—though he had not lived in the United States since 1923.[110]

Michael Shapiro was another leading figure among China's foreign friends in the 1960s. After the United States started bombing North Vietnam in 1965, Shapiro called a meeting of the English-speaking resident foreigners in Beijing. According to Morris Wills, then an English polisher in the Foreign Languages Press, Shapiro told the meeting:

> The Central Committee of the Party wanted the foreigners in Peking to show more enthusiasm for Chinese support of the North Vietnamese in the war. He explained that they had called this meeting to discuss what more they could do to develop the movement in America—on the campuses, among the Negroes, and anything else they could think of. There were suggestions about making recordings to send to North Vietnam and South Vietnam. In South Vietnam they would be broadcast to the American soldiers. Others suggested writing letters and propaganda sheets and getting these into America by various means. A select committee was elected to provide the means. They wanted to bring as many professors and students as possible into the chain. The Chinese envisioned that the start would be made on the campuses; the Party saw the war coming to a halt because of this movement in America.[111]

Whenever a crisis occurred in the world, Morris Wills records, the Chinese leadership would organize a demonstration to publicize Chinese feelings, "The small group of foreigners who worked with the Chinese politically was asked by the Chinese to organize all the foreigners to join the demonstrations. That's how I was brought into them. I joined the demonstrators because if you didn't join, you'd be on the blacklist and your treatment would be harsher. Most foreigners either wanted to join or had to."[112]

In the mid-1960s foreign friends based in China were asked by Chinese authorities to conduct a letter campaign, writing letters to friends all over the world to promote China's viewpoint.[113] The foreigners were also involved in supporting the anti-Vietnam War movement through their connections back home. In 1963 English polisher Douglas Lake, newly arrived from New Zealand, wrote to Maud Russell with an article on China for her magazine, telling her "I want also to do my share, however small it may be, to see that China, her people, and her problems are better understood in the rest of the world."[114] The Chinese authorities made a distinction in their treatment of foreigners between those who could write propaganda publicizing China and those who could not, as well as focusing attention on people who already had high standing in their own countries.

Unlike the Soviets, the CCP always made a point of being respectful to foreign communists who had supported their cause in the past. When Manya Reiss, a founder of the U.S. Communist Party, who had worked in Moscow and later in Beijing, was dying of cancer, Anna Louise Strong wrote to Maud Russell,

> in her last month Chou En-lai spent an afternoon at her bedside, giving her all the latest confidential interpretations of China and the world, while her comrades at work, stood around to get the information and Eppie [Israel Epstein] was asked by Chou to give it to me . . . That kind of thoughtfulness by high ranking people to rank and file comrades is done nowhere else that I know . . . 1200 came to her funeral and the wreaths exhausted the floral shops of Peking. Wires came from TASS and Prague and Rewi Alley wrote a very good poem on her passing which will be sent to *Mainstream*, and probably ignored. Not a word on her passing from the U.S. Party which she helped found . . . The Americans in Peking feel ashamed.[115]

Nevertheless, by the mid-1960s external and internal pressures contributed to a strong antagonism towards foreigners and foreign things in China. Neale Hunter and Colin Mackerras, who were based in Shanghai and Beijing respectively from 1965-1966 as foreign teachers, noted that in 1965 foreign art, literature, and music were frowned on; it was no longer part of mainstream society. Culture had increasingly become more "revolutionary," with a greater emphasis on Mao Zedong thought. Foreign things were attacked; even foreign-made cars had their names changed from Austin and Ford to "anti-imperialist" and "anti-revisionist."[116] As early as January 1965 Talitha Gerlach, among others, wrote to Maud Russell that "the Cultural Revolution is gathering momentum," telling her of reforms in the cultural sphere.[117] In July 1964, at Mao's behest, a Cultural Revolution Small Group had been set up to discuss cultural reform. Peng Zhen was the leader of this group.[118] As the cult of Mao grew, Maoist fever was building among some of the foreign friends. Elsie Fairfax-Cholmeley wrote to Russell of a peasant who discussed Mao Zedong's theories before deciding on a work plan, exclaiming to her, "It is so exciting."[119]

Notes

1. Rewi Alley, letter to Pip Alley, 7 May 1961, 4/6, Alley papers, ATL.

2. Jasper Becker, *Hungry Ghosts: China's Secret Famine* (London: John Murray, 1996), 289.

3. See Carl Riskin, *China's Political Economy—The Quest for Development since 1949* (New York: Oxford University Press, 1988), 136.

4. See for example the books of Felix Greene, *A Curtain of Ignorance* (London: Jonathan Cape, 1965); Anna Louise Strong, *China's Fight for Grain* (Peking: New World Press, 1963).

5. Emmanuel John Hevi, *An African Student in China* (London: Pall Mall Press, 1963), 71.

6. Michel Gordey, "White Russian Refugees Paint Blue Picture of Red China," newspaper clipping, source unknown, dated 13 April 1962, PM 264 3/1, MFAT.

7. Elsie Fairfax-Cholmeley, letter to Maud Russell, 26 March 1961, 1961 Correspondence, Box 5, MRP, NYPL.

8. Elsie Fairfax-Cholmeley, letter to Maud Russell, 1 December 1962, 1962 Correspondence, Box 5, MRP, NYPL.

9. Rewi Alley, letter to Maud Russell, 29 December 1960, Correspondence 1960, Box 5, MRP, NYPL. This section expands on research that was originally published in Brady, "Who Friend, Who Enemy? Rewi Alley and China's Foreign Friends," *China Quarterly* 151 (September 1997); and *Friend of China—The Myth of Rewi Alley*, chapter 8.

10. Rewi Alley, letter to Pip Alley, 19 December 1960, 4/5, Alley papers, ATL.

11. Becker, *Hungry Ghosts*, 94.

12. Rewi Alley, letter to Pip Alley, 27 January 1962, 3/3, Alley papers, ATL.

13. Rewi Alley, letter to Pip Alley, 22 June 1962, 4/7, Alley papers, ATL.

14. Becker, *Hungry Ghosts*, 283.

15. Hevi, *An African Student in China*, 41.

16. In 1961 Chinese university lecturers earned 40 yuan, a head of department earned 100 yuan, while foreign students received scholarships of between 100 and 150 yuan. Hevi, *An African Student in China*, 88.

17. Denise Lebreton, *Living in China*, 110.

18. Sonia Su, *Living in China*, 218.

19. Joan Hinton, interview, 19 December 1997.

20. Esther Holland Jian, *British Girl, Chinese Wife*, 184.

21. Frederick Nossal, *Dateline Peking* (London: Macdonald, 1962), 60. In 1959 there were still an estimated 3,000 White Russians living in Harbin, Nossal, 90.

22. Nossal, *Dateline Peking*, 211.

23. Canada's *Globe and Mail* (whose editors publicly advocated the recognition of the PRC) was the first Western newspaper to break this rule, with a journalist being granted a total of eight months. However at the end of that stay the journalist was ordered to leave China because of his "inaccurate" reports. Nossal, *Dateline Peking*, 172.

24. See Hans Koningsberger, *Love and Hate in China: A New Yorker's Chinese Notes* (New York: McGraw-Hill, 1966), 27; Nossal, *Dateline Peking*, 27; A. de Segonzac, *Visa for Peking*, xiii, 89.

25. Nossal, *Dateline Peking*, 27.

26. Hamrin, "Elite Politics and the Development of China's Foreign Relations," in *Chinese Foreign Policy*, ed. Robinson and Shambaugh, 87.

27. "Zhongyang xuanchuanbu guanyu jiaqiang guoji wenti yanjiu gongzuo de baogao," 18 January 1961, *DDXC*, vol. 1, 420-421.

28. Shambaugh, *Beautiful Imperialist*, 51.

29. S. Bernard Thomas, *Season of High Adventure*, 2. See also Edgar Snow, *Red China Today: The Other Side of the River* (Harmondsworth, Middlesex: Penguin [first published 1961] 1971), 24.

30. Thomas, *Season of High Adventure*, 186.

31. Edgar Snow Diary 2, 11 July 1960, Folder 131, Edgar Snow papers, UA-UMKC.

32. Tracy B. Strong and Helen Keyser, *Right in Her Soul: The Life of Anna Louise Strong* (New York: Random House, 1983), 304.

33. Edgar Snow, "Semantics Trouble," Diary 2, Peking 9-18 July 1960, 4, Folder 13, Edgar Snow papers, UA-UMKC.

34. Snow, *Red China Today*, 585.

35. Jia Wenhua and Gao Zhongyi, ed., *Sulian duiwai guanxi* (Zhengzhou: Henan jiaoyu chubanshe, 1989), 249.

36. Each Soviet expert was given a copy of the article "Long Live Leninism," published in the CCP Central Committee mouthpiece *Hong Qi* magazine in April 1960. The article expressed the CCP's views on the current international situation and the "correct" orientation of the international communist movement.

37. Leyda, *Dianying: Electric Shadows: An Account of Films and Film Audiences in China* (Cambridge: Massachusetts Institute of Technology, 1972), 304.

38. Yang Xianyi, interview, 13 September 1995.

39. Anna Louise Strong, letter to Maud Russell, 15 July 1962, 1962 Correspondence, Box 6, MRP, NYPL.

40. Alley, *At 90*, 246-249.

41. Tannenbaum, interview, 10 April 1997.

42. See for example, *Mao Zedong sixiang wansui* (Shijiazhuang: Hebei daxue Mao Zedong sixiang "ba yi, yi ba" hongwei bing xuanchuan bu, 1967); and *Jixu geming chengsheng qianjin* (Beijing: Zhongguo renmin daxue, 1970).

43. Mao Zedong, *Chairman Mao Tse-tung's Important Talks with Guests from Asia, Africa and Latin America* (Peking: Foreign Languages Press, 1960), 1.

44. For the figures on Latin America, see Cecil Johnson, *Communist China and Latin America 1959-1967* (New York: Columbia University Press, 1970), 9.

45. Leyda, *Dianying*, 316.

46. Zhao Pitao, *Waishi gaishuo*, 9.

47. They met on 9 February 1964, Li Jie, "Mao and Sino-Soviet Relations, 1949-69" (paper presented at the AACPCS/ANZSA International Conference of Communist and Post-Communist Societies, Melbourne, July 1998), 12.

48. Gerry Tannenbaum, interview, 10 April 1997.

49. See for example, *Mao Zhuxi lun shijie geming* (Beijing: Renmin ribao guojibu, 1968) and *Guoji zhengzhi cankao ziliao* (Beijing: Beijing daxue guoji zhengzhi xi, 1971).

50. Li Jie, "Mao and Sino-Soviet Relations," 13, citing "Two Diametrically Opposed Policies of Peaceful Co-existence—Sixth Comment on the Open Letter of the Central Committee of the Soviet Communist Party," *Renmin Ribao*, 12 December 1963.

51. Gerry Tannenbaum, interview, 10 April 1997.

52. Talitha Gerlach, letter to Russell, 21 October 1964, Correspondence July-December 1963, Box 7, MRP, NYPL.

53. Johnson, *Communist China and Latin America*, 22-23.

54. Sid Rittenberg, interview, 29 March 1998.

55. Gerry Tannenbaum, interview, 10 April 1997.

56. Mao Zedong, "Talks with African Friends," 8 August 1963, excerpted in *Quotations from Chairman Mao Tse-tung on Propaganda*, ed. Robert Friend (Peking: Foreign Languages Press, 1967), 26.

57. John Franklin Copper, *China's Foreign Aid* (Lexington, Mass.: Lexington Books, 1976), 17; Li Jie, *Mao and Sino-Soviet Relations*, 19, citing "Joint Communique of China and Mali" (21 January 1964) in *Long Live the Anti-Imperialist Great Unity among the Asian and African People—A Collection of Documents for the Chinese Leaders' Visit to the 13 Asian and African Countries* (Peking: People's Publishing House, 1964), 165-166. For the code of practice for PRC aid see, Pei Xiannong, *Zhou Enlai de waijiaoxue*, 212-214.

58. Philip Snow, "China and Africa," in *Chinese Foreign Policy*, ed. Robinson and Shambaugh, 288.

59. Snow, "China and Africa," 288; Becker, *Hungry Ghosts*, 81.

60. Marianne Bastid-Bruguière, interview, 26 March 1997.

61. Bastid-Bruguière, interview.

62. Nicholas Eftimiades, *Chinese Intelligence Operations* (Annapolis: Naval Institute Press, 1994), 98.

63. Fritz Schatten, *Communism in Africa* (New York: Frederick A. Praeger, 1966), 9. Students from Third World countries were invited on scholarships paid for by a range of Chinese organizations with *waishi* duties, such as the International Liaison Department, the All-China Federation of Labor, the All-China Federation of Women, the Afro-Asian Solidarity Committee, and the Sino-African Friendship Association. Hevi, *An African Student in China*, 115.

64. Hevi, *An African Student in China*, 9-11.

65. Hevi, *An African Student in China*, 131.

66. Hevi, *An African Student in China*, 162-170; and Barry Sautman, "Anti-Black Racism in Post-Mao China," *China Quarterly* 138, 414.

67. Sven Lindqvist, *China in Crisis*, trans. by S. Clayton (London: Faber and Faber, 1965), 28.

68. Former *waishi* cadre, interview, February 1999.

69. Lu Ning, *The Dynamics of Foreign-Policy Decisionmaking in China*, 47.

70. A. Doak Barnett, *The Making of Foreign Policy in China: Structure and Process* (Boulder: Westview, 1985), 90.

71. Lu Ning, *The Dynamics of Foreign-Policy Decisionmaking in China*, 48.

72. J. Robert Moskin and Morris Wills, *Turncoat, an American's 12 Years in Communist China* (Upper Saddle River, N.J.: Prentice-Hall, 1967), 171.

73. David Crook, "The Treatment of Foreigners Working in China and the Cultural Revolution," Correspondence January-March 1973, Box 9, MRP, NYPL.

74. Crook, "The Treatment of Foreigners Working in China."

75. For example in 1962 an anticorruption movement was launched, foreigners were told "they could join if they wanted to," previously participation had been automatic. Joan Hinton, interview, 19 December 1997.

76. Esther Holland Jian, *British Girl, Chinese Wife*, 183.

77. Holland Jian, *British Girl*, 191-192.

78. Lindqvist, *China in Crisis*, 22.

79. Lindqvist, *China in Crisis*, 16.

80. Joan Hinton, interview, 19 December 1997.

81. "Zhonggong zhong yang guanyu xiang quan dang quan ren jinxing jiaqiang tong ge guo renmin youhao de xuanchuan gongzuo de tongzhi," 8 May 1964, *DDXC*, vol. 1, 473-475, describes "unfriendly acts" towards foreigners that occurred in Beijing, Shanghai, Tianjin, Taiyuan, Changsha, and other locations; Hevi also mentions the hostility of some Chinese to foreigners in the 1960s, *An African Student in China*, 132-134.

82. Sid Engst and Joan Hinton, interview, 19 December 1997.

83. Eric and Marie Gordon, *Freedom Is a Word* (London: Hodder and Stoughton, 1971), 27.

84. Yang Xianyi, interview, 2 May 1996.

85. In Chinese "*you hong you zhuan.*" See Mao Zedong, "Gongzuo fangfa liushizhu" (1958), excerpted in *Selected New Quotations from Chairman Mao* (1 Jan. 1970-1 April 1975) (Beijing: Duiwaibu yingwen ziliao xiaozu, 1975), 76.

86. David Crook, letter to Maud Russell, undated late 1964, Correspondence July-December 1963, Box 7, MRP, NYPL

87. Crook, letter to Maud Russell.

88. Gordon, *Freedom Is a Word*, 32.

89. Endymion Wilkinson, interview, 2 May 1996. New study groups were set up for the arrivals; in this period there were Spanish, Portuguese, Italian, French, Arab, Belgian, Zanzabari, German, and Sri Lankan groups, as well as several English, French, and Japanese speaking groups, and *danwei*-based groups.

90. Gordon, *Freedom Is a Word*, 41.

91. Gordon, *Freedom Is a Word*, 44.

92. Gordon, *Freedom Is a Word*, 55.

93. Gordon, *Freedom Is a Word*, 48.

94. This and other discussions throughout the book relating to Rittenberg draw on Brady, "Review Article: The Political Meaning of Friendship: Reviewing the Life and Times of Two of China's American Friends," *China Review International* 9, no. 1 (2002).

95. Yang Kuisong, personal communication. See also Yang Kuisong, "The Soviet Factor and the CCP's Policy towards the United States in the 1940s," *Chinese Historians*, 5, no. 1 (Spring 1992), and Document no. 1 First Conversation of N. S. Khrushchev with Mao Zedong, Hall of Huaizhentan [Beijing] 31 July 1958, Vladislav M. Zubok, ed., The Khrushchev-Mao Conversations, http://cwihp.si.edu/files/zubok-mao.htm.

96. Sidney Rittenberg and Amanda Bennett, *The Man Who Stayed Behind* (New York: Simon and Schuster, 1993), 261.

97. Interview with former *waishi* official, December 1998.

98. Gordon, *Freedom Is a Word*, 35.

99. Sophia Knight, *Window on Shanghai, Letters from China, 1965-1967* (London: André Deutsch, 1967), 180.

100. Yang Xianyi, interview, 13 September 1995.

101. Winnington, *Breakfast with Mao*, 209.

102. Strong and Kayser, *Iron in Her Soul*, 316.

103.   Strong and Kayser, *Iron in Her Soul*, 319.

104.   For evidence of this, see Anna Louise Strong's letters to Maud Russell in the 1960s in the Maud Russell papers, NYPL.

105.   Anna Louise Strong, letter to Maud Russell, 12 January 1963, Correspondence January-March 1963, Box 6, MRP, NYPL.

106.   Rittenberg and Bennett, *The Man Who Stayed Behind*, 276.

107.   See Adler, Solomon, FBI File 65-58751.

108.   "US Scholar, Advisor to Beijing Government Dies," *Xinhua*, 2 September 1994.

109.   Gerry Tannenbaum, interview, 10 April 1997.

110.   Viviane Alleton, interview, 24 March 1997. David Finkelstein and Beverley Hooper, "57 Years inside China: An American Odyssey," *Asia* (January/February 1980): 10.

111.   Moskin and Wills, *Turncoat*, 151.

112.   Moskin and Wills, *Turncoat*, 30.

113.   Eva Hsiao, interview, 11 June 1996.

114.   Douglas Lake, letter to Maud Russell, 27 October 1963, Correspondence July-December 1963, Box 7, MRP, NYPL.

115.   Anna Louise Strong, letter to Maud Russell, 17 April 1962, April-June 1962 Correspondence, Box 6, MRP, NYPL.

116.   Colin Mackerras and Neale Hunter, *China Observed 1964/1967* (Melbourne: Thomas Nelson, 1967), 141.

117.   Talitha Gerlach, letter to Maud Russell, 10 January 1965, Correspondence January-March 1965, Box 7, MRP, NYPL.

118.   Yan Jiaqi and Gao Gao, *Turbulent Decade: A History of the Cultural Revolution*, translated and edited by D. W. Y. Kwok (Honolulu: University of Hawaii Press, 1996), 30.

119.   Elsie Fairfax-Cholmeley, letter to Maud Russell, 17 August 1964, Correspondence July-December 1964, MRP, NYPL.

Chapter 6

Red and Expert

The great achievements of China's Cultural Revolution are an inspiration to revolutionaries everywhere. As this base for the whole world revolution grows stronger day by day, it strengthens the fighting spirit and confidence of the revolutionary people everywhere.

—Sidney Rittenberg, 1967[1]

I wanted so hard to believe that I saw what I wanted to see, [I] bent reality to fit my own notions.

—Sidney Rittenberg, 1993[2]

On 10 November 1965, the Shanghai newspaper *Wenhui Bao* published a criticism of Wu Han's popular play *Hai Rui Dismissed from Office*, an article we now know as the first salvo in the Cultural Revolution. Published under the name of Shanghai *Liberation Daily* editor Yao Wenyuan, it was written with the assistance of Jiang Qing and the head of the Shanghai Propaganda Department, Zhang Chunqiao, and other interested parties, as well as being edited by Mao Zedong himself. It had taken more than eight months to write.[3] *Hai Rui Dismissed from Office* told the story of an upright official in the Ming dynasty who was punished for criticizing a tyrannical emperor. Mao's supporters and indeed Mao himself alleged the play was an attack on Mao's handling of Peng Dehuai's criticisms of the Great Leap Forward at the Lushan Plenum in 1959. Not long after the article was published, Mao, with Jiang Qing at his side, met in Shanghai with a select group of foreign friends. They had been flown in from their homes in Beijing to celebrate American journalist Anna Louise Strong's eightieth birthday in the company of other senior CCP leaders.[4] In a series of veiled allusions, Mao revealed the major shift in policy signaled by the publishing of the article: the launching of the Great Proletarian Cultural Revolution.[5] Mao told the group of foreigners that world revolution was in decline and in need of a vanguard party to lead it; the Chinese Communist Party would be that force.

Mao's assessment of the international scene was that the U.S. threat to China would decrease, while the threat of the USSR was likely to grow. He stated his desire to continue the struggle to reform Chinese society, regardless of what he described as his "minority" position in the CCP.

As they had been in the past, the foreign friends were proxies at that moment for the international revolutionary movement. They were symbols of Mao's theoretical position that China's revolution was part of a greater international trend, and indeed would now try to prove its leadership of that trend. At the time, most of the group of foreigners did not understand the significance of Mao's comments. Within a few months, however, the popular movement was launched and China's friends were swept up in it. From the earliest days of the Chinese revolution, internationalist support had been an essential aspect of the CCP's success. Now, in 1965, as Mao prepared to launch a movement that would have implications in the world revolutionary cause, he deemed the friends' support essential.

The 1966-1969 Cultural Revolution marks the peak of Mao's revolutionary line.[6] At its height, foreign policy and revolution were inextricably linked. Mao's claim that China was the center of the world revolution was part of his ideological disagreement with the Soviets and the battle to win the support of other communist parties and revolutionaries everywhere for his position. Writing in 1968, Robert Scalapino described how this appeared to Western eyes: "Mao sees a global revolution, not nation-to-nation competition, as China's route to power."[7] Mao's foreign policy in the 1960s was a combination of pragmatism and revolutionary internationalism. His concept of security envisaged world revolution with China at the center. According to this strategy, not only would Mao thought inspire Chinese people to create a new China, it would lead the revolutionary consciousness of the whole world. World peace, it was believed, was dependent on "people's revolutionary struggle."[8] Mao stated that his ultimate goal was the eradication of both class and state.[9] Since China was the leading revolutionary force in the world, the success of world revolution hinged on the success of the Chinese revolution. In 1966, a Xinhua report announced,

> China's Great Proletarian Cultural Revolution has strengthened the world's people's determination for revolution; it is a great encouragement for the revolutionary people of the whole world in their fight against U.S. imperialism, modern revisionism and all reactionaries. This Cultural Revolution is greater in its significance than any other revolution in history; it will greatly accelerate the historical process of the world revolution.[10]

From its very origins the Cultural Revolution had an internal as well as an external focus. Mao launched it both as a political movement to strengthen his power and as an ideological movement to strengthen ideological unity within China and beyond. The movement was the logical outcome of Mao's stated aim to remold Chinese society and his faith in the ultimate Marxist-Leninist goal, the liberation of the workers of the world. It would be wrong to assume that the ideological aims of the Cultural Revolution were merely a camouflage for rifts between the Chinese leadership or that the claim that China was the center of world revolution was simply a means to conduct a power struggle. Mao told the foreign friends that he believed that since Khrushchev's denunciation of Stalin, world communism faced a crisis of alarming proportions. With the unity of the international communist movement in disarray, Mao held that China alone could provide leadership; Mao's revolution would keep the faith.

Mao's supporters described him as the ideological leader of the third phase of world revolution: the first era, typified by liberal capitalism, was led by Marx and Engels; the second era, typified by anti-imperialism, was led by Lenin and Stalin, and the third era, heralding the victory of world revolution, would be led by Mao Zedong. Mao thought would reach out to the people of the world, to be a source of inspiration, as well as of practical knowledge on how to conduct a revolution.[11] Since Mao Zedong thought was the ideological heir to Marxism and Leninism, all true revolutionaries should study and carry out Mao's revolutionary line.

The paradox of the Cultural Revolution is that it was both internationalist and nationalist, in fact ethnocentric to the point of xenophobia. Western influence in China was rejected, which eventually led to attacks on foreigners. However, this was less contradictory than it might initially seem—Chinese nationalism was, as Mao himself had said, "applied internationalism." Maoists believed that if the Chinese revolution succeeded, this would be a victory for the worldwide revolutionary movement. In terms of foreign policy, "as long as China under Chairman Mao retained *the people* of the world, Chinese diplomacy was successful."[12] The PRC relied on international support in its cause, both from the point of view of practical assistance and the theoretical position that the Chinese revolution was more than a nationalist struggle. Mao and his supporters aimed to inspire the people of the world to follow China's revolutionary example. Hence publicizing the support of China's foreign friends—both in China and outside—for the new ideological movement would be crucial.

During the Cultural Revolution years the Chinese "proletariat" was exhorted to unite with the "proletariat" worldwide to fight the common enemy: imperialism and revisionism. According to one earwitness account, the Internationale was broadcast interminably in this period.[13] Mao's essay presenting Norman Bethune as a paragon of revolutionary internationalism was one of the three most widely read essays of the Cultural Revolution. The Cultural Revolution marked the high point of Mao's scheme to reform the psyche of the Chinese people and to create a new socialist culture. The septuagenarian leader not only sought a new future for China, he also hoped to set an example to the revolutionaries of the world to follow. Many of Mao's foreign admirers in China and abroad responded to this vision with a sense of optimism and fervor.

Foreign Activism

In the first phase of the Cultural Revolution, from the autumn of 1965 to mid-1966, the main role of China's foreign supporters was their continuing participation in China's foreign propaganda activities, both as polishers/translators and as authors of reports (usually disguised as chatty letters in order to evade Western censors), which were sent on to foreign correspondents such as Maud Russell. More recent arrivals who lacked the language or political skills to decipher the changes in the political environment were oblivious to the first rumblings of the cataclysmic movement.[14] To many outside observers, as to many Chinese, the public debate radiating out from the published criticisms of Wu Han's play appeared arcane and obscure.[15] Indeed, initially foreigners were deliberately kept uninformed about what was going on.

Throughout the early months of 1966, the criticisms of Wu Han gradually spread to attacks on other leading intellectuals and officials. In May 1966, the Politburo chaired by Liu Shaoqi (Mao was out of Beijing) met to discuss an alleged "anti-party plot," among the alleged conspirators were leaders in the Beijing party administration who had not done Mao's bidding on a number of crucial issues. On 25 May 1966 the first big character poster, *dazibao*, of the Cultural Revolution was posted up at Beijing University. The author of the poster, Nie Yuanzi, criticized the university authorities, some of whom also held positions in the Beijing central administration, for trying to suppress the new political movement. Nie had been encouraged to write the poster by Kang Sheng's wife, Cao Yi'ou, as Mao and his supporters sought ways to attack their opponents in the Beijing leadership. On 1 June 1966, Mao authorized the national broadcast of Nie's poster and on 2 June 1966, *Renmin Ribao* (which only days before had been taken under the control of the revised Cultural Revolution Group) published an editorial calling for "revolutionary types" to "accept unconditionally the central party leadership headed by Chairman Mao" and to "struggle resolutely against the 'black gang' that is opposed to Chairman Mao, to Mao Zedong thought, and to the directions of Chairman Mao and the Party Centre, no matter what banners they fly, no matter how high their positions, and how great their seniority."[16] Responding to this clarion call, letters of support for Nie Yuanzi's *dazibao* were received from all over the country and many newspapers printed approving articles. Mimicking the struggle at Beijing University, students and teachers at high schools and universities around the country held meetings to debate the *Renmin Ribao* article and began posting up their own *dazibao* attacking senior party leaders in their organizations. Other work units soon followed suit.

Also in June 1966, a Central Committee meeting directive was issued stipulating that "a clear distinction should be made between internal and external matters" (*bixu fenqing neiwai*), meaning that the Cultural Revolution should not affect China's foreign policy and foreign relations.[17] However this directive would ultimately have little affect in the face of the popular influence of Mao's radical worldview and the changing balance of power which meant that Mao's supporters in the Cultural Revolution Group came to have more power than the leaders in the Central Committee who were the ultimate targets of the Cultural Revolution. After Mao praised Nie Yuanzi's *dazibao*, personnel in the Ministry of Foreign Affairs began to put up their own posters criticizing the "decadence" of some leading officials in the Ministry of Foreign Affairs. This rebel activity was rapidly suppressed by means of "work teams" comprised of senior officials in the ministry.[18] Within a few months however, Mao had denounced the activities of the work teams, and rebels in the foreign affairs system renewed their attacks.

After *dazibao* began appearing at the Foreign Languages Press in Beijing, none of the Chinese staff would talk to journalist Eric Gordon on any matter other than those that were work related. A notice was put up above the Foreign Languages Press canteen where most of the *dazibao* were posted saying: "Foreigners Not Allowed In."[19] Neale Hunter reported that at his work unit, the Shanghai Foreign Languages Institute, foreigners were forbidden from viewing *dazibao*. The conflicts they reported were regarded as "internal contradictions," thus having nothing to do with foreigners.[20] Sophia Knight, working and living on campus at the nearby Shanghai Foreign Languages School, was allowed to attend two "accusation meetings" at her work unit where students and teachers vehemently denounced the "Black Line" of revisionists within the party.[21] Yet she too was forbidden to look at the *dazibao* posted up at her school and was told, "It concerns only Chinese people."[22] Many of the foreign friends wanted more than just a symbolic or observer's role in the Cultural Revolution: they too demanded the right to demonstrate their support for the Maoist line. The foreigners believed their role as internationalists entitled and obligated them to take an active part in the surging political movement.

Sidney Rittenberg, the American foreign expert, was the most high profile of these foreign activists. As a fluent Chinese speaker, Chinese citizen, CCP cadre and member of the senior management at Radio, Rittenberg had greater opportunity than most foreigners to participate in political activities in China. In early June 1966 Rittenberg wrote a self-criticism *dazibao* attacking his "bourgeois elitism" and other faults. His workmates at Radio responded with praise for his actions and he was cited as a model for other senior cadres to learn from.[23] Rittenberg became even more engaged in the movement after Mao Zedong's 5 August 1966 big character poster "Bombard the Headquarters" (*paoda silingbu*) was published. Mao's poster in all but name directly attacked Liu Shaoqi, exposing leading cadres whose "bourgeois dictatorship" had "struck down the surging movement of the Great Cultural Revolution."[24] To Rittenberg, Mao's directive "sounded like the guidelines for the American Revolution: elect your own leaders, assemble your own organization, print your own posters, publish your own newspapers. This, I thought, was a program for the end of party dictatorship."[25] As a supporter of the international revolution Rittenberg located the new stage of the Chinese revolution in the revolutionary upsurge that seemed to be sweeping many parts of the world in the latter half of the 1960s: "it appeared students all over the world, in Hong Kong, in France, in America—were all moved by the same revolutionary fervor."[26]

The second phase of the Cultural Revolution can be traced from the Eleventh Plenum of the CCP Central Committee in August 1966. The deliberations of the plenum were published as the Sixteen Point Decision on the Cultural Revolution. This laid out Mao's vision for the new political movement, which would entail a struggle to "change the mental outlook of the whole society."[27] The plenum's communiqué strengthened Mao's bid to regain power by endorsing the policies he had promoted on crucial issues throughout the 1960s and implicitly criticizing the policies of Liu Shaoqi. It also promoted a number of Mao's principal supporters, while demoting some of Liu's supporters, and those who had obstructed Mao's policies in the early phase of the Cultural Revolution.[28] Soon after the plenum ended, with Mao's encouragement and organized by the PLA, a series of massive Red Guard rallies began in Beijing.[29] The Red Guard movement had sprung up in Beijing in May 1966 as Qinghua University Middle School students debated the article criticizing *Hai Rui Dismissed from Office*. One student had signed a *dazibao* with the moniker "Red Guard" (after the Red Guard movement during the Russian Revolution) and it came to be the name adopted by those who wished to associate themselves with the Maoist line.[30] Mao gave his official support for the Red Guards in a letter to the students of Qinghua Middle School on 1 August 1966 (which was immediately publicized) when he affirmed that they had the "right to rebel," *zaofan you li*.[31] The Red Guards, made up of youth who had grown up in the revolutionary climate of new China were regarded as the literal embodiment of Mao's revolutionary vision for China.

On 29 August 1966, the day after Mao received the second great mass meeting of Red Guards in Tiananmen Square, four American foreign experts living in Beijing wrote a *dazibao* entitled: "What Monster Is Driving Us on the Road to Revisionism?" The group consisted of long-term residents Joan Hinton, Erwin (Sid) Engst, and Bertha Sneck (former wife of American author William Hinton), and a more recent arrival, Ann Tompkins.[32] The text was translated into Chinese by Sneck's daughter Carmelita Hinton, a student at the Beijing 101 Middle School, who spoke and wrote fluent Chinese. The group passed their poster on to a colleague in the Foreign Experts Bureau who posted it up in a room for "internal," *neibu, dazibao*. The *dazibao* demanded that revolutionary foreigners and their children be given the right to participate in thought reform, manual labor, and the current revolutionary movement and lashed out at the system of privilege that treated foreign experts as if they were bourgeoisie rather than "class brothers."[33] The *dazibao* was noted by some Red Guards from the Foreign Languages Institute (which in this period was a locus for advocates of a more radical line in foreign affairs) who copied it and put it up on their notice boards. A number of other foreign activists saw it and also wrote supporting *dazibao*.[34] Chairman Mao was shown a copy of their complaint, and he wrote a commentary, *pishi*, stating that he agreed with the writers of the *dazibao*, adding, "Revolutionary foreign experts and their children should be treated the same as Chinese people. No difference should be allowed. Please think about this matter. All those who want to, can live and so on in the same conditions (as Chinese people), according to circumstances."[35] Mao's support for foreign participation in the Cultural Revolution was in line with his dictum on intellectuals in new China that they must be both "red" (have high political consciousness) and "expert" (knowledgeable in their field). Foreign participation in CCP political campaigns was not new, but it had been discouraged in recent years. Nonetheless, the foreigners were not immediately informed about Mao's approval of their active participation in the movement and their involvement continued to be along the lines of witnesses and symbolic representatives of internationalist support for China's political line.

In order to publicize the new movement to the outside world, Anna Louise Strong and Sid Rittenberg sought out a meeting with Red Guard representatives in September 1966.[36] The meeting was written up in Strong's *Letters from China*. When the two Americans arrived at the Liaison Center for Red Guards of middle schools and colleges in Beijing, based in the Workers' Cultural Palace, part of the old imperial palace, they were initially turned away. However after Strong was recognized, they were invited to attend a discussion at the headquarters. To the delight of the two foreigners, in contrast to the formal treatment foreign friends usually received in China, the young rebels treated them as internationalist comrades. A Red Guard leader (who called herself "Fighting Red") told Strong that the Red Guards' revolutionary aims were as follows:

> Chairman Mao ha[s] defined [our] future as an armed revolutionary youth organization, legal under the dictatorship of the proletariat . . . So if Chairman Mao is our Red-Commander-in-Chief and we are his red soldiers, who can stop us? First we will make China red from inside out and then we will help the working people of other countries make the whole world red . . . And then the whole universe.

The desire to export China's revolution to other countries was a common theme among Red Guards in the period 1966-1967, though the wish to liberate "the whole universe" was perhaps a slight overstatement, even in the overblown rhetoric of the times. Following the discussion, Strong and Rittenberg were invited to become honorary Red Guards. The comments of Rittenberg sum up the internationalist idealism coming from both sides:

> I was thinking of John Reed in Leningrad and the *Ten Days That Shook the World*.[37] He talked with the Red Guards there and they accepted him as a fellow revolutionary from America. These Red Guards are International too. The youngest revolutionaries of China have given a membership to the oldest revolutionary from the United States.[38]

Rittenberg's comments were representative of the attitude many of the foreign friends held about the Cultural Revolution. The friends believed they had an important role to play in the movement, a role that had historical antecedents in earlier revolutions. After experiencing political and social isolation in previous years, the Cultural Revolution appeared to open new vistas for their activism, their internationalism, and their revolutionary enthusiasm. It was an exhilarating moment that held important implications for their place in the Chinese revolution and all aspects of their lives in China. American foreign experts resident in Peking at the outbreak of the Cultural Revolution, David and Nancy Dall Milton described the movement as a nascent expression of democracy in China, "An atmosphere of extraordinary freedom and purpose existed in those days, an intensity of life which has been noted in all the great revolutions. People talked about everything, speculated endlessly, and read anything they could get their hands on; ordinary folk had become political philosophers contemplating the years to come."[39] Sophia Knight described the outcome of one meeting she attended—held "to criticize ogres and monsters"—the outcome of which was "recognition of the need for "great (widespread and pure) democracy, to uproot the causes of revisionism, to consolidate the dictatorship of the proletariat, to guarantee the victory of the socialist line, to ensure progress right through to communism."[40] In order to achieve this the "Four Democracies" and "Six Freedoms" were to be used: 1) everyone to voice his or her opinion in big and small character posters; 2) propaganda leaflets and caricatures; 3) big debates in public and in work units; 4) argument and airing of views; and the freedoms of speech, publication, organization, movement, assembly, and thought.[41] The Miltons and many other non-Chinese supporters of the Chinese revolution, saw in the Cultural Revolution the natural successor to the great revolutions of the United States, France, and, although the Miltons didn't say so, the Russian Revolution too. In their words:

> The Chinese Cultural Revolution of the Sixties extended the concept of equality, first spread by the American and French revolutions and noted by De Tocqueville as an irreversible idea, to the vision of wiping out the age-old differences between mental and manual labor, town and country, leaders and led. Karl Marx recognized long ago that the state is founded upon the contradiction between public and private life. Mao Tse-tung has shown that those appointed to serve the public interest may use their positions of trust for public gain and that even leaders brought to power by popular revolutions may become a class in their own right, utilizing political as well as economic power to exploit another class. Both Marx and Mao would agree that the key question facing society is how to educate the educators, and the Chinese Cultural Revolution was the first social movement in history to attempt to put into practice the concept that leaders must become pupils of the masses and must be criticized and supervised by those who are led.[42]

For the foreign friends, support for the Cultural Revolution was furthermore an indicator of their support for the Chinese line in the Sino-Soviet dispute; it was a symbol of the ideological superiority of Mao's line versus that of the Soviet "revisionists." Ahmed Kheir, a Sudanese "freedom fighter" living in Beijing, was quoted in the Chinese media to lend support for China in the course of the bitter Sino-Soviet struggle, one of whose fronts was Africa:

> The Cultural Revolution helps the African people to clearly differentiate between genuine socialism and phony socialism, between the People's Republic of China and the Soviet Union. These two countries today present two entirely different pictures before the eyes of the peoples of the world. All that is opposed by the Cultural Revolution in China is precisely what is supported by the modern revisionists in the Soviet Union. What is being destroyed in China is precisely what is promoted and built up by the modern revisionists in the Soviet Union."[43]

For many of the foreign friends, the Cultural Revolution also appeared to be a means to reform Chinese society. In a letter to Maud Russell—echoing Lin Biao's call to eradicate "old ideas, culture, customs and habits of all exploiting classes" uttered when Mao first received the Red Guards at Tiananmen Square on 18 August 1966[44]—Rewi Alley admired the destruction of "old and useless" objects such as the altar at the Ritan in Beijing, the former imperial Temple of the Sun.[45] Talitha Gerlach was very supportive of the movement, writing to Maud Russell of her "counter-revolutionary" neighbors and even saying that "the cases of excessive actions" by Red Guards was a good thing because it brought these "elements" out into the open to be exposed.[46] She told Russell that she was watching denunciation meetings on television.[47] Doris Dawson, working in Kaifeng with her daughter Shirley Wood whose husband was Chinese, supported the criticisms against her son-in-law, a "black-liner" who was criticized for being bourgeois after securing privileged treatment for his son.[48]

The political upheavals in China attracted massive international attention and speculation as to what it was all about. Initially most of China's foreign supporters outside China supported the new movement and praised its aims. Over time, as awareness of the violence and chaos the movement had spawned became more widespread, many withdrew their public support or at least fell silent on China issues. Yet some foreign observers found what was happening in China inspiring and admirable. Some Maoists sought to copy the radical behavior of the Red Guards in their own countries;[49] others merely offered their support for Mao's efforts to revolutionize Chinese society. In September 1966 foreign Maoists who had attended an international conference in Vienna wrote to Chairman Mao to complain about the bourgeois appearance and behavior of Chinese diplomats they had met at the conference. Mao replied that embassy staff needed to be "revolutionized." This comment encouraged rebels in the Foreign Ministry to demand the recall of all Chinese personnel abroad to undergo struggle and criticism. This demand was resisted by Foreign Minister Chen Yi and Zhou Enlai, despite much protest from those who sought a more radical approach in China's foreign affairs.[50]

The China-based friends did not always like everything they saw in the early days of the Cultural Revolution, but a strong sense of loyalty to the CCP and perhaps an element of fear, held them back from writing everything they saw and thought to overseas correspondents. In the throes of revolutionary fervor, from June 1966 to August 1967, Red Guards and other rebel groups attacked ancient buildings and raided homes to destroy remnants of the decadent past. Their ideological targets were revisionism, imperialism, capitalism, and feudalism. The goal of the movement was to destroy the corrupting old and create a new revolutionary culture. Sophia Knight downplayed Western reports of Red Guard violence in a letter to her mother in September 1966, describing the activities of those she had personally observed as "restrained" and "disciplined."[51] Eric Gordon did not write home about Red Guard violence, "partly because I felt it would be too difficult to explain to people in England how I could feel enthusiastic about the Red Guards and yet have deep reservations about their actions . . . whatever was happening, I still felt that China was fundamentally socialist and that it needed defending."[52] Most of the foreigners were cocooned by their privilege, their foreignness, and, in many cases, their lack of Chinese language ability to know what was really going on. Even Doris Dawson, living a life in Kaifeng with her daughter, Chinese son-in-law, and their children that was closer to that of the average Chinese person than Russell's other correspondents in China, struggled to find something positive to say about the current situation as her personal world crumbled. Her letters of this time show her confusion—a conflict between her faith in revolutionary theory and what she saw at close hand.

Many of the foreigners who were attracted to work in China in the 1960s brought with them that decade's consciousness of antiauthoritarianism and youthful rebellion. Some began to insist that they wanted to be treated as comrades rather than as privileged foreign friends. Henri Dathier and his wife, Monique, who had only been in China for one year, wrote two (English) *dazibao* asking to be given the same living standards as the Chinese and suggesting that foreigners should be organized to join in with workers and peasants and participate in their labor. They stated,

> We don't want to be outsiders. We want to be the same as you all, to struggle alongside the revolutionary comrades of China and the whole world for the victory of Communism, for the annihilation of imperialism and all reaction and for the elimination of the system of exploitation of man by man.[53]

Michael Shapiro wrote in an open letter to the "Chinese comrades," "My life as a Communist is tied up with the work in China . . . 'Struggle is life!' and I keenly desire to take my part and do my share in the struggles of life in the interests of the proletarian revolution."[54] Foreign experts from the United States, France, and Belgium signed a *dazibao* declaring, "We want to fight side-by-side with the Chinese people against our common enemies—U.S. imperialism, modern revisionism and all reactionaries, for the world victory of Mao Tse-tung's

Edgar Snow meeting up for the first time with Ye Jianying, Zhou
Enlai, unknown military aide, Baijiaping, Shaanxi Province, 1936. Photo
Courtesy of Lois Wheeler Snow, Edgar Snow Archive at the University
of Missouri-Kansas City.

Dr. Norman Bethune, He Long, and Dr. Richard Brown, Yan'an, 1938. Photo
courtesy of the Rewi Alley Collection, Edgar Snow Archive at the
University of Missouri-Kansas City.

Mao Zedong with U.S. G.I. "progressives" in Chongqing, 1945.
Photo courtesy of Lois Wheeler Snow, Edgar Snow Archive at the
University of Missouri-Kansas City.

Cover of a 1952 propaganda cartoon booklet published in China
at the peak of the germ warfare scare. Needham Papers,
Imperial War Museum in London.

Alan Monteith, McGuigan, and Rewi Alley, some of the New Zealand delegates at the Asia-Pacific Peace Conference in Beijing, 1952. Photo courtesy of the Rewi Alley Collection, Macmillan Brown Collection at the University of Canterbury.

Hanoi Peace Conference, 1964. Rewi Alley, "Red Aristocrat" Saionji, and Willis Hariandji (Indonesian), speaking with South Vietnamese delegate. Photo courtesy of the Rewi Alley Collection, Macmillan Brown Collection at the University of Canterbury.

Guo Moruo, poet-president of the Chinese Academy of Sciences, toasting a foreign visitor to China. Photo courtesy of the Rewi Alley Collection, Macmillan Brown Collection at the University of Canterbury.

The Engst-Hinton family and their nanny before their move to Beijing in 1965. Photo courtesy of Joan Hinton.

Carma Hinton, Fred Engst, and companion on a reenactment of the Long March in 1967.
Photo courtesy of Joan Hinton.

Edgar Snow, translator, Mao Zedong, and Lin Bao in 1970. Photo courtesy of Lois
Wheeler Snow, Edgar Snow Archive at the University of Missouri-Kansas City.

Zhou Enlai pictured with a group of friends he convened to explain China's new foreign policy direction in 1971. Photo courtesy of Joan Hinton.

Thought."[55] As a symbolic indication of the revolutionary spirit among the foreigners, some suggested the Friendship Hotel in Beijing, where most of them resided, be renamed Bethune, after the Canadian doctor who Mao had singled out as the apotheosis of revolutionary spirit. Others advocated the setting up of an International Brigade to fight U.S. imperialism in Vietnam, along the lines of the International Brigade in Spain in the 1930s.[56] It was an exciting time for many. Denise Lebreton wrote:

> At the beginning, there was a great fraternity, our colleagues were eager for us to join their factions, took us to meetings and parades and we were happy in this warm camaraderie. We French recalled the Paris Commune where many foreigners had been admitted into the ranks like brothers.[57]

Foreign students in China in 1966 were generally less enthusiastic about participating in the Cultural Revolution. Marianne Bastid-Bruguière recalls that she and her fellow foreign students "saw the Chinese teachers being bullied and did not want to take part, had no thought of taking part. They saw it as inhumane."[58] She says it was different for the children of the foreign friends who had grown up in China: "they were familiar with the quarrels of the Chinese, they were indoctrinated."[59] Most foreign students were sent home following a ruling on 20 September 1966. Those remaining were from countries such as Albania, which were on good terms with China.[60] Soon even they could become targets. Esther Holland Jian reports seeing Red Guards in Hangzhou ordering Albanian students to remove their foreign leather pointed shoes and replace them with Chinese cloth ones.[61]

The New Zealand family of Doug and Ruth Lake and their three daughters Sara, Jo, and Pru were actively involved in Cultural Revolution activities. Sara, then a student at the Beijing University Middle School, says she "put up posters like everybody else."[62] She says there was no antiforeign feeling at her school, which was attended by a number of other foreign students, the children of foreign experts. In the late autumn of 1966 the Lake sisters along with some Beijing University students, like many Red Guard youth of the time, went on a staging of the Long March. The group traveled south on a train crowded with Red Guards. Their train tickets, food, and lodging were free, as they were for the Chinese students. In Hunan, the group stopped off to work in a porcelain factory for a few months.

The Bethune-Yan'an Rebel Group

In late 1966, rebels in the Foreign Experts' Bureau asked foreigners they knew to be sympathetic to the ideals of the Cultural Revolution to give support to their organization. This gave rise to the idea for the formation of a foreigners-only rebel group. Great upheavals were under way in the foreign affairs system, as rebel groups began to get the upper hand over more conservative forces. In De-

cember 1966 a liaison station to coordinate rebel activity was set up in the Ministry of Foreign Affairs. In January 1967 this rebel group attempted to seize
power in the Foreign Ministry. The group's bid for power was accepted by Zhou
Enlai, since with Mao's blessing, "power seizures" by rebel groups had become
official policy and it was preferable that such attacks came from within the Foreign Ministry, rather than from the students of colleges attached to the Foreign
Ministry.[63] It was at this stage that Zhou Enlai recalled virtually all of China's
diplomats from abroad. Each embassy was given the use of a large room at the
Ministry of Foreign Affairs in order to engage in its own mini-Cultural Revolution to smoke out revisionist, bourgeois, and reactionary elements.[64]

Reflecting these new developments in the foreign affairs system, in a meeting early in January 1967, Chen Yi, then minister of foreign affairs, addressed a
gathering of foreign experts and told them of Mao's reply to the Four Americans' *dazibao*. He told them that foreigners would now be allowed to actively
participate in the Cultural Revolution, even to the point of forming their own rebel group or participating in Chinese ones.[65] Responding to the criticisms in the
original *dazibao* of the privileged lifestyle led by the foreign experts, Chen told
them that anyone who wished to was free to reduce their salary, with the right to
revert to the higher scale if the gesture later proved to be rash. They were also
free to move into more humble accommodation. However, Chen Yi also pointed
out to the group some of the realities of living like Chinese: "To live like us,
foreign comrades, is to live without bathroom, telephone and elevator. Ours is a
hard life which we accept in the certainty of a better future."[66] Chen Yi also
noted that there might be some difference between the interests of the members
of the short- and long-term community of foreigners in Beijing. The American
dazibao supporters wrote an attack against this position saying there should only
be one policy towards foreigners. This attack brought the foreigners into the orbit of radical groups in the foreign affairs system who were attacking Chen Yi,
and through him, Zhou Enlai.[67]

After the January meeting Eric Gordon found his Chinese colleagues suddenly began talking to him again.[68] Sophia Knight also noted that the change in
policy led to an "enormous" improvement in foreigners' relationships with Chinese people. Under the new policy, Knight's colleagues and students were free
to visit her and talk freely, she was told that previously the foreigners were not
trusted and staff and students were discouraged from developing a relationship
with foreign teachers outside of lesson time. Now, Knight reported, "the new
line will be that foreigners are friends unless proved otherwise, and that they are
to be treated as equals, not as special but isolated guests."[69] Eric Gordon attended political meetings with his workmates and was allowed to work on a
commune together with his colleagues, picking vegetables for two weeks. His
colleagues talked relatively freely with him about political matters, even telling
him about those of his workmates who were considered bad elements. Gordon
wrote some *dazibao* of his own (in English) and began to take notes for a book
he planned to write explaining the Cultural Revolution to Western audiences.

Not long after the meeting with Chen Yi, the Bethune-Yan'an Rebel Group, *Baiqiuen-Yan'an zaofandui*, was set up. The name harked back to the Yan'an era, when foreigners like Norman Bethune and the CCP had collaborated to fight for the cause of the Chinese revolution. For some foreigners the motivation to join the group was to support Chinese rebels, rather than to reform their own position in Chinese society. For others it was to fight for the integration of foreigners into Chinese life. The internationalist ideals of Bethune-Yan'an were demonstrated by its organizational structure, which had delegates from five countries. The group aimed to unite the disparate group of foreigners around the common cause of support for China's line in the world revolution, but it also took a position on developments on the Cultural Revolution within China, especially those relating to foreign affairs.

Also in January 1967, after a protracted power struggle, Sid Rittenberg became one of the three top leaders at his work unit Radio, then the central government's most crucial national and international mouthpiece. From this point on, Rittenberg's political speeches were taped and broadcast all over China, a position of power that no foreigner had ever held in new China. As a leader of one of the most important organs of propaganda, Rittenberg had a crucial position. He had close connections with Wang Li, a leading ideologue of the Cultural Revolution Group who had a special interest in foreign affairs, and through Wang to Jiang Qing. Rittenberg became very influential, receiving preferential treatment wherever he went. People sought him out, hoping to benefit from his influence and connections. He was lauded at meetings with the title of "internationalist fighter for Communism."[70] In January 1967 Rittenberg was involved with Jiang Qing and other radical figures in pushing for the setting up of the "Beijing Commune," an attempt to reorganize the city government in Beijing (and later other cities) on similar lines to the Paris Commune. This proposal was eventually rejected by Mao, in favor of the new leadership model of the three-way alliance between revolutionary cadres, representatives from the PLA, and representatives from mass organizations.[71] In April 1967, Rittenberg was an important speaker at one of the most famous rallies in the Cultural Revolution, when Liu Shaoqi's wife, Wang Guangmei, was denounced at a meeting attended by thousands at Qinghua University. All other foreigners were prohibited from attending, while Rittenberg was given an honored place on the main platform indicating his high status at the time.[72] At the rally Rittenberg spoke on behalf both of the rebels at Radio as well as for international supporters of China's revolution.[73] A Chinese academic who was a young Beijing University student in 1966 remembers Rittenberg's speeches vividly: "He was a very good speaker, better than any of the Chinese rebel leaders. He spoke without notes. The Chinese students were very impressed with him, and glad to have him participate in their activities."[74]

By this time Sidney Rittenberg had also become the unofficial leader of political agitation among the activist foreigners in Beijing. Israel Epstein and Michael Shapiro were his lieutenants in Bethune-Yan'an, though he didn't formally join the group. Reflecting the atmosphere among this group in the early months of 1967, Israel Epstein wrote exultingly to Maud Russell, "We are indeed living through tremendous days, weeks, and months that do indeed 'shake the world'—rejuvenating, revivifying, scraping all the barnacles off the mind (and scraping off those who have themselves become barnacles on the cause)."[75]

Rittenberg was able to use his status as the highest-ranking foreign expert and the access to senior leaders his broadcasting position afforded him to get the support of Jiang Qing and Zhou Enlai for the Bethune-Yan'an Rebel Group at Broadcast Administration. Rittenberg proposed that the group sponsor a rally to hear Chen Lining, known as the "revolutionary madman" for his writings against Liu Shaoqi.[76] Chen had spent years in jail following his criticism of Liu, in the new world turned upside down of the Cultural Revolution he was now lionized by rebel groups for this. Bethune-Yan'an also received requests from Chinese groups in their various work units to lend their support at meetings "to indicate to all concerned that their cause had acquired world-wide significance."[77] Some regarded the foreign experts as "revolutionary sparks," *geming huozhong*, who could be radicalized and then sent back to their own countries to make revolution. Chinese activists divided the foreigners up into categories of "leftists, middle-of-the-road, and rightists."[78]

The children of the foreign friends formed their own rebel group, the Bethune-Yan'an Mao Zedong Thought Youth Corps. They took part in work experience at the Peking No. 1 Machine Tools Plant. They too were promoted in the Chinese press. A Xinhua news report quoted one internationalist youth, "Chairman Mao says that young people should not be revolutionaries just in talk, but should side with the revolutionary people by their actions. We aim to become true revolutionaries. So we've organized ourselves so as to study Mao Tse-tung's Thought and take part in the Great Cultural Revolution."[79] Many of the children also took part in rebel groups at their schools.

The Bethune-Yan'an Rebel Group suffered unique difficulties from the start. While Chinese rebel groups were based in work units and schools and responded to problems and people they were familiar with, the foreigners worked in a variety of organizations and most were unable to speak or read Chinese, hampering their ability to interpret the rapidly changing political environment.[80] Moreover, the foreigners lacked a common language and were dependent on multiple translators to conduct meetings. Bethune-Yan'an always lagged behind the Chinese rebel organizations in the progress of the Cultural Revolution. The children of the foreign friends wrote a *dazibao* criticizing the group, beginning with Mao's quotation, "No investigation, no right to speak." They warned their parents that by their ignorance of the complexities of the current political situation, they were allowing themselves to be used by "dubious" political groups.[81]

Foreign Propaganda

The Propaganda Department was one of the main loci for political struggle in the early days of the Cultural Revolution. Once Mao's supporters had taken control of this section of the administration the foreigners' support for the Cultural Revolution was widely publicized. From mid-1966 to late 1967, Chinese papers were flooded with articles promoting the support of foreign friends, especially those living in China, for the Cultural Revolution. Typical titles were: "Foreign Friends Acclaim China's Great Cultural Revolution," "Foreign Friends Praise China's Policy of Self-Reliance,"[82] "They Fight Side-by-Side with Us—Foreign Friends in Peking Support China's Great Cultural Revolution."[83] The latter article, written in October 1966 and sent out on Xinhua's international wire service, lauded the foreigners for their activism:

> Many foreign friends, while putting up big-character posters and putting forward revolutionary suggestions, put up portraits of Chairman Mao in their offices or homes. They also post on the wall quotations from Chairman Mao's works in their own handwriting. Many have organized themselves into small groups to study Chairman Mao's works and they persist in daily study and hold discussions regularly. "Chairman Mao's works are the truth guiding the world revolution, so we have to study them everyday and follow them," they said.[84]

In the same period, a deluge of information about the political movement was prepared directly for foreign consumption. The international dissemination of Mao Zedong thought had become the most important task in foreign affairs.[85] From April 1966 to April 1968 *Peking Review* ran a weekly series of articles depicting the adulation of foreigners all over the world for Mao Zedong thought. China's foreign broadcasts increased dramatically, transmitting to all parts of the world in thirty-three languages for a total of 1,103 hours a week. Millions of copies of *The Selected Works of Mao Zedong* and tens of million of the pocket-sized, *Quotations from Chairman Mao* were printed and translated into thirty-nine languages.[86] A number of foreigners also wrote material for external consumption in support of the Cultural Revolution. In the summer of 1967 a special group consisting of "foreign writers resident in Peking" (Rewi Alley, Sid Rittenberg, Anna Louise Strong, George Hatem, Robert and Mabel Williams, P. V. Sarma of the Malay League for National Liberation, and the Sudanese revolutionary Ahmed Kheir and his Austrian wife) were taken by the Foreign Experts' Bureau on a tour around China to enable them to report on current political developments at first hand.[87]

Many foreigners were involved in polishing translations of the massive output of propaganda for foreigners that appeared in this era explaining Mao Zedong thought and the Cultural Revolution. Although they were mostly supportive of the endeavor, they were critical of the style in which Chinese political articles were translated. At a meeting for Chinese propaganda workers, Mao responded with the "Directive on External Propaganda Work":

Some foreigners are critical of the way *Peking Review* and Hsinhua do foreign propaganda. Before, we didn't publicize Mao Tse-tung's Thought as a development of Marxism. Now, since the Cultural Revolution, we've been going all out. It's being pushed too hard. People can't accept it. Why should we be the ones to say certain things? We must be modest, particularly in what we send abroad. We should be more modest in what we're sending out. Of course, we must not abandon principle. Yesterday's announcement on the hydrogen bomb had "Great Leader, Great Teacher, Great Supreme Commander, Great Helmsman . . ." I crossed them all out. I crossed out "limitless rays" too. Where in the world do we have rays that are limitless? They all have a limit. So I crossed them out. In . . . "a joy and excitement of ten thousand degrees," I crossed out "ten thousand degrees." Not ten degrees, or a hundred, or a thousand, but ten thousand. I wouldn't even have one. I crossed it out completely.[88]

Also present at this meeting, Zhou Enlai told propaganda workers:

It's wrong to take what was intended for domestic readers and force it on people abroad. You're not using your heads. You don't care who the readers are or what they need. All you care about is what we want. Study your audience. Stick to principle and, at the same time get results. The characteristics (of foreign and domestic propaganda) are different.[89]

In November 1967 a group of foreigners based in China produced *Quotations from Chairman Mao Tse-tung on Propaganda*. The translators wrote in the preface of the need to "smash revisionism and establish the absolute dominance of Chairman Mao's principles in the field of foreign propaganda."[90] Two hundred copies of the book were printed. This was, the editors boasted "barely enough to stretch thin over the English sections of the different propaganda organizations in Peking."[91] The book was meant to be a manual for foreign propaganda workers and was divided under topics such as "Why We Say It, What We Say, To Whom We Say It, How We Say It, Who Says It, The Way We Work at Saying It."[92] The book's selection of quotes are a revealing source of the attitudes and goals of the activist foreigners living in China at this time who sought to be included in Mao Zedong's radical vision. The editors wrote: "We hold that the Chinese people's revolutionary camp must be expanded and must embrace all who are willing to join the revolutionary cause at the present stage. The Chinese people's revolution needs a main force and also needs allies, for an army without allies cannot defeat the enemy."[93] In a paraphrasing of Mao's speech on "The Foolish Old Man Who Moved the Mountains," the authors urged those involved in China's propaganda activities to embrace their mission to awaken the people of the world:

Our aim in propaganda is to build up the confidence of the world's peoples in the certain triumph of the revolution. We must first raise the political consciousness of the vanguard so that, resolute and unafraid of sacrifice, they will surmount every difficulty to win victory. But this is not enough. We must also raise the political consciousness of the world's peoples so that they may willingly and gladly fight together with us for victory. We should fire them with the conviction that the world belongs not to the reactionaries but to the people.[94]

Factionalism

Just as it did in the Chinese community, the Cultural Revolution brought to a boil the tensions and divisions among the foreigners. There was antagonism pitting the old hands versus the new, as well as among those of the newer arrivals who took a more radical line on Chinese politics than others. In October 1966 Sophia Knight reported that the foreigners in Shanghai were aligning themselves into openly pro- and anti-Cultural Revolution groups.[95] In Beijing, some of the newer arrivals were jealous of the privileged position of "old friends of China," such as Rewi Alley and George Hatem, and their apparently close relationship with the Chinese leadership. Meanwhile, the people who had shared the hardship of the pre-1949 era trusted each other and were suspicious of those who had come more recently.[96] Hatem and Alley were among a handful of foreign friends resident in China who asserted that foreigners should not involve themselves in Chinese political movements. They were strongly criticized for this stance by some within Bethune-Yan'an. Yet Alley edited Anna Louise Strong's *Letters from China*, which was pro-Cultural Revolution and pro-Jiang Qing, as was Alley (at least publicly). Remembering those difficult years, translator Yang Xianyi recalled, "Rewi behaved very wisely at this time. He remained friends with us [Yang Xianyi and his wife Gladys Yang who were under political suspicion], helped Anna Louise because that was the thing to do. But when he talked to us, sometimes he made sarcastic remarks . . . Rewi did not always stand on principle. You couldn't survive if you did."[97]

At the beginning of the political movement Chinese people were not allowed to criticize the foreign friends. But when Mao gave permission for foreigners to participate in the political movement this policy changed too. Han Suyin wrote,

> Some of the foreign translators living at the Friendship Hotel are having a hard time. One of them, a Frenchman, son of a prominent Party member (pro-China) says his father owns a dog. It is impossible, his Chinese comrades say, for a Marxist-Leninist to own a dog: he is vilifying his father. "But he does have a dog," replies the unhappy young Frenchman who refuses to make a self-criticism, though enjoined to do so . . . One night I hear great sobs. Someone rushes into an empty hotel room, and locks himself in. Somebody else comes after him. "Open, open, don't take it like that . . . it's only criticism . . ." There are muffled sounds, the door opens. Silence.[98]

Harry Lloyd and his wife went to teach English in Harbin in the mid-1960s. Lloyd, a longtime British Communist Party member made the mistake of disagreeing with some of the comments of the Red Guards at his university. He was accused of being anti-Mao, his wages were stopped, and he had a nervous breakdown from the strain. While he was in Beijing recuperating at the Friendship Hotel, a group of radical foreigners led by Bethune-Yan'an lieutenant, Michael Shapiro, came to his bedside to harangue him.[99]

The foreigners were conducting power struggles along the lines of "rebels" and "loyalists," mimicking the Chinese situation. Some informed the Chinese authorities about those foreign experts they accused of being "spies," "counterrevolutionaries," and "anti-Chinese."[100] Some went through books written by other foreign friends looking for evidence of counterrevolutionary ideas. One young American foreign expert promoted a theory that all the old hands were spies. Others took notes of every conversation with other foreigners.[101] Muslim foreign experts at the Friendship Hotel attacked Rittenberg, Israel Epstein, and Michael Shapiro, all of Jewish ancestry.[102]

At the same time that the Earth faction, *dipai*, the most radical of the rebel groups in Beijing, seized power in the Capital Red Guard Congress, the radicals seized power in the Bethune-Yan'an Rebel Group. The new leadership accused the original organizers of being "conservatives." The radicals among the foreigners supported the views of the Earth faction, which charged Foreign Minister Chen Yi of having a "bourgeois world outlook," due to his resistance to implementing the Cultural Revolution in the Foreign Ministry.[103]

Over the months of 1967, Bethune-Yan'an became increasingly radical. In April 1967 *Renmin Ribao* featured a two-part story "Foreign Friends Praise Chinese People's Liberation Army." The opening paragraph reads,

> Friends or comrades-in-arms from all over the world who have visited Chinese army units have acclaimed Chairman Mao's line in army building and the Chinese People's Liberation Army, founded by the most respected and great leader Chairman Mao, as a revolutionary army of the proletariat which is serving the Chinese people and all oppressed peoples and nations.[104]

At an August 1967 meeting of foreigners to study Mao's theory of people's war, speaker after speaker said they would follow Mao Zedong's teaching that "political power grows out of the barrel of a gun" and "take up guns and stick to armed struggle so as to bring about a new world without imperialism, capitalism and the system of exploitation."[105] These statements were not merely rhetoric for some. On two occasions in June 1967 a large group of foreign activists accompanied by Chinese media personnel (there to record the event) marched on the Office of the British Chargé d'Affaires in Beijing, broke windows, hit members of staff and burned the Union Jack; on the second occasion they even set fire to a diplomat's car.[106]

The radicalization of the foreigners involved in Bethune-Yan'an mirrored developments within the foreign affairs system as a whole. In the summer of 1967, as foreign rebels were participating in demonstrations against foreign embassies in Beijing, Kang Sheng and Wang Li were attempting to take control of the foreign affairs system. In June 1967 Kang Sheng met with rebel groups in the Foreign Ministry and, building on comments made by Mao in 1964, denounced the foreign policy of the three capitulations and one elimination (*san xiang yi mie*), meaning the surrender to imperialists, Soviet revisionists, and foreign reactionaries (three capitulations) and elimination of the revolutionary struggle of the suppressed people of the world (one elimination). Kang claimed that this was the foreign policy followed by Liu Shaoqi, and that it had prevented the implementation of Mao's foreign policy.[107] At a talk on 7 August 1967 Wang Li urged radicals in the foreign affairs system to directly oppose the foreign policy of the "three capitulations and one elimination" and advocated the adoption of a more revolutionary foreign policy.[108] Wang Li's speech was given wide publicity in the foreign affairs system and resulted in an intensification of radical activities.

Foreign Enemies

While for some the Cultural Revolution was an exhilarating time, to foreigners who were not friends of China and under official protection, the political movement was a horrifying experience. Antiforeignism, or rather antagonism to those people and their nations perceived to be imperialist or revisionist, was the other side to the catch cry for "internationalism" and the support for world revolution. In August 1966 the last foreign nuns in China, the seven sisters of the order of St. Francis who had been permitted to stay on after 1949 and run a school for the children of foreign diplomats in Beijing, were beaten and verbally abused by young activists and then forced to leave China. They were accused of being foreign spies and of working hand in hand with Chinese counter-revolutionaries. One of the group died soon after from the distress she suffered.[109] The graves of foreigners buried in Beijing were dug up and desecrated in the same period.[110] Such intense antagonism toward foreigners and foreign things was the result of two decades of intense antiforeign education. In the period from mid-1966 to mid-1967, these sentiments would come to a peak. Anthony Grey, Beijing correspondent for Reuters, recorded:

> from June 1966 to August 1967 eleven (diplomatic) missions were subjected to the now-familiar demonstration pattern: . . . the Soviet Union, Yugoslavia, Bulgaria, Mongolia and Czechoslovakia—the revisionists—Britain and France—the imperialists—Indonesia, India and Burma—the reactionaries— and Italy, so far unclassified . . . First come the poster stickers and the road painters. They arrive to deface the embassy compound walls and the road outside usually late at night before the main demonstrating day. Some sporadic groups march by shouting the appropriate "ism." The next day in the morning school-age Red Guards and students begin streaming by with portraits of Mao, slogan placards and colored paper flags bearing the same slogans.[111]

Foreigners were frequently attacked and humiliated during this period. According to a report made by the CCP Central Committee Organization Department and the Ministry of Public Security in 1982, a total of seventeen of those foreigners classified as foreign experts or foreign friends were detained or expelled from China in the Cultural Revolution years while eighty-one other foreigners were similarly treated.[112] Many other foreigners who were not formally charged or detained, suffered traumatic experiences in the Cultural Revolution years. Foreign journalists on short-term visas were harassed, as were foreign sailors passing through Chinese ports, the few tourists and business people who were allowed into China, foreign diplomats and virtually every other long-term foreign resident in China at this time. Foreigners from "revisionist" (the Soviet bloc) and "imperialist" countries (the West) were the initial targets. Sam Ginsberg, a foreign expert teaching in the Russian Department at Jinan University in Shandong Province, was singled out in 1966 by the rebel group in his university as a "monster." He was accused of being a "bourgeois academic authority." In February 1969, after three years of "investigation" he was "liberated," meaning he was absolved of his alleged crimes.[113] Ginsberg was one of a considerable number of White Russians or other displaced persons who had been resident in China before 1949, and had not left after the CCP came to power. There is little published information about the situation of these people in the Cultural Revolution, but from what is available, it appears that they had a much worse time than the high-profile foreigners who had the benefit of maintaining their foreign passports, or at the least, had expert status.[114] Ginsberg lived a more Chinese lifestyle than most of the Beijing-based foreigners. He had fewer privileges and was treated much the same as Chinese cadres when he was accused. Like his Chinese counterparts, at public accusation meetings he was made to stand in the "airplane" position for long periods of time, and was verbally, though seldom physically, abused. Ginsberg also had to endure forced labor and periods in the "cowshed," the detention center set up at his university to hold cadres under investigation.[115]

In June 1967 former CCP leader Li Lisan's Russian wife Lisa (Elisabeth Kischkin),[116] a Russian teacher at the Beijing Foreign Languages Institute, was detained along with her husband, as was the German photographer Eva Xiao (or Siao, née Sandberg) and her husband the poet Xiao San (Emi Siao).[117] Both couples were accused of spying for the Russians; in the era of Sino-Soviet friendship they had been given the task of "making friends" with Russian advisers and diplomats due to their pre-1949 activities in the Soviet Union. The two women were held in solitary confinement for seven years, then under semi-house arrest until 1979. Li Lisan committed suicide soon after his arrest, while Xiao San died not long after his release from detention in the late 1970s.[118]

Diplomats of both the Indian and the Soviet embassies were tormented at Beijing Airport as they left China, after repeated harassment at their compounds. Following on from the attacks by foreign activists on the Office of the British Chargé d'Affaires in June 1967,[119] on 22 August 1967 the office was actually burned down and its diplomats assaulted.[120] In all these situations the police stood by and did not intervene, they were clearly under instructions to allow what was described as the "revolutionary action of the masses." Had the police interfered they risked being accused of being antirevolution themselves. Other diplomatic missions were also attacked, both in China and abroad, and countries such as Kenya and Afghanistan were accused of being disrespectful to Chairman Mao.

A number of British nationals were detained in this period; Britain's relations were particularly sensitive with China in 1966-1969 as Maoism spilled over into British-run Hong Kong. Reuters journalist Anthony Grey was held under house arrest in his home in Beijing in retaliation for the detention of three Chinese journalists in Hong Kong; while Norman Barrymaine, a freelance journalist, was arrested in Shanghai and accused of espionage after taking photos of Shanghai street scenes;[121] Eric Gordon, his wife, and nine-year-old son, were arrested in Beijing as they were leaving the country to return home. Gordon was accused of "insulting Mao and trying to smuggle information out of China." Customs officials had found the notes for the book he had been writing on the Cultural Revolution, which he had foolishly hidden behind a portrait of Mao. Merchant Navy Captain Peter Wills was also held, accused of "insulting Chairman Mao."[122] In May 1968 British translator Gladys Yang (née Tayler) was arrested and detained, along with her husband Yang Xianyi; both were accused of being British spies.[123]

The Gordons were held in relative comfort in the Xinqiao Hotel for two years, although they were put on restricted rations after they refused to cooperate. The whole family was given political tracts to read in an attempt to remold their thinking. For a brief period, these had some effect, Gordon wrote,

> The whole mental atmosphere nibbled away at a person's conscience making him turn guiltily on himself to see whether he had transgressed the mores of society. It killed any rational enquiry into the essential forms socialism was taking. It corroded courage—how many men would deliberately express views that would brand them as enemies of society?[124]

The family was finally released in 1969 after they all developed serious health problems as a result of their poor diet.

1968: Antiforeignism

Although Mao had given permission for revolutionary foreigners to participate in the Cultural Revolution, there was concern from some leaders about the appropriateness of this decision. Jiang Qing and Lin Biao in particular were known to be disapproving of foreign involvement, or perhaps it would be more accurate to say that they were concerned about the role of foreigners who did not support their interests. In 1966 Jiang Qing told a meeting of the Congress of Red Guards of Universities and Colleges, "Don't allow foreigners to attend your meetings, to analyze the situation, or be your advisers."[125] In the late spring of 1967, rebel group July 16 criticized the Red Flag rebel group at the Foreign Languages Institute for enlisting the support of "foreign devils," *yang guizi*.[126] Tension grew about the foreigners' Cultural Revolution activities. On 17 October 1967, David Crook, an English teacher at the Beijing Foreign Languages Institute, was imprisoned and eventually held for five years after trying to intervene in a student dispute. It seems his arrest was the work of the Earth faction trying to bring down one of the foreign supporters of its opposition group, Heaven, *tianpai*, in retaliation for the opprobrium its own supporters (such as Rittenberg) were attracting.[127]

On 30 September 1967 a new campaign was announced to root out renegades (old cadres who worked in the Communist Party underground who had been arrested by the Nationalists); special agents (agents of foreign imperialism); and die-hard capitalist roaders (cadres deemed insufficiently revolutionary). Mao considered the excesses of 1967 (which he had incited)—including the Shanghai Commune, the Wuhan Incident and the burning of the British Chargé d'Affaires Office—to have gone too far. Mao decided to regroup his forces and unite the population by redefining the targets they were to rebel against. The foreign friends became victims of the new line, a line that encouraged already existent antiforeign feeling. At the beginning of the movement foreigners had been allowed to copy and later, to post, *dazibao*. By late 1967 the government threatened to accuse of spying those foreigners who copied wall posters or bought Red Guard publications. September 1967 also saw the downfall of Wang Li. This was an indication that the ideological aims of the revolution were being placed secondary to the goal of national unity. After the defeat of the rebel group to take over the Foreign Ministry, Zhou Enlai and Chen Yi's authority in the foreign affairs decision-making process was strengthened. Wang Li was purged, though Kang Sheng stayed in power.[128]

On 7 October 1967 the CCP Central Committee and State Council issued a directive banning unorganized, hostile demonstrations against foreigners.[129] (Presumably, officially approved and organized antiforeign demonstrations were still acceptable.) The radical foreign policy aims of the Red Guards and their government supporters had come to an end. For a short time the youthful rebels had held the stage in China, with the summer of 1967 being the peak of their activities. By autumn, the new line of the revolution proclaimed "Struggle against Self-Interest! Criticize Revisionism!" The dominant theme became ideological remolding. Chinese people were directed to "make themselves a target of the revolution" before trying to seize power from the power-holders.[130] The Red Guards were dispatched to the countryside to learn from the revolutionary masses while the position of the foreign friends in China became more and more awkward.

Sid Rittenberg was a protégé of Wang Li. By late 1967, with the fall of his patron, Rittenberg was vulnerable to attack. First posters appeared, accusing him of being an American spy. The charge of spying was used against Rittenberg and other foreigners to discredit them and justify their incarceration. A banner put up at his work unit asked "How is it that an American Adventurer Seized Red Power at Peking Radio?"[131] In the xenophobic climate of late 1967, it was considered very serious that a foreigner had seized power in such a sensitive organization, responsible for broadcasting the party line to the nation and abroad. Posters written by foreigners were pasted up at the Friendship Hotel, "He has climbed so high and fallen so low," "Rittenberg shows all the qualities we have long been accustomed to finding in the Jew."[132]

In December 1967 Rittenberg was put under house arrest; then in February 1968 he and his whole family were imprisoned. Rittenberg was not released until 1977.[133] He was not tortured or mistreated during this time. Indeed most of the foreign friends who were arrested received preferential treatment compared to Chinese prisoners.[134] Rittenberg wrote of the reasons for his incarceration, "They were trying to prove I ran a network of foreign spies; that I had recruited Wang Guangmei [to his alleged gang of spies], and through her the president of the People's Republic, Liu Shaoqi."[135]

As the campaign against Rittenberg grew, the reputation of Bethune-Yan'an declined as people linked the organization with him and called him its behind-the-scenes backer, *houtai*.[136] From January 1968 foreigners were forbidden to participate in the Cultural Revolution. They were to be excluded from Chinese political life, because, according to Zhou Enlai speaking five years later, "Some had supported this faction and some that, and then you have these bad people stirring up trouble."[137] The decision cordoned off the foreigners from any significant participation in China's revolutionary struggle. Not only were they excluded from participating in Chinese political activities, after the collapse of Bethune-Yan'an there were no longer even any foreigners' political study groups.[138]

At the January 1968 meeting Jiang Qing told other senior leaders, "we must watch out for foreign spies; she said there were spies who came into China for many years, even before Liberation, but they had been pretending to be friends and experts working for us."[139] After her speech, a number of foreign experts were held in detention. Among this group of foreign detainees was American foreign expert Bob Winter who later found out that an unnamed fellow American had falsely denounced him as a spy after his own arrest on spying charges in 1949. The accusation had been kept on his police file, though not investigated, until his file was released to rebels at his work unit, Beijing University.[140] Spy accusations had often been employed to topple Chinese leaders in the past. This particular phase of xenophobia was used by Jiang Qing and others as a means to attack Zhou Enlai, who they accused of being too pro-foreign. Most members of Bethune-Yan'an, excluding the leadership and a small band of followers, voted to close down the group after the arrest of Rittenberg. Soon after, the Chinese authorities detained the remaining leaders: Israel Epstein, Elsie Fairfax-Cholmeley, and Michael Shapiro, holding them in prison until 1973.

In March 1968 the article "A Mysterious American" was published in a number of newspapers around China. It described Sid Rittenberg as a "counter-revolutionary double-dealer," he was accused of having usurped the leadership of the Broadcasting Affairs Administrative Bureau for six months with the help of Wang Li, of joining *Quanhong zong*, (an ultra-leftist group which was declared an illegal organization) as well as having expressed support for the uprising in Wuhan in 1967:

> he was allowed to take part in the Party's organizational life. However, he retained his American citizenship, drew high pay, and regularly visited the embassies of capitalist countries. He is of doubtful antecedents and one to be suspected . . . A bourgeois magazine in Rittenberg's home country—the United States—cried with pride: "Peking is led by an American!" What cannot be tolerated if this can be?[141]

There was a deep sense of bewilderment and fear among foreigners in China in 1967-1968. In 1968 Anna Louise Strong asked the writer Han Suyin, "Can you tell me what really happened during the Cultural Revolution?"[142] Despite living in and writing about China for her *Letters,* Strong could not understand the turn the revolution had taken. Both Strong and Rewi Alley were, unusually so, quite outspoken in their criticism of the turn the movement was taking when they spoke to a group of New Zealand and Australian students in January 1968.[143] By contrast, Talitha Gerlach's letters to Maud Russell after 1967 were extremely cautious. It is uncertain whether she was afraid of Chinese eyes or Western, or indeed both. It wasn't until May 1971 that any of Russell's China correspondents wrote to her directly about the imprisoned foreigners. Gerlach wrote to Russell not to defend them against the slurs of spying that had been made against them, but rather to ask her to remove the names of Israel Epstein, Elsie Fairfax-Cholmeley, and David Crook from the list of earlier publications displayed in issues of *Far Eastern Reporter.* Gerlach told her, "Though we do not know the full score, we have absolute confidence in the judgment of those who removed them from work and circulation several years ago."[144] Interestingly, also in 1971, Russell also received a letter from a group calling itself "The Anti-Communist Group of Students of the Kaifeng Normal School." The letter is one of the few instances of plain speaking about the situation in China in the whole of Russell's collected papers. The group wrote,

> After reading your publication "Far East Report" [sic] we have a strong feeling that your analysis of problems are far from the fact and ignore the truth completely. You have totally forgotten the value of freedom and democracy and have utilized the theory of being deceived and deceiving others to carry out the propaganda for Mao Tse-tung, the Chinese mad man. We can not understand what your mind and purpose are![145]

Naturally Russell declined to publish the letter in her journal, which continued to promote a pro-CCP line, whatever direction this took. Another of Russell's China-based correspondents, Doris Dawson, mentioned "one day in July" in

1967 when something awful had obviously happened to her, but she did not elaborate. Dawson's letters to Russell from 1967-1968 were very confused as she struggled to reconcile her political beliefs with the reality around her. By January 1968, Dawson was living under guard in Kaifeng. Many of those foreigners who had homes to go to, left China in 1967-68. Some were refused exit visas for several months. When they finally left, their bags were rigorously searched.[146] The numbers of foreign experts declined so much in this period that at the lowest point, there were only 59[147] in the whole of China compared to 411 at the start of the Cultural Revolution period,[148] and more than 1000 per annum during the era of Sino-Soviet cooperation.

Although only a relatively small number of foreigners were arrested, many others were kept under partial or full house arrest for the next two years. Some of their privileges were removed at the same time. Now only overseas visitors were allowed to go to the Friendship Store to purchase special provisions unavailable elsewhere.[149] Rewi Alley, Hans Mueller, and George Hatem were deprived of their annual holiday at Beidaihe for three years. Alley was not allowed to receive hospital treatment for skin cancer,[150] and a police guard followed his every movement, even sleeping in his house, until 1972. He told Han Suyin in that year, "The old cadres of my organization came back and they liberated me."[151] A banner had been put up outside Alley's front door "*Da dao di xiu fan*" (Down with the Imperialist-Revisionist-Counterrevolutionary, meaning a foreigner who was anti-Mao).[152] Alley's foster son, Deng Bangzhen, was interrogated by the workers' propaganda team of Alley's work unit about his relationship with Alley. Several of Alley's former students from Shandan days were arrested by the guards at the gate of his residence in the Friendship Association, when they came to visit him in 1968.

Nonetheless, however difficult this time was for the foreign friends and other foreigners resident in China, the consequences of the xenophobic turn were much more serious for their Chinese families and those who associated with them, whether in a private or professional capacity. Having relatives abroad or mixing with foreigners was a crime in the Cultural Revolution. Sidney Rittenberg was relatively well treated during his ten-year imprisonment while his Chinese family suffered beatings and torture because of him. Rittenberg's father-in-law was forced to kneel on broken glass. Rewi Alley's adopted son Alan was badly beaten. Anthony Grey's chauffeur was forced to attend a "struggle meeting" in front of 15,000 Red Guards, his only crime being that he was regarded as having been too friendly to a foreign enemy.[153]

After 1968 the foreign friends became virtually indistinguishable from other foreigners in China. They had become stuck between the desire of rebels within the foreign affairs system to attack Chen Yi and Zhou, and Mao's desire to unite the disparate forces of the Cultural Revolution around a common foe: agents of foreign powers. Foreigners became mere pawns in this power struggle that reverberated and tore apart the highest levels of Chinese politics. The *Renmin Ribao* editorial of 16 March 1968 sums up the new mood:

> For a long time, U.S.-led imperialism, modern revisionism with Soviet revi-
> sionism at its centre and all reactionaries have ceaselessly pursued their sub-
> versive plots and engaged in sabotage activities against our country. They have
> co-operated with and made use of a handful of class enemies within China. In
> addition, they have continuously sent spies and secret agents of all descriptions
> in the guise of legitimate occupations into China to carry out all kinds of
> criminal activities. Particularly since the launching of China's Great Proletar-
> ian Cultural Revolution the class enemies at home and abroad have wantonly
> intensified their espionage and sabotage activities because they feared and
> hated this revolution and imagined it to be an opportunity for them to fish in
> troubled waters. The unearthing of the British spy case shows once again that
> the counter-revolutionary nature of imperialism, modern revisionism and all
> reaction will never change.[154]

The antiforeignism that erupted in the Cultural Revolution demonstrates the intense nationalism which underpins the Chinese revolution. Despite the fact that
many of the foreign friends were Communist Party members or sympathizers,
some of them even members of the CCP and Chinese citizens, they were not accepted as equal participants. The activities of the friends were cited as examples
of international support for the Chinese revolution, but later this could be used
against them. The experience of David Crook while in prison was telling. Chinese warders told him, "The Thought of Mao is having a worldwide effect, you
need have no thought of your masters the imperialists rescuing you, Mao
Zedong Thought is on the upgrade."[155] Though Mao spoke of the internationalist
principles underpinning the Chinese struggle, claiming that the Cultural Revolution was an important part of the world revolution, in the end nationalism pre-
vailed over the international cause. While it suited Mao's purposes the foreign
friends were allowed to participate in the revolution, when it no longer suited
they were moved off center stage.

From June 1968 a new ruling prohibited the use of the claim that "Beijing is
the centre of world revolution."[156] While propaganda aimed at both Chinese citizens and foreigners still promoted the notion that Mao Zedong thought had had
a great impact worldwide, the support of individual foreigners for China's revolutionary line was no longer sought.[157] The international aspects of the movement were confined to party-to-party relations, with only the pro-Maoist views
of revolutionary groups outside China and nameless foreigners—from tourists to
Soviet sailors—cited.[158] China's revolution was to be for Chinese alone, the
CCP did not want any new Norman Bethunes. The foreign friends wanted to be
like Bethune, to work for the Chinese revolution, to be internationalists. But to
the CCP, even those foreigners who had taken on Chinese citizenship would always be outsiders. The antiforeign spy hysteria beginning in 1968 made all foreigners, not just those automatically under suspicion such as diplomats and journalists, even more isolated than before.

The party's central foreign policy advisory body, the Foreign Affairs Leading Small Group, ceased to exist in 1969, with most of its senior members (with

the notable exception of Zhou Enlai) in disgrace. Most of the other main foreign affairs organizations were barely functioning at this time, with the majority of their staff exiled to the rural labor camps known as May 7th Cadre Schools.[159] As xenophobia reached its peak, China turned inward.

Notes

1. "China's Cultural Revolution Opens Channel to Communism Says US Journalist," New China News Agency (NCNA)-English, 10 April 1967, *Survey of China Mainland Press* (hereafter *Survey*), no. 3918, 35.
2. Rittenberg and Bennett, *The Man Who Stayed Behind*, 448.
3. See Yan Jiaqi and Gao Gao, *Turbulent Decade*, 27. This chapter is based on my essay, "Red and Expert: China's 'Foreign Friends' in the Great Proletarian Cultural Revolution," *China Information* XI, nos. 2/3 (Autumn/Winter 1996): 110-137.
4. The foreign guests at this occasion were: Anna Louise Strong, Sid Rittenberg, Rewi Alley, George Hatem, Israel Epstein, Frank Coe, Sol Adler, Julian and Donna Schuman, David and Nancy Dall Milton, Jose and Delia Venturelli. Rittenberg's Chinese wife Yulin was also allowed to attend. The meeting with Mao is described in David and Nancy Dall Milton, *The Wind Will Not Subside: Years in Revolutionary China* (New York: Pantheon Books, 1976), 106; Strong and Keysser, *Right in Her Soul*, 329-330.
5. Mao confirmed in a meeting with a delegation from Albania in 1967 that he dated the true beginning of the Cultural Revolution from the publishing of the article criticizing *The Dismissal of Hai Rui*. See David Milton, Nancy Milton, and Frank Schurman, eds., *The China Reader, People's China: Social Experimentation, Politics, Entry onto the World Scene 1966 through 1972* (New York: Random House, 1974), 261.
6. Since 1981, the official Chinese line has designated the Cultural Revolution era as "Ten Years of Chaos," beginning in 1966 and ending in October 1976. However, the original official boundaries of the Cultural Revolution were from May 1966 to April 1969, when the ninth Party Congress brought it to a close. The periodization of the Cultural Revolution is debatable depending from which angle we examine it—power struggle, ideological battle, or a social conflict. However, for the purposes of considering the internationalist aspects of the Cultural Revolution and the role of China's foreign friends in this, the Ninth Party Congress in April 1969, when Mao Zedong and Lin Biao declared the successful resolution of the Cultural Revolution, is the logical conclusion for the movement. (See *Zhongguo gongchandang di jiu ci quan guo daibiao dahui wenjian huibian* (Beijing: Renmin chubanshe, 1969). By 1969, the foreign friends were either arrested, under house arrest, had returned home, or were keeping a very low profile in China. The need for them as internationalist supporters of Mao's revolutionary line had been discarded for political reasons and China was about to begin a new era in foreign relations, which would place the foreign friends in a new role altogether.
7. Robert Scalapino, "The Cultural Revolution and Chinese Foreign Policy," *Current Scene: Developments in Mainland China* VI, no. 13 (1 August 1968), 4.
8. *Mao Zhuxi lun shijie geming* (Beijing: Renmin Ribao guojibu, 1968), 59.
9. *Mao Zhuxi lun shijie geming*, 63.
10. "Foreign Friends Praise China's Cultural Revolution," NCNA-English, 17 November 1966, *Survey*, no. 3825, 27.
11. *Lin fuxi yulu* (Beijing: n.p., 1969), 10-17.

12.   Scalapino, "The Cultural Revolution and Chinese Foreign Policy," 11.

13.   Miltons, *The Wind Will Not Subside*, 214.

14.   Sophia Knight, living in Shanghai as a foreign expert at the Shanghai Foreign Language School, makes first mention of the new political movement on 21 May 1966 when she describes the attacks on Deng Tuo, Liao Mosha, and Wu Han, *Window on Shanghai*, 196.

15.   For a detailed chronology of the events of the early phases of the Cultural Revolution, see Yan Jiaqi and Gao Gao, *Turbulent Decade*, 23-55.

16.   *Turbulent Decade*, 41-42.

17.   Barbara Barnouin and Yu Changen, *Chinese Foreign Policy during the Cultural Revolution* (London and New York: Kegan Paul International, 1998), 57.

18.   Barnouin and Yu, *Chinese Foreign Policy*, 4-5.

19.   Eric Gordon, *Freedom Is a Word*, 68.

20.   Mackerras and Hunter, *China Observed*, 140.

21.   Knight, *Window on Shanghai*, 212.

22.   Knight, *Window on Shanghai*, 212.

23.   Rittenberg and Bennett, *The Man Who Stayed Behind*, 307.

24.   *Renmin Ribao*, 5 August 1966, 1. This translation of the poster appeared in *Peking Review*, no. 33 (11 August 1967): 5.

25.   Rittenberg and Bennett, *The Man Who Stayed Behind*, 315.

26.   Rittenberg and Bennett, *The Man Who Stayed Behind*, 377.

27.   Harry Harding, "The Chinese State in Crisis, 1966-9," *The Politics of China: The Eras of Mao and Deng* (2nd ed.), ed. Roderick MacFarquhar (Cambridge, U.K.: Cambridge University Press, 1997), 178.

28.   Harding, "The Chinese State in Crisis," 177.

29.   Harding, "The Chinese State in Crisis," 181.

30.   Yan Jiaqi and Gao Gao, *Turbulent Decade*, 56-57.

31.   *Turbulent Decade*, 59.

32.   Carmelita Hinton, e-mail to the author, 4 October 1996.

33.   "Gei waiguo zhuanjiaju de dazibao," in He Shu, "Wenge yijun—waiguo zaofanpai," unpublished paper.

34.   Joan Hinton, e-mail to the author, 2 October 2001.

35.   *Ziliao xuanbian* (Beijing: n.p., 1967), 326.

36.   Anna Louise Strong, "I Join the Red Guards," *Letters from China*, no. 41 (20 September 1966): 4.

37.   An American journalist, John Reed's account of his experiences in the Russian Revolution.

38.   Anna Louise Strong, "I Join the Red Guards," 4.

39.   Miltons, *The Wind Will Not Subside*, 239.

40.   Knight, *Windows on Shanghai*, 229.

41.   Miltons, *The Wind Will Not Subside*, 239.

42.   *The Wind Will Not Subside*, 376. See also Gordon, *Freedom Is a Word*, 85.

43.   "China's Cultural Revolution and African People's Struggle for Liberation: Interview with Ahmed Kheir," NCNA-English, 18 April 1967, *Survey*, no. 3924, 28.

44.   *Renmin Ribao*, 19 August 1966, 2.

45.   Rewi Alley, letter to Maud Russell, undated approximately September 1966, Correspondence July-December 1966, Box 7, MRP, NYPL.

46. Talitha Gerlach, letter to Maud Russell, 18 September 1966, Correspondence July-December 1966, Box 7, MRP, NYPL.

47. Talitha Gerlach, letter to Maud Russell, 7 May 1967, Correspondence April-June 1967, Box 8, MRP, NYPL.

48. Doris Dawson, letter to Maud Russell, 28 October 1966, Correspondence July-December 1966, Box 7, MRP, NYPL.

49. On Maoists and the international left-wing movement, see Klaus Mehnert, *Peking and the New Left: At Home and Abroad* (Berkeley: Center for Chinese Studies, University of California, Berkeley, 1969), 61-69, 154-156. For an account of the impact of Maoism in France in the 1960s, see Christophe Bourseiller, *Les Maoïstes: La Folie Histoire des Gardes Rouges Français* (Paris: Plon, 1996). For a comprehensive site on foreign Maoists worldwide in the twenty-first century, see http://www.geocities.com/CapitolHill/Lobby/8317/rmc/links.html. See also the site of the Maoist International Movement, http://www.etext.org/Politics/MIM/wim/index.html.

50. Barnouin and Yu, *Chinese Foreign Policy during the Cultural Revolution*, 13.

51. Knight, *Windows on Shanghai*, 219, 221.

52. Gordon, *Freedom Is a Word*, 72-73.

53. "They Fight Side-by-Side with Us—Foreign Friends in Peking Support China's Great Cultural Revolution," 9 October 1966, *Survey*, no. 3800, 37.

54. "They Fight Side-by-Side with Us," 37.

55. "They Fight Side-by-Side with Us," 37.

56. David Crook, interview, 23 April 1996.

57. Denise Lebreton, "My Love for a Country," *Living in China*, 75.

58. Marianne Bastid-Bruguière, interview, 26 March 1997.

59. Marianne Bastid-Bruguière, interview.

60. Scalapino, "The Cultural Revolution and Chinese Foreign Policy," 6, 14.

61. Esther Holland Jian, *British Girl, Chinese Wife*, 197.

62. Sara Lake, phone interview, 1 February 1996.

63. Barnouin and Yu, *Chinese Foreign Policy during the Cultural Revolution*, 10-11.

64. *Chinese Foreign Policy during the Cultural Revolution*, 13.

65. Shapiro, *An American in China*, 235. Sophia Knight describes the change in policy taking affect in Shanghai at the same time in *Windows on Shanghai*, 237.

66. "Forgotten Americans in China Have Few Regrets," *Washington Post*, 14 March 1972, A13. Some foreigners did move out of the Friendship Hotel and took reductions in their salary. But all eventually returned to the comfort of their luxury (by Chinese standards) accommodation in the post-Cultural Revolution period.

67. Miltons, *The Wind Will Not Subside*, 218.

68. Gordon, *Freedom Is a Word*, 77.

69. Knight, *Window on Shanghai*, 251.

70. Rittenberg and Bennett, *The Man Who Stayed Behind*, 334.

71. Miltons, *The Wind Will Not Subside*, 195-201.

72. *The Wind Will Not Subside*, 225.

73. William Hinton, *Hundred Day War: The Cultural Revolution at Tsinghua University* (New York: Monthly Review Press, 1972), 105.

74. Anonymous source.

75.   Israel Epstein, letter to Maud Russell, 27 April 1967, Correspondence April-June 1967, Box 8, MRP, NYPL.

76.   Miltons, *The Wind Will Not Subside*, 233. It was later discovered that Chen had also been compiling a record of the inaccuracies of Mao's works. After this he was discredited and declared a counterrevolutionary. Chen was called a "revolutionary madman" in reference to Lu Xun's famous story *Diary of a Madman*, where the narrator feigns madness to protest against the brutality of Chinese political society.

77.   Miltons, *The Wind Will Not Subside*, 230.

78.   Zhao Pitao, *Waishi gaishuo*, 132.

79.   "Children of Foreigners Working in Peking Take Part in Voluntary Labor," NCNA-English, 29 March 1967, *Survey*, no. 3909, 38.

80.   Shapiro, *An American in China*, 235.

81.   Miltons, *The Wind Will Not Subside*, 230.

82.   "Foreign Friends Praise China's Policy of Self-Reliance," 15 September 1966, *Survey*, no. 3784, 31.

83.   "They Fight Side-by-Side with Us," *Survey*, no. 3800, 37.

84.   "They Fight Side-by-Side with Us."

85.   Zhao Pitao, *Waishi gaishuo*, 198; see also Lin Biao, "Zai shoudu renmin jinian shiyue geming wushi zhounian dahui shang de jianghua," 6 November 1967, in *Guoji xingshi he wo guo de duiwai zhengce* (publisher and location unknown, 1969), 13.

86.   Henry Noyes, *China Born: Memoirs of a Westerner* (London: Peter Owen, 1989), 136. The sole distributor of books from the PRC in the U.S. in the 1960s, China Books and Periodicals, sold more then one million copies of the "Little Red Book" in the U.S. from 1967-1983 (Noyes, 82). The manager of Xinhua Printing Press told Noyes on a visit to Beijing in 1975 that in the five years before 1966, his press published "only ten million copies of Chairman Mao's works," but after 1966, "several hundred millions" were published in the following five years (Noyes, 139).

87.   Talitha Gerlach, letter to Maud Russell, 27 July 1967, Correspondence July-December 1967, Box 8, MRP, NYPL. Rewi Alley's turgid *Travels in China, 1966-71* (Peking: New World Press, 1971) was one of the few tangible results of this trip.

88.   Mao Zedong, "Directive," June 1967, Robert Friend, ed., *Quotations from Chairman Mao Tse-tung on Propaganda* (Peking: Foreign Languages Press, 1967), 97.

89.   *Quotations from Chairman Mao on Propaganda*, 66.

90.   *Quotations from Chairman Mao on Propaganda*, i.

91.   *Quotations from Chairman Mao on Propaganda*, ii.

92.   *Quotations from Chairman Mao on Propaganda*, iii.

93.   Mao Zedong, "Carry the Revolution through to the End," *Selected Works*, vol. 4, 304-305, excerpted in *Quotations from Chairman Mao on Propaganda*, 18.

94.   Extended from Mao Zedong, "The Foolish Old Man Who Moved Mountains," *Selected Works*, vol. 3, 321-322, excerpted in *Quotations from Mao Zedong on Propaganda*, 14.

95.   Knight, *Windows on Shanghai*, 224.

96.   York Young, interview, 20 January 1996.

97.   Yang Xianyi, interview, 13 September 1995.

98.   Han Suyin, *My House Has Two Doors* (London: Jonathan Cape, 1980), 438-440.

99.   Harry Lloyd papers, held in the possession of Joan Hinton; Joan Hinton, interview, 22 December 1997.

100.   Gordon, *Freedom Is a Word*, 101.

101.   Joan Hinton, interview, 19 December 1997.

102.   York Young, interview, 20 January 1996.

103.   Miltons, *The Wind Will Not Subside*, 257.

104.   "Foreign Friends Praise Chinese People's Liberation Army," *Renmin Ribao*, 10 April 1967, *Survey*, no. 3918, 23.

105.   "Foreign Friends in Peking Hail the Great Victory of Chairman Mao's Theory of People's War," NCNA-English, 31 August 1967, *Survey*, no. 4014, 40.

106.   See http://www.ace.lu.se/documentation/engelsk.html for text and photos of the events. According to Joan Hinton, who participated in the demonstration, the protest had been peaceful initially, but erupted into violence when the British representative refused to come out to hear a petition. The crowd of foreigners became enraged and threw flowerpots through the windows, hitting a portrait of the queen. They took the front door off its hinges and stormed in. After the chargé d'affaires came downstairs the crowd calmed down and the petition was read to him. As a final act of defiance, outside the building some of the foreign demonstrators pulled down the flagpole and burned the British flag. Joan Hinton, e-mail to author, 16 October 2001.

107.   Barnouin and Yu, *Chinese Foreign Policy during the Cultural Revolution*, 60.

108.   *Chinese Foreign Policy during the Cultural Revolution*, 155-9.

109.   Stuart and Roma Gelder, *Memories for a Chinese Granddaughter* (London: Hutchinson, 1967), 58-61.

110.   *Memories for a Chinese Granddaughter*, 205.

111.   Anthony Grey, *Hostage in Peking* (London: Michael Joseph, 1970), 96.

112.   Zhong gong zhongyang zuzhibu, Zhong gong gong'anbu dang zu, "*Guanyu waiguo zhuanjia pengyou luoshi zhengce qingkuang baogao*," 11 February 1982.

113.   Sam Ginsberg, *My First Sixty Years in China* (Beijing: New World Press, 1982), 289.

114.   For the experiences of one such individual, see Ury Ivanov, *Ten Years of My Life in the Cultural Revolution* (Dandenong: Dandenong College of TAFE, 1985).

115.   Ginsberg, *My First Sixty Years in China*, 293.

116.   On the life of Li Lisan and Elisabeth Kischkin, see Patrick Lescot, *L'empire rouge: Moscou-Pékin, 1919-1989* (Paris, 2001).

117.   For Eva Xiao, see *China, Mein Traum, Mein Lieben* (München: Taschenbuch, 1994).

118.   Interview with Eva Xiao, 11 June 1996.

119.   See footnote 106.

120.   Grey describes the terror of this night, 122-127. See also Percy Cradock, *Experiences of China* (London: John Murray, 1994).

121.   Norman Barrymaine, *The Time Bomb, a Veteran Journalist Assesses Today's China from the Inside* (London: Peter Davies, 1971).

122.   Grey, *Hostage in Peking*, 340.

123.   Yang Xianyi, *Autobiography*, unpublished typescript, 156. The Yangs were held in prison until 1 May 1972.

124.   Gordon, *Freedom Is a Word*, 202.

125.   "A Mysterious American—How Rittenberg Usurped the Leadership of the Central Broadcasting Bureau," *Wenge tongxun*, no. 13, March 1968, *Survey*, 26 April 1968, no. 4165, 3.

126. Miltons, *The Wind Will Not Subside*, 235.
127. *The Wind Will Not Subside*, 301.
128. Hamrin, "Elite Politics and the Development of China's Foreign Relations," in *Chinese Foreign Policy*, ed. Robinson and Shambaugh, 88.
129. Grey, *Hostage in Peking*, 201.
130. Miltons, *The Wind Will Not Subside*, 295.
131. *The Wind Will Not Subside*, 303.
132. Rittenberg and Bennett, *The Man Who Stayed Behind*, 383.
133. *The Man Who Stayed Behind*, 431.
134. Unlike Chinese prisoners who lived in crowded and unsanitary conditions, foreigners had their own cells, they did not even share cells with other foreigners. For some this was a bonus, giving them privacy and some control over their own surroundings, for others the enforced isolation led to psychological problems.
135. Rittenberg and Bennett, *The Man Who Stayed Behind*, 407.
136. Miltons, *The Wind Will Not Subside*, 302.
137. Miltons, *The Wind Will Not Subside*, 372.
138. Pat Adler, interview, 10 December 1997.
139. Yang Xianyi, *Autobiography*, unpublished typescript, 1990, 156. David Crook, interview, 23 April 1996.
140. David Finkelstein and Beverley Hooper, "57 Years Inside China: An American's Odyssey," *ASIA* (January/February, 1980): 46.
141. "A Mysterious American," *Wenge tongxun*, 1.
142. Han Suyin, *My House Has Two Doors*, 496.
143. Brian Shaw, "Report on a Visit to China," 5 April 1968, PM 58/11/4, MFAT.
144. Talitha Gerlach, letter to Maud Russell, 16 May 1971, Correspondence April-June 1971, Box 9, MRP, NYPL.
145. The Anti-Communist Group of Students of the Kaifeng Normal School, letter to Maud Russell, 28 August 1971, Correspondence July-September 1971, Box 9, MRP, NYPL.
146. Joan Hinton, interview, 19 December 1997.
147. Zhao Pitao, *Waishi gaishuo*, 132.
148. Zhonggong zhongyang zuzhibu, Zhonggong gong'anbu dang zu, "*Guanyu waiguo zhuanjia pengyou luoshi zhengce qingkuang baogao*" (A Report on the Situation and Implementation of Policies on Foreign Experts and Foreign Friends), 11 February 1982.
149. Talitha Gerlach, letter to Maud Russell, 10 July 1969, Correspondence July-December 1969, Box 8, MRP, NYPL.
150. Han Suyin, *My House Has Two Doors*, 495.
151. *My House Has Two Doors*, 564.
152. Deng Bangzhen, interview, 6 December 1993.
153. Grey, *Hostage in Peking*, 47.
154. "Deal Resolute Blows at Enemy Spies," *Renmin Ribao*, 16 March 1968, *Survey*, no. 4142, 32.
155. David Crook, interview, 16 May 1996.
156. *Current Background*, no. 622, 6 August 1968, 3.
157. See for example, "Revolutionary People in Western Europe, North America, Oceania, Study Marxist-Leninism-Mao Tse-tung Thought in Surging Mass Movements," NCNA-English, 1 May 1969, *Survey*, no. 4410, 22.

158.   See for example, "The International Situation," *Dongfang hong dianxun*, no. 3, July 1968, *Survey*, no. 4231, 20. "Revolutionary People of Soviet Union and East Europe Love Chairman Mao," NCNA-English, 28 August 1968 *Survey*, no. 4250, 33, "World People Look Up to Peking Their Hearts Turning to Chairman Mao," NCNA-English, 1 April 1969, *Survey*, no. 4391, 25, Xibei gongye daxue geming weiyuanhui zhengyizu, *Mao Zhuxi shijie renmin re'ai nin*, Xibei gongye daxue, 1969.

159.   Lu Ning, *The Dynamics of Foreign-Policy Decisionmaking in China*, 155. The Chinese Association for Cultural Exchange changed its name in 1966 to the Chinese People's Association for Friendship with Foreign Countries (*Zhongguo renmin duiwai youhao xiehui*, commonly abbreviated as *Youxie*). However its operations were soon after closed down when cadres became involved in Cultural Revolution activities. *Youxie* didn't become active again until 1969. Han Xu, "Mao Zedong de minjian waijiao sixiang he zhongyao juece" in *Mao Zedong waijiao sixiang yanjiu*, ed. Pei Jianzhang, 53.

Chapter 7

Bridge Building

In the early seventies you had the feeling the Chinese government had a purpose for every foreigner . . . and this was exhilarating for some people.[1]

Threats of a "surgical" nuclear attack from the Soviet Union in the summer of 1969 forced Beijing to reconsider China's strategic relationships. Facing a choice between improving relations with the Soviet Union or the United States, Mao chose the United States. The improvement in China-U.S. relations was founded on the goal of forging a new international united front against the Soviet Union. Mao Zedong's decision was undoubtedly strengthened by a series of private and public comments from President Nixon in the summer of 1969 stating his desire to improve Sino-U.S. relations. What caught Mao's attention in particular was Nixon's language of a multipolar world and the context of the U.S. withdrawal from Vietnam. In July 1969, the United States withdrew a routine patrol in the Taiwan Strait that had been in place since the Korean War. In December 1969, Nixon directed the U.S. ambassador to Poland to contact Chinese diplomats about the resumption of bilateral ambassadorial talks. The talks only lasted two sessions after China criticized the U.S. invasion of Cambodia. However, in June 1970, the U.S. forces withdrew from Cambodia. Soon after, President Nixon announced a loosening of import restrictions on products originating from the PRC. In August of that year, Mao Zedong personally authorized a new visit to China by journalist Edgar Snow. Mao apparently believed that Snow was a CIA agent and a channel for information to the highest levels of the U.S. government.[2] During China's 1970 National Day celebrations Snow and his wife, Lois Wheeler Snow, were invited to stand on the rostrum of Tiananmen[3] with Mao and other senior leaders. This was given front-page coverage in *Renmin Ribao* the following day. Placing a foreigner (above all an American) on the Tiananmen rostrum was a powerful symbolic act. Its significance was, however, completely missed by Washington. But Nixon continued to send his own secret messages, informing intermediary countries such as Romania and Pakistan that he was willing to send a secret envoy to China. Mao signaled his willingness for Nixon to visit China in an interview with Snow on 18 December 1970.

Edgar Snow found this high-profile role grating at times. During the visit, Snow told his wife that he felt he was a "symbol to be paraded here and there by an ambassador with no chance to really talk to anybody long enough to learn anything."[4] He was not well (within months he would be diagnosed with cancer), and he wanted to return home to rest and avoid the harsh Beijing weather. Nevertheless, Snow was kept waiting in China for months for talks with Zhou and Mao. When the meetings finally eventuated, to Snow's annoyance, all interviews had to be edited, even his own notes had to be "cleared" and "amplified" and he was not given permission to leave China until this was done. "On top of all that," he complained, "they kept giving me banquets, I don't know how many unnecessary farewells there were."[5]

Not long after Edgar Snow returned from China, in March 1971 U.S. Democrat senator and presidential candidate George McGovern told Snow he hoped to visit China later that year, and that he planned to make the following statement:

> If I were appointed president of the U.S. I would be prepared to recognize Peking as the sole legitimate government of China, leaving the future status of Taiwan to a peaceful resolution by the Chinese people.[6]

McGovern asked for Snow's assistance to negotiate the visit with the Chinese authorities. But Beijing was cool to McGovern's suggestion; having already begun negotiating with the incumbent, Richard Nixon, to come. Though the CCP had supported the left-wing movement in the U.S. and other Western countries in the 1960s, they were realistic about the impossibility of a successful revolution there. From the 1970s on, Beijing cooperated with mainstream organizations in the United States, simply because they were closest to power.[7] Mao made the decision to deal with those in power, *dangquanpai*, to conduct Sino-U.S. relations.[8] Nonetheless, Chinese officials still had contact with more left-leaning organizations, but now this was in order to utilize existing channels in order to come closer to the mainstream. At a meeting with senior leaders in 1972, Mao stated "we must win over one of the two big powers, and we cannot fight on two fronts."[9] Of course fighting on two fronts was precisely what China had done since 1960, but from now on a more pragmatic policy would prevail. After Nixon visited China in 1972, the Chinese government described him as a friend of China, a label that appalled many of China's stalwart foreign admirers. Chinese officials explained that Nixon had come to China, and on the basis of his acts and their potential for building U.S.-China relations, he would be considered a "friend." In the long run, CCP decision makers cared little about the left-wing movement in the United States.[10] Mao told Edgar Snow in 1970:

> I don't like the Democratic Party, I prefer the Republican Party. I like Nixon in power. Why? Because though he is deceitful, he is a little bit less so. He resorts

more to tough tactics, though also some soft ones. If he wants to come to Peking, you may bring him a message, tell him to come in secret and not to make
it known to the public; he can just get on the plane and come. It doesn't matter
whether or not the talks will be successful. Why continue such a stalemate?[11]

Remarkably, Mao also unburdened himself to Snow on the subject of who he
said were his only real "friends": Snow and the leader of the tiny breakaway
pro-China Australian Communist Party (Marxist-Leninist), Ted Hill,

> You and I are old friends. I don't have many friends. In fact there are only two
> people I can talk to . . . one of them is [Ted] Hill (you know the Australian
> Communist) and the other is you. Hill told me the same thing you did about the
> Cult. He is an honest man. So I value your friendship. We have known each
> other for thirty years . . . I have no reason to distrust you . . . the important
> thing is not to lie . . . and you haven't told any lies . . . and I haven't told any
> lies about you.[12]

Curiously, when speaking with Snow at this meeting Mao used the word "*pengyou*" (friend) as if it was a title, *Sinuo pengyou*, Friend Snow. In modern Chinese usage, this was equivalent to other titles common in the era, such as
Teacher Wang, or Engineer Zhang. In Mao's usage, being called a friend of
China was not just an act of courtesy, it was a job classification.

Ping-Pong Diplomacy

Nineteen-seventy-one was a momentous year in CCP diplomacy. In a flurry of
activity, the numbers of foreign visitors to China (among them prominent politicians of the Western world such as Henry Kissinger and Australian Labor leader
Gough Whitlam) increased dramatically after the isolation of the last decade, especially the last five years, and, at the end of the year, the PRC finally took up
the China seat in the United Nations. The improvement in the PRC's diplomatic
relations was part of a general trend both in the Western world and China, most
notably the formation of an anti-Soviet united front between China and the
Western world.

The major paradigm shifts involved in the improvement of Sino-Western
relations were symbolized by what came to be known as "ping-pong diplomacy." In March 1971 the Chinese Ping-Pong team attended the World Table
Tennis championships, held in Japan, for the first time since the Cultural Revolution began. The team's participation was personally supported by Mao and
Zhou. The Foreign Ministry prepared guidelines for the Chinese players on how
to interact with competitors from the United States. They were told not to initi-
ate conversations or greetings with them, and not to exchange team flags if they
played together, but they were allowed to shake hands with them after a match.[13]

This cautious contact was taken still further when the U.S. contestants expressed a wish to visit China and play table tennis there. On 10 April 1971 the

U.S. team arrived in China. Zhou Enlai met with them soon after their arrival, and he told them, "You have opened a new page in Sino-U.S. relationships."[14] The visit was significant as the first public indication of the improvement in Sino-U.S. relations.

The Australian China specialist Ross Terrill visited China in mid-1971 to assist with the visit of Gough Whitlam. Before the Whitlam delegation arrived, Terrill's minder, Zhou Nan (later to take up high-profile postings at the UN and Hong Kong), gave him a list of the Australian journalists who would be attending and asked him to give an ideological background on all of them. Terrill agreed to do so. Terrill was well rewarded for his information, he says the Chinese "showered me with goodies," including flying him to meet with Cambodian prince Sihanouk in Xi'an.[15] On his travels throughout China during the trip, Terrill noted prominently displayed banners that proclaimed: "Make the foreign serve China," *yang wei Zhong yong*.[16] This served both as a signal to the Chinese population of the new direction in China's foreign policy and as a justification for rapprochement with the old foe, Western imperialists. This slogan was also featured prominently in a series of articles on China's foreign affairs in the party magazine *Hong Qi* in mid-1972 and presented in translated form in *Peking Review*.[17] Ross Terrill wrote a number of reports based on the visit for the *Atlantic Monthly*, which later became the highly successful book *800,000,000: The Real China*. (It was so influential in its day that Henry Kissinger recommended President Nixon read it before he visited China in 1972.) Terrill's writing was both known about and encouraged by his Chinese hosts.

The changes in foreign policy tactics observed by Terrill were a result of shifts in the leadership structure leading up to the fall of Lin Biao in September 1971, and a realignment of strategic understandings. Zhou Enlai's power base was strengthened, and two close associates of Zhou, Li Xiannian and Ye Jianying, took up senior roles in *waishi* decision making. (Mortally ill with cancer, Chen Yi passed away in 1973.) The restoration to power of Deng Xiaoping in 1974 also assisted the process toward the new diplomatic opening to the United States and the West generally. Nevertheless, the last years of the Mao era were troubled by severe factional struggle, discouraging complete control over foreign affairs by Zhou and his associates.[18] As a result, the PRC's new direction in foreign policy would tend to zigzag between radicalism and a new openness to the outside world for some years to come.

China Opens the Door

On 5 October 1971 Zhou Enlai hosted a special reception at the Great Hall of the People for a large group of U.S. citizens. People from a wide range of political backgrounds were invited to attend, and all expenses for their trip in China were paid for by Beijing: members of the Black Panthers were there; as were delegates from an American youth group; former State Department official Jack Service who had been part of the Dixie Mission to Yan'an in 1944; Max and Grace Granich who had worked for the Comintern in Shanghai in the 1930s, putting out a pro-CCP newsletter, and importantly, had taken the Chinese side in the Sino-Soviet split; and a number of American foreign friends resident in Beijing such as Ione Kramer, who had been released from prison especially for the meeting. Two non-American foreign friends also attended, Austrian doctor Hans Mueller and veteran CCP propagandist, the New Zealander, Rewi Alley.

The transitional state of China's foreign relations in this period was shown by the way the CCP treated former prominent foreign supporters such as the leaders of the New Zealand Communist Party and Australian Communist Party (Marxist-Leninist) both of whom privately criticized the new direction. Both had been among the handful of communist parties who sided with the Chinese in the Sino-Soviet split. Now, although Beijing began inviting a succession of Western politicians to China, in public it continued to champion leftist supporters such as Wilcox and Hill.[21] This outward solidarity would continue at least until 1978-1979, when both the NZCP and ACP (Marxist-Leninist) virtually collapsed after their members were unable to stomach the radical economic and political changes of their patron party, the CCP.

The dual policy of outwardly supporting leftists and revolutionaries, while negotiating with those it had formerly called enemies, was summed up at Mao's meeting with U.S. president Nixon in 1972. Mao told Nixon that even though relations between the United States and the PRC had improved, "the Chinese press would still carry articles attacking the U.S., and he expected the American press to keep up its criticisms of China. The peoples of both countries were so used to the criticisms that readjusting to the new friendship would take time."[22] Similarly, speaking to U.S. secretary of state Henry Kissinger, Mao dismissed the anti-American slogans that had marked his rule since 1949 as merely "the sound [of] a lot of big cannons."[23] From this period on, party propaganda organs began producing materials aimed at helping to "readjust" popular concepts of Sino-foreign relations.[24] In the latter half of 1972 up to three-quarters of the then six-

Zhou Enlai explained to the group that Nixon was to come to China and why this was so. He asked them to help promote the friendship between the United States and China and to work to improve China's image there.[19] Zhou discussed the history of U.S.-Chinese relations mentioning Snow's visit to the CCP base at Bao'an in 1936, General Stilwell's support for the CCP during World War II, and the good relationships the Chinese communists established with U.S. officials such as Jack Service before 1949. The reception was part of the buildup to Nixon's visit to China, and was emblematic of the beginnings of the Sino-U.S. rapprochement. After the talk, former U.S. State Department diplomat Service apologetically informed Chinese officials that he would have to report back to the State Department on his return. This was exactly what the Chinese had hoped for. Before he left China, Zhou Enlai met with Service in private, giving him a three-hour summary of Chinese foreign policy.[20]

page *Renmin Ribao* were devoted to foreign affairs.[25] Such materials were used in nationwide political study sessions in order to introduce the Chinese population to the radical new direction in China's foreign relations.

Most of China's foreign friends needed some time to adjust to the new "friendship" too. Former Beijing-based foreign experts David and Nancy Milton's comments summed up the feelings of many, when back in the United States they wrote,

> We watched with strangely mixed emotions as television brought us the view of President Nixon and his entourage in Peking. Again and again in the months which followed, we would see some of our closest Chinese teaching colleagues and former students performing professionally as interpreters for the leading statesmen of the Western world. The American press campaign was skillfully orchestrated to overcome any major opposition to the opening to China. It soon proved not to exist.[26]

It was necessary for Beijing to ensure that its China-based foreign friends supported the new policy toward the United States, since their opposition could cause a public relations headache, both in China and the West. They would also be called into action to sell the new policy to Americans, including those on the left, but more importantly to "middle America." Soon after negotiations for the Sino-U.S. rapprochement began, George Hatem and Sidney Shapiro were sent to the United States (in Hatem's case the first visit home since he had arrived in China in the 1920s) where both engaged in extensive speaking tours disguised as "family visits." Rewi Alley took on a similar task in Australia and New Zealand. In 1971 and 1972, the small number of Americans based in China were repeatedly given special treatment. The *Washington Post* reported in 1972, "Premier Chou En-lai has had them all over to the Great Hall of the People several times in the past year or so, spending a couple of hours on each occasion talking about old times and discussing the world situation."[27] The friends' support was important from a symbolic point of view. But it was also important because, despite the fact that China's formal state-to-state relations increased rapidly from this point on, people's diplomacy took on a new significance as China worked on improving its image in the Western world. Even more so than before, the activities of the foreign friends as interlocutors and supporters of the CCP were useful and important in this task. The friends' views on the changes in China were sought after and quoted by a new generation of foreigners eager to believe in and be accepted by the rulers of new China.[28]

In October 1971, the U.S. government lifted travel restrictions on Americans visiting the PRC. From this period on, increasing numbers of foreigners, particularly from Western countries, began arriving in China, though there were quotas on how many could visit per year.[29] From 1973, after a break of seven years, small numbers of foreign students were allowed to study in Chinese universities.[30] Satirizing the revolutionary rhetoric of the times, the foreign students jokingly referred to themselves as "worker-peasant-soldier foreign students," *gong nong bing liuxuesheng.* They were accommodated in separate dormitories and ate at separate dining halls from Chinese students, but were permitted to participate in "voluntary" labor in the countryside and factories. Nineteen-seventy-three also marked the period when a mini import boom of technology and equipment from the West, particularly Japan, began. This was known as the "4-3" policy, because the government planned to spend US$4.3 billion on the plan.[31]

In these early days of opening up to the outside world, foreign visitors were taken to both traditional tourist spots as the Forbidden City, in addition to sites more in keeping with China's revolutionary ideology such as the Beijing Coking Plant, the No. 1 State Cotton Mill, the Beijing General Petroleum Chemical Works, and the Beijing No. 3 Deaf-Mute School.[32] As in the 1950s and 1960s the Chinese interpreters and guides who accompanied the tours were still obliged to encourage ideological orthodoxy among the visitors. Orville Schell, who visited China in 1975, wrote of the "ideological remolding" he received on one such trip,

> Almost every day the interpreters meet, they discuss the trip, its problems, us and what political approaches are correct to follow. It is not uncommon in one day for two or three interpreters to find time to sit down next to the same person on a bus or during a meal, and all raise the same point. It is a kind of political education. If one is resistant, one feels a distinct coolness—a withdrawal of approval, even friendship, during these probationary moments.[33]

Though the Chinese guides spoke frequently of the "friendship" between the Chinese and American people, Schell found it all rather empty:

> Sometimes I sit in the meeting halls, listening to the platitudes, the "welcome of foreign friends," the "B.I." [background information], the blank recitation of how many tons of grain have come from how many mou of land after Liberation and the Cultural Revolution, the stories of "rooting out those who have taken the capitalist road" and the "wrong line," and find myself yearning for a more tangible kind of contact; something warmer, more real, more human: something we seem to be on the verge of grasping when we stay put in one place and work without interruption.[34]

"Real," "human" contact in China was not easy to achieve for foreign visitors like Schell in the 1970s.[35] Most Chinese were too wary of getting into political trouble to risk talking with a foreigner outside of official *waishi* duties.[36] Even if they were discontented with the situation in China, foreign admirers of the regime (as many foreign visitors in this period still were) were not always the safest people to confide in.[37] The new stress on "friendship," rather than ideological goals, was reflected in changes in the bureaucratic structure of the main *waishi* organization involved in hosting foreign groups, the Friendship Association, when in 1972, the formally high-profile Peace Association was formally merged into its counterpart.[38]

Instead of human contact with Chinese, foreign visitors to China in the 1970s were frequently offered the opportunity to meet with some of the resident foreigners. A number of the long-standing resident foreign friends were involved in hosting the guests and answering their questions on the new, new China. In 1972 Talitha Gerlach was moved out of her formerly cramped accommodation into a spacious house with a garden (and an air-raid shelter for her personal use—potentially quite useful at a time when China still feared the USSR might launch a nuclear attack). Gerlach's work unit, the China Welfare Institute, told her the new accommodation was so she could "entertain [foreign] guests."[39] To the visitors, many of whom had never visited China before, the foreign friends had an aura of relative objectivity, knowledge, and approachability compared to the stiffness of many of the Chinese *waishi* personnel who accompanied them on their escorted travels in the PRC. In fact, the friends were extremely cautious to follow the official line in their interactions with foreign visitors, they well knew that from both the point of view of the visitors and the Chinese officials who inevitably came with them, deviation was not advisable. Mentioning his old friend Rewi Alley, Max Granich, who visited China frequently throughout the 1970s and 1980s as a leader of U.S. friendship delegations, told an interviewer why he was careful to avoid talking politics with foreign friends and Chinese:

> They don't want to, especially foreigners. Especially foreigners. And [Rewi Alley] is a, is really a foreigner. He's never been taken into Chinese citizenship. I mean he could be deported tomorrow. So you don't want to discuss too many things with Rewi. When things occur Rewi makes a quick comment that gives you the slant and you understand that you don't push for details. You could pick those up elsewhere, easily.[40]

On 8 March 1973, as part of continuing efforts to get the foreign friends' support for the new foreign policy direction, a meeting was held for foreigners and Chinese *waishi* cadres in the Great Hall of the People, to commemorate International Women's Day. Also at the meeting were Jiang Qing, Zhang Chunqiao, Yao Wenyuan, Wang Hongwen (the coterie later reviled as the Gang of Four), Liao Chengzhi, Qiao Guanhua, and other senior *waishi* officials.[41] About two hundred foreign experts, their families, and four hundred Chinese cadres attended.[42] By 1973, all the foreigners who had been detained in 1968 (except Sid Rittenberg) had been released from prison, though some were still kept under semi-house arrest. David Crook sent both Maud Russell and the Marxist U.S.-journal *Monthly Review* a report of the talk Zhou Enlai gave at the meeting. It was an act of personal justification after the vilification and five years in prison he had received in the Cultural Revolution years.

The meeting was broadcast on CCTV news that night. Zhou told the group that 8 March 1973 marked a new stage in the revolution, especially for foreigners living in China:

> He cited concrete examples of the wrong treatment of foreigners in China

(strikingly enough they were all from English-speaking countries). He apologized to all of them, including some who were present at the reception . . . Premier Zhou concluded with a forthright condemnation of chauvinism, racialism, exclusivism, etc. in the treatment of foreigners in China, and upheld the principle of internationalism. He said that Chairman Mao recently said that the Chinese tend to be conservative, cliquish and rather reluctant to contact foreigners and to marry foreigners. Such an attitude, he said, could not promote internationalism and world revolution, nor enable China to make its proper contribution to mankind.[43]

It was indeed striking that Zhou had chosen to single out those foreigners from English-speaking countries for mention, since some of the foreigners who had received the worst treatment in the Cultural Revolution were those accused of being spies for Moscow, such as German Eva Xiao or Li Lisan's Russian wife, Lisa Li. In 1973, however, China was striving to improve its relations with the Western world, in a united front against its then main enemy the Soviet Union. Canada, Australia, and New Zealand had established relations with the PRC in the previous two years and relations with the United States were improving rapidly. Now was the time when China needed to call on the help of its foreign friends from Western countries, above all the United States, to facilitate the new phase in China's international relations.

At the March meeting, Zhou stated that the mistreatment of foreign experts during the Cultural Revolution was due to excesses in the movement caused by the subversive actions of Lin Biao and his "anti-party clique."[44] The mistreatment of foreigners was divided into three categories. The first category consisted of those who had been cold-shouldered or made to feel unwelcome. The second category included those who were treated discourteously before they left. Zhou said that if they wished to "they are welcome to come back so we can make up for the mistake of not looking after them well." The third category were those who, in the course of taking an active part in the Cultural Revolution, had become entangled in the subversive activities of some "bad elements." Sidney Rittenberg was cited as the ringleader of this group. Rittenberg had been accused of being involved in a counterrevolutionary plot with Wang Li, Guan Feng, and Qi Benyu, as were Israel Epstein, Elsie Fairfax-Cholmeley, and Michael Shapiro (though these three were assessed as being "taken in and deceived"). Thus, in typical CCP-scapegoating style, the fate of the foreign friends who became politically active in the Cultural Revolution era was explicated economically, with only a minority suffering the consequences. A further round of debts against foreigners was settled in 1977 when a public meeting in the Beijing Workers' Stadium announced the sentences of those who had burned down the British Chargé d'Affaires in 1967. Those foreign friends still resident in China attended, as did Foreign Ministry officials and representatives from all bureaus dealing with foreigners. York Young, then working for *Peking Review*, recalls that the meeting was held "as a lesson to you [meaning the Chinese] as much as anything."[45]

Despite all they had suffered, most of China's foreign supporters retained their idealism and optimism in the Chinese revolution—at least for a few more years. Sam Ginsberg in response to a question by an American professor as to whether he felt he had made the right choice in staying on in China after 1949, replied:

> I have acquired as my Motherland a vast fair country which has not given me birth, most of whose territory I have not yet seen, whose language I speak with a lamentable absence of tonality that gives me away as soon as I open my mouth. But China has accepted me for what I am, in which everything pulls at me and the pull is getting stronger as the years pass. It's not because there is no anti-Semitism in this country—this is more than most great countries in the world can say today. Here I feel myself not a Jew, but a citizen because here it's not things that own me, as they used to in the old society, but I own everything I have. It is because this country has given me a sense of belonging, a sense of oneness with its people, a craft, a realization of usefulness.[46]

Just released after five years in prison on false charges, David Crook wrote to Maud Russell,

> I'm fitter than I have been for decades (63 this summer). I was back at work within a few days of my return. Of course the experience has in no way changed my convictions, in fact it's strengthened them. A revolution is not a dinner party. During such an unprecedented and massive one as the cultural revolution it was unavoidable that there should be some casualties, some price to pay, some painful experiences. But the gains are the overwhelming aspect, not the losses.[47]

In public, Crook was positive about the effect of his prison experience. He told Han Suyin that, following the 1973 meeting, "Then I understood much better how complicated the revolution was and we wanted to stay in China more than ever."[48] But actions speak louder than words; not long after his release Crook traveled to his native England and investigated possibilities of starting a new life there.[49] He soon found he was too old and too underqualified to make a new start in the West, but many other formerly loyal friends of China had already left China by this stage, though none spoke publicly of their reasons for going. Those who stayed behind were either too old to move on to make a new life in another country, stateless, or on short-term contracts only.

While the friends welcomed the improvement of China's international relations and an end to the terror of the late 1960s, the changes marked the beginnings of a disillusionment with the CCP among many foreign friends. This disillusionment became increasingly pronounced, as the government moved further and further away from socialist principles. This is not to say that anyone would really wish to return to the climate of 1966, simply that a generation of extremely idealistic individuals came to feel themselves to have been misled and misused by the leader and party they once worshiped.

Reform and Opening Up

It took some time for the shifts in the Sino-U.S. relationship to have an effect on Sino-foreign relations within China. The ongoing political power struggles of the 1970s meant that change came only in fits and starts. In January 1976, Zhou Enlai died, followed by Mao Zedong in September that year. It was more than two years after Mao's death before the new leadership structure was established. During the rule of Mao's designated successor Hua Guofeng from 1976-1978, *waishi* decision making was dominated by Zhou's associates Li Xiannian and Ye Jianying. The CCP Central Committee Foreign Affairs Leading Small Group was reestablished with Li Xiannian in charge and Zhao Ziyang as his deputy.[50] In this period the policy of gradually improving relations with the Western world was continued, as part of the anti-Soviet united front.[51] A further import boom began, later derided as the "Western Leap Forward," whereby billions of dollars worth of new industrial plant was imported from the West. This plan ended in failure as some of the technology was found to be inappropriate for China's needs, but most importantly, because the overspending caused a massive budget blow out.

The Third Plenary Session of the eleventh Central Committee of the CCP in December 1978 confirmed Deng Xiaoping in power. The December 1978 meeting was important not only because it established the new leadership structure, but also because it formalized a radical turnaround in economic policy that had had a number of false starts in earlier eras, but under Deng would finally come into fruition. This shift in economic policy would in turn have a significant impact on China's *waishi*. The new direction was known initially as the Four Modernizations, *si ge xiandaihua*,[52] a policy that had first been proposed by Zhou Enlai in 1965.[53] As reforms deepened throughout the 1980s, the term "reform and opening up," *gaige kaifang*, came into general use. The policies were not a blueprint as such, rather a cautious approach, which Hua Guofeng summed up with the phrase "crossing the river by feeling the stones," *mozhe shitou guo he*.[54] In 1979, the first experimental Special Economic Zones (SEZs) were set up in twelve coastal cities in southern China's Guangdong and Fujian Provinces. They were planned as designated zones with an economic and financial environment that would be attractive to foreign investors, luring both investment and the transfer of foreign technology.[55]

From this period on, the economy increasingly became the primary focus of government activity. China urgently required the assistance of foreign technology and investment in order to speed up its modernization process. Following nearly thirty years of CCP rule where foreigners had clearly been unwelcome and even foreign friends only allowed there on sufferance, China had to convince the world that it had changed. Beijing began to conduct an ongoing campaign to alter global perceptions about the country and encourage foreign assistance. A major propaganda effort was launched, both in China and abroad, critiquing the Cultural Revolution era and promoting the government's new line.

Deng Xiaoping took on an important frontline role of promoting China's Four Modernizations and the open door policy in the 1980s. His official visits to the United States, Japan, France, and countries in Southeast Asia were a visible example of China's new openness to the outside world.[56] So too were many more personal gestures he made, such as wearing a ten-gallon cowboy's hat at a barbecue he attended during his visit to the United States in 1979 (the first ever of a PRC leader) and revealing his fondness for French croissants. As Zhou Enlai had done in earlier eras, Deng made a point of cultivating the international media to promote China's aims.

The reforms launched by Deng in late 1978 were further strengthened in 1980-1981 when he consolidated his leadership role by becoming chairman of the Military Commission and established his protégés Hu Yaobang, Zhao Ziyang, and Wan Li in key leadership roles in the Party Secretariat and State Council respectively.[57] In 1981, the "Resolution on Certain Questions in the History of Our Party Since the Founding of the People's Republic of China" was published, which sharply criticized the policies of the Mao era. Also in 1981, as part of efforts to standardize and professionalize *waishi*, the State Council issued Article 157, regulating the basic activities and responsibilities of provincial and local *waishi* offices.[58]

Deng Xiaoping told party cadres that the three great tasks of the 1980s were "oppose hegemony, uphold world peace, and implement the unity of China and its economic reconstruction." *Waishi* was to be the primary activity uniting and working for all these tasks, with particular emphasis on the economy.[59] After 1978, the government began a dramatic expansion of *waishi* activities and organizations, with a corresponding increase in numbers of personnel with *waishi* duties. From this period on, officials called for greater professionalism in *waishi* and a more thorough training.[60]

Attempts to focus on greater "professionalism" in *waishi* in the new era were part of a wider debate on improving the quality, *suzhi*, of *waishi* cadres and indeed an ongoing obsession of the CCP and many Chinese intellectuals in the post-Mao era of improving the general "quality" of the entire nation. Improving the quality of *waishi* cadres meant both bringing those already involved in foreign affairs activities up to date with the dramatic changes China was undergoing, as well as increasing the numbers of trained staff available to work in foreign affairs offices. It also meant a greater focus on skills such as language abilities and university qualifications, rather than just political trustworthiness.[61] It was an indication of the radical turnaround in thinking within the CCP that those of good class origin (workers and poor peasant origins) were implicitly no longer regarded as of "high quality." As senior cadres returned to power, who had suffered during the Cultural Revolution years precisely because of the taint of the West and the relatively high levels of education which had made them such effective *waishi* workers, they instituted a system that rewarded the educated and the skilled, rather than those of modest (that is, ideologically high) class origin. In the 1980s the knowledge and experience of those from the former elite classes who had dominated CCP *waishi* from its earliest days had once more become an asset. In this new era, even those with bad class origins who were able to pass entrance exams were allowed to attend university. In 1978 the College of International Relations, which had been closed down from 1966-1976, reopened its doors to students and the College of International Politics, *Guoji zhengzhi xueyuan*, was set up, also in Beijing.[62] In 1983, specialized courses for *waishi* cadres were set up at six leading universities. These four-year courses provide training in foreign propaganda and foreign cultural exchange. It was proposed that graduates should not be permitted to leave China,[63] although this would prove impossible to enforce. Beginning in 1984, in addition to these degree courses, a number of other universities as well as the Ministry of Foreign Affairs supervised intensive refresher courses for senior and middle-rung *waishi* cadres.[64]

The founding of the journal *Reference Reports on Foreign Affairs Matters* (*Duiwai baodao cankao*)[65] in 1981 was an important indication of the new direction in *waishi* that Deng and his associates ascribed to. This restricted access, *neibu*, journal, published by Xinhua News Service, became a channel to publish articles by experienced *waishi* cadres coming from a wide range of organizations. This was useful to educate the generations of Chinese who had grown up after 1949 and had experienced little contact with outsiders, especially Western businesspeople, other than as targets of political hate and derision. The new journal also provided an important forum for theorizing on and for promoting practical training on issues related to dealing with foreigners. In the early days of the reform era, advice to cadres found in the journal's pages appears quite "revisionist," if one considers the line of only a few years before. Still, as Lenin's authoritative article on left-wing communism had argued, for Marxists not to be able to shift political lines according to circumstances was "infantile."[66] The CCP obviously took such dictums to heart.

One aspect had not changed at all however; the journal articles still reflected a strong sense of the foreigner as the Other. According to this understanding, foreigners were alien and different from Chinese people, who needed to be instructed on how to deal with them. The phrase "treat insiders and outsiders differently," *neiwai you bie* (here referring to the political divide between foreigners and Chinese) featured prominently in *waishi* literature of the 1980s. Although China was opening up to the West, this did not mean that the old divisions between foreigners and Chinese could be ignored. As one cadre admonished his readers, "don't forget, foreigners are not Chinese."[67] At the same time, the principle "be strict internally, relaxed on the outside," *nei jin wai song*, was also stressed when dealing with foreigners in the new era, meaning that foreigners should not be made to feel overly aware of the potential restrictions and controls on their presence in China or dealings with Chinese officials.[68]

Though the goals of China's *waishi* activities changed somewhat from the Mao to the Deng period, as the authors of innumerable articles in the journal pointed out, there was continuity in the methodology. Noticeable was a complete omission of any mention of the *Soviet* influence on China's *waishi* activities. Along with almost everything else in the PRC since the Sino-Soviet split, China's *waishi* system and activities were presented as a uniquely Chinese, indigenous response to the outside world. Indeed, as the reforms deepened throughout the 1980s, phrases from the Confucian classics such as "*you peng zi yuanfang lai, bu yi le hu*"[69] (Is it not delightful to have friends coming from afar!) were commonly used in *waishi* manuals to stress the "Chineseness" of Chinese-style foreign affairs in the post-Cultural Revolution period. Having passed through a period of what was euphemistically and diplomatically described as "leftism"—in other words the Mao era—the true Chinese Self was now revealed as being Confucianist, or rather State-Confucianist, after all. It was a highly ironic turnaround, but one which *waishi* publications of the post-Mao period were careful to ignore. Increasingly throughout the 1980s, the official construction of the Chinese Self began to embrace Orientalist popular notions of Chineseness that earlier generations of Chinese revolutionaries, including some that were still alive in this period, had once emphatically rejected.

As economic reform spread throughout China and contact between Chinese and foreigners increased in the form of foreign investment, trade, educational exchanges, and tourism, an increasing number of organizations and enterprises needed to know the basics of managing foreigners. From the mid-1980s as the emphasis in foreign affairs moved to localized activities rather than high-level high-profile visits conducted from Beijing, individual provinces with a large *waishi* workload were encouraged to expand their operations to include their own monthly journal. These regional journals introduced to the ever-growing *waishi* corps the basics of handling foreigners, Chinese laws and regulations related to foreigners, information on foreign customs and society, policy on Chinese citizens going abroad to study or work, and the latest regulations or guidelines on *waishi* work itself. The journals' contents were virtually indistinguishable from that of the Beijing-published *Report on Foreign Affairs Matters*, apart from local information or *waishi* experience.

Foreign Propaganda with Chinese Characteristics

In the 1980s, foreign propaganda was regarded as an integral part of China's economic modernization process. Its task was to gain the "understanding and friendship of the people of various countries, in order to create international conditions beneficial to the implementation of China's Four Modernizations."[70] In 1980, the importance of foreign propaganda designed for the needs of the reform period was recognized with the formation of a Foreign Propaganda Group, *duiwai xuanchuan xiaozu*, within the CCP Central Committee bureaucracy. This group was charged with formulating policy guidelines and strategies for promoting China to the outside world; these guidelines in turn were passed on to the Propaganda Department.[71] In an early directive, the Foreign Propaganda Group recommended the rapid expansion and modernization of foreign propaganda activities.[72] After a national meeting of local propaganda bureaus in 1982, each area in China was instructed to focus on localized propaganda in order to encourage foreign investment and tourism to their areas.[73]

The propaganda of the 1980s was markedly different in nature from that of the Mao era. Instead of paeans to Mao Zedong or exhortations in support of world revolution, foreign propaganda cadres were told they must de-emphasize the "political content" (meaning the Marxist-Leninist aspects) of their work and stress that China was a democratic country with a proper legal system.[74] Officials in the reform era stressed the creation of "foreign propaganda with Chinese characteristics," *you Zhongguo tese de duiwai xuanchuan.*[75] This was a euphemistic term for moving away from Maoist propaganda with its discussions of world revolution and class struggle. The emphasis on the "Chineseness" of the new-style propaganda was part of the process of legitimating the great changes China was going through. Even so, in the reform period the government published summaries of *waishi* and propaganda material from earlier periods of CCP rule as instructive reading for the new generation of *waishi* cadres. All such materials passed over the Cultural Revolution decade from 1966-1976, or at best devoted only a paragraph describing it as a "mistake." This was an implicit criticism of a period when the PRC also attempted to reach out to the world with a high-output propaganda effort, but portrayed itself as a center of world revolution rather than of economic investment.

A common complaint among those engaged in *waishi* work in this period was that for a long time, due to "the pernicious influence of Lin Biao and the Gang of Four,"[76] foreign propaganda had been boring, and hence, ineffectual. Beginning in 1980, the new goal of propagandists was to create material that would overcome foreign suspicions about China, material that would be written to suit foreign tastes. This was a dramatic shift from past practice, where the notion of creating propaganda to suit foreign tastes was formerly criticized as "pandering to capitalists."[77] A writer in 1984 argued that, "This requires knowledge of the audience's special characteristics, doubts and opinions. Only by 'knowing the enemy and knowing oneself,' only by 'adjusting the medicine to the illness' can we increase the effectiveness of propaganda."[78] In a speech published in *Report on Foreign Affairs Matters* in 1983, senior propaganda chief Zhu Muzhi bluntly informed *waishi* cadres that from now on when talking about new China, they must stop all their "boasting and verbiage" about the "so-called world revolution," and they must, "stop stuffing Socialism! Communism! And other revolutionary stuff down [foreigners'] throats [*sic*]!" In this way Zhu argued, other countries could better understand China.[79] Such a radical about-turn in China's foreign propaganda style took some explaining to often skeptical and cynical foreign audiences. To overcome the awkwardness of the sudden change in line, in the early and mid-1980s *waishi* officials were provided with model answers on difficult questions foreigners might ask such as "Do you still believe in communism?"[80] Writers of propaganda for foreign audiences were also told to drop pejorative descriptions of terms such as humanitarian and humanism, which in the Mao era had always been prefaced with "reactionary" or "so-called."[81]

Deng Xiaoping, in an earlier speech also published in *Report on Foreign Affairs Matters*, told a group of foreign visitors that China welcomed foreign investment and trade, and that it wanted foreign help to set up factories and improve technology.[82] He explained to them that the Cultural Revolution was wrong, as was the Red Guard theory "rebellion is justified," *zaofan you li*, and informed them that China was now moving towards opening up, *kaifang*, and freedom, *ziyou*. Publishing the speech in the journal was a means to instruct foreign affairs workers on the new line, and by addressing his talk to foreigners, Deng hoped that the outside world would get the message too.

Perceptions about China after the Cultural Revolution took some time to change in the West. A single speech from China's new leader would not be enough to convince foreign investors that the country was a safe place to invest their money. In the early 1980s, senior officials focused on issues such as how to explain to foreigners why the Cultural Revolution was incorrect and how to deal with other questions of concern to them, such as the situation of "minority" peoples, religious freedom, and human rights in Tibet. In the 1980s the five targets of foreign propaganda (other than journalists) within China were identified as: 1) embassy officials and diplomats, 2) tourists and people visiting relatives, 3) teachers, scholars, and students, 4) engineers and technicians, 5) foreign business people.[83] These groups were regarded as both prime recipients and prime passers-on of CCP propaganda.[84] This followed the CCP's tried-and-true methodology of "using foreign strength to propagandize for China," *liyong waili wei wo xuanchuan*.[85] Government organizations were instructed to diversify their approach in dealing with foreigners according to their category. For example, teachers were to have seminars organized, students were to be taken on cultural activities, tourists would be propagandized through their tour commentaries, and reporters through question and answer sessions—with the information given out of a higher quality than that given to other foreign groups.[86]

Following the same principle, in addition to assisting writers and journalists, the government also encouraged joint-venture projects with foreign television, radio, and film groups. The worldwide success of Bertolino Bertolucci's 1987 film *The Last Emperor* was frequently cited as an example of the effectiveness of such collaboration. A further long-term propaganda strategy for using foreign strength was the decision to promote the study of Chinese language internationally. Proponents of this strategy argued that foreigners who invested time and effort into learning Chinese language were likely to "establish normal, long-lasting relationships with [China] and they will develop a special feeling, *ganqing* [towards China]. This will be very useful in the long run."[87] As a result, a steadily increasing number of Chinese universities were allowed to open their doors to privately funded foreign students, as well as the already existing small numbers of government-funded foreign students. In this way these universities were both able to gain access to foreign exchange and perform a useful political role.

At the same time as utilizing foreign strength for China's propaganda work, Chinese citizens who had contact with foreigners, whether those directly involved in *waishi*, ordinary personnel, or those traveling abroad, were also supposed to engage in China's propaganda work on foreigners. A 1980 directive instructed:

> The Foreign Propaganda Group and relevant departments should organize forces to compile a series of propaganda materials including viewpoints and policy on important national and international topics [that would be] suitable for people in all ranges of occupations to explain issues to foreigners.[88]

Propagandists in the 1980s were advised to use political slogans sparingly, and if they had to use them at all, explain them in terms that foreigners could understand. For example the phrase *jingshen wenming* was to be explained as "intellectual and moral development," a more palatable euphemism than the direct translation "spiritual civilization" (though this advice seems to have been universally ignored).[89] They were also told to absorb techniques from the West.[90] From the mid-1980s, in English and other foreign languages, the more neutral phrase "public relations" was used in preference to "propaganda" to describe the government's publicity and information activities. This was regarded as a term both more acceptable to foreigners in general, as well as being more acceptable to the foreign friends China now most wanted to attract: senior politicians and business people.[91] It was also an indication of the overlap between political and economic goals in the new era. Increasingly, China began to mimic many Western-style approaches and organizational structures while maintaining the same basic methodology of *waishi*.

After 1980, every province and administrative area in China formed its own foreign propaganda unit; previously this had been done from Beijing. More than forty government departments and organizations established their own official media spokespersons, where before there was none. (The most important media event was the Foreign Ministry's weekly press conference, which became a major forum for presenting the PRC's perspective on global events.) The number of officials involved in foreign propaganda work at both the central and local level increased considerably, and foreign propaganda news bureaus, broadcasting, films, television, and publishing all underwent major restructuring and modernization. Before 1980 China published only a handful of magazines for foreign readers; in the 1980s over twenty new titles were added. In 1981 the PRC began publishing an English newspaper, soon to become ubiquitous in China, *China Daily*, targeted at foreign residents as well as an edition of *Renmin Ribao* for overseas Chinese readers. More than ever before, reports from China's own news service, the New China News Agency, *Xinhua*, were broadcast worldwide and picked up by other news organizations. The numbers of Sino-foreign cultural exchange activities increased considerably, as did books published for foreign readers.[92] Sino-foreign cultural exchanges were a popular and benign way of improving China's international image. However PRC materials for foreigners in the 1980s appeared dated and out of step with the non-ideological times. Though economic reform was changing China, the political system had not changed, and this was obvious in the heavy-handed rhetoric of many publications from the Foreign Language Press of this period.

"Bridge Builders": Foreign Friends in the 1980s

When China's reform and opening up policies began, foreign friends like Rewi Alley and George Hatem continued to be useful. Hatem met privately with Jimmy Carter and Ronald Reagan when they visited China. On his first visit to China in 1978, Senator Edward Kennedy visited Hatem in hospital. Rewi Alley reported, "Ma [Hatem] gave a very excellent résumé of medical work in China since 1936. Masterly."[93] Alley met with Canada's Pierre Trudeau; New Zealand's Robert Muldoon (who refused to be photographed with him);[94] and many other important and not so important figures. The friendship language of the late 1970s and 1980s changed to reflect the new role of the foreign friend in China. Long-standing friends such as Alley and Hatem were now described as "bridge builders" and "friendship ambassadors," symbolizing the relations China sought with their respective countries—amicable, equal, and peaceful. The friends were to be a means to improve state-to-state relations, as well as working on people's diplomacy. After 1978, all the resident foreign friends became pro-Deng and his reforms (at least publicly), with few exceptions.

Still, in private many of the resident foreigners were frequently uncomfortable with the new China that developed out of the reforms. Though they tried to make their concerns known, they frequently found themselves rebuffed or ignored. In 1978, in response to her criticism that the Beijing Hotel and other hotels for foreigners were becoming more capitalistic, senior party leader Wang Zhen defiantly told Joan Hinton, "Foreigners have got money, so why shouldn't we get some of it?!"[95] Beginning in the late 1970s there was a dramatic change within the party in the attitude towards foreigners, as Beijing turned its focus from revolutionary change to seeking out foreign capital and technology. This led to a corresponding change in attitudes to China's old friends, now regarded disparagingly as "leftists." As the economic changes progressed, like most Chinese citizens, the old friends' salaries failed to keep pace with inflation and they lost many of the perks they had once had. Meanwhile foreign correspondents and business people began to be treated comparatively well. Leftist foreign friends felt neglected, on the outer of decision making. Frank Coe, based in the International Liaison Department, formerly regarded by other foreigners as an "insider," was ignored. Julian Schuman, who had worked periodically in China since the late 1940s, was so hurt about the change in treatment that he used to burst into tears when he talked about it.[96] Rewi Alley's death in 1987 is even rumored to have been caused by an apoplectic fit brought on as a result of his anger over being asked to pay for a cup of tea in a Beijing hotel with Foreign Exchange Certificates (F.E.C.), the special currency for foreigners introduced in 1980.[97]

Apart from the formal apologies of 1973 and 1978, there was also some attempt at material compensation for those foreigners who had suffered under the worst excesses of the Maoist years. Eva Xiao had been arrested in June 1967, along with her husband, Xiao San, a poet and former schoolmate of Mao Zedong. She was held in solitary confinement for seven years and was kept under semi-house arrest until 1979. In 1980 she was assigned a large apartment in Muxidi, under the control of the State Council. Many others who were imprisoned during the Cultural Revolution were also assigned apartments there. The New China News Service, which had briefly employed Xiao in the 1950s, took her back on the payroll, became the work unit responsible for her, and gave her a comfortable pension and medical benefits.[98] Some of the other friends were sent on all-expenses-paid trips back home; in the case of Rewi Alley, too old and sick to travel, his family in New Zealand was invited to China to stay with him. The aging friends were also assured of high-quality medical care when they fell ill. American Bob Winter, who had also suffered badly in the Cultural Revolution years, was given the best possible treatment when he went into hospital for hip surgery. The U.S. embassy seemed to compete with the Chinese in according him special treatment.[99] U.S. embassy officials visited him every week during his hospital stay, though in the 1950s the U.S. government had taken away his passport. Winter's passport was reinstated after the United States formally recognized the PRC in 1979. A further gesture of reconciliation was the invitation to a select group of foreign friends with Chinese citizenship to participate in the Chinese People's Political Consultative Conference (CPPCC), a united front rubber-stamp political organization. The foreigners' presence was singled out in television coverage at CPPCC meetings.

Nevertheless, in the new era, the foreign friends whom China coveted were clearly those with money or with influence such as U.S. political figures Alexander Haig, Henry Kissinger, Edward Kennedy, George Bush, British foreign policy adviser Percy Cradock, and former British prime minister Edward Heath (the latter two useful for presenting the Chinese view on the question of Hong Kong to the British government). From the early 1970s on, much work was done to cultivate the support of such individuals.[100] From 1978 on, in addition to increasing numbers of foreign experts, China welcomed large numbers of foreigners from across the political spectrum. In the years after 1949 the government had mainly encouraged leftists who came to China as pilgrims, or after the Sino-

Soviet split had determined relationships on the basis of the opposite party's attitude toward the Soviet Union. In the Deng era the policy was to welcome as a
foreign friend anyone who was influential and might help China in some way.[101]
After 1978 as *waishi* work expanded, the work of the Friendship Association
"entered a new phase."[102] The organization became more active than ever before
with hosting foreign delegations. It was hoped that the increasing numbers of
foreign visitors, no longer selected by political criteria, would return home to
become "friendship with China activists" creating a fifth column of pro-China
supporters.

Under the new system, former enemies were especially welcome, one suspects, if they had connections with the U.S. military, big business, or politics. A
classic example was John Downey, a CIA pilot imprisoned in China from 1952-
1973 after his plane crashed on Chinese soil. Downey was finally released after
the Nixon visit to China. During his twenty-year imprisonment he was allowed
four visits from his mother and taken on trips around Beijing. He appears to
have left China with a good impression. Downey revisited the PRC in 1983;
Wang Bingnan, president of the Friendship Association, which hosted his stay
told him, "Yesterday you were my enemy, today you are my honored guest."[103]

In a similar vein, Sidney Rittenberg, who had been imprisoned for more
than ten years for his activities in the Cultural Revolution, in the 1980s, after
leaving China for a new life in the United States, reinvented himself as a highly
successful broker of U.S.-China trade and investment. Rittenberg was able to
draw on his contacts (and those of his wife) with senior government officials in
China built up from his years as a political insider. These contacts in turn enabled him to attract high prestige clients such as Levi Strauss, ARCO, Digital
Equipment, Polaroid, Campbell, ABC's Mike Wallace, and television evangelist
Billy Graham, which were highly valued by his Chinese contacts.[104] A (1993)
China Daily review of Rittenberg's biography praised him as a "self-denying
revolutionary," praise that was regarded as "preposterous" and "ironic" by foreign friends who remained behind in China.[105] What the "leftist" foreign friends
sometimes found hard to accept was that under Deng, and later Jiang Zemin,
practical assistance or psychological support for the new economic and political
goals of the new era—symbolized by the Four Cardinal Principles and the Four
Modernizations—took precedence over political correctness.

Former U.S. Dixie Mission participants and other U.S. soldiers based in
China during World War II were also suddenly treated as friends again. In the
early 1980s, government propaganda promoted the idea that Chinese people
"loved" them for their contribution to China's fight against the Japanese, stressing that the Chinese and Americans had cooperated in the 1940s, therefore im-
plying they could do so again in the future.[106] There was of course no mention
that the United States was mostly involved in supporting the Nationalist government's war effort, or that even in the brief period of CCP-U.S. cooperation
from 1944-1945 there existed a high level of mistrust and caution on both sides.
This propaganda was used to strengthen the notion that because the Chinese and

United States were allies in the war, they had a long friendship, and hence should be friends in the 1980s, in particular, eliding the experience of the civil war, the Korean War, and the Vietnam War. The claim of the long-standing friendship between the Chinese and American peoples also strengthened the legitimacy of CCP rule in China. Though they had not been the government at this time, to assert that the United States and China were allies implied that the CCP represented China then too, and that the PRC was the legitimate successor to the Republic of China. Chinese propaganda on the United States in the 1980s differed markedly from that in the early years of CCP rule, with its deliberate campaigns to promote hostility toward the United States.

In 1985, the Chinese government organized a tour for American journalists who had reported favorably on the CCP in the 1940s. They were treated to a three-week all-expenses-paid trip, which included a long session in the Great Hall of the People with Deng Xiaoping, a reception in their honor at the same place, meetings with top officials, trips by chartered plane to Yan'an, Xi'an, Chongqing, and a cruise down the Yangzi River. To Peter Rand, whose father was one of the "old China hand" journalists and who took part in the trip on his dead father's behalf, "The trip was a gesture, finally of thanks, and a way of healing some old wounds."[107] But from the Chinese perspective, the trip was also an attempt to make use of old contacts to garner favorable publicity for Deng's China.[108] Former journalist at Chongqing in the 1940s Hugh Deane also participated in the tour. His view was a little less idealistic than Rand's:

> The Chinese were hoping they'd get some favorable writing about China from these veteran correspondents. But they didn't get very much because most of these people were very conservative to begin with. They spent a lot of money on it . . . I sat next to Deng Xiaoping and Deng Liqun at the Great Hall of the People . . . we interviewed him . . . he trotted out all the truisms.[109]

From the late 1970s, the government began to publish books and articles about "friendly personages," foreigners who had assisted the Chinese revolution in some way. These foreigners were not only those who were ideologically sympathetic to Chinese communism, they encompassed ordinary individuals who had stayed on in China for personal reasons. Swiss-born missionary Rudolph Alfred Bosshardt, who had been kidnapped and held for ransom by a section of the Red Army during the Long March and later was forced out of China along with other foreign missionaries in the early 1950s, was rediscovered as an "old friend" under this new policy. In 1984 he was featured in a wildly inaccurate article in *Renmin Ribao* on his "participation" in the Long March and his "assistance" to the Red Army forces.[110] According to Xiao Ke, this entailed helping him read a French-language map of Guizhou. There was no mention of the other assistance he gave in the form of a massive ransom paid out by the China Inland Mission to the Red Army for Bosshardt's release or his role as a target in anti-imperialist propaganda campaigns. Following on from this article, Bosshardt featured in numerous newspaper articles and television programs commemorating the Long

March where he was described as the "second" foreigner to go on the march (after Otto Braun).

In addition to this sort of writing, from 1979 on, virtually every prominent figure in China's cast of old friends either wrote an autobiography or had an officially approved and assisted biography written about them.[111] Whether by Chinese or non-Chinese authors, these biographical accounts tended to be what the authorities would call "friendly," *youhao*, that is, noncritical, not to say insipid. This outpouring of biographic material was useful both in internal, *duinei*, and external, *duiwai*, propaganda. The old friends of China were part of the idealized revolutionary past, the myth that established the legitimacy of the regime and linked it with the present day. Material on nonpolitical foreigners who had lived in China demonstrated the positive contribution many foreigners had made to China's modernization. The books and other published materials were part of the government's efforts to reeducate the Chinese population, to get them used to the new economic policies after twenty years of telling them that the West was evil, and to accustom them to accepting a wide range of foreigners in China, not just revolutionaries and Maoists. They were also aimed at guiding and encouraging a new generation of sympathetic foreigners, who would assist China's modernization.

A further method by which more foreigners were encouraged to become well disposed to the goals of the CCP government in the 1980s was through the promotion of even more numbers of prominent individuals to the status of "friends of China." Foreign friend was not, however, a title to be used lightly, nor did reform and opening up mean that the government had relaxed its policy on managing foreigners. Concerned at misunderstandings that had arisen in China on such points, a 1985 *waishi* handbook warned:

> Overcome the erroneous tendency of failing to draw a clear line and relaxing vigilance: When propagandizing to foreigners we must act in accordance with our nation's foreign policy of acting independently and maintaining the initiative, we should defend our nation's self-respect and treat people as equals. While opposing blind xenophobia, we should also oppose worship of foreign things and toadying to foreigners, we must be warm and polite, but we must not act obsequiously. We must stop putting foreigners on a pedestal and we must also stop discriminating against black people. Foreigners who come to China should, as a rule, be referred to by their own status, we can not just call them all without distinction "foreign friends," "international friends," and "foreign guests," regardless of what their status or attitude to us is. This sort of excessive usage can easily lead to our people feeling inferior and have the disastrous effect of slackening the vigilance we should maintain . . . We must both trust that most foreigners and Overseas Chinese, Hong Kong, Macau and Taiwanese compatriots are good people, while at the same time realizing that a small minority of agents and bad people will sneak in. We must raise vigilance, and establish an awareness of enemy activity.[112]

In the post-Mao period there were to be no particular criteria on who could be a friend of China, as long as they followed the Chinese government's line on crucial issues such as the status of Taiwan and Tibet and kept away from Chinese dissidents. The new, new China of the reform period was very appealing to many foreigners. In the 1980s, membership of China Friendship Societies increased dramatically in the Western world.[113] China also established numerous Friendship City and Friendship State relationships, mostly with Western countries. Officials of the Friendship Association justified the Friendship Cities program in the following terms, "The development of friendship city relationships helps attract foreign capital and promote Chinese investments in other countries, mostly in the form of joint ventures."[114]

On the whole, most Chinese people seemed to welcome the change in policies toward the outside world. In fact popular enthusiasm for contact with the outside world became so strong in the 1980s that government publications began to warn of the tendency to adulate the West at the expense of China. In addition to anxieties about an internalized racism resulting in a decline in patriotism, there was also some concern that the focus on Western countries for the purposes of the reform and opening up policies was leading to racism and chauvinism toward Third World nations. *Waishi* publications strongly criticized the tendency "to look down on black people" while "worshipping white people and feeling inferior to them."[115] As always, one of the important tasks of the *waishi* system was to balance and delineate the relations between Chinese citizens and foreigners, avoiding both the extremes of foreign adulation and xenophobia.

"Make Friends with Everyone": People's Diplomacy in the 1980s

Although by the late 1970s the PRC had established diplomatic relations with most nations, rather than declining in importance, during the 1980s, people's diplomacy activities actually increased. Like other senior leaders before him, Deng Xiaoping recognized the value of people-to-people relations, even under the new conditions of the reform period. Indeed, *waishi* historians in China even argue that the policies of the Deng Xiaoping era have advanced China's distinctive foreign relations style beyond their original parameters toward a concept of "total diplomacy," *zongti waijiao*.[116] "Total diplomacy" means that all possible channels will be used to facilitate inter-national exchanges and interaction, without the ideological restraints on some interactions that had inhibited earlier eras. This new approach was summed up by Deng Xiaoping's adage to *waishi* workers in the era of reform and opening up, "Have exchanges with everyone, make friends with everyone," *tong shei dou laiwang, tong shei dou jiao pengyou*.[117] Nevertheless, despite the opening up and diversifying of inter-national relations, as before all *waishi* activities were ultimately still tightly controlled and overseen by central authorities.

In the Mao era, most people's diplomacy was channeled through the Chinese People's Association for Friendship with Foreign Countries, *Zhongguo renmin duiwai youhao xiehui*, and other organizations such as the CCP International Liaison Department or the Peace Committee. In the 1980s a plethora of new groups operated. Some of them appeared to duplicate each other's functions;[118] others focused on particular tasks such as publishing biographies of foreign friends. The China Association for International Friendly Contact, *Zhongguo guoji youhao lianluohui*, a parallel association to the Friendship Association was set up in 1984. It is a front organization for the International Liaison Department of the PLA General Political Department.[119] This organization provides political and economic information for the Political Department as well as conducting people's diplomacy on similar lines to the Friendship Association. In the 1980s and 1990s it had close links to Deng Xiaoping. According to senior cadres of this organization, the difference between themselves and the Friendship Association (in terms of their people's diplomacy activities) was that "rightists, leftists, we see them all." In contrast, they said, in the 1980s the Friendship Association continued to focus on "friendly personages," meaning those who the CCP now (privately) called "foreign leftists."[120] One important function of the China Association for International Friendly Contact was to take over host duties from the Foreign Ministry when leaders of countries that did not have diplomatic relations with China came to visit.[121]

Rather than declining, as might be expected, the public activities of the CCP International Liaison Department expanded in the Deng era. Instead of being restricted to pro-China communist parties, the bureau's open activities began to include forging links with any foreign political party that was willing to meet with it. These links were slow to get started, but throughout the 1980s and even more so after the end of the Cold War, the International Liaison Department expanded its international relations significantly with parties all over the political spectrum.[122]

Recognizing the spread of and increasing influence globally of NGOs (nongovernmental organizations), the Chinese government also created a range of equivalent front organizations in the 1980s such as the Centre for Peace and Development Studies, *Fazhan yu heping yanjiu zhongxin*, and the Centre for Religious Research on China, *Zhongguo zongjiao yanjiu zhongxin*. These organizations were nominally nongovernmental, *feizhengfu zuzhi*, though from their organizational structure and funding, they were clearly organs of party and government policy. Many of these organizations existed in name alone, forming part of another foreign affairs organization under the well-established *waishi* practice of having one office with two (or more) nameplates. Cadres in many of these new organizations were given academic titles to enable them to attend international academic forums, though their qualifications and "research" were often questionable. At the same time as creating its own front NGOs, the Chinese government firmly restrained the spread of genuinely nongovernmental organizations in China. Beijing also increased its participation in intergovernmental organizations, going from involvement in a mere handful before 1978, to membership of 500 in 1983.[123] Membership continued to grow throughout the 1980s.[124] The government clearly saw this as a means to further extend China's international influence. Both international NGO and intergovernmental organization meetings were utilized to promote China's views on issues such as human rights and to isolate Taiwan in the international community. Considerable effort was put into building alliances with Third World countries on the broad issues of opposition to imposed "Western notions" of human rights and the importance of respect for national sovereignty. China received other significant benefits from its membership in such organizations. A remarkable indication of the pragmatism of the new era was the move from 1981 onward to begin accepting foreign aid for disaster relief and economic development through various international aid organizations and soon after, directly from foreign governments.[125] In the same period China's own foreign aid program, whether to foreign insurgents or the countries of the Third World, was reduced considerably.

By the late 1980s the numbers of organizations involved in foreign affairs had proliferated to almost unmanageable levels. Though policies varied somewhat in different aspects of *waishi*, such as diplomacy, technology transfer, intelligence, and foreign propaganda, they were all guided by the principles of reform and opening up, which stressed the economy and the modernization of China over ideological goals. In 1985, the State Council Foreign Affairs Office, *Guowuyuan waishi bangongshi*, took over responsibility for coordinating *waishi* policies from the CCP Central Committee Secretariat. In the same year, Premier Zhao Ziyang's influence in *waishi* decision making strengthened, as he became head of the CCP Central Committee Foreign Affairs Leading Group.[126] Zhao's influence was shown in the expanding numbers of advisory bodies or think tanks involved in researching *waishi* activities, which came to overshadow the traditional bureaucratic structures for a period.[127]

Opening the Window without Letting the Flies and Mosquitoes In[128]

Reflecting the Chinese government's attempt to limit the negative effects of opening up China to the outside world in the 1980s, rather than declining in the era of reform and opening up, control of the foreign presence in China actually increased. Following the principle of being "relaxed on the outside, strict on the inside" these controls were not always apparent to the increasing numbers of foreigners who began to flood into China during the 1980s.

Spreading knowledge about how to interact with foreigners in the reform era was necessary in order to create a disciplined workforce capable of serving the needs of the international investors China now hoped to attract. A 1984 directive from the CCP Central Committee and the State Council ordered that all those whose occupations were likely to bring them into close contact with outsiders without being *waishi* personnel as such, for example customs officials, border police, personnel in clinics and hospitals for foreigners, airline staff, hotels, restaurants, shops, and theaters targeted at foreigners and so on, were to be given detailed instructions on the limits of Sino-foreign interaction in the new era. For ordinary Chinese citizens, both education on nationalism/patriotism, *aiguozhuyi*, and internationalism, *guojizhuyi*, was to be stepped up.[129] According to foreign propaganda expert Zhu Muzhi, "the masses will not necessarily all be directly having contact with and talking to foreigners, but every person's actions can have a foreign propaganda purpose. From this point of view it is necessary to conduct some education among them."[130]

The regulations controlling Sino-foreign contact had certainly become considerably less restricting than they had been in the previous thirty years—but this was all in the interest of doing more effective *waishi* work and attaining China's goal of utilizing foreign investment and technology to modernize China. By no means did it mean a slackening of discipline. From 1979, also toward the goal of increasing Sino-foreign exchanges, Chinese citizens studying foreign languages were officially permitted to listen to foreign shortwave broadcasts such as the Voice of America and NHK (though in politically sensitive times broadcasts would be jammed by the authorities).[131] During periodic political campaigns against the excessive influence of political liberalization throughout the 1980s, *waishi* controls tightened. In 1983, during the campaign against bourgeois liberalization, the government sent out a directive that all foreign articles or other publications from foreign countries had to be submitted to the Propaganda Department for approval before being translated and published in China. It was forbidden to directly publish materials without approval. This directive was particularly concerned with foreign publications in the arts which were "creating a bad impression" among the Chinese reading public.[132] In 1988, when the Republic of China eased restrictions on mainland residents visiting family in Taiwan, Chinese citizens with Taiwanese relatives were given detailed instructions preparing them for such visits including the admonishment "don't tell people how poor you are or speak of your hardships, don't demean yourself."[133]

Foreign tourism expanded dramatically in the reform period and became an important source of foreign exchange. In the interests of encouraging more tourists, more and more areas of China were opened up to foreigners. Each new "open area" established local foreign affairs offices within various government bodies that would have contact with or responsibility for dealing with foreigners. In a 1978 meeting with cadres from the China Travel Service, senior leader Chen Yun discussed the reasons for maintaining strict though subtle controls on foreign visitors, these were: fear of spies, fear that Chinese people would be corrupted by foreigners, and fear that foreigners would realize how backward China is. At the same time he maintained that such problems were insignificant compared to the benefits to be gained from opening up China to foreign tourists.[134]

As part of the attempts to reform China's international image away from the antiforeignism of the Mao era, the government worked hard to convince foreigners that they were welcome and safe there. Crimes against foreigners were punished much more severely than those committed against Chinese citizens. The Public Security Bureau had specially trained officers who were called in when there was a crime involving foreigners. Even in death, foreigners were to receive special treatment. The Ministry of Public Security had to be notified in the event of a foreigner dying in China, and their passport and other identification documents handed in.[135] As the number of foreigners marrying Chinese citizens increased, the Ministry of Civil Administration opened suboffices in cities with large foreign populations dealing only with marriages between foreigners and Chinese. Numerous directives informed Chinese officials that such marriages were no longer prohibited, but if a Chinese person wished to leave the country to marry a foreigner outside China, both the foreigner and the Chinese citizen were to be subject to a police investigation.[136] Chinese citizens in some occupations, such as those who worked for the military, were prohibited from marrying foreigners.

The new influx of foreigners into China was required by law to live in foreigners-only accommodation, such as foreigners' hotels, *shewai binguan*, foreign students' dorms, *liuxuesheng sushe*, foreign experts' buildings, *waiguo zhuanjia lou*, and diplomatic quarters, *waijiao gongyu*, and they were required to register at these places of residence. Most residential quarters for foreigners had at least one member of staff who also covered security responsibilities. When necessary, this person spied on foreign residents, reporting to more senior public security personnel. Chinese workers in the specially designated compounds for foreigners and foreign journalists were provided by the Ministry of Foreign Affairs Diplomatic Services Bureau who reported on the daily activities of the foreigners they worked for. Eavesdropping on their home and work telephones was routine. All visitors to foreign residences were required to register at the building entrance and hand in their ID card.

In addition to foreigners registering at their normal place of residence, section 30 of the 1988 Administrative Law of the Entry and Exit of Foreigners stipulated,

> If foreigners stay in the residences of Chinese citizens in cities and towns, within 24 hours of their arrival they, or the person they are staying with, must take their passport, foreign resident's pass and the residence card of the person they are staying with and report with these to the local public security authorities, filling out a temporary residence registration form. Foreigners who stay with people living in the countryside, must report within 72 hours to the nearest police station or household registration office.[137]

Not only did foreigners need to register when they stayed with Chinese people or in hotels or other accommodation, if they stayed with other foreigners their movements also had to be accounted for:

> Foreigners in China who stay with foreign organizations or in other foreigners' homes, within 24 hours of their arrival, the organization they are staying with, the person they are staying with or the individual themselves must take their passport or residence permit to report to the local public security bureau. Foreigners who are staying in a moving vehicle and who are stopping over temporarily must report to the local Public Security Bureau within 24 hours.[138]

Though such regulations were taken quite seriously in the late 1970s and early 1980s, as the economic and political reforms of the new era impacted on society there was a gradual weakening of vigilance. By the late 1980s the increasing numbers of low-budget foreign travelers in the PRC broke through the restrictions on foreigners staying in foreigner-only hotels and it even became possible in some of the larger cities for foreigners to illicitly rent Chinese housing.

In the early years of economic reform, a further means to control foreign residents and visitors' movements within China was the highly unpopular system of a separate currency for foreigners, F.E.C., *waihui quan*, which had to be bought with foreign currency. This was an attempt to restrict foreigners to the limited number of hotels, tourist shops, and transportation offices that accepted F.E.C. As these locations often charged higher prices than those that accepted Chinese *yuan*, it was also a means to make foreigners spend more foreign currency while in China. In fact, however, a thriving foreign exchange black market sprang up to cope with foreigners' need for *renminbi* and Chinese citizens' desire for foreign dollars. In addition to the requirement to pay for goods in F.E.C., foreigners were also forced to pay almost double the cost of Chinese citizens for travel and accommodation. Only foreign experts and government-sponsored foreign students were issued "white cards," *bai ka*, partially exempting them from this system.

From the late 1970s onward, the number of foreign journalists based in China increased considerably. New regulations to control the activities of foreign journalists were established in 1981.[139] Their most striking feature was the requirement that journalists apply to the local foreign affairs office to obtain permission for every interview they conducted with Chinese citizens. Nevertheless, even in the earliest days of the reform period, this requirement was frequently ignored, except on occasions when officials felt a journalist had pushed the boundaries too far. Foreign journalists were, overall, handled carefully after 1979. Although they often published different views from those of the Chinese government, it was believed they could still be used to promote the government's opinions in their reports.[140] Beginning in 1980, officials were instructed to "be brave about meeting with them," "hold regular press conferences with them," and "relax the rules a bit when they are visiting areas outside Beijing."[141] As had been the custom in the Mao era, officials were instructed to investigate foreign reporters' political viewpoint, their attitude toward China, previous work experience, and their employing news service's political stance before allowing them to meet with senior Chinese leaders.[142] In 1988, new regulations were established on the control of foreign journalists and foreign news services in China, which strengthened the existing system without departing markedly from it.[143]

In the Mao era, foreigners doing research on China found it virtually impossible to conduct research in country, whether on contemporary or historical themes. Only in special cases and under carefully controlled conditions, was it possible to conduct research in this period. Beginning in 1978, foreign researchers, especially those engaged in social science research, were both appreciated for their potential as pro-China propagandists[144] and mistrusted for their predisposition to investigate taboo topics. The government understood this was a necessary quid pro quo for sending thousands of Chinese students to study abroad in the reform period, especially in the United States.

In contrast to social scientists, foreign specialists on science and technology were considered much less problematic and gaining access to their knowledge was regarded as an essential task of those involved in the management of foreign visitors. In 1979, Chinese scientists were instructed to make friends with foreign scientists. Toward the goal of increasing Sino-foreign scientific exchanges or more pertinently, obtaining foreign research findings, they were now permitted to meet with foreigners without the need to have another Chinese staff member present. They were also allowed to meet with foreigners in a private capacity, to give and receive gifts, and, as long as their work did not touch on secret topics, to send their research papers overseas.[145]

From the earliest days of the reform era the government made a special effort to attract a new generation of foreign talent, *wai zhili*, foreign experts who would help China develop its economy and catch up technologically.[146] *Waishi* personnel were under special instructions to focus attention on hospitality to these foreign experts in order to gain what "money could not buy": skills and insider knowledge that often was not part of the original contract. A cadre experienced in *waishi* work in a certain oil company reported how his work unit worked on their foreign experts in the new era:

> Following many years of hospitality work the company managers and technicians have realized that equipment and installations can be purchased with money, but the foreign expert's friendly feelings toward the people of China, along with their active skills and knowledge, cannot be bought with money. For all of these, only after patient and meticulous propaganda work, can a true friendship be won over.[147]

Before the arrival of foreign experts in the company, workers were given a month-long course in *waishi*. They were instructed to "express warmest friendship, work hard, treat them politely, be neither servile nor supercilious, and be natural and graceful."[148] It was considered particularly important to provide the foreigners with good housing and Western food, to take them on outings, invite them to their colleagues' houses for dinner, all of which would build up *gan-qing*. However, the report warned, "Regarding their unreasonable requests or non-friendly acts, we will wage a righteous, effective and controlled struggle."[149]

Although in the reform era, the Chinese government began to court foreign scholars and experts for the kudos and information they brought the country, at the same time it attempted to control foreigners' research outside of officially proscribed activities. Foreigners who worked with the close cooperation of Chinese officials were under strong pressure to produce work that was "friendly" to China. Ross Terrill—who had benefited in terms of access to China denied to other foreign academics in the early 1970s—by the late 1970s was no longer considered a friend of China after he took opposing views to the official line.[150] Even one of the leading U.S. Sinologists David Shambaugh, in the preface to his book on Sino-American relations, *Beautiful Imperialist*, felt obliged to apologize that some readers might not find his book "friendly to China."[151] Orville Schell, author of a number of high-profile books on post-Mao China, in the 1980s an influential China journalist, and, from the mid-1990s dean of the School of Journalism, University of California, commented in an interview on the pressure he felt to be seen to be "friendly" to the Chinese government, and admitted that he made a point of considering the reaction of the Chinese government to what he wrote,

> I try incredibly hard not to allow myself to be blown off course. I try to say, "Okay, here is what I think, what I understand; what I think I see, have learned, and read." Then, I try and think through what the Chinese government's reaction will be. I try to be very clear in my mind so that these two imperatives don't become confused. And then I try to be as truthful as I can in a way that is respectful and unprovocative but that is not pandering. China has a tremendously highly evolved capacity to create panderers both among its own people and foreigners who become involved with them.[152]

The pressure on foreign researchers to be "friendly to China" at the same time as being allowed to conduct social science research there demonstrated the inherent tensions and contradictions of the reform era. On the one hand the CCP sought foreign investment and expertise and worked hard to reclaim China's place on the international stage. On the other hand, such policies threatened to undermine the party's hold on power. These tensions were reflected in a series of political campaigns in 1983, 1987, and 1988 to combat "spiritual pollution," in other words, Western bourgeois influences. Of concern were matters such as the potential corruption of cadres through contact with decadent Western civilization. During the 1983 campaign, Deng Xiaoping told cadres they should "open the window without letting the flies and insects come in." Bourgeois notions such as human rights and democracy were just the sort of "flies" and "mosquitoes" the government was attempting to keep out:

As we implement the policies of opening up to the outside, we will uphold the assimilation of the healthy aspects of Western thinking and culture, and progressive things, but we will not introduce things which harm our nation and people. At the same time, we will teach our people to oppose the invasion of decadent and moribund capitalist thinking. We can be certain that our Chinese people will treat this issue consciously and correctly, Chinese society will not change its nature.[153]

Not only did the government fear the corrosive influence of foreigners, it was anxious about the tendency of Chinese citizens to seek out foreigners for personal gain. The 1985 *Foreign Affairs Personnel Handbook* warned:

We should actively make friends with well-off, trustworthy foreigners, especially foreign experts, scholars and reporters, but we should not take the initiative to make connections with foreigners for selfish motives, plotting with foreigners to resort to deception and cheating, damaging national interests.[154]

As the 1980s came to a close, the contradictions between the government's plan to open up China to the outside world while attempting to control the process and popular demands for more radical change became increasingly apparent. As both 1969 and 1979 had proved to be the cusp of a decade of changes, so too would 1989, the beginning of a return to political conservatism and economically, to radical reforms much more drastic than could have been imagined at the beginning of the experiment.

Notes

1. Ross Terrill, interview, 29 July 1997.
2. Li Zhisui, *The Private Life of Chairman Mao: The Inside Story of the Man Who Made Modern China*, ed. Anne F. Thurston (New York: Random House, 1994), 105.
3. Tiananmen, the "gate of heavenly peace," is one of the most potent symbols of power and authority in modern China. Tiananmen is the outermost southern gate of the imperial palace in Beijing.
4. Edgar Snow, letter to Lois Wheeler, 17 February 1971, Folder 80, Edgar Snow papers, UA-UMKC.
5. Edgar Snow, letter to Lois Wheeler, 17 February 1971.
6. Edgar Snow, notes from a phone call with Senator McGovern, 17 March 1971, Folder 80, Edgar Snow papers, UA-UMKC.
7. Gerry Tannenbaum, interview, 10 April 1997.
8. Lu Ding, *The Dynamics of Foreign-Policy Decisionmaking in China*, 85.
9. Li Jie, "Mao and Sino-Soviet Relations," 29, citing Wang Yongqin, "1969—Turning Point of Sino-US Relations," *Dang de wenxian* 6 (1995): 77.
10. Gerry Tannenbaum, interview.
11. Edgar Snow's own notes of Mao Zedong interview, 18 December 1970, 3, Folder 197, Edgar Snow papers, UA-UMKC.

12.   Edgar Snow's own notes of Mao Zedong interview, 18 December 1970, 7. This comment is omitted in the version of the interview produced by Mao's translator Nancy Tang.

13.   Lu Ning, *The Dynamics of Foreign-Policy Decisionmaking in China*, 85-86.

14.   Ji Tao, "Ping-Pong Influences Sino-US Ties," *China Daily*, 21 August 1997.

15.   Ross Terrill, interview, 15 November 1998. Based on his travels in the early 1970s, Terrill also wrote *Flowers on an Iron Tree: Five Cities of China* (Boston: Little Brown, 1975).

16.   Ross Terrill, *800,000,000: The Real China* (Boston: Little Brown, 1972), 91.

17.   See Milton, Milton, and Schurman, eds., *The China Reader, People's China: Social Experimentation, Politics, Entry onto the World Scene 1966 through 1972*, 439.

18.   One of the symptoms of the factional struggle was Jiang Qing's bid to be immortalized in the same way that Mao had been by Edgar Snow in *Red Star over China*. In 1972 she invited an American historian, Roxanne Witke, to interview her for a biography. "Let me dissect myself before you," she told Witke (see Witke, *Comrade Chiang Ch'ing* ([London: Wiedenfield and Nicolson, 1977], 5). At the conclusion of their first interview, Jiang told Witke, "I hope you will be able to follow the road of Edgar Snow and the road of Mrs Snow" (Witke, 33). At the second interview Jiang again mentioned Snow, saying that he had "the advantage of time for long exploratory talks with Chairman Mao, Premier Chou, and other revolutionaries of the older generation" (Witke, 39). After her downfall in 1976, Jiang was accused of self-aggrandizement and telling "personal affairs and party secrets" to a foreigner (Witke, 4).

19.   Joan Hinton, interview, 19 December 1997 and E. J. Kahn, Jr., *The China Hands: America's Foreign Service Officers and What Befell Them* (New York: The Viking Press, 1972), 293.

20.   Kahn, *The China Hands*, 294. Jack Service had been one of the early victims of McCarthyism, purged under orders from Patrick Hurley.

21.   See Ross Terrill, *China in Our Time: The Epic Saga of the People's Republic of China from the Communist Victory to Tiananmen Square and Beyond* (New York: Simon and Schuster, 1993), 106, and Brady, *Friend of China*, 91.

22.   Li Zhisui, *The Private Life of Chairman Mao*, 565.

23.   Henry A. Kissinger, *The White House Years*, 749.

24.   See, for example, *Women de pengyou bian tianxia: fazhan tong ge guo renmin de youyi tongxun xuan* (Beijing: Renmin chubanshe, 1972).

25.   Milton, Milton, and Schurman, eds., *The China Reader*, 432.

26.   Miltons, *The Wind Will Not Subside*, 365.

27.   "Forgotten Americans in China Have Few Regrets," *Washington Post*, 14 March 1972, A13.

28.   See for example the books of economists J. K. Galbraith and Joan Robinson, both of whom were guided in their travels around China in the 1970s by former U.S. government economists turned defectors, Sol Adler and Frank Coe. Galbraith, *A China Passage* (London: André Deutsch, 1973); Robinson, *Economic Management, China 1972* (London: Anglo-Chinese Educational Institute, 1973).

29.   The U.S. quota was approximately 2000-3000 per year. Open entry did not begin until the mid-1980s. Tom Grunfeld, e-mail to author, 3 January 2001. Interest in China after 1970 was intense in the Western world. China Books and Periodicals, sole U.S. distributor of books from the PRC in this period reported a 1200 percent increase in distribution from 1970-1977, Noyes, *China Born*, 91.

30.   Zhao Pitao, *Waishi gaishuo*, 142.

31.   Zhang Guang, e-mail to author, 24 October 2001. See also Lee Chae-jin, *Japan Faces China: Political and Economic Relations in the Post-war Era* (Baltimore: The Johns Hopkins University Press, 1976).

32.   *Waishi gongzuo renyuan yingyu jiben cihui* (Sichuan sheng di si jixie gongyeju qingbao zhan, 1979), 40-41.

33.   Orville Schell, *In the People's Republic* (New York: Vintage Books, 1978), 174.

34.   *In the People's Republic*, 237.

35.   See also Schell, *Watch Out for the Foreign Guests!* (New York: Pantheon Books, 1980); and Simon Leys, *Chinese Shadows*, 2-5, 19-27, 69-72.

36.   The strict *waishi* discipline imposed on Chinese who had contact with foreigners at this time is illustrated by the experience of U.S. economist John Kenneth Gailbraith, who traveled to China with two other senior U.S. economists in 1973. One of his traveling companions lost a plastic bag with some old clothes in it on a train, and did not discover it was lost until some days later. The group's Chinese minders told them the bag would be found and returned to them, and it was, see Gailbraith, *A China Passage*, 24. Many other travelers to China reported similar stories of discarded items being returned to foreign visitors in this era.

37.   For example former Maoist Jan Wong reported on a Chinese classmate at Beijing University who asked her help to leave the country. See Jan Wong, *Red China Blues: My Long March from Mao to Now*, 106-108.

38.   Han Xu, "Mao Zedong de minjian waijiao sixiang he zhongyao juece" in *Mao Zedong waijiao sixiang yanjiu*, ed. Pei Jianzhang, 54.

39.   Talitha Gerlach, letter to Maud Russell, 30 January 1972, Correspondence January-March 1972, Box 9, MRP, NYPL.

40.   Granich, interview transcript, 184.

41.   Jiang Qing's views on the meeting were made very clear when she refused to accompany Zhou Enlai and his entourage to greet the foreigners after his speech. According to David Crook she stayed at her table "glowering." Interview, 23 April 1996.

42.   Correspondence January-March 1973, Box 9, MRP, NYPL.

43.   Correspondence January-March 1973, Box 9, MRP, NYPL.

44.   Miltons, *The Wind Will Not Subside*, 371-2.

45.   York Young, phone interview, 20 January 1996.

46.   Ginsberg, *My First Sixty Years in China*, 368.

47.   David Crook, letter to Maud Russell, 22 March 1973, Correspondence January-March 1973, Box 9, MRP, NYPL.

48.   Han Suyin, *My House Has Two Doors*, 592.

49.   Joan Hinton, interview, 19 December 1997.

50.   Lu Ning, *The Dynamics of Foreign-Policy Decisionmaking in China*, 107.

51.   Hamrin, "Elite Politics and the Development of China's Foreign Relations," in *Chinese Foreign Policy*, ed. Robinson and Shambaugh, 88. An example of the gradual opening up to West in this period was the drive to get more foreign tourists to visit China, local *waishi* bureaus held meetings on this topic as early as April 1978, see *Nanchang waishi zhi*, 51.

52.   The Four Modernizations were Science and Technology, Industry, Agriculture, Defense.

53.   See Jin Chongji, *Zhou Enlai zhuan* (1949-1976) (Beijing: Zhongyang wenxian chubanshe, 1998), 832-833.

54.   Although this phrase is usually attributed to Deng, it was in fact uttered by Hua Guofeng. Cheng Zhongyuan, Wang Yuxiang, Li Zhenghua, *1976-1981 nian de Zhongguo* (Beijing: Zhongyang wenxian chubanshe, 1998), 255.

55.   David Goodman, *Deng Xiaoping and the Chinese Revolution: A Political Biography* (London: Routledge, 1994), 94.

56.   David Goodman, *Deng Xiaoping and the Chinese Revolution*, 120.

57.   Hamrin, "Elite Politics and the Development of China's Foreign Relations," in *Chinese Foreign Policy*, ed. Robinson and Shambaugh, 88.

58.   *Nanchang waishi zhi*, 90-91.

59.   Qi Huaiyuan, "Deng Xiaoping de minjian waijiao sixiang yu shixian, in *Deng Xiaoping waijiao sixiang yanjiu wenji*, ed. Wang Taiping (Beijing: Shijie zhishi chubanshe, 1993), 180; Zhu Muzhi, "Guanyu duiwai xuanchuan de jige wenti," 10 September 1981, *ZMZ*, 23.

60.   Zhu Muzhi, "Duiwai baodao yao wei shehuizhuyi xiandaihua jianshe fuwu," April 12, 1978, *ZMZ*, 1-13.

61.   "Zhonggong zhongyang guanyu jianli duiwai xuanchuan xiaozu jiaqiang duiwai xuanchuan gongzuo de tongzhi," 16 September 1980, *DDXC*, vol. 2, 714.

62.   Barnett, *The Making of Foreign Policy in China*, 90-91.

63.   "Deng Liqun de jianghua: Peiyang duiwai wenhua he xuanchuan renyuan," *DWBDCK*, no. 21 (1983): 3. The six universities are: Beijing University and Beijing Foreign Languages Institute where students major in International Culture, studying foreign languages and international cultures and societies; and Fudan University, Shanghai International Studies University, Beijing Broadcasting University, and Jinan University where students major in International News, learning to write foreign propaganda for foreign news services, newspapers, radio, and television. The Central Party School in Beijing also offers occasional courses in foreign propaganda. Previously *waishi* cadres were mostly graduates of Beijing Foreign Languages Institute, People's University, and the Foreign Affairs Institute.

64.   *Nanchang waishi zhi*, 92-93; *Zhejiang sheng waishi zhi*, 57; Zhu Muzhi, "Tigao duiwai xuanchuan ganbu de suzhi," 7 September 1987, *ZMZ*, 177. The Beijing Broadcasting Institute was to be responsible for holding specialized refresher courses for cadres involved in foreign propaganda work as well as training new generations of propaganda workers, "Zhongyang xuanchuanbu guanyu zhuanfa 'Quan guo dianshi duiwai xuanchuan gongzuo huiyi jiyao' de tongzhi," 29 August 1983, *DDXC*, vol. 3, 1176.

65.   In the mid-1980s, its name was changed to *Duiwai xuanchuan cankao*. As the collection I viewed had a number of issues missing from 1984-1985, I was unable to ascertain the exact date when the name changed.

66.   V. I. Lenin, *"Left-Wing" Communism, an Infantile Disorder* (Moscow: Foreign Languages Publishing House, 1950).

67.   "Qian tan neiwai you bie," *DWXCCK*, no. 9 (1985): 14.

68.   Former *waishi* cadre, interview, December 1998.

69.   This is in the first section of the Confucian *Analects*. See Zhong gong Guangzhou shiwei duiwai xuanchuan xiaozu bangongshi, *Shewai renyuan shouce* (Guangzhou: Xinhua shudian, 1985), 1.

70.   Zhu Muzhi, "Guanyu duiwai xuanchuan de jige wenti," 19 September 1981, *ZMZ*, 26.

71.   "Zhonggong zhongyang guanyu jianli duiwai xuanchuan xiaozu jiaqiang duiwai xuanchuan gongzuo de tongzhi," 707-712. The group included representatives from the CCP Central Committee Propaganda Department, International Liaison Department, Investigation Department, Taiwan Relations Leading Small Group, Foreign Ministry, Ministry of Culture, Central Government Propaganda Department, Overseas Chinese Bureau, Hong Kong and Macao Office, Chinese Academy of Social Sciences, Xinhua, *Renmin Ribao*, Department of Broadcasting and the Foreign Languages Bureau.

72.   "Zhonggong zhongyang guanyu jianli duiwai xuanchuan xiaozu jiaqiang duiwai xuanchuan gongzuo de tongzhi," 714.

73.   Zhu Muzhi, "Zai quanguo duiwai xuanchuan gongzuo huiyi shang de jianghua," 30 October 1990, *ZMZ*, 269.

74.   "Sifabu Zou Yu fubuzhang tan zhengzhi gongzuode duiwai xuanchuan," *DWBDCK*, no. 8 (1983): 2-4; Zhu Muzhi, "Zai quan guo duiwai xuanchuan gongzuo huiyi shang de jianghua," 26 November 1986, *ZMZ*, 120.

75.   "Kaizhan you Zhongguo tese de duiwai xuanchuan," DWBDCK, no. 14 (1983): 4-6.

76.   "Zhonggong zhongyang guanyu jianli duiwai xuanchuan xiaozu jiaqiang duiwai xuanchuan gongzuo de tongzhi," 710.

77.   "Zhonggong zhongyang guanyu jianli duiwai xuanchuan xiaozu jiaqiang duiwai xuanchuan gongzuo de tongzhi," 711.

78.   "Xuanchuande zhenduixing jiaqiang waishi de jiedai," *DWXCCK*, no. 11 (1984): 6.

79.   "Zhu Muzhi tan duiwai wenhua jiaoliu he xuanchuan gongzuo," *DWBDCK*, no. 9 (1983).

80.   See for example "Guanyu gongchanzhuyi xinren de duihua," *Liaoning waishi tongxun*, no. 6 (1986): 15-16.

81.   "Zai rendaozhuyi he renxin liang ge ci qian bu yao jiao 'fandong' er zi," *Liaoning tongxun waishi*, no. 3 (1985): 23.

82.   "Deng Xiaoping yu waibin tan sihua jianshe he 'sige jianchi,'" *DWBDCK*, no. 12 (1981): 2-4.

83.   "Xuanchuan de zhenduixing jiaqiang waishi de jiedai," *DWXCCK*, 1984, no. 11, 6; See also, Zhu Muzhi, "Duiwai xuanchuan yu fandui zichan jieji ziyouhua," 23 March 1987, *ZMZ*, 146.

84.   "Zhonggong zhongyang guanyu jianli duiwai xuanchuan xiaozu jiaqiang duiwai xuanchuan gongzuo de tongzhi," 712.

85.   "Zhonggong zhongyang guanyu jianli duiwai xuanchuan xiaozu jiaqiang duiwai xuanchuan gongzuo de tongzhi," 713; "Guanyu liyong waili wei wo xuanchuan" *DWXCCK*, no. 23 (1985): 4; Zhu Muzhi, "Duiwai xuanchuan bixu jiji zhudong gengjia kaifang," *ZMZ*, 204.

86.   "Xuanchuan de zhenduixing jiaqiang waishi de jiedai," DWXCCK, no. 11 (1984): 6.

87.   Zhu Muzhi, "Ba duiwai xuanchuan gongzuo tigao yibu," 22 June 1986, *ZMZ*, 71.

88.   "Zhonggong zhongyang guanyu jianli duiwai xuanchuan xiaozu jiaqiang duiwai xuanchuan gongzuo de tongzhi," 713

89.   Duan Liancheng, *Duiwai chuanboxue*, Chinese-English Bilingual edition (Beijing: Zhongguo jianshe chubanshe, 1988), 277.

90.   "Duiwai bianji jiagong de ABC," *DWBDCK*, no. 2 (1983): 29.

91.   Zhu Muzhi, "Fahui neizai dongli, zuohao duiwai xuanchuan," 29 August 1986, *ZMZ*, 82.

92.   Zhu Muzhi, "Zai quan guo duiwai xuanchuan gongzuo huiyi shang de jianghua," 26 November 1986, *ZMZ*, 121-123.

93.   Rewi Alley, letter to James Bertram, 13 January 1978, 93-105-05, Bertram papers, ATL.

94.   30 July 1980, 59/264/11, MFAT.

95.   Joan Hinton, interview, 19 December 1997.

96.   Sid Rittenberg, phone interview, 29 April 1998.

97.   Brady, *Friend of China*, 208.

98.   Eva Xiao, interview, 11 June 1996.

99.   Viviane Alleton, interview, 24 March 1997.

100.   Wu Qinghe, "Deng Xiaoping renmin waijiao de zhengce sixiang ji qi shixian," in *Deng Xiaoping waijiao sixiang yanjiu wenji*, ed. Wang Taiping, 201.

101.   Qi Huaiyuan, "Deng Xiaoping de minjian waijiao sixiang yu shixian," in *Deng Xiaoping waijiao sixiang yanjiu wenji*, ed. Wang Taiping, 182-183.

102.   "Report on the Work of the CPAFFC," *Voice of Friendship*, February 1987, 5.

103.   *Voice of Friendship*, February 1984, 21.

104.   Sidney Shapiro, *I Chose China, the Metamorphosis of a Country and a Man* (New York: Hippocrene, 2000), 300, citing an interview with Rittenberg and Seattle-based journalist Nick Gallo.

105.   Shapiro, *I Chose China*, 300.

106.   Chu Yin, Su Ming, Pei Hwa, "Rescue and Reunion," *China and Us* [sic], (June-August 1979): 1-4.

107.   Rand, *China Hands*, 315.

108.   In a similar vein, see Harrison Salisbury's highly successful *China's New Emperors: China in the Era of Mao and Deng* (Boston: Little, Brown and Company, 1990).

109.   Hugh Deane, interview, 2 April 1997.

110.   Zhang Guoqi, "Chang Zheng tu zhong de ling wai yi ge waiguoren," *Renmin Ribao*, 21 October 1984.

111.   I have discussed this topic in more detail in my article "FriendLit, or, How to Become a Friend of China," *Revue Bibliographique de Sinologie*, 1998.

112.   *Shewai renyuan shouce* (Guangzhou: Xinhua shudian, 1985), 19-20.

113.   Jack Ewen, interview, 29 June 1992.

114.   "Friendship Cities Bear Fruits," *Voice of Friendship* (February 1988): 17.

115.   *Shewai renyuan shouce*, 8. See also "Zhonggong zhongyang guowuyuan guanyu jiaqiang guojizhuyi jiaoyu, kefu daguozhuyi sixiang he zhongzuzhuyi qingxu de tongzhi," 7 May 1984, *DDXC*, vol. 3, 1219.

116.   Tang Yan, "Deng Xiaoping waijiao sixiang shi xin shiqi dang de duiwai gongzuo de guanghui zhinan," in *Deng Xiaoping waijiao sixiang yanjiu wenji*, ed. Wang Taiping (Beijing: Shijie zhishi chubanshe, 1996), 191.

117.   Tang Yan, "Deng Xiaoping waijiao sixiang," 192.

118.   For example, the China Exchange Association (*Zhongguo jiaoliu xiehui*), the International Public Relations Association (*Guoji gonggong guanxi xiehui*), the China Cultural Association (*Zhongguo wenhua xiehui*), the Friendship Association, and the China Association for International Friendly Contact all perform similar activities.

119. http:/www.fas.org/irp/world/china/pla/gpd_ild.htm.

120. Interview with *Youlian* officials, March 1997.

121. http:/www.fas.org/irp/world/china/pla/gpd_ild.htm.

122. See Jiang Guanghua, *Fangwen waiguo zhengdang jishi* (Beijing: Shijie zhishi chubanshe, 1997); Tang Yan, "Deng Xiaoping waijiao sixiang shi xin shiqi dang de duiwai gongzuo de guanghui zhinan," in *Deng Xiaoping waijiao sixiang yanjiu wenji,* ed. Wang Taiping, 191-193.

123. Chan, *China and International Organizations,* 1.

124. Chan, *China and International Organizations,* 15.

125. Chan, *China and International Organizations,* 76.

126. Hamrin, "Elite Politics and the Development of China's Foreign Relations," in *Chinese Foreign Policy,* ed. Robinson and Shambaugh, 89.

127. Hamrin, "Elite Politics," 90.

128. *"Ba chuanghu dakai, nanmian hui you cangying wenzi pao jinlai,"* Deng Xiaoping, 10 October 1983, uttered at the Second Plenary Session of the twelfth Central Committee of the CCP as part of the campaign against "spiritual pollution," *jingshen wuran.*

129. "Zhonggong zhongyang guowuyuan guanyu jiaqiang guojizhuyi jiaoyu, kefu daguozhuyi sixiang he zhongzuzhuyi qingxu de tongzhi," 7 May 1984, *DDXC,* vol. 3, 1218-1219.

130. Zhu Muzhi, "Ba duiwai xuanchuan gongzuo tigao yibu," 22 June 1986, *ZMZ,* 74; see also Zhu Muzhi, "Guanyu duiwai xuanchuan de ji ge wenti," 10 September 1981, *ZMZ,* 30.

131. "Zhongyang xuanchuanbu guanyu shouting 'Meiguo zhi yin' Huayu guangbo zhong Yingyu jiaoxue jiemu ji shifou keyi xiang 'Meiguo zhi yin' zhu Xianggang banshi jigou han suo Yingyu jiaocai deng wenti de tongzhi," 5 January 1979, *DDXC,* vol. 2, 667-668.

132. "Zhongyang xuanchuanbu zhuanfa wenhuabu dangzu guanyu cong kongzhi xinjian chubanshe liang ge baogao de tongzhi," 2 October 1983, *DDXC,* vol. 3, 1195.

133. "Zhongyang xuanchuanbu zhongyang dui Taiban guanyu zuo hao fu Tai renyuan sixiang jiaoyu gongzuo de yijian," 18 November 1988, *DDXC,* vol. 4, 1795.

134. Chen Yun, "Guanyu dangqian jingji wenti de wu dian yijian," 10 December 1978, *Chen Yun wenxuan* (1956-1985) (Beijing: Renmin chubanshe, 1986).

135. *Shewai renyuan shouce,* 104.

136. *Shewai renyuan shouce,* 182.

137. Wang Rihua, ed. *Shiyong shewai changshi shouce* (Beijing: Renmin Zhongguo chubanshe, 1993), 101.

138. *Shiyong shewai changshi shouce,* 101.

139. Gong'anbu yiju, ed., *Waishi minjing gongzuo shouce* (Beijing: Qunzhong chubanshe, 1981), 111.

140. Fang Qi, "Zenmeyang jiedai waiguo jizhe," *DWXCCK,* no. 14, (1985): 6-7.

141. "Zhonggong zhongyang guanyu jianli duiwai xuanchuan xiaozu jiaqiang duiwai xuanchuan gongzuo de tongzhi," 713; see also "Zhonggong zhongyang bangongting zhuanfa Zhonghua quan guo xinwen gongzuozhe xiehui guanyu zhaokai Zhongwai jizhe zhaodaihui jieshao qingkuang de qingshi," 13 August 1980, *DDXC,* vol. 2, 718-719; Zhu Muzhi, "Ba duiwai xuanchuan gongzuo tigao yibu," 22 June 1986, *ZMZ,* 65, 70-71.

142.   "Zhonggong zhongyang bangongting zhuanfa zhongyang duiwai xuanchuan xiaozu 'guanyu gaijin dang he guojia lingdaoren huijian haiwai xinwen congye renyuan guanli banfa de ji dian jianyi' de tongzhi," 2 May 1987, *DDXC*, vol. 3, 1593-1594.

143.   *Zhejiang sheng waishi zhi*, 66.

144.   Zhu Muzhi, "Ba duiwai xuanchuan gongzuo tigao yibu," 22 June 1986, *ZMZ*, 71.

145.   "Guowuyuan pizhuan guojia kewei, Zhongguo kexueyuan, waijiaobu guanyu banfa kexue jishu renyuan duiwai tongxun lianxi he jiaohuan shukan ziliao liang ge guiding de qingshi," 1 February 1979, *DDXC*, vol. 2, 648.

146.   Zhao Pitao, *Waishi gaishuo*, 132.

147.   "Ruhe zuohao zhu chang waiguo zhuanjia de xuanchuan gongzuo," *DWXCCK*, no. 2 (1984): 7.

148.   "Ruhe zuohao zhu chang waiguo zhuanjia de xuanchuan gongzuo," 7.

149.   "Ruhe zuohao zhu chang waiguo zhuanjia de xuanchuan gongzuo," 7.

150.   Ross Terrill, interview, 15 November 1998.

151.   David Shambaugh, *Beautiful Imperialist: China Perceives America, 1972-1990* (Princeton, N. J.: Princeton University Press, 1991), xi.

152.   Orville Schell, interviewed by *Media Studies Journal* 13, no. 1 (Winter 1999): 72.

153.   *Shewai renyuan shouce*, 248.

154.   *Shewai renyuan shouce*, 3-4.

Chapter 8

China Says Yes and No

The whole Western imperialist world is contriving to make our nation re-
nounce the Socialist path and to become a vassal state of international monopoly capital. They are using all kinds of means to carry out political and ideological infiltration, sparing no effort to propagate hypocritical capitalist "democracy" and "human rights," instigating and supporting the trend of bourgeois liberalism within China. We must take a clear-cut stand, engaging in a
long term and resolute struggle against these kinds of "peaceful evolution"
plots and operations.[1]

In the wake of what became known internationally as the Tiananmen Massacre,
or June 4 (a direct translation of the Chinese, *liu si*), when PLA soldiers attacked
unarmed civilians in Beijing on 4 June 1989, the Chinese leadership took a sharp
swerve to the left. Soon after crushing the protest movement, the government
began to step up antiforeign propaganda within China, blaming the political upheaval on foreign interference. What the Chinese authorities called the "counter-
revolutionary rebellion," *fangeming baoluan*, was the result of six weeks of nationwide protests. Sparked by the death of CCP-moderate Hu Yaobang, the protests had focused on demands for political liberalization and concerns about
economic inflation and political corruption. There was strong support for the
protests throughout both the party and society at large.

The protest movement had attracted strong international attention, not least
because it coincided with the historic Sino-Soviet rapprochement in May 1989,
marked by the visit to China of Soviet leader Mikhail Gorbachev. Scores of foreign journalists arrived in late May to report on Gorbachev's visit and stayed on
to watch the drama unfolding in the streets of Beijing. International reaction to
the events of June 4 was severe. Most Western countries imposed sanctions on
China and canceled state visits, as well as invitations to Chinese leaders to visit.
In the months after June, it appeared that China might become isolated once
again in the international scene, undoing the work of the past ten years of re-

form. The sanctions not only threatened China's position in international politics; they were also potentially damaging to the country's efforts to attract foreign capital and technology.[2]

Beijing adopted a multilevel strategy to combat the impact of the sanctions and ameliorate their effects. Political education was increased, initially to justify the government's actions and more generally to strengthen the authority of CCP rule. Newspaper editorials of late 1989 and the early 1990s were filled with dire warnings of the potential effects of "peaceful evolution," *heping yanbian*, and policy documents focused on how to combat it.[3] The phrase stemmed from a comment by U.S. secretary of state John Foster Dulles in 1955 that Chinese communism would be undermined by means of the gradual influence of Western ideas and culture, a peaceful evolution rather than violent invasion.[4] In an important directive soon after June 4, party propagandists were told to focus on the economy, stressing how the economic situation was gradually improving in China, that reform and opening would bring prosperity for all, and that prosperity could only come about through political stability.[5] There was an effort to reassert control over the publishing industry, in order to make it harder for dissident voices to be heard—though it was acknowledged that with the rapid expansion of publishing outlets in recent years, this would be extremely difficult.[6] Soon after, the government also attempted to control the sale of foreign newspapers and magazines in China, restricting most to selected locations such as hotels for foreigners or a restricted number of government work units that needed them as research materials. Some newspapers that were regarded as extremely reactionary were banned altogether.[7] Orders were given to publicize incidents of foreign spying on China, to heighten public awareness of the threat China faced from the outside world.[8]

In the first year after June 4, China's foreign policy followed a more conservative line than in previous years.[9] Sino-foreign contacts were reduced, as was foreign trade. Despite the imposition of sanctions by Western countries, most of these were symbolic only, with minimal impact. Much of China's isolation at this time was actually self-imposed, a temporary turning inwards. Within China, relations between foreign residents and Chinese citizens returned to a level of caution and distance familiar to those who had lived through earlier periods of political crackdown. In the immediate months after June 4, as the witch-hunt went on all over the country for the ringleaders of the demonstrations, Chinese students who had been regular visitors to foreign students' university dorms were a subject of suspicion and some criticism by state education authorities. Many foreign students and other foreigners resident in China had been both participants and observers in the demonstrations; many had given money, taken photos of the movement, and afterwards helped Chinese citizens to escape the authorities. Most foreign students were evacuated home by their embassies after June 4, but those who returned for the September term found a much stricter regime controlling contact with Chinese citizens than had been the case in the relatively liberal late-1980s. In many universities, from this period on, first-year students were sent off on "military training" (*jun xun*) for periods from three months and, in the case of a number of key universities, up to a year. Students undergoing this "training" were kept under strict military discipline in an attempt to indoctrinate them before they formally began their university life. Contact between Chinese citizens and foreign diplomatic personnel was theoretically once again strictly controlled after 1989. Throughout the 1980s, numerous directives had been published warning Chinese citizens not to view films, books, and other materials provided by foreign embassies and consulates. These regulations had largely been ignored in the past, and apparently, even in the cold political climate post-1989, many continued to ignore such warnings.[10]

Saying Yes: Rebuilding Foreign Relations after 1989

Immediately after the events of June 4, Beijing had been defiant and hostile in the face of Western criticism. By late 1990 the Chinese government began to gradually try and improve its foreign relations by means of a number of old and new approaches. First, authorities adopted the tried-and-true method of manipulating contradictions, *liyong maodun*, in this case those between the Western countries.[11] For example the PRC began to work on improving relations with Israel, which it had previously ignored because of its support for the Palestinians. Beijing formally established diplomatic relations with Israel in 1991. By developing closer relations with the Israelis, China was able to get access to high-level technology, in particular military technology, denied it by U.S. sanctions. When European nations attempted to chastise China for its human rights violations, the government rewarded those few countries who refused to join in the criticism with greater trade access and punished those who did criticize it with temporary sanctions of its own.

At the same time, China worked hard to alter its international profile, replacing the violent images of June 4 with more positive ones. In March 1990, the CCP Central Committee Foreign Propaganda Group was revived (it had been closed down in 1988) to focus on the urgent task of improving China's foreign image abroad. Veteran propagandist Zhu Muzhi was put in charge of the group, in addition to his responsibilities on the CCP Central Committee Ideological Work Group.[12] Efforts were made to increase foreign propaganda to explain to foreigners "the basics of China's achievements in constructing Socialist spiritual and material civilization."[13] In January 1990, regulations regarding foreign journalists were tightened. When foreign journalists visited China, local departments, police, and the State Security Bureau were instructed to be extremely vigilant in managing them. Under no circumstances were they to be allowed to wander around on their own (although this would prove impossible to enforce).[14] Considerable efforts were made to "normalize" and "systemize" the task of guiding foreign journalists' impressions of China, and prevent them from relying on "hearsay," *dao ting hu shuo*, for their reports.[15] In a further attempt to improve the PRC's international profile in the early 1990s, the authorities also worked hard to bid for a number of important international events to be held in China. The bid to host the 1995 UN International Forum for Women was successful, though the proposal to hold the Year 2000 Olympics in Beijing was not. Nevertheless, June 4, symbolized by the lone figure who dared to brave the tanks on Chang'an Avenue, became the icon for a negative picture of China in the West. After 1989, the PRC suffered from a severe image problem in Western eyes and to date, the propaganda attempts of the government to reinvent perceptions of it have had only limited success.

The third approach adopted by Beijing to overcome Western hostility post-1989 was to make use of personal contacts, figures of political prominence "friendly to China," to influence Western governments. Soon after June 4, new senior leader Jiang Zemin instructed *waishi* personnel to step up their activities.[16] Chinese cadres responsible for *waishi* activities in the 1990s commonly cite Henry Kissinger and George Bush as being particularly helpful to blunt the effects of sanctions in this period. At the same time as this gradual attempt to restore and improve relations with as many nations as possible, Beijing also made it clear that it would act to defend its own interests in future, and that it would negotiate bilateral differences from a position of strength.[17] A statement made repeatedly by senior leaders throughout the 1990s summed up this new stance, "no country has the right to interfere in China's internal politics." Concerned with the new world order after the collapse of the Soviet Union and other Eastern European states in 1989 and 1990, and the consequent end of the Cold War, Beijing stressed the equality of all nations and its fundamental opposition to "hegemony," the overwhelming influence of larger powers over others.

A further important aspect that developed in the wake of June 4 was a change in China's strategy for attracting foreign investment. After 1989, China turned increasingly to its Southeast Asian neighbors for investment. These countries tended to be much less critical of the Chinese government's moves to crush dissent and most of them had substantial overseas Chinese elites who could be wooed to invest in the PRC as much for patriotic reasons, as for good economic sense. Taiwan was a further source of investment that boomed in the 1990s. In the long run, China's economic planners hoped to make the nation less dependent on foreign investment, and eventually, capable of generating its own finance capital.

Finally, after 1989, a diplomatic principle known as "looking for things in common and letting disputed points lie," *qiu tong cun yi*, became an important theme in PRC foreign policy in relations with Western countries, the nations of South East Asia, the Third World, and the former Soviet bloc. Although Zhou Enlai had articulated the principle in the 1950s,[18] both external pressures and domestic factors of the time meant that it was not always in evidence in the early years of the People's Republic. According to this principle, common points included respect for national sovereignty and equal status among nations; they could also include sharing an enemy. As the PRC deepened its relations with the countries of Southeast Asia in the 1990s, China's *waishi* representatives were instructed to stress the common history and culture they shared. However, the Chinese government's policy toward Western countries was to be treated slightly differently. After the establishment of "peaceful coexistence, mutually beneficial economic equality and technology exchange," any actions which were considered as interfering in China's affairs were to be brought to light appropriately and criticized. This was called "curbing differences," *yi yi*. With the United States, China followed a more aggressive approach, what was called the principle of "looking for commonalities and facing up to differences," *qiu tong li yi*.[19]

The results of this policy are most obvious if we look at China's propaganda on the United States in this period. As they had done in the 1980s, Chinese propagandists stressed that the United States and China had a shared history that both countries could be proud of. In 1995, when the wreck of a World War II U.S. bomber plane was discovered in Henan Province, reports described the plane as "a symbol of Sino-U.S. friendship" saying that it would be exhibited to the public in a museum.[20] Prior to Jiang Zemin's visit to the United States in 1997, *China Daily* outlined the positive side of U.S.-China contact in the last 200 years,

> As early as 1784, the American clipper ship, Empress of China, visited a number of Chinese port cities . . . During World War II Chinese and Americans fought shoulder to shoulder against fascists defending human justice and dignity and promoting word peace and progress. The Chinese will forever cherish the memory of the American airmen who laid down their lives in China during the war . . . Against the backdrop of profound changes now taking place on the world scene, the common interests between China and the United States have increased rather than decreased and the potential for co-operation has steadily expanded.[21]

At the same time as such benign rhetoric on Sino-U.S. goodwill (frequently even in the same edition of a newspaper), on matters where the Chinese government's viewpoint differed from that of the United States, media reports in the 1990s were increasingly belligerent and unsubtle. As we have mentioned, the issue of human rights was one where the United States and China were frequently in conflict. Although China also disagreed with other Western countries on this matter, it did not pull them up on their own human rights abuses in the way it did with the United States. As it once had done on the topic of black civil rights abuses in the United States in the 1960s, the Chinese media pointedly published frequent critiques of the human rights situation in the United States. This served both as a rebuttal to its most powerful and frequent international critic and an antidote for popular Chinese perceptions of the United States of America as the bastion of human rights and democracy. In 1998, Beijing released a lengthy official report hitting back at U.S. criticism of the mainland's human rights record. It ranked the United States as "the world's number one" in the growth of juvenile crime, the private possession of firearms, violent crime and the use of high technology to suppress prisoners. Amnesty International's 1998 worldwide human rights report was cited to reveal "persistent and widespread patterns of human rights violations in the U.S.," which was urged by the Chinese government to "mind its own business." The United States was also accused of police brutality, the execution of juvenile and mentally ill criminals, as well as foreign citizens. The Chinese government report said that the results of *US research* (note the use of "foreign strength" to promote CCP aims) indicated that rampant discrimination existed among Americans. Moreover, poverty, hunger, and homelessness continued to plague the United States "due to serious polarization of wealth distribution," freedom of the press in the United States was "a myth" and its political framework a "dollar democracy."[22]

Old Friends and New

The events of 4 June 1989 were profoundly distressing to the tiny community of resident "old friends," the foreigners who had committed their lives to the Chinese revolution. In private many of them expressed their rage and incomprehension at the actions of the Chinese government against their own people, though of those resident in China none chose to speak out publicly at the time,[23] and unlike other momentous periods in PRC history, such as the Sino-Soviet split or the Cultural Revolution, none chose to leave China in protest. Following the radical shifts in Chinese politics and the economy that had occurred after 1978, the public role and private realities of China's revolutionary friends had become a contradiction. The internationalism they represented did not exist anymore in China, if indeed it ever had. Hence when they spoke out about their true beliefs it was a dangerous act, as they were well aware. Unlike other political crises in the PRC's history when the CCP could always rely on the foreign friends to promote its own version of events, few of the PRC's foreign supporters openly condoned the actions of the Chinese government in June 1989. Interviewed in 1990, the writer Han Suyin told a journalist "the students had gone too far," while former U.S. secretary of state Henry Kissinger is reported to have said during a meeting with senior leaders in Beijing in November 1989 that "the events of the Tiananmen incident are much more complex than Americans understand," and regarding international perceptions of the massacre "China's propaganda work has been insufficient."[24]

The paucity of public support from China's old friends on the government's actions in June 1989 undoubtedly contributed to the decline in importance of their propaganda role. Perhaps it is best that some of the CCP's most loyal foreign supporters were long dead by 1989, Anna Louise Strong in 1970, Edgar Snow in 1972, Rewi Alley in 1987, and George Hatem in 1988. Many others were aging and incapacitated. The events of June 4 made the old friends even more marginal in Chinese politics. By the early 1990s, they had become cultural relics, wheeled out on symbolic occasions only. They continued to be celebrated ritually throughout the 1990s, but it was for appearances only, to symbolize CCP control of the foreign presence in China, and as a form of political education to Chinese and foreigners alike. As one *waishi* cadre told me, "When Chinese people think of the foreign friends they have a warm feeling for the countries they come from."[25]

Since generating "warm feelings" toward other countries was an important requirement in this period and the revolutionary ideals of China's old friends became irrelevant and dated in the increasingly consumer-oriented protocapitalist PRC of the 1990s, the most famous foreign "friend" of this period was, appropriately enough, a young Canadian, Mark Rowswell, known universally by his Chinese name Da Shan. Rowswell became a national hit after he performed Beijing-style comic "cross talk" on a nationally-televised New Year celebration program in 1988 to an estimated audience of 550 million viewers, but he did not really become a household name until the following year on a similar program in late 1989. The public appearance of this rising foreign star on CCTV's popular New Year variety show was highly significant in propaganda terms. In the post-June 4 freeze, most other foreigners, including those traditionally known as "friends," were clearly shunning any public association with the Chinese government. Da Shan's December 1989 performance was an indication both that Sino-foreign relations were becoming slightly more relaxed than they had been immediately after June 4, when the Chinese authorities had accused the "whole Western imperialist world" of a plot to overthrow CCP rule,[26] and a reminder to Chinese people that despite Western criticism of its political system, China still had foreigners willing to support its regime. Throughout the 1990s, the Da Shan persona grew into a major marketing tool, involved in both soft politics (being asked to host successively, Li Peng, Zhu Rongji, and Jiang Zemin at televised welcoming banquets in Canada) and hard-sell economics (forming his own company, Dashan Incorporated, which focused on the China market and promoted everything from Canadian ginseng to telecommunications equipment). The rapid rise of Da Shan, the Norman Bethune for the 1990s, received the active support of both the Chinese propaganda system and the Canadian government and Canadian businesses, an arrangement of benefit to all parties.[27]

As television increasingly became the most important medium for party propaganda throughout the 1990s, it was only logical that foreigners would have a starring role. In the 1990s, a series of popular programs showcased resident foreigners' "talents" in various Chinese cultural forms such as Beijing Opera, Chinese pop songs, and martial arts. Never were they asked to perform examples of their own culture and customs, the objective of the activities was clearly to show Chinese people how much foreigners admired and wanted to learn from Chinese society. In the late 1990s as the numbers of foreigners rose in China, other programs featured foreigners-only game shows and documentaries about their lifestyles in China aimed at normalizing their presence in the country and encouraging acquiescence for the policies of opening up to the outside world.

Foreigners selected for such activities were cast in deliberately nonpolitical roles; they were not friends of the revolution, but rather friends of the economic changes China was going through. It was a radical turnaround from the explicit campaigns to alienate foreigners and Chinese citizens in the pre- and early post-1949 period.

After 1989 *waishi* organizations had been instructed to focus their energies on attracting foreign investment and technology to China.[28] Throughout the 1990s, the high-profile Friendship Association redirected much of its attention to setting up economic links between China's hinterland provinces and foreign countries and "incorporated business into its agenda."[29] Friendship Societies continued to function in most Western countries, though their influence was now minimal. Beijing no longer relied on their help to develop foreign relations, nor did those foreigners who wanted to have contact with China need to go through them to get access to the country. The societies often had to struggle to find a meaning for existence in the wake of a general antipathy in the West toward China after 1989. The Chinese authorities maintained limited contact with the foreign-based Friendship Societies, but gave the impression of setting little store in their usefulness. The disdain was often mutual, and relationships maintained for self-serving purposes only.

In any case, true friends of the Chinese revolution had become very scarce by the 1990s. June 4 marked the end of all residual idealism towards the CCP-led Chinese revolution in both China and the West. Most of China's resident foreign friends remained so for pragmatic reasons, rather than because they still supported the government. A tiny few were bitterly opposed to the rightist-deviationist policies of Deng and his successors, but did not promote their views. Revolutionary foreigners became an embarrassment or even a joke to many foreigners and Chinese alike after 1989. Foreign journalists tended to sneer at the old friends of China.[30] And according to a historian in the Shanghai Academy of Social Sciences in 1997, Chinese researchers were also no longer interested in researching revolutionary foreigners.[31] Writing by Chinese scholars focused increasingly on nonpolitical foreigners. In this period the majority of research on foreigners in China was on the Jews, with some on the Japanese, and a little on Russians (both Soviet and White Russians).[32]

In terms of personalities, *waishi* activities of the 1990s were much more colorless than in the past. By 1989, most of the important figures, both Chinese and foreign, had either passed away or passed from power. Under the hegemony of Deng Xiaoping and then Jiang Zemin, in accordance with the notion of the "core leadership," *lingdao hexin*, power at the macro level was extremely concentrated. There would be no Zhou Enlai's or Chen Yi's in this era, and Da Shan notwithstanding, nor were there many foreigners willing to step forward to be the new Edgar Snow or Rewi Alley.

Nevertheless, *waishi* organizations continued to foster publications on former foreign friends. Even more so than in the 1980s, in the 1990s, frequent newspaper articles and TV programs appeared promoting other less-famous longtime resident Western friends of China, emphasizing the positive role of foreigners from Western countries in the PRC's development.[33] In contrast, materials on the contribution made by Soviet experts or long-term residents from non-Western countries were scarce. In 1997 an eleven-volume series of books for children on China's "old friends," including Rewi Alley, Edgar Snow, and Norman Bethune, was published.[34] A forum to discuss the contribution of these old friends to the Chinese revolution was held at the Diaoyutai State Guesthouse. In attendance were Vice-Premier and Foreign Minister Qian Qichen, Huang Hua, and other senior leaders involved in foreign affairs, as well as embassy representatives from countries associated with the "friends" (Austria, United Kingdom, Canada, India, Russia, and New Zealand), although representatives from the U.S. Embassy were notably absent. New Zealand diplomats who attended reported, "The forum was a useful reminder that the memory of China's old friends still runs strong, and that the Chinese government continues to put great store in the linkages generated by these individuals."[35]

Despite the optimistic view of New Zealand diplomats that the linkage generated by their compatriot Rewi Alley might offer them extra leverage with the Chinese government, as material in *waishi* publications made clear, in this era more than ever before the old friends were merely figures of idealized Sino-foreign relations. The ideal of internationalism and fraternal relations between Chinese and supportive foreigners was long outdated, and most of the Chinese leaders who had formerly had close personal relations with China's foreign friends had passed away. Indeed, in this period of downsizing the government bureaucracy one has to suspect that the expansion of *waishi* publications on old friends of China was as much to justify the overpadding of staff numbers in organizations such as the Friendship Association and indeed part of a justification for the organizations' very existence in their competition with rival organizations with duplicate functions, as it was to fulfill any perceived need for such materials. The same could be said for the increase of newspaper articles on foreign friends, rather than a specific policy seeking such materials, from my interviews with *waishi* propaganda writers, it appears that a number of journalists realized that writing about foreign friends such as Alley and George Hatem was a sure way to get published in the *Renmin Ribao* and other leading newspapers. Similarly, one can only suspect personal advantage to be the main motive for the setting up in the 1990s of numerous individual organizations, museums, memorials, and conferences to commemorate less well-known foreign friends of the Chinese revolution such as George Hogg, Helen Foster Snow, and Joseph Needham. Local authorities in remote areas, obscure writers, and underemployed local-level *waishi* personnel all had noted a gap in the market, which though not overly lucrative, did have potential appealing benefits such as the possibility of overseas trips, personal fame, opportunities for foreign investment, and the virtually guaranteed blessing of central authorities.

Though many of the traditional approaches for attracting foreign support remained, *waishi* personnel adopted some new strategies. One noticeable change was the introduction of awards for foreigners who had helped China in some way.[36] These had the benefit of being low cost, highly flattering to the individual foreigners and useful for meeting the goals of both local and foreign propaganda work. Beginning in the early 1990s, a plethora of these awards was established, whether nationwide, provincial, or ones specific to individual workplaces. Founded in 1991, Friendship Awards were handed out annually by the Foreign Experts Bureau to a number of foreign experts "in recognition of their outstanding contribution to the development of China's economic construction, science, technology and culture."[37] The Marco Polo Award was given to "commend those who have made a contribution to sponsoring volunteer experts working in China." Former U.S. president George Bush and the presidents of Motorola and Ford have been recipients of the award.[38] The International Award on Agricultural Science and Technology Co-operation was given out to foreign experts who had made an "outstanding achievement in agricultural co-operation and exchange."[39] (This award was established in 1986.) Another award for foreign experts was called the "China International Science and Technology Award"; British scientist and historian Joseph Needham was a posthumous recipient.[40] Shandong Province awards foreign experts the Qilu Friendship Prize. These awards began in 1993 and are awarded annually.[41] There is also the Rewi Alley Co-operation Foundation Award, which was occasionally given out to foreigners involved in the co-operative movement.[42] The title of friendship ambassador, *renmin youhao shizhe*, was bestowed on a few old leftist foreign friends such as the writer Helen Foster Snow.[43] Foster Snow was also the recipient of the first "Literature Prize for Contributing to International Understanding and Friendship" in 1991 from the Chinese Literature Fund for her writing on China and work on U.S.-China Friendship. The PRC also adopted the Western practice of granting honorary doctorates and academic titles to important figures. In 1998 an honorary professorship at Beijing University was conferred on Hans-Dietrich Genscher, the former vice-chancellor and foreign minister of Germany. Naturally, the university president lauded Genscher as "an old friend of the Chinese people."[44]

The slogan which summed up the pragmatic approach of *waishi* propaganda in the Deng/Jiang era was the phrase "use foreigners as a bridge," *yi qiao wei qiao*, which appeared repeatedly in 1990s *waishi* materials.[45] In a crude sense, both "leftist" foreigners such as Sidney Shapiro, ex-leftists such as Sidney Rittenberg, the Deng/Jiang-era friends such as Da Shan, and senior politicians, and business people such as French president Jacques Chirac, businessman Rupert Murdoch, and Australian former prime minister R. J. Hawke, all had their uses bridging multiple opportunities for both public and personal profit-making as well as political education and point-scoring. Like many other aspects in Chinese society in the 1990s, politics and economic profit were a natural match.

Diplomacy with Chinese Characteristics

Despite the blip in China's international relations caused by June 4, by the mid-1990s, China had established diplomatic relations with 159 countries as well as developing economic, trade, scientific, technological, and cultural exchanges with over 220 countries and regions.[46] In theory, China need no longer rely on "people's diplomacy" to conduct its international relations. In practice however, people's diplomacy and other traditional practices of what, in the late-Deng era, Chinese diplomats started to call "diplomacy with Chinese characteristics" still played an important role.[47] The PRC continued to use people's diplomacy as a means to avoid pressure from foreign governments and establish its position in the world. Cultural, academic, and military exchanges, "friendship" cities, political tourism, and so on, were still regarded as helpful. In what Beijing perceived as a new Cold War of international antagonism toward China, people's diplomacy was an important guerrilla tactic.

In the 1990s, China particularly focused on "rightists," *youpai*, in its people's diplomacy because, officials argued, they were the most influential globally, and most anti-China policies came from them.[48] In the 1990s several "close friends of U.S. presidents" were invited to China on all-expenses-paid trips. These have included former senior diplomat Henry Kissinger, who was escorted by staff of *Youlian* on a personal tour of the Three Gorges. The point of such visits, officials told me, was to establish *ganqing*, or feeling. "One can only have friendship," they say, "after gradually establishing feeling."[49] After the visits some of their influential American guests immediately "telegraphed" the U.S. president urging him to support Most Favored Nation (MFN) status for China.[50] In return, apart from lavish banquets and free tours, China's politician friends often made use of their high-level connections in Beijing to engage in a little networking on their own account, building relationships for such clients as major Western corporations with their Chinese counterparts.

An important boost for people's diplomacy activities in the 1990s was Deng Xiaoping's Southern Tour, *nan xun*, in spring 1992. Though officially retired, Deng still held effective power as the self-proclaimed "core" of the CCP leadership structure.[51] In an effort to get the economic reform process moving again after the swerve to the left following June 4, Deng visited the Pudong Economic Zone in Shanghai and special economic zones in Guangdong Province. The comments that Deng made at the time were not publicized at first, due to opposition within the party. However by late 1992 these, at times, almost incoherent ramblings, had been edited into an important new text that justified a more rapid expansion of economic reform than had been planned in the first tentative years after 1978-1979.[52] This in turn led to an expansion of people's diplomacy activities, more than ever before, tailored to lure foreign business and technology into China.

Particularly after 1992, in the 1990s, as the government became aware of the important role that NGOs were coming to play in international politics, China increased its participation in international nongovernmental activities. In 1992 the China Society for Human Rights Studies, *Zhongguo renquan yanjiuhui*, and the Human Rights Theoretical Research Association, *Renquan lilun yanjiuhui*, were set up to promote China's views on human rights at international forums. Although the two groups were in fact government-funded and organized, they used the NGO label to get into international human rights forums such as those organized by the UN and to send individuals from their organization to as many international forums as possible.[53] Zhu Muzhi, a veteran cadre involved in high-level foreign propaganda strategy was in charge of both groups. Rather than supporting and encouraging an improvement in human rights in China, their main activities appeared to consist of combating foreign criticism of China's human rights behavior.

Many other Chinese "NGOs" were involved in propagating the Chinese government's views on human rights and political conditions. A 1997 conference on women's and human rights issues held in Beijing was typical. Topics for discussion at the event (which had received substantial European Union funding) included legislation, violence against women, poverty, health, the environment, education for women, and their involvement in politics. Approximately sixty representatives from Chinese women's groups and forty European representatives attended. While European speakers saw women's rights as part of the overall debate on human rights, Shen Shuji, vice-president of the All-China Women's Federation, focused on "dialogue." In a word-perfect rendering of the *waishi* policy of "looking for things in common and letting disputed points lie," *qiu tong cun yi*, Shen told reporters at the meeting: "Only through dialogue and exchanges, seeking common ground while reserving differences, making up each other's deficiencies, can we co-operate with vitality and go along with the trends of peace and development in the world today."[54]

"Dialogue" is also the theme of discussion sessions on human rights the Chinese authorities have regularly held with a number of Western countries since the mid-1990s. In the wake of June 4, and due to strong interest in Tibet in the West, many Western governments were pressured by citizen lobby groups to make a principled stand on human rights abuses in China. Though Beijing is critical of "interference in China's internal politics," "human rights dialogue" gives Western governments "face" and releases them from doing anything serious about China's human rights situation. As a 1995 handbook on *waishi* noted, rather than being an indication of weakness, to the Chinese authorities: "Talks are a tool for furthering contact, and they are a weapon to oppose and subdue opponents."[55] Meetings were held between senior Chinese leaders and foreign delegations representing one nation only, whereby the foreign delegation expressed their concerns behind closed doors and on a unilateral basis only. Any attempt by Western countries to create a concerted response on human rights in China was strenuously undermined.

Serve the Economy: Foreign Propaganda in the 1990s

Serve the economy, give impetus to opening up the economy, and establish a positive image.[56]

One of the immediate consequences of the themes of Deng's Southern Tour being adopted was the stepping up of foreign propaganda work, especially that which targeted foreign journalists. In 1993, officials were instructed to encourage and assist foreign journalists who were regarded as "relatively objective and fair" towards China, to visit areas engaged in economic reform.[57] Since so much of China's foreign investment in recent years had come from the Asian region, journalists working for publications with an Asian focus were particularly sought after, as well as those from overseas Chinese newspapers. Throughout the 1990s, foreign propaganda activities primarily focused on the economic changes China was undergoing, stressing the improvement in people's material conditions. Local propaganda, *difang xuanchuan*, took on greater importance as the government opened up new areas of China, especially in the Western hinterland, to foreign investment, trade, and tourism.[58] Of slightly lesser importance, but with a higher profile, was China's defense of its human rights situation, to combat what *waishi* officials described as a "strong anti-Chinese feeling" in the United States.[59]

Foreign propaganda organizations continued to expand and modernize in the 1990s. China's shortwave radio service (renamed China Radio International and given a more Westernized format) was broadcast in thirty-eight languages and four Chinese dialects. Via satellite, Chinese Central Television (CCTV) sent out special news reports and other programs to the rest of the world. A satellite TV channel, CCTV 4, was set up targeted at foreign viewers. A number of new print publications was established to reflect the changing focus of *waishi* activities toward economic goals. The old established magazines such as *People's China* and *Beijing Review* continued to be published, though one had to wonder who actually read them. Reflecting the influence of Western ideas and approaches that had begun in the 1980s, cadres continued to prefer to use the phrase "public relations" and "publicity," rather than "propaganda" to describe Beijing's political indoctrination activities, especially in foreign language material. A considerable number of books in Western languages on the subject of public relations was translated into Chinese. Chinese authorities continued to encourage joint-venture projects between foreign television, radio, and film groups. Beijing increasingly focused on television as a means to propagandize both to its own people and to other countries. China's propaganda strategists recognized that in the modern era most people received their news and information from the electronic media. Collaborating with foreign television groups enabled China to get into markets normally inaccessible. The government also made use of the Internet to promote its views; government-controlled web pages made available China's own reports on the human rights situation and other highly topical issues.

Nevertheless, despite technological innovations, China's propagandists continued to favor familiar approaches for influencing foreign and Chinese public opinion, such as getting foreigners to speak out on behalf of China's interests. The English-language *China Daily* frequently featured this type of material under headings such as "Ex-Pats Admire Changes in China,"[60] "Western Scholars Refute Congressman's Remarks,"[61] (regarding the criticisms of U.S. congressman Frank Wolfe on conditions in Tibet). The paper also published a regular column written by foreigners entitled "China through My Eyes" about their experiences of living in or visiting China. Naturally, only those with a "friendly" perspective were printed (minute criticisms were acceptable). There seemed to be a strong need on the part of Chinese authorities to gain acknowledgment and acceptance for China's achievements and certain of its struggles.

Propaganda targeted at Chinese citizens, *duinei xuanchuan*, often followed similar themes. In 1997, three foreign students (accentuating their exoticism, though only one of them actually had blue eyes, one popular newspaper described them as "three big nosed blue-eyed foreign youths") were paid to go on a restaging of the CCP's historic Long March. The excursion was filmed by CCTV and publicized in numerous newspaper articles.[62] In 1998 the idea was raised that Chinese filmmakers should produce a Chinese version of *Schindler's List*, portraying the efforts of foreigners trying to rescue local residents during the Nanjing massacre. About twenty foreigners had been involved in helping Chinese citizens to escape the Japanese.[63] In January 1999, veteran film director Xie Jin announced his plans to film *Rabe's Diary*, a German Nazi's record of the Nanjing massacre.[64] "Foreign strength" was also used during the commemorations of the twentieth anniversary of the reform period in late 1998-early 1999. In addition to foreign participation in China-based symposiums organized to discuss the reform era, a number of "friendly" foreigners wrote articles or were interviewed on television during the anniversary period. Lisa Carducci, a Beijing-based Canadian writer, wrote an article that appeared both in Chinese and English comparing the improved conditions of the present era with those before.[65] Shanghai-based American teachers Robert and Susan Spellman wrote on freedom of religion in China, stating "Some people in the West claim that religious freedom is suppressed in China and that Christians are persecuted. That is not an accurate description of the China we know."[66]

Making the Foreign Serve China: Foreigners in China in the 1990s

Uphold the policy of reform and opening up and "making the foreign serve China"; study and draw lessons from it, use that which is beneficial for the construction of our nation's spiritual civilization.[67]

As Deng Xiaoping's 1992 Southern Tour led the way to a further opening up of the Chinese economy to foreign investment and foreign contact, the new slogan of the era was "expand opening up and bring in foreign investment," *kuoda kaifang, yinjin waizi*.[68] From late 1992, the Foreign Experts' Bureau began to expand its operations, inviting even more numbers of foreigners to share their skills and knowledge. In 1996, *China Daily* reported there were "about 180,000 foreigners working in China, 70,000 of them employed by government bodies, and 100,000 working for foreign institutions or overseas-funded ventures."[69] (Where the other 10,000 worked was not accounted for.) The new foreign experts were not solely from Western countries. According to *China Daily*, "Since 1992, nearly 4,000 Russian experts have worked in China, mainly in the Northeast in the chemical, oil, and metallurgical industries, medicine and agriculture, or as translators and teachers."[70] China made the most of the expertise of specialists from the former Soviet Union's massive military complex, providing a major boost to the country's military modernization.

Controls were also further relaxed on the quota of foreign students allowed to study in China in the 1990s. Numbers trebled in the five-year period 1991 to 1996. In 1997 there were 40,000 foreign students studying in China at some 332 universities, an increase of 190 since 1992. Since the reform policies began in 1979, around 258,000 foreign students had studied in China. By the late 1990s, 90 percent of these students were self-funded.[71] In February 1998 the State Education Commission gave all universities in China the right to enroll foreign students, without having to get the individual approval of the commission. Teaching foreigners Chinese was seen as an important tactic to increase international understanding of and "friendship" toward China, creating even more economic, cultural, and other links between China and the outside world. Since 1997, in a further turnaround from the policies of the Mao era, higher learning institutions in China were encouraged to cooperate with overseas universities, institutes, and individuals involved in science and technology, all for the goal of improving the Chinese economy.[72]

Foreign nonprofit organizations (often surreptitiously engaging in missionary activities) supplied much of the "foreign talent" required in China in the 1990s. The Chinese authorities generally turned a blind eye to their proselytizing work, as long as it was discreet. The government especially welcomed retired professionals to work in China, drawing on their skills and experience. They were also preferred because they were less likely to want to stay long term, and usually had retirement incomes that could supplement the pitiful salaries they received as "foreign experts." In the 1990s, the privileges of "foreign experts" had been undermined so much that working in China financially disadvantaged most foreigners. Long gone were the free trips around the country during the winter and summer vacations, and salaries no longer kept up with inflation—indeed they were considerably lower than many Chinese people earned.

The numbers of foreign tourists in China continued to soar in the 1990s, as did the areas where they were allowed to visit. In 1997 approximately 7.428 million foreigners and 99,000 visitors identified as overseas Chinese entered and departed China. The bulk of China's visitors on tourist visas were still from Hong Kong or Macao.[73]

From the mid-1990s a number of important changes were instigated in foreigner management that made life in China for the foreign visitor or sojourner more convenient. In 1994 the dual currency system was finally done away with and foreign exchange became much more readily available. Increasingly the distinction between foreigners-only and Chinese-only hotels became blurred, most hotels would accept whoever had money to stay. After 1996, foreigners no longer had to pay higher charges for long-distance travel. By 2001, even the special counters for foreigners at travel offices had disappeared, as had the special extracomfortable waiting rooms exclusively for their use. According to staff at Beijing's main Xike Train Station, this was because many Chinese people had complained that Chinese and foreigners should be treated equally.[74] As the Chinese urban middle class expanded throughout the mid- to late 1990s, the notion of special privileges for foreigners became less acceptable. Foreign travelers in China were minuscule in number compared to the huge numbers of Chinese (deliberately encouraged under government policies aimed at boosting consumer spending) now traveling within China for business or pleasure. In China of the late 1990s, money talked and foreigners were only admired if they had money or special skills China required. Officially, by 1996, special foreigner's prices for items such as museum entrance fees were disallowed. In fact, the practice continued in many locations, and in other situations such as taxi fares or buying goods in a market, Chinese people often stated that the price for foreigners was higher "because they can afford it."

The Iron Fist in the Velvet Glove: Managing the Foreign Presence

As the number of foreigners in China continued to increase, the government was still concerned to maintain some level of control over the process. As activities and cooperation between Chinese and foreigners grew, so too did the range of regulations aimed at controlling these interactions. In 1996, the State Bureau of Foreign Experts announced that China would hire more foreign experts in "a regulated employment process."[75] China began to host annual international talent fairs to attract skilled workers, where Chinese officials met with foreign employment agencies.[76] According to the new legislation, "Regulations on the Management of Foreign People's Employment in China," all foreigners working in the PRC were required to have an employment certificate from a local government labor office. The legislation aimed to prevent low-skilled foreigners competing for jobs with Chinese workers and to cut down on "criminal activity" by nonresidents. The Ministry of Public Security claimed that many foreigners were engaged in prostitution, smuggling, and drug trafficking, "causing adverse effects on social order."[77] In 1997, further regulations were issued to control aspects of the entertainment industry that involved foreigners. Beijing banned the establishment of all foreign equity, contractual joint venture, or solely overseas-funded theatrical troupes, performing venues, and booking institutions. Also prohibited were all shows that might "endanger State security and social stability, promote division among ethnic groups or spread pornography, superstition or violence."[78] Overall, foreign criminal activity in China was treated very carefully, a 1994 manual on security issues regarding foreigners noted, "Handling cases or incidents involving foreign nationals is an extremely political, policy-driven, principle-driven task. Not only does it involve protecting national sovereignty and interests; it also involves our foreign policy."[79]

In accordance with *waishi* regulations, throughout the 1990s most foreigners were still required to live in officially or unofficially designated "foreigners quarters" within the large cities of China. Those with Chinese spouses were entitled to live in Chinese areas that were open to foreigners, as long as they registered their presence with the local police. However from 2001, most foreigners in ten key cities were basically allowed to live wherever they wanted to.[80] Nevertheless this change in policy, though important, was cosmetic compared to the number of areas that continued to be closed or restricted.[81] Moreover, if foreigners intruded into areas, which while not officially closed, were not usually frequented by non-Chinese, plainclothes police checked to ensure their activities were legitimate. And foreigners who were caught visiting areas closed off to outsiders without applying for a permit to enter were summarily expelled. With the use of a national computerized database, also from 2001, public security officials involved in *waishi* were able to keep an even closer watch on foreigners' movements.[82] The post office continued to maintain its interest in foreigners' mail, as well as foreign mail received or sent by Chinese citizens.[83] Such mail frequently arrived weeks or even months late, already opened. Security files were still kept on foreign experts, keeping track of their behavior during their time in China and whether they were "friendly" to the regime or not.[84] Diplomatic personnel were still required to hire their Chinese staff through the Ministry of Foreign Affairs agency, the Diplomatic Service Bureau, and the hiring of Chinese staff for foreign enterprises became even more regulated and controlled than it had been in the 1980s.

Attempts to control personal contacts between Chinese citizens and foreigners continued, and in theory at least, government personnel could only form friendships with foreigners for official purposes.[85] In 1999, a Hebei worker was sentenced to three years imprisonment for writing to the U.S. news service Voice of America.[86] Chinese dissidents were warned by police not to contact foreign journalists or organizations, if caught, those who ignored such warnings tended to face much harsher sentencing.[87] Even visits between foreigners and their Chinese friends and family were still meant to be carefully controlled, and of course, if that visit required an overnight stay it still required registering of the foreigner's presence with the local Public Security Bureau. Foreigners' visits to Chinese people's homes, especially those of official guests of the Chinese government, were not regarded as a solely personal matter, according to one *waishi* manual, "composing an important part of the hospitality and liaison work of *waishi* personnel, it is a task that is very political, having a wide effect, deep in human feeling, complex, and interesting."[88] Meetings between official visitors and their contacts were meant to be carefully scripted and organized in advance. *Waishi* personnel were instructed to ascertain the details of the person to be visited, their work unit, their relationship with various people, and so on. They were told to liaise with the work unit of the person being visited so that appropriate preparations could be made, as well as with the host so that they could "ideologically, and in terms of etiquette and gifts, be completely prepared."[89] Afterwards *waishi* staff were instructed to make a report of the outcome of such visits. Foreigners who were the guests of the Chinese government, whether on official or nonofficial business, were perhaps the most controlled of all. Those who could speak Chinese were especially watched. All official guests were assigned a minder, who, as in earlier years, was instructed to note and report back their views on all matters. A 1993 manual on *waishi* work instructed staff:

> Be completely familiar with the foreign guest's work situation and personal requirements, as well as their response to every activity and event, and report them to senior staff promptly. Reports must be accurate and reliable; it is not acceptable to exaggerate or to downplay matters. Shelving foreign guests' responses and ignoring them, concealing and not reporting them show a lack of organization and discipline.[90]

Periodic security campaigns were conducted throughout China in the 1990s in an attempt to maintain discipline on the theoretical distance that was supposed to be kept between Chinese citizens and foreigners. Concerned that there was confusion over the meaning of reform and opening up, the government increased its efforts to spread awareness of *waishi jilü* and other guidelines regulating the relationship between foreigners and Chinese people.[91] That these messages have been absorbed at least on some levels in the new, new China can be seen by the commercialization of the word "friendship" by nonstate-owned Chinese companies. "Friendship," *youyi*, attached to the name of a Chinese product or company came to imply foreigners or foreign things. Hence a new Sino-Australian project to build offices and accommodation for Chinese companies working in Australia was named the *Sino-Australian Friendship Village* and a number of large private department stores in China have now attached "friendship" to their name.

Apart from official visitors, the group that attracted the greatest attention from the Chinese government were foreign journalists. Strong action was taken against journalists who reported on subjects the CCP did not want exposed. Throughout the 1990s, foreign journalists were detained, in some cases physically assaulted, as well as being expelled from the country.[92] When necessary, regulations requiring foreign journalists to get official permission for all reporting activities (since 2000 available on the Internet) were used to prevent journalists from speaking with critics of the Chinese government.[93] Overall however, coercion rather than violence was preferred. A 1996 *China Daily* article criticizing foreign journalists for biased reporting urged them to "learn from Edgar Snow." The newspaper singled out Snow for his "accuracy, objectivity and impartiality" in his coverage of China.[94]

Among the "points for attention" regarding the hosting of foreign journalists in the 1990s, *waishi* staff were instructed,

> As for some journalists, who, as a result of not understanding China put forward questions that seem to be unfriendly to China, we should patiently explain to them, being careful not to act impetuously and make a brusque retort. And as for the one or two journalists who, from their behavior, really have raised unfriendly questions, we should simply explain our viewpoint, not quibble and try all possible explanations in order to win over the sympathy of the other journalists.[95]

Journalists who were perceived as "friendly" toward China could expect slightly better treatment than those who were not, though the rewards were not great—at least officially. If the authors of a 1993 *waishi* manual are to be believed, in the era of reform and opening up, instead of free trips around the country to visit senior leaders as pro-China journalists in the early 1970s (such as Snow and Ross Terrill) were given, or a permanent retirement base as Anna Louise Strong was offered in 1958, the most pro-China journalists could hope for was an annual greeting card:

> Allowing oneself to be interviewed by journalists is within the realm of public relations hence one should use the opportunity to do some extra work. Make contact at the emotional level, discuss appropriately the friendly exchanges between the two countries, and emphasize that through tourism the two peoples can improve their mutual understanding and friendship, and that you hope the journalist will stay in touch and that they will send a copy of their article. To some journalists who are friendly to us and who have written many reports or quite lengthy articles, we can express our thanks by sending them a New Year card.[96]

 The Chinese authorities have long regarded the legitimate activities of foreign journalists and university researchers as a form of spying. Repeating the warnings of the 1980s, in 1993 *The Practical Handbook of Foreign Affairs Knowledge* urged:

> We should be extremely vigilant against foreigners using various opportunities and means to seek connections in high places, corroding and seducing, spying out information on our nation's politics, military, economy and culture, and engaging in illegal activities. If foreigners ask our citizens to distribute "survey forms" or "opinion polls" the work unit hosting the foreigner or accompanying

person must put a stop to it, and our citizens must refuse to fill out the forms, and report the incident immediately.[97]

In late 1990, in a direct response to perceived Western involvement and support for the 1989 protest movement, the State Education Commission had issued a directive prohibiting Chinese universities and research institutes from collaborating with foreign researchers.[98] Official approval for foreigners to conduct research in China became more difficult to obtain at this time.[99] Foreign social science experts working in Chinese research institutes and universities were supposed to be monitored more closely than other foreigners.[100] Nevertheless, as was the case in many issues involving foreigners in China in the 1990s, the official line and actual practice were frequently very different. In theory, the government tried to limit foreign research activities in China by means of requiring foreign researchers to apply for research visas and be attached to a Chinese university or research institute. In practice, however, in the 1990s it became quite possible for researchers to work independently of official scrutiny, as long as they kept a low profile. Even in the first three years after 1989, most foreign researchers were able to conduct their research in China, as long as they were not obviously involved in or encouraging antigovernment activities. In 1999 Beijing issued new regulations requiring all market research companies and social science investigators operating in China to submit virtually every stage of their work for government examination and approval.[101] However, despite the new regulations, foreign market research companies reported that no one seemed to be complying.[102]

The government's efforts to control foreign social science researchers were frequently undermined by the attitude of Chinese academics, many of whom for personal and professional reasons supported the right of their foreign colleagues to engage in untrammeled China-based research. The era of reform and opening up, which maintained a weakened state system alongside a burgeoning private sector, left much more room for covert rule breaking than the Mao era did. As many underpaid, underappreciated Chinese intellectuals sensed the CCP-led system was slowly sinking, they were not averse to establishing other links that might help them if the situation were to take a turn for the worse. These surreptitious, unofficial, undeclared networks, *guanxi wang*, between foreigners and Chinese were further encouraged by official policies expanding academic links between Chinese universities and research institutes and their foreign equivalents.

As in the past, foreign academics, diplomats, journalists, and so on were not only seen as threats to China's safety, they were also regarded as potential agents of influence or expertise who could be used and manipulated for Chinese needs. Again, as in the past, part of the task of *waishi* cadres and government personnel who come into contact with such foreigners was to do "work" on them through activities such as political hospitality. *Waishi* cadres and those whose jobs brought them into contact with foreigners were particularly encouraged to work on foreigners under their care who were critical of China, explaining China's viewpoint.[103] Cadres were urged to take the "long-term view" on political friendship.

In the 1990s *waishi* cadres had to be capable of doing both "political friendship work" and "economic work," meaning engaging in activities to encourage greater foreign investment and trade.[104] The training of *waishi* personnel became increasingly formalized, with many more universities than the original six proposed in the early 1980s providing courses on subjects such as foreign expert management, joint venture management, foreign investment, tourism, *waishi* public relations, and so on. Some cadres were sent overseas for more specialized training in these matters.[105]

The enormous increases in the numbers of foreigners living in and visiting China in the 1990s led to a need for much wider awareness of *waishi* practice, not only among those whose jobs were specifically concerned with *waishi* or *shewai* activities, but also among the general public. While promoting reform and opening up and "friendship" with foreign peoples, the government constantly attempted to remind the Chinese people that "insiders and outsiders are different," and that economic reform did not mean a slackening of discipline.[106] Through direct means such as formal instructions to state employees, popularization of *waishi* information through formats such as desk diaries, to more subtle methods such as spy scares, carefully selective reporting of international news, a constant harking back to China's past humiliations, and even a deliberate policy of "not encouraging" Sino-foreign marriages, Chinese people were made uncomfortably aware of the difference between foreigners and themselves.

An important and useful means of indoctrination for the enormous numbers of personnel engaged in *waishi*-related activities in the 1990s was the mass-production of handbooks on how to deal with foreigners.[107] These materials were not only aimed at those who had contact with foreigners within China, they were also designed for the large numbers of government officials who had opportunities to travel abroad, as well as the general public. Though a number of these guides existed previously, their circulation had been restricted to the small number of officials involved in *waishi* work from the 1950s to the 1970s. *Waishi* in the Mao era had been controlled by a tiny core of senior leaders who were the primary sources for new China's foreign relations style. As these leaders passed away, it became necessary to create textbooks to analyze and codify the strategies and practices they had initiated, in order to pass on their traditions and knowledge, as well as to standardize *waishi* practices for the increasing numbers of *waishi* personnel.[108]

Some of the topics the handbooks focused on reflected a growing anxiety about China's image abroad both by the government and among Chinese intellectuals, as more Chinese traveled overseas and more foreigners visited China.[109] The *waishi* handbooks of the 1990s gave instruction on subjects as wide-ranging as personal hygiene ("be sure to wash *both* hands," and "never pick your snot, eye detritus, or earwax in front of foreigners"),[110] as well as how to establish "friendly relations" with foreigners, and the basic rules of contact between foreigners and Chinese ("don't reply to questions that don't relate to work matters").[111] *Waishi* cadres were given instructions on "the art of saying no," and "the art of criticism" as well as humor and praise.[112] Books on specialized aspects of *waishi* also became common, such as those for hotel workers, secretaries, lawyers, writers and translators, and so on.

Much as late-Qing dynasty reformers legitimized their reforms by finding models in Chinese history, the handbooks all made a point of stressing the historical and uniquely Chinese cultural origins of *waishi*. The author of a 1995 handbook on *waishi* claimed that China's people's diplomacy had its origins in cultural practices going back as far as the Western Zhou period. No mention was made of the Soviet origins of the system or why the CCP had been so dependent on people's diplomacy throughout its foreign relations history. According to Zhao Pitao's *Waishi gaishuo* (Foreign Affairs Outline), published in 1995, the PRC's distinctive form of foreign affairs occurred "spontaneously":

> Spontaneous people to people contact became the origin of people to people diplomacy. People to people diplomacy shows how people to people contact has an official backdrop and support, consciously and deliberately representing national interests, implementing national policies of people to people friendship. In fact, people to people relations is a foreign affairs activity which is "half official half popular." Emerging as the times require, people to people diplomacy is a follow on of the development of international people to people contact. Our nation still has its own unique and fresh ideas on people to people relations.[113]

A further codifying of *waishi* behavior in the 1990s came from the publication of materials on the *waishi* theory and practice of senior leaders Mao Zedong, Zhou Enlai, and to a lesser degree, that of Deng Xiaoping. These materials aimed to educate the next generation of *waishi* workers on Chinese-style foreign affairs, but they may also be seen as an attempt to emphasize some positive aspects of the Mao era and establish pride in Chinese communist traditions.

Despite all the regulations and guidelines however, with the increased foreign contact that came about through the expansion of the economic reforms, many Chinese people refused to accept the necessity of this distance. Most Chinese citizens, even government employees, chose to ignore the regulations and guidelines aimed to separate them from foreigners. Police or work-based security enforcement of the regulations was also much less stringent. *Waishi* regulations tended to be applied, and lawbreakers punished, when police were concerned about other activities not specifically covered in Chinese law, which were politically unacceptable to the government.

In any case, regardless of how effective or meaningful it really was, large numbers of *waishi* personnel continued to engage in the various forms of *waishi* activities, simply because it was what they were employed to do. In a time of growing unemployment, any government attempts to reduce the *waishi* bureaucracy would have been met with much opposition. As globalization pushed open the doors of the Chinese market, especially encouraged and welcomed by leaders and businesspeople in the eastern coastal regions who had the most to gain from it, CCP *waishi* policies and practices seemed increasingly at odds with the realities of much Sino-foreign interaction. But like so many other aspects of Chinese society in this transitional period, Maoist bureaucracy had to coexist uneasily with the free market, or rather the free market had to learn to coexist, even ignore, the bureaucracy that often got in its way.

Saying No: 1990s Nationalism

As we have noted, following the events of 1989, the Chinese government had deliberately fostered a notion of foreign "enemies" seeking to undermine China's prosperity and prevent its development. With the decline in faith in Marxist-Leninist-Maoist thought the CCP faced the difficult task of finding a suitable replacement for communist ideology's unifying role. Nationalism, or rather chauvinism, came to be an important tool to unite the Chinese nation.[114] Throughout the 1990s, CCP propagandists worked to foster a sense of antagonism towards Western countries, especially focusing on the imperialist past. Talk of the West's "peaceful evolution" policies in the early 1990s set the tone for a decade of reintensified hostility toward the Western world, especially the United States. Numerous books, films, television programs, and exhibitions continually reminded Chinese citizens of the wrongs enacted against Chinese society by foreign countries. Beginning in the mid-1990s Beijing raged that in addition to "peaceful evolution" plots, Western countries were now trying to "contain China," *ezhi Zhongguo*, and attacked the "China threat" theory proposed by some Western analysts as the fig leaf for justifying China's containment.[115] A leading article in *Liberation Daily* in 1995 claimed that "proponents of the 'China threat theory'" were mobilizing public opinion "to secure a bigger slice of the enormous Asian arms purchasing pie for the U.S." The article stated the theory's supporters were trying to sow discord between China and its Asian neighbors, creating a leading role for Washington in the region.[116] A 1996 article in the *Liberation Army Daily* declared,

> History tells people that most of those countries who advocate the "China threat" theory have invaded China before. During the Opium war in the middle of the 19th century, Western powers launched heavy attacks on China. As a result, the country was destroyed and the people had no means of livelihood, throwing the nation into a semi-colonial society . . . the "China threat" theory maintains that relations between China and its neighboring countries will inevitably be tense. In fact, China has close and friendly relations not only with its Asian neighbors, but also with most countries throughout the world . . . The real threat to the world today is those countries which go against these historical trends and try to violate other countries' sovereignty, interfere with others'

internal affairs, and sabotage others' territorial and national unity under the
pretence of "freedom, democracy, and human rights."[117]

As a response to the "plots" of peaceful evolution and the "containment of
China," or perhaps simply to make his mark on Chinese politics as his place in
the leadership role became more stable, in 1995 Jiang Zemin proposed a "spiritual civilization" campaign advocating a return to "traditional" socialist and
Chinese values. In the same year, he also publicly urged cadres to "stress politics," an indirect reference to the perceived corrupting influences of excessive
Westernization. Deng Xiaoping had of course earlier launched similar campaigns and warnings in the 1980s. Where Jiang differed was his stress on "traditional" Chinese values, as well as "traditional" Marxist-Leninist ones. The goals
of Jiang Zemin's spiritual civilization campaign followed a pattern familiar from
late-Imperial China, stressing the superiority of Chinese culture and advocating
a selective adopting of Western "technique" only. Beginning in 1997, in a direct
reference to the slogans of the Qing "self-strengthening" movement, a thirty-
second patriotic message was flashed across TV screens during ad breaks on
CCTV channels with the slogan "self-strengthen, create, and be glorious,"
ziqiang chuangzao huihuang. Before the nightly CCTV1 seven o'clock news
(which had come to be the modern equivalent of a daily political study session),
a one-minute-long, MTV-style version of the national anthem flashed a succession of split-second images of China's past and present. The emphasis was on
China's strengths and achievements both in the present era, represented by the
high-tech skyscrapers of Shenzhen, and to those of the past, symbolized by the
Great Wall.

The spiritual civilization campaign was combined with an attempt to root
out unsavory Western bourgeois influences within Chinese society. Hoping to
break the influence of Western culture on China in the 1990s, the government
tried to foster homegrown icons, such as investing in a cartoon industry so that
Chinese children could have cartoon characters that reflected Chinese culture.[118]
In December 1996, a *Renmin Ribao* editorial criticized unnamed Chinese writers
and academics accusing them of being "unpatriotic and betraying Chinese culture by championing all things foreign."[119] The government announced a policy
on the importation of foreign cultural items, "vowing to firmly ban decadent
ideas and practices from abroad." Yuan Xue, a deputy director in the Ministry of
Culture, said China would encourage some imports "based on the principles of
making foreign things serve China, enriching people's cultural lives and developing the people's cultural sphere."[120] *Waishi* cadres were instructed to study the
experiences of other recently developed countries in managing to control the
process of accepting the positive cultural contributions of other societies, while
keeping out the negative.[121] In 1997, the central authorities put pressure on
Western advertisers to produce public service announcements promoting the
"spiritual civilization" campaign. The State Administration for Industry and

Commerce said Western companies that frequently advertised in the PRC would be "urged" to put out morality messages in the Chinese media.[122]

Symbols which echoed China's bitter past under imperialism featured prominently in the Jiang era. In 1996 the People's Publishing House of China published, an "atlas of shame." *China Daily* told readers it charted in "graphic detail China's humiliation at the hands of world powers over the past century."[123] Just before Hong Kong returned to Chinese control in July 1997, two major anti-foreign films were released. Work units around the country organized tickets for their staff to view the movies, *The Opium War* and *Red River*. (The latter was a violent account of the British invasion of Tibet in 1904.) One man was reported as saying after seeing *Red River* in Beijing, "The foreigners could not do this now. We have nuclear bombs. In those days we were too weak and the foreigners cheated us."[124] In an interview, Xie Jin, the director of *Opium War* compared Britain's role in the Opium Wars to Germany's massacre of the Jews in World War II, Japanese militarism in the 1930s and China's own Cultural Revolution. Xie said he hoped his new film would make the British "face up to their mistakes ahead of the handover."[125] In Guangdong Province tourists were invited to visit a theme park dedicated to British imperialism in China. *South China Morning Post* journalist Jasper Becker reported:

> At Sandy Point Fortress where Captain Elliot fired the first cannon shots of the Opium War; you can now personally destroy the barbarian invaders with a laser gun. Inside the battlements which once guarded the entrance to the Pearl River is a chamber of horrors where grinning automatons with red hair, glide along rails rasping "Bastard! I'll chop you," in harsh mechanical voices. Visitors are invited to take part in a "Search and destroy drug smuggler mission" and blast the figures modeled on the creatures featured in "Night of the Living Dead." Gazing over the Pearl River estuary also stands the statue of Commander Chen Liangsheng, who together with his son perished in resisting the British attack. The authorities even erected a separate statue glorifying his horse "Jie Ma" whose memory is cherished because it kicked every Englishman who came near it.[126]

Beginning in 1996 foreign investors talked of a spirit of "China can say no" coming from the political arena and influencing business deals. Despite the official policy of opening up to foreign investment, investors found the government slow in approving foreign investment deals.[127] Moreover, a tension began to develop between the Chinese government's manipulation of nationalism as a social adhesive and the need to have its population accepting of foreign investment and other activities in China. In 1996, the extremely nationalistic *China Can Say No* (*Zhongguo keyi shuo bu*), written by a group of independent writers, was the most popular, as well as the most controversial, book of the year. The authors adopted a lowbrow, antiforeign tone aimed at a mainstream audience. *Megatrends China* (*Zhongguo da qushi*) written by government officials and originally published in a government magazine came out soon after, and it too became a best-seller. That book contained articles warning of U.S.-led efforts to "contain" China through such methods as environmental lobbying, human rights pressure, and even direct military intervention.[128] According to the book's editor, Cao Weibin, "[the authors] views reflect the general debate in government and academic circles about how China should greet the next century."[129] One of the authors, Lieutenant-General Mi Zhenyu, vice-commandant of the Academy of Military Sciences in Beijing, advocated that China should engage in a covert arms buildup to seek a balance of power with the United States, while at the same time maintaining friendly relations. "For a relatively long time, it will be absolutely necessary that we quietly nurse our sense of vengeance. We must conceal our abilities and bide our time."[130] A number of other books appeared on the same themes within months: *Chronicles of Sino-U.S. Contest, Why Does China Say No? The China That Does Not Only Say No, Overpass U.S.A.*, and *The Background to the Demonizing of China.* Most of the authors and editors were intellectuals in their thirties and forties, the Cultural Revolution generation. Some were specialists in international affairs; a number had studied in the United States. An article in *Beijing Review* summarizing the various works commented:

> The strong message that all these publications send to the United States is that there have been people in Washington who have long misunderstood, isolated and remained hostile to China; that it is high time for Chinese to stand up to defend China and say no to Washington if it continues to pursue power politics and assume bellicose attitudes; and that while the Chinese people are doing their best to avoid confrontation, that doesn't mean they fear confrontation, will yield to pressure and can easily be bullied . . . The fact that these books have emerged from fresh pens suggests that younger intellectuals are disappointed and even disgusted with American values, politics and especially, the country's China policy. It also implies that Washington's non-secret scheme to nurture a "pro-U.S." generation among younger Chinese has come to little avail.[131]

The books were representative of a growing antagonism towards the West, especially the United States, which developed among Chinese intellectuals from the early 1990s. This antagonism exploded in government-supported and in some cases, government-organized demonstrations all over China in early May 1999, after NATO's alleged accidental bombing of the Chinese embassy in Belgrade during a routine attack in the war against Yugoslavia. During the week of the demonstrations, Chinese citizens physically and verbally abused foreigners from Western countries—particularly Americans—and foreign embassies were barricaded and stoned in scenes reminiscent of August 1967.[132] To China's leaders, the notion that came to dominate international politics in the 1990s, that human rights take precedence over national sovereignty was anathema. Though the demonstrations were clearly government orchestrated and approved, they still had strong popular support. Many ordinary Chinese citizens had become alienated by the West's constant singling out of China for criticism at international forums. Chinese press reports on Kosovo frequently referred to "gunboat diplomacy," a trope for the humiliations suffered by China in the Opium War period.[133] The NATO intervention into the Kosovo conflict served to inflame both societal and governmental paranoia about the West. The last year of the twentieth century ended in an atmosphere of popular and officially orchestrated ultranationalism, most visible during the fiftieth anniversary celebrations of the founding of the PRC and in the Chinese response to R.O.C. President Lee Teng-hui's claim that Taiwan and China shared a "special state-to-state relationship." It was an outcome deliberately fostered by fifty years of CCP indoctrination on the topic of the difference between Chinese and foreigners and the damage caused by contact with the West.

Notes

1.   "Zhonggong zhongyang guanyu jiaqiang xuanchuan, sixiang gongzuo de tongzhi," 28 July 1989, *DDXC*, vol. 4, 1812-1813.

2.   David Goodman, *Deng Xiaoping and the Chinese Revolution*, 112.

3.   Zhu Muzhi, "Zai jianchi gaige kaifang qingkuang xia jiaqiang fan heping yanbian," 16 October 1989, *ZMZ*, 235.

4.   Teng Wensheng, ed., *Fan heping yanbian jiaoyu da wen lu* (Beijing: Falu chubanshe, 1992), 16; see also Liu Honghu, ed., *Xifang zhengyao he baokan guanyu heping yanbian de zuixin yanlun* (Wuhan: Hubei renmin chubanshe, 1992); Xin Can, *Xifang zhengjie yaoren tan heping yanbian* (Beijing: Xinhua chubanshe, 1991).

5.   "Zhonggong zhongyang guanyu jiaqiang xuanchuan, sixiang gongzuo de tongzhi," 28 July 1989, *DDXC*, vol. 4, 1815-1816.

6.   "Zhonggong zhongyang guanyu jiaqiang xuanchuan, sixiang gongzuo de tongzhi," 1817.

7.   "Zhongyang xuanchuanbu xinwen chubanshu guanyu jiaqiang dui waiguo he Gang, Ao, Tai baokan jinsuo guanli de yijian," 2 December 1989, *DDXC*, vol. 4, 1900-1903.

8.   "Zhongyang xuanchuanbu guojia anquanbu guanyu gongkai baodao jiandie tewu anjian de you guan guiding de tongzhi," 5 July 1989, *DDXC*, vol. 4, 1868-1869.

9.   See Robinson, "Chinese Foreign Policy 1940s-1990s," in *Chinese Foreign Policy*, ed. Robinson and Shambaugh, 588.

10.   "Zhongyang xuanchuanbu guanyu zhongshen yanjin renhe danwei he geren xiang waiguo zhu Hua shi, lingguan jiedu yingshipian ji shu bao zazhi de tongzhi," 4 November 1989, *DDXC*, vol. 4, 1898.

11.   See Zhu Muzhi's instructions on how to do this in relation to foreign propaganda activities, "Zai quanguo duiwai xuanchuan gongzuo huiyi shang de jianghua," 30 October 1990, *ZMZ*, 277.

12.   "Zhonggong zhongyang guanyu huifu zhongyang duiwai xuanchuan xiaozu de tongzhi," *DDXC*, vol. 4, 1904.

13.   "Zhongyang xuanchuanbu zhuanfa 'guanyu gaijin feimaoyi duiwai wenzi xuanchuanpin chuban faxing gongzuo de yijian' de tongzhi," 22 February 1990, *DDXC*, vol. 4, 1956.

14.   "Guowuyuan guanyu jiaqiang waiguo jizhe guanli wenti de tongzhi," 20 January 1990, *DDXC*, vol. 4, 1941-1945; see also Zhu Muzhi, "You jihua de zuohao waiguo jizhe de gongzuo," 24 November 1990, *ZMZ*, 288.

15.   Zhu Muzhi, "Yao you zhenduixing de jinxing xinwen fabu gongzuo," 5 December 1990, *ZMZ*, 290.

16.   Zhao Pitao, *Waishi gaishuo*, 79. See also Qi Huaiyuan, "Deng Xiaoping de minjian waijiao sixiang yu shixian, in *Deng Xiaoping waijiao sixiang yanjiu wenji*, ed. Wang Taiping, 182, on Deng Xiaoping's efforts in this regard.

17.   Robinson, "Chinese Foreign Policy 1940s-1990s," in *Chinese Foreign Policy*, ed. Robinson and Shambaugh, 590.

18.   The term was first used when a delegation from the British Labour Party visited China in 1954. Pei Xiannong, *Zhou Enlai de waijiaoxue*, 404.

19.   Wang Yonghua, "Zhou Enlai de waijiao yishu," *DWXCCK*, no. 7 (1994): 5-8.

20.   Guo Nei, "Plane Wreck Unveils Tribute to Friends," *China Daily*, 9 January 1995.

21.   "Principle Basis of Good Sino-US Relations," *China Daily*, 29 October 1997.

22.   Oliver Chou, "Amnesty Cited in Counter-attack over Human Rights," *SCMP*, 2 March 1999.

23.   In a book published in 2000, longtime resident friend Sidney Shapiro did, however, publish sharp criticisms of the government's response to 1989. See *I Chose China: The Metamorphosis of a Country and a Man* (New York: Hippocrene Books, 2000), 318-319. These criticisms were left out of the Chinese version of his book, while retaining his critical comments on the students' behavior. See Brady, "The Political Meaning of Friendship: Reviewing the Life and Times of Two of China's American Friends," *China Review International*, 9 (2001):1.

24.   Liu Hongchao, Cai Guangrong, eds., *Waiguo yaoren mingren kan Zhongguo*, (Beijing: Zhonggong zhongyang dangxiao chubanshe, 1992), 189 and 224 respectively.

25.   *Waishi* cadre, interview, December 1997.

26.   "Zhonggong zhongyang guanyu jiaqiang xuanchuan, sixiang gongzuo de tongzhi," 28 July 1989, *DDXC*, vol. 4, 1812-1813.

27.   See http://www.dashan.com.

28.   *Zhejiang sheng waishi zhi*, 67.

29.   "Association Bridges International Exchanges," *China Daily*, 16 December 1995. See also, Qi Huaiyuan, "Deng Xiaoping de minjian waijiao sixiang yu shixian, in *Deng Xiaoping waijiao sixiang yanjiu wenji*, ed. Wang Taiping, 186-187.

30.   See for example, "Party's Over for Foreign Friends of Mao's China," *Daily Telegraph*, 25 March 1999; Marcus Brauchli, "True Believers," *Asian Wall Street Journal*, 13 September 1999, S3.

31.   Zheng Zu'an, personal communication, 21 March 1996. According to Zheng, since the early 1990s there was a "slight" change in policy on researching and writing about foreigners in China. The reasons for this are both economic and political. The Jews are generally perceived as rich potential investors in China. After a 1994 conference in Shanghai on the Jews in China, Chinese officials took conference participants on a tour of the Pudong Special Economic Zone. Research on the Jews in China is funded by a New York-based organization. The Japanese are researched for similar reasons to the Jews, while the Russians are researched to strengthen Sino-Russian relations. Research

on missionaries in China has also increased in recent years, see Shen Dingping and Zhu Weifang, "Western Missionary Influence on the People's Republic of China: A Survey of Chinese Scholarly Opinion between 1980 and 1990," *International Bulletin of Missionary Research*, 22 (October 1998): 154.

32. In the 1990s, as Sino-Russian relations have improved, the Chinese have recognized a few Russian nationals as old friends of China. Many of the senior leaders in China today studied in the former Soviet Union and maintain an affection and nostalgia towards it.

33. See for example, Hu Qihua, "A Couple Devoted for Life, China," *China Daily*, 26 January 1999. In July 1999, Beijing announced that a film based on Edgar Snow's *Red Star over China* would be made, as part of the celebrations for the fiftieth anniversary of the founding of the PRC.

34. See also the twelve-volume collection published by Shijie zhishi chubanshe (the Ministry of Foreign Affairs' publishers) on International Friends (*guoji youren*); Ma Xianglin, *Lan yanjing, hei yanjing, guoji youren yuan Hua kangri jishi* (Beijing: Jiefangjun wenyi chubanshe, 1995); *Mao Zedong and International Friends: Selected Collections of the International Friendship Museum* (Beijing: Xiyuan chubanshe, 1994).

35. New Zealand Embassy report, April 1997.

36. For the specific policy encouraging the handing out of such awards, see *Shiyong shewai changshi shouce* (Beijing: Renmin chubanshe, 1992), 105; see also Zhao Pitao, *Waishi gaishuo*, 140.

37. "Foreign Experts Awarded," *China Daily*, 30 September 1997.

38. "US Expert Given Award," *China Daily*, 12 June 1998.

39. "US Expert Wins Science Award," *China Daily*, 18 October 1995.

40. Cui Ning, "Six Foreign Scientist Experts Honoured," *China Daily*, 15 May 1996.

41. "Foreigners Get Taste of Success," *China Daily*, 26 September 1995.

42. *China Daily*, 2 December 1997.

43. "Helen Snow Awarded for Friendship," *China Daily*, 14 June 1996.

44. "Honorary Title," *China Daily*, 26 January 1999.

45. See for example *DWXCCK*, no. 8 (1997). Here *qiao* could mean both *waiguo qiaomin* (foreigners) and *huaqiao* (overseas Chinese).

46. "Tian Zengpai Notes Diplomacy in New Period," Beijing Central People's Radio Network, 4 October 1994, FBIS-CHI-94-195.

47. "China's Diplomacy Attracts World Attention," *Renmin Ribao Overseas Edition*, 24 October 1994, FBIS-CHI-94-217.

48. *Waishi* cadre, interview, March 1997.

49. "Man man de jianli ganqing cai you youyi."

50. *Waishi* cadre, interview, March 1997.

51. Lu Ning, *The Dynamics of Foreign-Policy Decisionmaking in China*, 8.

52. See Deng Xiaoping, "Gist of Speeches Made in Wuchang, Shenzhen, Zhuhai and Shanghai," *Beijing Review* (7-20 Feb. 1994): 9-20, see also *Deng Xiaoping Selected Works*, vol. III, 1982-1992, Internet edition, www.peoplesdaily.com.cn.

53. Zhu Muzhi, "Gaoju renquan de qizhi," 20 December 1994, *ZMZ*, 570. See also Wu Qinghe, "Deng Xiaoping renmin waijiao de zhengce sixiang ji qi shixian," in *Deng Xiaoping waijiao sixiang yanjiu wenji*, ed. Wang Taiping, 204, for comments on the success of this policy.

54. "Women's Rights Conference Opens," *SCMP*, 27 October 1998.

55. Zhao Pitao, *Waishi gaishuo*, 157.
56. *Fuwu jingji, tuijin kaifang, shuli xingxiang,* Liu Luxiang, *Shewai gonggong guanxi*, 167.
57. Zhu Muzhi, "Dui wai xuanchuan yao guanche Deng Xiaoping nan xun tanhua jingshen," 9 April 1993, *ZMZ*, 475-476.
58. Du Cheng "Nuli kaichuang dianshi waixuan gongzuo xinjumian," *DWBDCK*, no. 8 (1997): 14-16.
59. *Waishi* cadres, interview, December 1997.
60. *China Daily*, 4 September 1997.
61. *China Daily*, 26 August 1997.
62. "San ge laowai zou chang zheng," *Beijing guangbo dianshi bao*, no. 23/32 (1997): 1. Veteran American journalist Harrison Salisbury, his wife Charlotte, and former U.S. State Department official Jack Service had earlier reenacted the Long March in 1984 accompanied by a Ministry of Foreign Affairs interpreter and other officials, see Salisbury, *The Long March: The Untold Story* (New York: Harper and Row, 1985).
63. "China's Own 'List' Suggested," *China Daily*, 8 January 1998.
64. Zhu Xiaoyong, "Rabe's Diary Hits Big Screen," *China Daily*, 15 January 1999.
65. Lisa Carducci, "Wo shenghuo zhong de Zhongguo," *Beijing Youth Daily*, 25 January 1999.
66. Robert and Susan Spellman, "Going to Church in China," *Beijing Youth Daily*, 25 January 1999.
67. Zhao Pitao, *Waishi gaishuo*, 97.
68. *Zhejiang sheng waishi zhi*, 73.
69. "Foreign Workers Required to Apply for New Licences," *China Daily*, 2 May 1996.
70. "Sino-Russian Experts Exchanges Continue," *China Daily*, 25 April 1996.
71. "State Frees All Colleges to Register Foreigners," *China Daily*, 17 February 1998; see also "Foreign Students Wise Up to China," *China Daily*, 18 April 1996.
72. Cui Ning, "Overseas Education Exchange Encouraged," *China Daily*, 21 August 1997.
73. China Data Centre, University of Michigan, http://0www.umich.edu/~iinet/chinadata/stat.
74. Personnel from what was formerly the Booking Office for Foreigners, Xikezhan, interview, May 2001.
75. "State to Regulate Hiring: Foreign Experts Sought," *China Daily*, 9 April 1996.
76. "Head-Hunt for Talented Foreigners," *China Daily*, 13 December 1995.
77. "Head-Hunt for Talented Foreigners."
78. "State Keeps Reins Tight on Theatre," *China Daily*, 30 August 1997.
79. Shao Zhenxiang, *Shewai gong'an zhishi wenda* (Beijing: Zhongguo fangzheng chubanshe, 1994), 209.
80. Interview with *waishi* official, May 2001. Foreign journalists (and, presumably, diplomats) in Beijing were restricted to living in the Chaoyang or Dongcheng districts, see http://www.fmprc.gov.cn/eng/15127.html.
81. For a list of regions open to foreigners, see http://www.fmprc.gov.cn/eng/15138.html.
82. Interview with *waishi* official, May 2001.

83. See Wang Zhongnong, ed., *Duiwai jiaoliu shouce* (Wuhan: Hubei renmin chubanshe, 1995), 706-707, for the regulations on this.

84. Zhao Pitao, *Waishi gaishuo*, 139, and in general, discussing the "management" of foreign experts in China in the 1990s see 129-141.

85. Wang Rihua, ed., *Shiyong shewai changshi shouce* (Beijing: Renmin Zhongguo chubanshe, 1993), 40.

86. "241 'Still Paying' for Tiananmen," *SCMP*, 29 April 1999.

87. Agence France Presse, "Drop Meeting Plan, Activists Told," 15 February 1999; and also "China Defends Dissident Arrest," *SCMP*, 3 December 1998.

88. Wang Rihua, ed., *Shiyong shewai changshi shouce*, 94.

89. *Shiyong shewai changshi shouce*, 94.

90. See *Shiyong shewai changshi shouce*, 48, and Li Jinwei, *Waishi zhishi daquan* (Shanghai: Shanghai yiwen chubanshe, 1992), 774.

91. Zhao Pitao, *Waishi gaishuo*, 201-204; see also Huang Zhizhong, *Duiwai kaifang yu guofang jiaoyu* (Beijing: Guofang daxue, 1990).

92. See for example Jasper Becker, "Newsman Accused of Stealing Secrets," *SCMP*, 19 November 1998. *Der Spiegel* journalist Juergen Kremb was arrested during an intensified crackdown on leakage and theft of classified material. "Appeal for Crackdown on Leaks," *SCMP*, 20 November 1998; see also "All the News That's Fit to Print" (Chinese secrecy and foreign journalists), *The Economist* 323, no.7761 (30 May 1992): 34.

93. See for example, "Purged Aide Silenced after Talk with Media," *SCMP*, 5 June 1998; "One and a Half Month before New Millennium: Troubled Times," *FCCC Newsletter* (November 1999). For current regulations on handling foreign journalists, see http://www.fmprc.gov.cn/eng.

94. Scott Hill, "China: China Urges Western Media to Study Model Reporter," Reuter News Service, 31 October 1996.

95. Wang Rihua, ed., *Shiyong shewai changshi shouce*, 96.

96. *Shiyong shewai changshi shouce*, 96.

97. *Shiyong shewai changshi shouce*, 100. See also *Shewai renyuan shouce* (1985), 3.

98. Daniel J. Curran and Sandra Cook, "Doing Research in Post-Tiananmen China," in *Researching Sensitive Topics*, ed. Claire M. Renzetti and Raymond M. Lee (New York: Sage Publications, 1993), 72.

99. Curran and Cook, "Doing Research in Post-Tiananmen China," 78.

100. Zhao Pitao, *Waishi gaishuo*, 136.

101. "Provisional Measures on Foreign-Related Social Investigations," promulgated 15 August 1999 by the State Statistical Bureau, see *China Economic News*, 17 January 2000.

102. "Mainland Urged to Ease Survey Controls," *SCMP*, 29 September 1999.

103. Zhao Pitao, *Waishi gaishuo*, 196.

104. Zhao Pitao, *Waishi gaishuo*, 187.

105. Zhao Pitao, *Waishi gaishuo*, 190.

106. Duiwai maoyi jingji hezuobu jiaojishi, *Shewai liyi ABC* (Beijing: Zhongguo renmin chubanshe, 1997), 8; Zhao Pitao, *Waishi gaishuo*, 136; Zhonghua renmin gongheguo gonganbu waishi ju, *Libin gongzuo shouce* (Beijing: Jingguan jiaoyu chubanshe, 1997), 9.

107. These publications are too numerous to list here, but I have listed them in my bibliography.

108.   Zhu Muzhi, "Guanyu duiwai xuanchuan de ji ge wenti," 10 September 1981, *ZMZ*, 30; and Zhu Muzhi, "Ba duiwai xuanchuan gongzuo tigao yibu," 22 June 1986, *ZMZ*, 74.

109.   Many nonofficial books on how to deal with foreigners have been appearing in recent years, see for example Li Xinshi, ed., *Ruhe yu waiguoren zuo shengyi* (Beijing: Dizhen chubanshe, 1993). Li Xinshi informs his Chinese readers the basic rule in doing business with foreigners is not to forget that they *themselves* are the foreigner (Li, 1).

110.   Wang Rihua, ed., *Shiyong shewai changshi shouce*, 51 and 50.

111.   *Shiyong shewai changshi shouce*, 48.

112.   Hao Meitian, *Shiyong libinxue*, 77-85.

113.   Zhao Pitao, *Waishi gaishuo*, 72.

114.   See the document "Realistic Responses and Strategic Choices for China after the Soviet Upheaval," published in *Zhongguo qingnian bao* in 1991. This *neibu* document renounced the Marxist-Leninist legacy and advocated nationalism as a unifying force, combining Western rationalism with Chinese culture. Cited in Gu Xin and David Kelly, "New Conservatism: Intermediate Ideology of a 'New Elite,'" in *China's Quiet Revolution*, ed. David S. Goodman and Beverley Hooper (Melbourne: Longman Cheshire, 1994), 219-233.

115.   Proponents of the China threat theory believe that China is becoming increasingly belligerent and will threaten the interests of the West in the future, see for example Richard Bernstein and Ross H. Munro, *The Coming Conflict with China* (New York: A. A. Knopf, 1997); Samuel P. Huntington, *The Clash of Civilizations and the Remaking of World Order* (New York: Simon and Schuster, 1996).

116.   "China Poses No Threat to Others," *China Daily*, 7 November 1995.

117.   "China Holds High Banner of Peace," *China Daily*, 29 June 1996.

118.   "Disney's Donald Takes a Ducking," *China Daily*, 25 May 1996. From a new production base in Chengdu, sixty-two new comic books for juveniles and children were to be published. China planned to build five cartoon publication bases, publishing fifteen comic book serials and five cartoon magazines for children.

119.   "Writers Guilty of 'Betrayal,'" *SCMP*, 14 December 1996.

120.   "Cultural Imports Minus Vulgarity," *SCMP*, 13 December 1996.

121.   "Zhonggong zhongyang guanyu jiaqiang he gaijin xuanchuan sixiang gongzuo, geng hao de wei jingji jianshe he gaige kaifang fuwu de yijian," 3 September 1992, *DDXC*, vol. 4, 2107.

122.   Tom Korski, "Western Advertisers Urged to Push Ethics," *SCMP*, 14 May 1997.

123.   "Atlas of Shame," *China Daily*, 22 June 1996.

124.   Mark O'Neill, "Thousands Mobilized for Imperial 'War Crimes' Films," *SCMP*, 13 June 1997.

125.   Alison Smith and Reuter, "Director Blasts 'Hitlerish' Britain," *SCMP*, 6 May 1997.

126.   Jasper Becker, "Opium City on a High," *SCMP*, 7 June 1997.

127.   "No Leverage," *FEER* (24 October 1996).

128.   Bruce Gilley, "Potboiler Nationalism," *FEER* (3 October 1996): 23.

129.   "Potboiler Nationalism," 23.

130.   "Potboiler Nationalism," 23.

131.   Li Haibo, "Snapshot," *Beijing Review* 40, no. 20 (19-25 May 1997): 4.

132.   See Christopher Thiele, "Fallout from the Bomb," *Amida* (June/July 1999): 18; Jane Hutcheons reporting from Beijing, ABC 7 p.m. News, 16 May 1999.

133.   Frédéric Bobin, "Kosovo Comes to Haunt China," *Le Monde*, 22 June 1999.

Chapter 9

Friends All over the World?

Looking at the history of the CCP foreign affairs system in the period from its origins in the 1920s to the beginning of the twenty-first century, one might question the well-known CCP slogan "we have friends all over the world," *women de pengyou bianyu quan shijie.*[1] Rather than the numerousness of China's international friends, the structures and ideology of the *waishi* system imply a perception of the outside world, particularly the West, as hostile and intrinsically opposed to the PRC. In CCP terms, "friendship" might be read as doublethink for "hatred," or at the very least, "distrust."

The CCP's *waishi* system developed out of a deliberate and calculated response to its perception of a hostile world beyond China's borders. It is both a system for managing the foreign presence in China and China's contacts with the outside world, as well as having an implicit role in controlling the Chinese population. It is a defensive response from a society that has felt its worldview, a sense of the greatness of Chinese society and culture, profoundly challenged. It reflects a cultural crisis, a reaction against events such as the Opium War, the treaty port system, the Taiping Rebellion, the Washington Treaty of 1919, the Japanese invasion, the Cold War, and in more recent years, the Western response after the events of 4 June 1989, the NATO bombing of the Chinese embassy in Belgrade in 1999, and the February 2001 U.S. spy plane incident on Hainan Island. As an approach and means to managing both foreigners and the people of China, it has proved to be one of the most effective tools in the repertoire of the Chinese Communist Party for building and then sustaining its hold on power.

Waishi has played an essential role in the CCP's "mytho-logical" national narrative, forming part of a larger project of a government-controlled reinvention of what constitutes "Chineseness." As we have seen, Maoist historiography officially relegated exploitative foreign relations to the past, the bad years of "semicolonialism, semifeudalism" before 1949. From Year Zero (1949), in contrast to what had gone before, all contact with the foreign was to be controlled by the Chinese people, or rather, their vanguard leaders, the CCP. One of the most basic themes of CCP foreign policy has long been that it should not be seen to be dominated by the will of foreign powers (though as was shown in the Sino-Soviet talks in the early 1950s, CCP leaders were willing to make concessions as long as these were not publicized). During the West's containment of the PRC in the Cold War era, Mao made a virtue out of China's self-reliance. And when U.S.-China relations improved in the early 1970s, the CCP presented itself as victorious and in control of the situation. The Sino-Soviet split came about because the CCP was willing to cut links with its closest ally when it felt it was being exploited. Mao's criticism of Soviet "revisionism" might have been more subdued had the Soviet Union accepted a more equal relationship with China. In the years after the split, CCP historians promoted the idea that Mao Zedong had frequently been in conflict with Moscow's policies in the pre-1949 years and that any mistakes in policy had originated from following Moscow's advice too closely. In the years after 1949, the CCP set out to eradicate "foreign influence" in China, meanwhile imposing a whole new set of foreign institutions and ideology courtesy of the Soviet Union. And throughout the 1980s and 1990s and on into the early years of the twenty-first century, as Western investment in China has deepened and Western-style economic reform has seen the country adopting an economic system that bears more resemblance to raw capitalism than socialism, the CCP propaganda machine has been careful to emphasize the unique "Chinese characteristics" of this transformation and the party's total control of the whole experience.

Party spokespersons claim that the *waishi* system itself has uniquely Chinese antecedents, which has led to the development of "diplomacy with Chinese characteristics." Howsoever we might dispute these claims, they are revealing in themselves. In the era of Jiang Zemin, such claims have been part of a deliberate project to weaken the influence of Marxist-Leninist-Maoist ideology in Chinese society (at the same time as continuing to mouth the same old truisms) and to erase or obfuscate the past history of the CCP's close relations with the Soviet Communist Party and the Comintern, or in recent years, the absorption of Western ideas and methodology. The CCP has from the late 1930s encouraged the invention of a notion of "Chineseness" that draws selectively from China's ancient history as well as various foreign influences, which themselves can quickly become "Chinese" by dint of their translation into familiar terms. An examination of the *waishi* system confirms the analysis of many foreign scholars of the abiding influence of nationalism (or in the term Mao preferred "patriotism") on CCP foreign policy decision making. Although the CCP's Marxist-Leninist ideological origins demanded allegiance to an internationalist revolutionary cause, internationalism can only be seen as having a significant influence on CCP foreign policy when it suited China's national interest. Indeed Mao justified the strongly nationalist elements of the Chinese revolution by calling it "applied internationalism." The importance of nationalism over internationalism in Chinese foreign policy was even sanctioned by Stalin in 1949, when he ac-

knowledged that imperialism was the main contradiction in the Chinese revolution. Though Marxist-Leninist ideology has been used to justify the foreign policy decisions of the government, it does not decide them. As a close reading of
classified CCP leaders' speeches and memorandum from the pre- and post-1949
period reveals, pragmatism, *real politik*, a bitter hatred of China's past humiliations, combined with a strong sense of insiders and outsiders, and the ability to
size up who is a friend, however temporary, and who is an enemy, have been the
deciding factors in the foreign policy decision making of the People's Republic
of China.

The CCP foreign affairs system has constructed a highly politicized image
of foreigners as the "Other" in contrast to the Chinese Self. The image of the
foreign Other has by no means been purely negative, government-orchestrated
xenophobia has always been selective and controlled, as has government-
orchestrated admiration of foreigners and foreign things. One of the objectives
of *waishi* is to manage a balance between the two extremes among the Chinese
population, drawing on and manipulating pro- or anti-foreign sentiment in accordance with the political needs of the time. Hence there is a close link between
domestic policy, *neishi*, and foreign policy, *waishi*, in the Chinese political system. In the early years of the Mao era, the domestic economy required the workforce to unite behind the CCP government; so antiforeign feeling was manipulated to bring disparate forces together. In the China of Deng Xiaoping and after,
the domestic economy requires a docile, moderately educated population capable of working for low wages for overseas investors, yet still mindful of the difference between "insiders" and "outsiders"; so the government promotes positive propaganda about the role of foreigners in China's economic transformation
at the same time as incessant, pernicious propaganda on the past and present
wrongs done against China by foreign countries.

The positive symbol of the objectified foreign Other in new China is the
"foreign friend." The foreign friend's moral antithesis is the foreign imperialist
or foreign spy, who unlike foreign friends is usually generic. "Foreign friends"
and "friendship" have become the key words to the CCP's ideology of the foreign in China. On a subconscious level, like so many other elements of the CCP
revolution, the language of "friendship" has fundamentally altered the vocabulary of Sino-foreign interaction in the Chinese mainland and beyond. After more
than fifty years of assiduous propaganda work on Sino-foreign relations, both
foreigners and Chinese alike now frequently find themselves, wittingly or not,
enmeshed in a worldview which evaluates Sino-foreign interactions in terms of
whether they are "friendly" or not to China, a "China" which implicitly means
that ruled by the CCP. Breaking through such a paradigm to establish genuine
interaction and a genuine exchange of ideas and opinions is one of the chal-
lenges of Sino-foreign interaction in the future.

One of the key tasks of China's *waishi* cadres has long been to garner more
friends for China, at the same time as discrediting or silencing those who did not
support the interests of the Chinese Communist Party. CCP leaders used for-

eigners from Edgar Snow to Henry Kissinger and others less famous to advance Chinese interests outside China; they also used their support for Chinese government policy as an example to the Chinese population. For some foreigners, especially in the Mao era, being a friend of China was a full-time job, defining their whole life. For many others it was merely flattering, at times embarrassing, to be described in such terms. In the Mao era, senior leaders often acted as if the foreign friends were the repository of the power of the West, spending enormous amounts of time "exchanging views" with them on their high-profile visits or meeting with a select few resident friends of China as if they truly were ambassadors of the "people of the world." In the Deng era comparatively less money and pomp is expended on foreign friends than in the past, but then in the 1980s and 1990s far larger numbers of foreigners of influence and power have regarded it as in their interests to be on good terms with the Chinese government. As always, the foreign friends have not been required to be in complete agreement with the CCP, they need simply share a common interest or goal and preferably, keep silent about the points they disagree on.

Waishi has had an important role to play in the process of nation building and modernizing that has enabled China to move from its weak state at the end of the Qing dynasty to a position as one of the world's major powers. One of the early themes of Chinese nationalism was the preoccupation with reestablishing China's rightful place in the hierarchy of nations. China's traditional worldview posited the Middle Kingdom at the center of the universe; all other cultures were on the periphery. Western incursions from the mid-nineteenth century on, Western technical and political superiority, and the collapse of the Chinese Empire in 1911 challenged historical notions of China's cultural superiority and left the country divided by warlords and foreign imperialists. The CCP has made a point of nurturing and maintaining popular resentments about this painful past. China's *waishi* has been primarily directed at the West, both because the West has what modern China most needs, technology, finance for development, and power and dominance in the global system, and because the imperialist or neo-imperialist policies of the West against China are an important part of the CCP's claim to rule. In the 1950s and 1960s, China's stance on international relations won it much support in the decolonizing, underdeveloped world, and by the end of the 1990s, its stand on human rights was gaining it a new set of allies among some of the countries of the former Soviet bloc, most noticeably Russia and Serbia, as well as in the developing world.

An indication of the nation-building role of *waishi* has been the prominence placed on foreign propaganda from the earliest years of CCP *waishi* institutions. In line with its vision of a new, strong, and independent China, the CCP has worked hard to change international perceptions of a nation that was once regarded as the "sick man of Asia." In the 1950s and 1960s one of the tasks of *waishi* cadres was to broadcast new China's revolutionary vision to the world and urge others to follow it. Beginning in the late 1970s, *waishi* cadres were ordered to replace that earlier vision with one of China as a great market, open to the outside world. Although the slogans have changed, the goal of China's foreign propaganda has not. China's propagandists are tasked with presenting the PRC as strong, united, and in control of its own destiny under any circumstances, whether in famine or economic boom time, rebellion or revolution.

This study has offered a political history of *waishi* from 1921-2003, outlining its origins and showing how a bureaucratic system and ideology defining the foreign and China's place in the world has evolved in the last eighty years. By nature of the vastness of the topic it has not been possible to plumb all the depths of the *waishi* system, nor have I attempted to do so. There is much more work to be done on this crucial area of research, some of which will only be revealed when the equivalent of China's own Stasi files are opened.

It is likely that for both psychological and strategic reasons, as long as there is a CCP government in power in China, "diplomacy with Chinese characteristics," or the *waishi* system, will continue. Managing the foreign Other is an essential element in the CCP's hold on political power. Though China will continue to open its markets to the outside world, and indeed World Trade Organization (WTO) membership requires it to do so, the CCP will maintain its attempt to control that process and limit any potential damage. From the CCP's point of view, to relinquish its grip on Sino-foreign contact and limit government control to matters such as diplomacy and trade policy would be potentially regime threatening. Regardless of a relatively peaceful international strategic environment, the CCP perceives the major threat to its hold on power to be an ideological one, the impact of bourgeois liberal notions of democracy, with a secondary threat the potential of economic instability due to a failure to successfully reform the Chinese economy. Hence *waishi* will continue to have two crucial roles to play in the future: 1) to maintain a notion of the foreign threat to China among the Chinese people, and 2) to stimulate, encourage, and manage increased foreign investment and technology exchange to China, as well as to continue to build up China's international prestige.

"Use the past to serve the present, make the foreign serve China," Mao Zedong's aphorism neatly sums up the *waishi* system and its far-reaching implications. The slogan indicates that the People's Republic of China will aim to make use only of what it needs from the outside world, fully in control of the process of cultural transformation, while maintaining its own traditions. Rather than an example of naïve, quaint, cultural practice, China's foreign affairs system, with its stress on "friendship" and building "feeling," reflects a complex, systemized approach to engaging with the outside world, incorporating matters as large as diplomacy and as small as the tone of conversations between Chinese and foreigners. As China increases its global influence and strengthens its ties with other countries, it is important that we acknowledge and are aware of the current Chinese government's approach to foreign affairs, its perspective on the foreign and its impact on public opinion. *Waishi* is a window on how China's leaders see increased contact with the outside world, both as a threat and an opportunity. It should not be regarded as simply an example of mere paranoia or xenophobia. From the point of view of an overpopulated, resource-rich but technologically backward, developing nation, Chinese-style foreign relations are a means to speed up modernization, while attempting to protect national interests against foreign incursions. And from the viewpoint of the last 150 years of Chinese history, the *waishi* system is a matter of both national pride and dignity.

Notes

1.   This slogan appears prominently in locations frequented by foreigners in China, such as the lobby of the Beijing Hotel. It originates from Mao Zedong's speech to the first meeting of the Chinese People's Consultative Conference on 21 September 1949, published in *Renmin Ribao* the following day. The full version of this quote is "Our revolution has already gained the sympathy and acclaim of all the people in the world, we have friends all over the world." Excerpted in *Zui gao zhishi* (Important Instructions) (Beijing, n.p., 1969), 286.

Appendix

Regulations for Foreign Affairs Staff (*waishi jilü*)

1. Be loyal to the Motherland, loyal to the people. Resolutely defend our nation's sovereignty and national dignity, do not say things that are not to the advantage of the Motherland, do not do things that harm our nation's dignity or integrity.
2. Have a firm standpoint, uphold principles, guard against, and resist the plots of hostile forces' to promote peaceful evolution. Consciously resist the corrosion of decadent bourgeois ideology and lifestyle, be one who can not be debauched by riches and honor, is unmovable in straightened and humbled circumstances, and can not be subdued by force.
3. Resolutely implement the Party and State line and policies; conscientiously abide by laws and regulations. Report conditions strictly according to the facts, strictly implement the system of asking for instructions and reporting back.
4. Guard State secrets, strictly implement security laws and regulations. Adhere to the policy of treating insiders and outsiders differently; do not divulge internal matters.
5. Be faithful in the discharge of one's duties; fulfill one's duty and responsibilities. Heighten vigilance; guard against traitors, combat espionage, and combat plots of insurrection.
6. Strengthen organizational attitudes, consciously observe discipline. When outside China obey the leadership of the Chinese embassy and consulate in that country, abide by the laws of that country, abide by the customs of that country. Do not practice chauvinism or racial discrimination.
7. Do not engage in private dealings with foreign organizations or foreign individuals, do not utilize the powers of office or work connections to seek private gain or profits. It is strictly forbidden to demand or accept bribes, do not violate State regulations by keeping any honorariums or commissions received, strictly adhere to the regulations on receiving gifts.

8. Be hardworking and thrifty, be honest in performing one's official duties, draw a clear distinction between public and private, strictly adhere to the finance rules.
9. Be modest, speak and act discreetly, be neither obsequious nor supercilious. Make an effort to be civilized and polite, pay attention to dress and appearance. It is forbidden to drink alcohol excessively.
10. Bear in mind the overall situation and the development of approach, coordinate and work together, cooperate in dealing with outsiders.[1]

Notes

1.   These are translated from a standard *waishi* handbook *Shiyong shewai changshi shouce*, 40.

Glossary

aiguo 爱国

aiguozhuyi 爱国主义

ba chuanghu dakai, nanmian hui you canying wenzi pao jinlai 把窗户打开，难免会有苍蝇蚊子跑进来

ba fangwu dasao ganjing zai qing ke 把房屋打扫干净再请客

baquanzhuyi 霸权主义

bai ka 白卡

Baiqiuen-Yan'an zaofandui 白求恩延安造反队

baogao hui 报告会

Beijing baoluan 北京爆乱

bin li 宾礼

bixu fenqing neiwai you bie 必须分清内外有别

bu yao wangji lao pengyou 不要忘记老朋友

changqi zhu He Da 长期住 "和大" (和平大会)

chaoji daguo 超极大国

chong yang mei wai 崇洋媚外

daguozhuyi 大国主义

da yuejin 大跃进

dazibao 大字报

da zu yi rong zhong, de zu yi huai yuan 大足以容众，德足以怀远

dangquan pai 当权派

dao ting tu shuo 道听途说

dipai 地派

difang xuanchuan 地方宣传

diguozhuyizhe 帝国主义者

duikou 对口

duinei 对内

duinei xuanchuan 对内宣传

duiwai 对外

duiwai guanxi 对外关系

duiwai huodong 对外活动

duiwai xuanchuan xiaozu 对外宣传小组

duiwai zhengce 对外政策

ezhi Zhongguo 遏制中国

ermu 耳目

Fazhan yu heping yanjiu zhongxin 发展与和平研究中心

fei guanfang waijiao guanxi 非官方外交关系

feizhengfu zuzhi 非政府组织

fengjian shi zhong 丰俭适中

fengsuo 封锁

gaige kaifang 改革开放

ganqing 感情

gao bizi 高鼻子

gaomizhe 告密者

geming huozhong 革命火种

gong nong bing liuxuesheng 工农兵留学生

gongtongdian 共同点

gu wei jin yong, yang wei Zhong yong 古为今用，洋为中用

guangjiao pengyou 广交朋友

guanxi 关系

guanxi wang 关系网

guanzhong pengyou 观众朋友

Guoji gonggong guanxi xiehui 国际公共关系协会

guoji youren 国际友人

guojizhuyizhe 国际主义者

guojiazhuyi 国家主义

Guowuyuan waishi bangongshi 国务院外事办公室

heping yanbian 和平演变

houtai 后台

Huai, lai, rou, an 怀，来，柔，安

huai rou 怀柔

huai rou bai shen 怀柔百神

huairou zhengce 怀柔政策

jizou fangzhen 挤走方针

jie 接

jiedai keren 接待客人

jielu diren 揭露敌人

jing jiu 敬酒

jingshen wenming 精神文明

jun xuan dao ti feng, huai rou bai yue 君宣导体风，怀柔百越

kaifang 开放

Kang Mei yuan Chao 抗美援朝

kuoda kaifang, yinjin waizi 扩大开放，引进外资

laoshi 老师

ling qi luzao 另起炉灶

lingdao hexin 领导核心

liuxuesheng sushe 留学生宿舍

litong waiguo 里通外国

liyong maodun 利用矛盾

liyong waili wei wo xuanchuaṇ 利用外力为我宣传

liyong waizi 利用外资

liu si 六四

mangren mo xiang 盲人摸象

mei you gongchandang, jiu mei you xin Zhongguo 没有共产党 就没有新中国

mie yang 灭洋

minjian waijiao 民间外交

minjian zuzhi 民间组织

minzuzhuyi 民族主义

mozhe shitou guo he 摸着石头过河

nan xun 南巡

neibu 内部

nei jin wai song 内紧外松

neishi 内事

nei wai you bie 内外有别

nongmin pengyou 农民朋友

paoda silingbu 炮打司令部

pantu 叛徒

peixun ban 培训班

pengyou 朋友

pishi 批示

qin Mei, chong Mei, kong Mei 亲美崇美恐美

qing 轻

qiu tong cun yi 求同存异

qiu tong li yi 求同立异

qunzhong jiandu 群众监督

renmin youhao shizhe 人民友好使者

rou yuanren 柔远人

rouyuan 柔远

san dou yi duo 三斗一多

sannian ziran zaihai 三年自然灾害

sanxiang yimie luxian 三向一灭路线

shanyu zuo ren de gongzuo 善于做人的工作

shewai 涉外

shewai binguan 涉外宾馆

shezhan 舌战

si ge xiandaihua 四个现代化

song 送

Sulian de jintian shi women de mingtian 苏联的今天是我们的明天

suzhi 素质

tanzi 探子

tianpai 天派

tizhi 体制

tongshi 同室

tongxiang 同乡

tongxiao 同校

tongzhi 同志

waiguo 外国

waiguo pengyou 外国朋友

waiguo qiaomin guanli ke 外国侨民管理科

waiguo tongzhi 外国同志

waiguo zhuanjia 外国专家

waiguo zhuanjia lou 外国专家楼

waiguoren fang de pi dou shi xiang de 外国人放的屁都是香的

waihui quan 外汇卷

waijiaobu 外交部

waijiao gongyu 外交公寓

waijiao shiwu 外交事物

waili 外力

waishi 外事

waishibu 外事部

waishichu 外事处

waishi bangongshi 外事办公室

waishi gongzuo 外事工作

waishi jilü 外事纪律

waishi kou 外事口

waishi lingdao xiaozu 外事领导小组

waishi xitong 外事系统

waishi xiaozu 外事小组

waiyi 外夷

wai zhili 外知力

women de pengyou bianyu tianxia 我们的朋友遍于天下

wuqin 五勤

xitong 系统

xiao pengyou 小朋友

Xinhuashe 新华社

xuanchuan ziji 宣传自己

yang guizi 洋鬼子

yi binli qin bangguo 以宾礼亲邦国

yi bian dao 一边倒

yi min cu guan 以民促官

yiyi 抑异

yi qiao wei qiao 以侨为桥

yin shui bu wang jue jing ren 饮水不忘记掘井人

yong yi bian Xia 用夷变夏

youhao guanxi 友好关系

Youlian 友联

youpai 右派

youyi 友谊

Youxie 友协

you Zhongguo tese de duiwai xuanchuan 有中国特色的对外宣传

yumin pengyou 渔民朋友

zaofan you li 造反有理

zhanyou 战友

zheng ming 正名

zhi bi zhi ji, bai zhan bu dai 知彼知己，百战不殆

Zhongguo jiaoliu xiehui 中国交流协会

Zhongguo guoji maoyi cujin weiyuanhui 中国国际贸易促进委员会

Zhongguo guoji youhao lianluohui 中国国际友好联络会

Zhongguo renmin de lao pengyou 中国人民的老朋友

Zhongguo renmin duiwai wenhua xiehui 中国人民对外文化协会

Zhongguo renmin duiwai youhao xiehui 中国人民对外友好协会

Zhongxue wei ti, Xixue wei yong 中学为体，西学为用

Zhongguo zongjiao yanjiu zhongxin 中国宗教研究中心

zijiren 自己人

zi qiang 自强

ziqiang chuangzao huihuang 自强创造辉惶

ziyou 自由

zougou 走狗

zuguo 祖国

Select Bibliography

Interviews

Pat Adler, Beijing, 10 December 1997.
Viviane Alleton, Paris, 24 March 1997.
Courtney Archer, Christchurch, 4-6 July 1993.
Jean Chesneaux, Paris, 23 March 1998.
Marianne Bastid-Bruguière, Paris, 26 March 1997.
David Crook, Beijing, 23 April and 16 May 1996.
Isabel Crook, Beijing, 23 April and 16 May 1996.
Hugh Deane, New York, 2 April 1997.
Deng Bangzhen, Beijing, 24 June 1991; Auckland, 6 December 1993.
Ces English, Canberra, 2 February and 25 July 1997.
Karen Engst, Beijing, 19 December 1997.
Sid Engst, Beijing, 28 November, 19 and 22 December 1997.
Israel Epstein, Beijing, 5 November 1990 and 8 August 1996.
Jack Ewen, Auckland, 29 June 1993.
Tom A. Grunfeld, New York, 7 April 1997.
Carmelita Hinton, Beijing, 15 January 1998.
Joan Hinton, Beijing, 28 November, 19 and 22 December 1997.
David Kidd, Kyoto, 30 October 1994.
Sara Lake, Nelson (telephone), 4 December 1993 and 1 February 1996.
Nyrene Masson, Auckland (telephone), 26 January 1996.
Past and present *waishi* cadres of the All-China Trade Union Federation, Centre for Peace and Development Studies, China Travel Service, China Welfare Institute, Foreign Experts' Bureau, Foreign Languages Press, Chinese Association for Friendship with Foreign Countries, Friendship League, International Liaison Bureau, Ministry of Foreign Affairs, Peking Radio, Public Security Bureau, Xinhua News Service, various interviews 1996-2000
Sid Rittenberg, Chapel Hill (telephone), 29 April 1998.
Gerry Tannenbaum, Santa Barbara, 10-11 April 1997.
Ross Terrill, Canberra, 29 July and 5 May 1997, 15 November 1998.
Anne Turner, Canberra, 26 April 1999.
Ruth Weiss, Beijing, 13 March 1996.

Endymion Wilkinson, Beijing, 2 May 1996.
Alex Yang, Beijing, 5 and 8 November 1990.
Yang Xianyi, Beijing, 13 September1995 and 2 May 1996.
Eva Xiao, Beijing, 11 June 1996.
York Young, Wellington, 18 January 1993 and (telephone) 20 January 1995.

Unpublished Materials

Rewi Alley papers, Alexander Turnbull Library, Wellington, New Zealand.
Harry Lloyd papers, in the possession of Joan Hinton, Beijing.
Maud Russell papers, New York City Public Library.
Heinz Shippe papers, in the possession of Ruth Weiss, Beijing.
Edgar Snow papers, University Archives, University of Missouri, Kansas City.
Helen Foster Snow papers, L. Tom Perry Special Collections, Harold B. Lee Library,
    Brigham Young University.

Published Sources

Aarons, Eric. *What's Left? Memoirs of an Australian Communist*. Sydney: Penguin
    Books Australia, 1993.
Allen, Ted and Sydney Gordon. *The Scalpel and the Sword: The Story of Dr. Norman
    Bethune*. Revised edition. New York: Monthly Review Press, 1971.
Alley, Rewi. *At 90: Memoirs of My China Years*. Beijing: New World Press, 1987.
Anagnost, Ann. *National Past-Times: Narrative, Representation, and Power in Modern
    China*. Durham and London: Duke University Press, 1997.
Anti-Japanese Bases in North China as Seen by Westerners. Pamphlet. Chongqing: CCP
    Foreign Propaganda Group, March 1943.
Auden, W. H., and Christopher Isherwood. *Journey to a War*. London: Faber and Faber,
    1939.
Bair, Deidre. *Simone de Beauvoir: A Biography*. London: Vintage, 1991.
Band, William, and Claire Band. *Two Years with the Chinese Communists*. New Haven:
    Yale University Press, 1948.
Bao Ruo-wang (Jean Pasqualini), and Rudolph Chelminski. *Prisoner of Mao*. New York:
    Coward, McCann and Geoghan, 1973.
Barghoorn, Frederick C. *The Soviet Cultural Offensive: The Role of Cultural Diplomacy
    in Soviet Foreign Policy*. Princeton: Princeton University Press, 1960.
Barnett, A. Doak. *The Making of Foreign Policy in China: Structure and Process*. Boul-
    der, Colo.: Westview Press; and the Johns Hopkins University School of Advanced In-
    ternational Studies, Foreign Policy Institute: SAIS Papers in International Affairs,
    1985.
Barnouin, Barbara, and Yu Changen. *Chinese Foreign Policy during the Cultural Revolu-
    tion*. London and New York: Kegan Paul, 1998.
Barrett, David D. *Dixie Mission: The United States Army Observer Group in Yenan,
    1944*. Centre for Chinese Studies, University of California, Berkeley, China Research
    Monograph no. 6, 1970.

Barrymaine, Norman. *The Time Bomb, a Veteran Journalist Assesses Today's China from the Inside.* London: Peter Davies, 1971.

Bartkè, Wolfgang. *The Economic Aid of the PR China to Developing and Socialist Countries.* 2d and revised edition. München: K. G. Saur, 1989.

de Beauvoir, Simone. *The Long March.* London: Andre Deutsch, 1958.

Becker, Jasper. *Hungry Ghosts, China's Secret Famine.* London: John Murray, 1996.

Belden, Jack. *China Shakes the World.* New York: Victor Gollancz, 1951.

Bennett, Milly. *On Her Own, Journalistic Adventures from San Francisco to the Chinese Revolution 1917-1927,* edited and annotated by A. Tom Grunfeld. New York: M. E. Sharpe, 1993.

Benton, Gregor. *Mountain Fires, the Red Army's Three-Year War in South China, 1934-1938.* Berkeley: University of California Press, 1992.

Bertram, James. *Capes of China Slide Away: A Memoir of Peace and War.* Auckland: Auckland University Press, 1993.

———. *First Act in China: The Story of the Sian Mutiny.* Reprint of 1937 edition *Crisis in China.* Westport, Conn.: Hyperion Press, 1973.

———. *Return to China.* London: Heineman, 1957.

———. *The Shadow of a War: A New Zealander in the Far East 1939-1946.* Australia and New Zealand: Whitcombe and Tombs Ltd., 1947.

———. *Unconquered: Journal of a Year's Adventures among the Fighting Peasants of North China.* New York: John Day and Co., 1939.

Bisson, T. A. *Yenan in June 1937: Talks with Communist Leaders.* Berkeley: Centre for Chinese Studies, University of California, 1973.

Bodde, Derk. *Peking Diary: A Year of Revolution.* London: Jonathan Cape, 1951.

Bosshardt, R. Alfred. *The Guiding Hand.* London: Hodder and Stoughton, 1973.

———. *The Restraining Hand: Captivity for Christ in China.* London: Hodder and Stoughton, 1936.

Bourseiller, Christophe. *Les Maoïstes: La Folie Histoire des Gardes Rouges Français.* Paris: Plon, 1996.

Brady, Anne-Marie. "The Curious Case of Two Australasian 'Traitors,' or, New Zealand, Australia and the Cold War." *The New Zealand Journal of History* 35, no. 1 (April 2001): 85-110.

———. *Friend of China—The Myth of Rewi Alley.* Richmond, Surrey: Curzon, 2002.

———. "'FriendLit,' or, How to Become a Friend of China." *Revue Bibliographique de Sinologie* (1998): 389-397.

———. "The Political Meaning of Friendship: Reviewing the Life and Times of Two of China's American Friends." *China Review International* 9, no. 1, 2002.

———. "Red and Expert: China's 'Foreign Friends' in the Great Proletarian Cultural Revolution." *China Information* 11, nos. 2/3 (Autumn/Winter 1996): 110-137.

———. "'Treat Insiders and Outsiders Differently': The Use and Control of Foreigners in China." *China Quarterly* 164 (December 2000): 943-964.

———. "West Meets East: Rewi Alley and Changing Attitudes towards Homosexuality in China." *East Asian History,* no. 9 (June 1995): 97-120.

———. "Who Friend, Who Enemy? Rewi Alley and China's Foreign Friends." *China Quarterly* 151 (September 1997): 614-632.

Braun, Otto. *A Comintern Agent in China 1932-1939,* translated by Jeanne Moore. London: C. Hurst and Company, 1982.

Burchett, Wilfred, and Alan Winnington. *Koje Unscreened.* Published by the authors, Peking, 1953.

Burchett, Wilfred. *Plain Perfidy*. London: British-China Friendship Association, 1954.

Cameron, James. *Mandarin Red*. New York: Rinehart and Company, 1955.

Carlson, Evans Fordyce. *Twin Stars of China*. Reprint. Westport, Conn.: Hyperion Press, 1975.

Caute, David. *The Fellow Travellers: A Postscript to the Enlightenment*. London: Wiedenfeld and Nicholson Limited, 1974.

Chan, Gerald. *China and International Organizations: Participation in Non-Governmental Organizations since 1971*. Hong Kong: Oxford University Press, 1989.

Chen Benlin. *Shewai zhishi daquan*. Shanghai: Shanghai renmin chubanshe, 1989.

Chen Jian. *China's Road to the Korean War: The Making of the Sino-American Confrontation*. New York: Columbia University Press, 1994.

———. *CCP Leaders' Selected Works and the Historiography of the Chinese Communist Revolution*. Cold War International History Project, Woodrow Wilson International Centre for Scholars.

———. *A Crucial Step toward the Sino-Soviet Schism: The Withdrawal of Soviet Experts from China, July 1960*. CWIHP, Woodrow Wilson International Centre for Scholars.

———. "The Ward Case and the Emergence of Sino-American Confrontation, 1948-1950." *The Australian Journal of Chinese Affairs*, no. 30 (July 1993): 149-170.

Chen Liangxuan. *Shewai yingyu shiyong jiaocheng*. Kaifeng: Henan daxue chubanshe, 1994.

Chen Xiaomei. *Occidentalism: A Theory of Counter-Discourse in Post-Mao China*. New York: Oxford University Press, 1995.

Chen Xuezhao. *Surviving the Storm: A Memoir*. Edited with an introduction by Jeffrey Kinkley, translated by Ti Hua and Caroline Greene. New York: M. E. Sharpe, 1990.

Chen Yun. *Chen Yun wenxuan (1956-1985)*. Beijing: Renmin chubanshe, 1986.

Cheng Zhongyuan. "Zai Sinuo 'xixing' zhi qian." *Dang de wenxian*, no. 1 (1992).

China and the Asian African Conference. Peking: Foreign Languages Press, 1955.

Chuguo renyuan zhishi. Beijing: Jingguan jiaoyu chubanshe, 1995.

Cohen, Raymond. *Negotiating across Cultures: Communication Obstacles in International Diplomacy*. Washington, D.C.: United States Institute of Peace Press, 1991.

Copper, John Franklin. *China's Foreign Aid*. Lexington, Mass.: Lexington Books, 1976.

Curran, Daniel J., and Sandra Cook. "Doing Research in Post-Tiananmen China." In *Researching Sensitive Topics*, edited by Claire M. Renzetti and Raymond M. Lee. New York: Sage Publications, 1993.

Cressy-Marcks, Violet. *Journey into China*. New York: E. P. Dutton, 1942.

Deng Shengshou, "Xibei geming genjudi de waishi huodong." Ma Gongwu, ed., *Zhongguo geming genjudi shi yanjiu*. Nanjing: Nanjing daxue chubanshe, 1992.

Croft, Michael. *Red Carpet to China*. London: The Travelling Book Club, 1958.

Dimond, E. Grey. *Inside China Today: A Western View*. New York: W. W. Norton, 1983.

Duan Liancheng. *Duiwai chuanboxue*. Chinese-English bilingual edition. Beijing: Zhongguo jianshe chubanshe, 1988.

Duiwai baodao cankao. In the mid-1980s name changed to *Duiwai xuanchuan cankao*. Beijing: Xinhuashe duiwai xinwen bianji bu, 1981-1999.

Duiwai maoyi jingji hezuobu jiaojishi, ed., *Shewai liyi ABC*. Beijing: Zhongguo renmin chubanshe, 1997.

Endicott, Stephen L. "Germ Warfare and 'Plausible Denial.'" *Modern China* 5, no. 1 (January 1979): 79-104.

Enzensberger, Hans Magnus. "Tourists of the Revolution." In *Raids and Reconstructions*, 224-252. Edited London: Pluto Press, 1976.

Epstein, Israel. *The Unfinished Revolution in China.* Boston: Little, Brown and Company, 1947.

————. *I Visit Yenan.* Bombay: People's Publishing House, 1945.

————. *Woman in World History Song Qingling (Madame Sun Yat-sen).* 2d ed. Beijing: New World Press, 1995.

Ewen, Jean. *China Nurse, 1952-1939: A Young Canadian Witness of History.* Toronto: McLelland and Stewart, 1981.

Fan Changkun, ed. *Waishi zhishi shouce.* Shijiazhuang: Hebei kexue jishu chubanshe, 1987.

Farnsworth, Robert. *From Vagabond to Journalist: Edgar Snow in Asia 1928-1941.* Columbia and London: University of Missouri Press, 1996.

Fensui Meiguo xijun zhan. Dongbei yixueyuan chubanshe, 1952.

Fitzgerald, John. *Awakening China: Politics, Culture, and Class in the Nationalist Revolution.* Stanford: Stanford University Press, 1996.

Fokkema, D. W. *Report from Peking: Observations of a Western Diplomat on the Cultural Revolution.* London: C. Hurst and Company, 1970.

Ford, Robert. *Captured in Tibet.* London: George Harrap and Co., 1957.

Fox, R. M. *China Diary.* London: Robert Hale Ltd., 1959.

Fraser, John. *The Chinese: Portrait of a People.* Toronto: Collins, 1980.

Friend, Robert, ed. *Quotations from Chairman Mao Tse-tung on Propaganda.* Peking: Foreign Languages Press, 1967.

Gailbraith, John Kenneth. *A China Passage.* London: André Deutsch, 1973.

Gale, G. S. *No Flies in China.* London: Allen and Unwin, 1955.

Garland, Margaret. *Journey to New China.* Christchurch: The Caxton Press, 1954.

Gao Xiaofang, Zhang Qin, eds. *Waishi yingyu.* Wuhan: Cehui keji daxue chubanshe, 1997.

Garner, Karen. *Challenging the Consensus: Maud Muriel Russell's Life and Political Activism.* Ph.D. diss., University of Texas at Austin, 1995.

Garver, John. *Sino-Soviet Relations 1937-1945.* New York: Oxford University Press, 1988.

————. *Foreign Relations of the People's Republic of China.* Englewood Cliffs, N.J.: Prentice Hall, 1993.

Ge Weide, ed. *Shewai wenmi yingyu.* Beijing: Zhongguo duiwai jingji maoyi chubanshe, 1996.

Gelder, Stuart, and Roma Gelder. *The Long March to Freedom.* London: Hutchinson, 1962.

————. *Memories for a Chinese Granddaughter.* London: Hutchinson, 1967.

————. *The Timely Rain, Travels in New Tibet.* London: Hutchinson, 1964.

Ginsberg, Sam. *My First Sixty Years in China.* Beijing: New World Press, 1982.

Gong Guan, ed. *Shewai mishu xiuyang he shiwu.* Beijing: Zhongguo shengji chubanshe, 1996.

Gonganbu yiju, ed. *Waishi minjing gongzuo shouce.* Beijing: Qunzhong chubanshe, 1981.

Goodman, David. *Deng Xiaoping and the Chinese Revolution: A Political Biography.* London: Routledge, 1994.

Gordon, Eric and Marie Gordon. *Freedom Is a Word.* London: Hodder and Stoughton, 1971.

Gu Qingchun. *Waishi shengya ershi nian.* Lanzhou: Gansu renmin chubanshe, 1993.

Gu Xin, and David Kelly. "New Conservatism: Intermediate Ideology of a 'New Elite.'" In *China's Quiet Revolution*, edited by David S. Goodman and Beverley Hooper, 219-233. Melbourne: Longman Cheshire, 1994.

Guangdong waishi. Guangzhou: Guangdong sheng zhengfu waishichu, 1985-1999.

Guangxi waishi. Nanning: Guangxi sheng zhengfu waishichu, 1995-1999.

Guo Huimin, ed. *Guoji gonggong guanxi jiaocheng*. Shanghai: Fudan daxue chubanshe, 1996.

Guo Meisheng, ed. *Shewai gongan yingyu huihua*. Taiyuan: Shanxi renmin chubanshe, 1993.

Guoji shishi cidian. Beijing: Shangwu yinshudian, 1984.

Guoji xingshi he wo guo de duiwai zhengce. Publisher and location unknown, 1969.

"Guoji youren zai kangRi zhanzheng zhong de gongxian he zuoyong," *Lishi Dang'an*, no. 3 (1998).

Guoji zhengzhi cankao ziliao. Beijing: Beijing daxue guoji zhengzhi xi, 1973.

Grey, Anthony. *Hostage in Peking*. London: Michael Joseph, 1970.

Grunfeld, A. Tom. "Friends of the Revolution: American Supporters of China's Communists 1926-1939." Ph.D. thesis, New York University, 1985.

Hamilton, John Maxwell. *Edgar Snow: A Biography*. Bloomington and Indianapolis: Indiana University Press, 1988.

Hamm, Harry. *China: Empire of the 700 Million*. Translated by Victor Anderson. New York: Doubleday, 1966.

Han Nianlong et al., eds. *Diplomacy of Contemporary China*. Hong Kong: New Horizon, 1990.

Han Suyin. *Wind in the Tower: Mao Tse-tung and the Chinese Revolution 1949-1975*. Boston: Little Brown, and Company, 1976.

———. *Phoenix Harvest*. London: Triad Granada, 1982.

———. *My House Has Two Doors*. London: Jonathan Cape, 1980.

Hao Meitian, ed. *Shiyong libinxue*. Shantou: Shantou daxue chubanshe, 1996.

Harding, Harry. *A Fragile Relationship, the United States and China since 1972*. Washington, D.C.: The Brookings Institute, 1992.

Haylen, Leslie. *Chinese Journey: The Republic Revisited*. Sydney: Angus and Robertson, 1959.

Hevi, Emmanuel John. *An African Student in China*. London: Pall Mall, 1963.

Hevia, James L. *Cherishing Men from Afar: Qing Guest Ritual and the Macartney Embassy*. Durham: Duke University Press, 1995.

Hinton, William. *Hundred Day War, the Cultural Revolution at Tsinghua University*. New York: Monthly Review Press, 1972.

Hogg, George. *I See a New China*. London: Victor Gollancz, 1945.

Holland Jian, Esther. *British Girl, Chinese Wife*. Beijing: New World Press, 1985.

Hollander, Paul. *Political Pilgrims: Travels of Western Intellectuals to the Soviet Union, China, and Cuba*. New York: Oxford University Press, 1981.

———. "Pilgrims on the Run, Ideological Refugees from Paradise Lost." Special pamphlet. *Encounter* (1986).

———. "Durable Significance of Political Pilgrimage," *Society* 34, no. 5 (July-August 1997): 45-55.

Homer, Joy. *Dawn Watch in China*. Boston: Houghton Mifflin Company, 1941.

Hooper, Beverley. *China Stands Up: Ending the Western Presence 1948-1950*. Sydney: Allen and Unwin, 1986.

Horn, Joshua. *Away with All Pests*. London: Paul Hamlyn, 1969.

How the 8th Route Army Helped Us to Escape from Peiping. Chongqing: CCP Foreign Propaganda Group, September 1942.

Hoyt, Frederick B. "Protection Implies Intervention: The U.S. Catholic Mission at Kanchow." *The Historian* 38, no. 4 (August 1976): 709-727.

Hu Qiaomu. *Hu Qiaomu huiyi Mao Zedong.* Beijing: Renmin chubanshe, 1994.

Hu Xiaoji. *Shewai huodong yingyu zhinan.* Beijing: Yuhang chubanshe, 1991.

Hua Xingbang. *Waishi gongzuo shiwu quanshu.* Beijing: Qiye guanli chubanshe, 1996.

Huang Dexun, Huang Jianhua, eds. *Shewai huodong sucheng yingyu kouyu.* Nanning: Guangxi kexue jishu chubanshe, 1990.

Huang Zhizhong. *Duiwai kaifang yu guofang jiaoyu.* Beijing: Guofang daxue, 1990.

Hunt, Michael H. "CCP Foreign Relations: A Guide to the Literature." *CWIHP*, Woodrow Wilson International Centre for Scholars, n.d.

———. "Constructing a History of Chinese Communist Party Foreign Relations." *CWIHP*, Woodrow Wilson International Centre for Scholars.

———. *The Genesis of Chinese Communist Foreign Policy.* New York: Columbia University Press, 1996.

Hunt, Michael H., and Niu Jun, eds. *Chinese Communist Foreign Relations 1920s-1960s: Personalities and Interpretive Approaches.* Washington, D.C.: Asia Program, Woodrow Wilson Centre for Scholars.

Hunter, Edward. *Brainwashing in Red China: The Calculated Destruction of Men's Minds.* New York: The Vanguard Press, 1951.

Hunter, Neale. *Shanghai Journal.* New York: Frederick Praeger, 1969.

I Fight against the War-Makers with the 8th Route Army. Chongqing: CCP Foreign Propaganda Group, March 1943.

Illsley, Walter. *An American in China.* Unpublished typescript, 1953-1954.

Isaacs, Harold R. *Re-encounters in China, Notes of a Journey in a Time Capsule.* New York: M. E. Sharpe, 1985.

Ivanov, Ury. *Ten Years of My Life in the Cultural Revolution.* Dandenong: Dandenong College of TAFE, 1985.

Jensen, Lionel M. *Manufacturing Confucianism: Chinese Traditions and Universal Civilisation.* Durham and London: Duke University Press, 1997.

Ji Bin, ed. *Guowuyuan jigou gaige gailan.* Beijing: Xinhua chubanshe, 1998.

Jia Wenhua, and Gao Zhongyi, eds. *Sulian duiwai guanxi.* Zhengzhou: Henan jiaoyu chubanshe, 1989.

Jiang Guanghua. *Fangwen waiguo zhengdang jishi.* Beijing: Shijie zhishi chubanshe, 1997.

Jiangsu waishi. Nanjing: Jiangsu sheng weiyuanwei waishi bangongshi, 1997-1999.

Jiangxi waishi. Nanning: Jiangxi sheng waishi weiyuanhui, 1993-1999.

Jin Zengkun, Miao Ying, ed. *Shewai jiaoji liyi.* Beijing: Kexue puji chubanshe, 1991.

Jixu geming chengsheng qianjin. Beijing: Zhongguo renmin daxue, 1970.

Johnson, Cecil. *Communist China and Latin America 1959-1967.* New York: Columbia University Press, 1970.

Johnson, Hewlett. *The Upsurge of China.* Peking: New World Press, 1961.

Kampen, Thomas. *Mao Zedong, Zhou Enlai and the Evolution of the Chinese Communist Leadership.* Copenhagen: Nordic Institute of Asian Studies, 1999.

Kidd, David. *Peking Story: The Last Days of Old China.* London: Aurum Press, 1988.

Kipnis, Andrew B. "'Face': An Adaptable Discourse of Social Surfaces." *Positions* 3, no. 1 (Spring 1995): 119-148.

————. *Producing Guanxi: Sentiment, Self, and Subculture in a Northern China Village.* Durham, N.C.: Duke University Press, 1997.

Kirby, William C. "The Internationalization of China: Foreign Relations at Home and Abroad in the Republican Era." *China Quarterly* 150 (June 1997): 432-458.

————. "Intercultural Connections and Chinese Development: External and Internal Spheres of Modern China's Foreign Relations." In *China's Quest for Modernisation: A Historical Perspective*, edited by Frederick Wakeman Jr. and Wang Xi, 208-223. Berkeley: Institute of East Asian Studies, University of California, 1997.

Klochko, Mikhail A. *Soviet Scientist in China.* English translation. New York: Frederick A. Praeger, 1964.

Knight, Sophia. *Window on Shanghai: Letters from China, 1965-1967.* London: Andre Deutsch, 1967.

Koch, Stephen. *Double Lives: Spies and Writers in the Secret Soviet War of Ideas against the West.* New York: The Free Press, Macmillan, 1994.

Kovalev, Ivan. "The Stalin-Mao Dialogue." *Far Eastern Affairs*, no. 2 (1992): 94-111.

Khrushchev, Nikita. "Mao Zedong and the Split." *Far Eastern Affairs*, no. 3 (1990): 91-103.

Lapwood, Ralph, and Nancy Lapwood. *Through the Chinese Revolution.* London: Spalding and Levy, 1954.

Ledovsky, Andrei. "Mikoyan's Secret Mission to China in January and February 1949." *Far Eastern Affairs*, no. 3 (1995): 74-89.

————. "The Moscow Visit of a Delegation of the Communist Party of China in June to August 1949." *Far Eastern Affairs*, no. 4 (1996): 64-86; no. 5 (1996): 84-97.

Leitenberg, Milton. *The Korean War Biological Warfare Allegations Resolved.* Centre for Pacific Asia Studies at Stockholm University, Occasional Paper 36, May 1998.

Lenin, V. I. *"Left-Wing" Communism, an Infantile Disorder.* Moscow: Foreign Languages Publishing House, 1950.

Leyda, Jay. *Dianying: Electric Shadows: An Account of Films and Film Audiences in China.* Cambridge: Massachusetts Institute of Technology, 1972.

Leys, Simon. *Chinese Shadows.* Middlesex, England: Penguin, 1974.

Li Bin. *Guoji liyi yu jiaoji lijie.* Beijing: Shijie zhishi chubanshe, 1985.

Li Guosheng, Wang Enhong, eds. *Waishi zhishi gailan.* Shenyang: Baishan chubanshe, 1993.

Li Jie. "Mao and Sino-Soviet Relations, 1949-69." Paper presented at AACPCS/ANZSA International Conference of Communist and Post-Communist Societies, Melbourne, July 1998.

Li Jinwei. *Waishi zhishi daquan.* Shanghai: Shanghai yiwen chubanshe, 1992.

Li Tianming. *Xiandai guoji liyi zhishi— zenmeyang jinxing duiwai huodong.* Beijing: Shijie zhishi chubanshe, 1994.

Li Xiangcun, ed. *Shewai jingjixue.* Jinan: Shandong renmin chubanshe, 1995.

Li Xueqin. *Shewai wenshu xiezuo zhinan.* Beijing: Beijing keji jishu chubanshe, 1993.

Li Yongtai, ed. *Mao Zedong yu Meiguo.* Kunming: Yunnan renmin chubanshe, 1993.

Li Yuanjiang, ed. *Duiwai xuanchuan jichu.* Guangzhou: Guangdong renmin chubanshe, 1987.

Li Yuanzi. *Shewai qiye zhongfang guanli renyuan bidu.* Guangzhou: Guangdong gaodeng jiaoyu chubanshe, 1991.

Li Yun, ed. *Nanchang waishi zhi.* Nanchang: Jiangxi renmin chubanshe, 1994.

Li Zhenzhong. *Duiwai tanpan jiqiao.* Beijing: Duiwai maoyi jiaoyu chubanshe, 1987.

Li Zhisui. *The Private Life of Chairman Mao: The Inside Story of the Man Who Made Modern China*, edited by Anne F. Thurston. New York: Random House, 1994.

Li Zihua. *Chuguo renyuan zhishi shouce*. Beijing: Jiangguan jiaoyu chubanshe, 1996.

Liao, San. *Peking Blues*. Hong Kong: Dragon Fly Press, 1959.

Liaowang, ed. *Guowuyuan jigou gaige gailan*. Beijing: Xinhua chubanshe, 1998.

Lieberthal, Kenneth G. *Governing China: From Revolution to Reform*. New York: W. W. Norton, 1995.

Lin Biao. *Lin Fuxi yulu*. Beijing: n.p., 1969.

Lindquist, Sven. *China in Crisis*. Translated by S. Clayton. London: Faber and Faber, 1965.

Lindsay, Michael. *China and the Cold War*. Melbourne: Melbourne University Press, 1955.

———. "Report of a Visit." *International Affairs* 26, no. 1 (January 1950): 22-31.

———. *The Unknown War: North China 1937-1945*. London: Bergstrom and Boyle Books, 1975.

Litten, Frederick S. "The Noulens Affair." *China Quarterly* 138 (June 1994): 492-512.

———. "Otto Braun's Curriculum Vitae—Translation and Commentary." *Twentieth Century China* 23, no.1 (November 1997): 31-62.

Liu Congrong, Lu Chenyue. *Shewai fandian guanli yu fuwu*. Kunming: Yunnan renmin chubanshe, 1993.

Liu Hongchao, Cai Guangrong, eds. *Waiguo yaoren mingren kan Zhongguo*. Beijing: Zhonggong zhongyang dangxiao chubanshe, 1992.

Liu Honghu, ed. *Xifang zhengyao he baokan guanyu heping yanbian de zuixin yanlun*. Wuhan: Hubei renmin chubanshe, 1992.

Liu Hongzhang. *Shewai mishu shiwu yu yingyu*. Shanghai: Jiaotong daxue chubanshe, 1994.

Liu Kang, Li Xikuang. *Yaomohua Zhongguo de beihou*. Beijing: Zhongguo shehui kexue chubanshe, 1996.

Liu Luxiang. *Shewai gonggong guanxi*. Dalian: Dalian chubanshe, 1996.

Liu, Lydia H. "Translingual Practice: The Discourse of Individualism between China and the West." In *Narratives of Agency: Self-Making in China, India, and Japan*, ed. Wimal Dissananyake. Minneapolis: University of Minnesota Press, 1996.

———. *Translingual Practice: Literature, National Culture, and Translated Modernity—China, 1900-1937*. Stanford, Calif.: Stanford University Press, 1995.

Liu Renmin, Li Qun, eds. *Xiandai shewai liyi*. Beijing: Zhongguo huanjing kexue chubanshe, 1997.

Liu Yuxue, Liu Zhengchang, eds. *Shewai lisu zhishi bidu*. Beijing: Zhongguo luyou chubanshe, 1990.

Living in China: By Twenty Authors from Abroad. Beijing: New World Press, 1979.

Lu Guohua, ed. *Shewai falu yu qianti*. Jinan: Shandong daxue chubanshe, 1991.

Lu Ning. *The Dynamics of Foreign-Policy Decisionmaking in China*. Boulder, Colo.: Westview Press, 1997.

Lu Yufang. *Waishi gongguan*. Shanghai renmin chubanshe, 1991.

Ma Gongwu. *Zhongguo geming genjudi shi yanjiu*. Nanjing: Nanjing daxue chubanshe, 1992.

Ma Xianglin. *Lan yanjing, hei yanjing, guoji youren yuan Hua kangri jishi*. Beijing: Jiefangjun wenyi chubanshe, 1995.

Ma Yongshun. *Zhou Enlai zujian yu guanli zhengfu shilu*. Beijing: Zhongyang wenxian chubanshe, 1995.

Mackerras, Colin and Neale Hunter. *China Observed 1964/1967*. Melbourne: Thomas Nelson, 1967.

MacKinnon, Janice R., and Stephen R. MacKinnon. *Agnes Smedley: The Life and Times of an American Radical*. Los Angeles: University of California Press, 1988.

Mai Renzeng, ed. *Waishi gongzuo renyuan yingyu changyong fenlei cihui*. Beijing: Beijing chubanshe, 1983.

Mancall, Mark. *China at the Centre: 300 Years of Foreign Policy*. New York: The Free Press, 1984.

Mao Zedong and International Friends: Selected Collections of the International Friendship Museum. Beijing: Xiyuan chubanshe, 1994.

"Mao Zedong on the Comintern's and Stalin's China Policy." *Far Eastern Affairs*, no. 4-5 (1994): 132-144.

Mao Zedong. *Chairman Mao Tse-tung's Important Talks with Guests from Asia, Africa and Latin America*. Peking: Foreign Languages Press, 1960.

———. *Jianguo yilai Mao Zedong wengao*. 13 vols. Beijing: Zhongyang wenxian chubanshe, 1993.

———. *Mao Zedong sixiang shengli wansui*. Beijing: n.p., 1969.

———. *Mao Zedong sixiang wansui*. Shijiazhuang: Hebei daxue Mao Zedong sixiang "ba yi, yi ba" hongwei bing xuanchuan bu, 1967.

———. *Mao Zedong waijiao wenxian*. Beijing: Zhonghua renmin gongheguo waijiaobu, 1994.

———. *Mao Zhuxi lun shijie geming*. Beijing: Renmin ribao guojibu, 1968.

———. *Selected Works of Mao Tse-tung*. 5 vols. Beijing: Foreign Languages Press, 1977.

Marcuse, Jacques. *The Peking Papers*. London: Arthur Baker Ltd., 1968.

Margulies, Sylvia R. *The Pilgrimage to Russia: The Soviet Union and the Treatment of Foreigners, 1924-1937*. Madison: The University of Washington Press, 1968.

McEwan, Keith. *Once a Jolly Comrade*. Brisbane: Jacaranda Press, 1966.

Meisner, Maurice. *Mao's China and After: A History of the People's Republic*. New York: The Free Press, 1986.

Meng Xianwei, Wang Yujie. *Shewai hunying jiating yu fa*. Guangzhou: Guangdong renmin chubanshe, 1995.

Milton, David, and Nancy Dall. *The Wind Will Not Subside, Years in Revolutionary China*. New York: Pantheon Books, 1976.

Mitchell, J. M. *International Cultural Relations*. London: Allen and Unwin, 1986.

Mo Qibo, ed. *Gongmin churu jing guanli*. Nanning: Guangxi renmin chubanshe, 1997.

Moskins, J. Robert. *Turncoat, an American's 12 Years in Communist China*. Upper Saddle River, N.J.: Prentice-Hall, 1967.

Nixon, Richard. *The Memoirs of Richard Nixon*. New York: Grusset and Dunlap, 1978.

Nie Rongzhen. *Nie Rongzhen huiyilu*. 3 vols. Beijing: Junshi chubanshe, 1983.

Niu Jun. *Cong Yan'an zou xiang shijie—Zhongguo gongchandang duiwaiguanxi de qiyuan*. Fuzhou: Fujian renmin chubanshe, 1992.

Niu Zhongdong, ed. *Shewai yingyu changyong huihua*. Beijing: Wenjin chubanshe, 1994.

North, Robert C., and Xenia J. Eudin. *M. N. Roy's Mission to China: The Communist-Kuomintang Split of 1927*. Berkeley: University of California Press, 1963.

North, Robert. *Moscow and the Chinese Communists*. Stanford, Calif.: Stanford University Press, 1953.

Nossal, Frederick. *Dateline Peking*. London: Macdonald, 1962.

Noyes, Henry. *China Born: Memoirs of a Westerner*. London: Peter Owen, 1989.

Pan Xinming. *Waishi shiyong wenshu daquan.* Shenyang: Liaoning renmin chubanshe, 1994.

Pan Zhangxian. *Waishi jiedai shiyong yingyu.* Hangzhou: Zhejiang keji xueshu chubanshe, 1997.

Panikkar, M. *In Two Chinas.* London: George Allen and Unwin, 1955.

Passin, Herbert. *China's Cultural Diplomacy.* New York: Frederick A. Praeger, 1963.

Peck, Graham. *Two Kinds of Time.* Boston: Houghton Mifflin Company, 1950.

Pei Jianzhang, ed. *Mao Zedong waijiao sixiang yanjiu.* Beijing: Shijie zhishi chubanshe, 1994.

———. *Zhonghua renmin gongheguo waijiaoshi 1949-1956.* Beijing: Shijie zhishi chubanshe, 1994.

Pei Xiannong. *Zhou Enlai waijiaoxue.* Beijing: Zhonggong zhongyang dangxiao chubanshe, 1997.

Pei Xiaolin, ed. *Shewai jiben changshi.* Suzhou: Suzhou daxue chubanshe, 1994.

Porter, Edgar A., *The People's Doctor: George Hatem and China's Revolution.* Honolulu: University of Hawaii Press, 1997.

Priestly, K. E. "The Sino-Soviet Friendship Association." *Pacific Affairs* 25, no. 3 (September 1952).

Pu Litian. *Shewai gongzuo.* Guangzhou: Huanan ligong daxue chubanshe, 1991.

Qian Jiang. *Ping pang waijiao muhou.* Beijing: Dongfang chubanshe, 1997.

Quan guo renmin daibiao dahui changwei yuanhui dianliju. *Jiedai waibing xuzhi.* Beijing, 1956.

Rand, Peter. *China Hands, the Adventures and Ordeals of the American Journalists Who Joined Forces with the Great Chinese Revolution.* New York: Simon and Schuster, 1995.

Reardon-Anderson, James. *Yenan and the Great Powers.* New York: Columbia Press, 1980.

"Reminiscences of Veterans." *Far Eastern Affairs*, no. 6 (1989): 22-33.

Ren Minggao, Li Wenye. *Weida de gongchanchuyi zhanshi, Ke Dihua.* Beijing: Shangwu yinshudian, 1984.

Ren Wenyuan. *Shewai mishu jichu duben.* Jinan: Shandong jingji chubanshe, 1996.

Report of the International Scientific Commission for the Investigation of the Facts Concerning Biological Warfare in Korea and China. Peking: n.p., 1952.

Rickett, Allyn, and Adele Rickett. *Prisoners of Liberation: Four Years in a Chinese Communist Prison.* New York: Anchor Press, 1973.

Rittenberg, Sidney, and Amanda Bennett. *The Man Who Stayed Behind.* New York: Simon and Schuster, 1993.

Robinson, Robert, with Jonathan Slevin. *Black on Red: My 44 Years inside the Soviet Union.* Washington, D.C.: Acropolis Books, 1988.

Robinson, Thomas W., and David Shambaugh, eds. *Chinese Foreign Policy: Theory and Practice.* Oxford: Clarendon Press, 1994.

Saich, Tony. *The Origins of the First United Front in China: The Role of Sneevliet (alias Maring).* 2 vol. Leiden: E. J. Brill, 1991.

Saich, Tony, ed. *The Rise to Power of the Chinese Communist Party: Documents and Analysis.* New York: M. E. Sharpe, 1996.

Salisbury, Harrison. *China's New Emperors: China in the Era of Mao and Deng.* Boston: Little, Brown and Company, 1990.

———. *The Long March: The Untold Story.* New York: Harper and Row, 1985.

Sargant, William. *Battle for the Mind: A Physiology of Conversion and Brainwashing.* London: Pan Books, 1957.

Satow, Ernest Rt. Hon. Sir. *A Guide to Diplomatic Practice.* London: Longmans Green and Co., 1957. Translated into Chinese in 1957, published by New World Press.

Scalapino, Robert A. "The Cultural Revolution and Chinese Foreign Policy." *Current Scene Developments in Mainland China* 6, no. 13 (1 August 1968).

Schaller, Michael. *The U.S. Crusade in China, 1938-1945.* New York: Columbia University, 1979.

Schatten, Fritz. *Communism in Africa.* New York: Frederick A. Praeger, 1966.

Schell, Orville. *In the People's Republic of China.* New York: Vintage Books, 1978.

Schram, Stuart R., ed. *Chairman Mao Talks to the People.* New York: Pantheon Books, 1974.

———. *Mao Tse-tung Unrehearsed: Talks and Letters: 1956-71.* Harmondsworth: Penguin, 1974.

———. *The Political Thought of Mao Tse-tung.* New York: London, 1969.

———. *The Thought of Mao Tse-tung.* Cambridge: Cambridge University Press, 1989.

Schuman, Julian. *China: An Uncensored Look.* New York: Second Chance Press, 1979.

de Segonzac, A. *Visa for Peking.* Translated by Marion Barwick. Kingswood, Surrey: Windmill Press, 1956.

Selected New Quotations from Chairman Mao, 1 January, 1970-1 April, 1975. Beijing: Duiwaibu yingwen ziliaozu, 1975.

Sendy, John. *Comrades Come Rally! Recollections of an Australian Communist.* Melbourne: Thomas Nelson Australia, 1978.

Sewell, William G. *I Stayed in China.* New York: A. S. Barnes and Co., 1966.

Shai, Aron. *The Fate of British and French Firms in China, 1949-1954: Imperialism Imprisoned.* London: MacMillan, 1996.

Shambaugh, David. *Beautiful Imperialist: China Perceives America, 1972-1990.* Princeton, N.J.: Princeton University Press, 1991.

———. "The Soviet Influence on China's Worldview." *The Australian Journal of Chinese Affairs,* no. 27 (January 1992).

Shao Zhenxiang. *Shewai gongan zhishi wenda.* Beijing: Zhongguo fangzheng chubanshe, 1994.

Shapiro, Sidney. *An American in China, Thirty Years in the People's Republic.* Beijing: New World Press, 1979.

——— *I Chose China, the Metamorphosis of a Country and a Man.* New York: Hippocrene, 2000.

———. *Ma Haide: The Saga of an American Doctor George Hatem in China.* New York: Cypress Press, 1993.

Schell, Orville. *In The People's Republic.* New York: Vintage Books, 1978.

———. *Watch Out for the Foreign Guests!* New York: Pantheon Books, 1980.

Sheng, Michael M. *Battling Western Imperialism: Mao, Stalin, and the United States.* Princeton, N.J.: Princeton University Press, 1997.

Shewai ganbu bibei. Shijiazhuang: Hebei jiaoyu chubanshe, 1996.

Shewmaker, Kenneth E. *Americans and Chinese Communists, 1927-1945: A Persuading Encounter.* Ithaca and London: Cornell University Press, 1971.

Shi Zhifu, ed. *Zhonghua renmin gongheguo duiwai guanxi shi,* 1949/10-1989/10, October 1949-October 1989. Beijing: Beijing daxue chubanshe, 1994.

Shijie zhishi chubanshe. *Guanyu ge guo gongchandang he gongrendang daibiao huiyi shengming wenji.* Beijing: Shijie zhishi chubanshe, 1962.

Shimada Masao. *Wei youyi jiaqiao sishi nian*. Beijing: Xinhua chubanshe, 1992.
Shishi zhengce wenxuan. Waibin jiedai bangongshi, n.d.
Snow, Edgar. *Random Notes on Red China (1936-1945)*. Cambridge, Mass.: China Economic and Political Studies, Harvard University, 1957.
———. *Red China Today: The Other Side of the River*. Harmondsworth, Middlesex: Penguin, 1971.
———. *Red Star over China*. London: Victor Gollancz, 1937, and New York: Grove Press, 1968.
———. *Scorched Earth*. London: Victor Gollancz, 1941.
Snow, Helen Foster. *Inside Red China*. New York: Da Capo Press, 1977.
———. *My China Years*. New York: William Morrow and Company, 1984.
Solomon, Richard H. *Chinese Negotiating Behaviour: Pursuing Interests through "Old Friends."* Washington, D.C.: United States Institute of Peace Press, 1999.
Song Changmei, ed. *Duiwai jiaowang zhong de liyi lijie*. Harbin: Heilongjiang renmin chubanshe, 1996.
Song Qiang, et al. *Zhongguo keyi shuo bu*. Beijing: Zhongguo wenlian chuban gongsi, 1996.
———. *Zhongguo haishi neng shuo bu: "Zhongguo keyi shuo bu" xuji*. Beijing: Wenlian chuban gongsi, 1996.
Stanley, Margaret. *Foreigners in Areas of China under Communist Jurisdiction before 1949: Bibliographical Notes and a Comprehensive Bibliography of the Yenan Hui*. Reference series no. 3. Centre for East Asian Studies, University of Kansas, 1987.
State Bureau of Foreign Experts, PRC. *The Foreign Experts' Handbook—A Guide to Living and Working in China*. Beijing: New World Press, 1988.
Strong, Anna Louise. *The Chinese Conquer China*. Garden City, N.Y.: Doubleday, 1949.
Strong, Tracy B., and Helene Keysser. *Right in Her Soul: The Life of Anna Louise Strong*. New York: Random House, 1983.
Stuart, John Leighton. *Fifty Years in China: The Memoirs of John Leighton Stuart, Missionary and Ambassador*. New York: Random House, 1954.
Sues, Ilona Ralf. *Sharks Fins and Millet*. Boston: Little, Brown and Co., 1944.
Suigi, Carlo. *In the Land of Mao Tse-tung*. London: Allen and Unwin, 1953.
Sun Tzu. *The Art of War*. Translated by Lionel Giles. London: Hodder and Stoughton, 1995.
Teng Wensheng, ed. *Fan heping yanbian jiaoyu da wen lu*. Beijing: Falu chubanshe, 1992.
Terrill, Ross. *800,000,000: The Real China*. Boston: Little, Brown and Company, 1972.
———. *China in Our Time: The Epic Saga of the People's Republic of China from the Communist Victory to Tiananmen Square and Beyond*. New York: Simon and Schuster, 1993.
Thomas, Bernard S. *Season of High Adventure: Edgar Snow in China*. Berkeley, Calif.: University of California Press, 1996.
Thornton, Richard C. *The Comintern and the Chinese Communists, 1928-1931*. Seattle: University of Washington Press, 1969.
Tikhvinsky, S. "China in My Life." *Far Eastern Affairs*, no. 4 (1989): 89-105, and no. 5 (1989): 112-128.
Topping, Seymour. *Journey between Two Chinas*. New York: Harper and Row, 1972.
Townsend, Peter. *China Phoenix*. London: Jonathan Cape, 1959.
Van Slyke, Lyman P. *Enemies and Friends: The United Front in Chinese Communist History*. Stanford, Calif.: Stanford University Press, 1967.

Vladimirov, Peter. *The Vladimirov Diaries: Yenan, China: 1942-1945.* New York: Doubleday and Co., 1975.

Vorontsov, Vladilen. "Mikhail Borodin: Life Exploit and Tragedy." *Far Eastern Affairs,* no. 1 (1991): 208-226.

Waijiaobu waijiaoshi yanjiushi. *Dangdai Zhongguo shijie waijiao shengya.* Beijing: Shijie zhishi chubanshe, 1995.

Waishi gongzuo renyuan yingyu jiben cihui. Sichuan sheng di si jixie gongyeju qingbao zhan, 1979.

Waishi gongzuo shouce. Hangkong gongye bu diyi jishu qingbao wang, 1983.

Waishi gongzuozhe yuekan. Liaoning sheng waishi bangongshi, 1985-99. (Pre-1989 known as *Liaoning waishi tongxun.*)

Waishi tiandi. Chongqing: Sichuan sheng zhengfu waishichu, 1993-99. (Previously known as *Sichuan waishi,* n.d.)

Waldron, Arthur. "Friendship Reconsidered." *Free China Review* (April 1993): 52-57.

Wan Weitai, ed. *Waishi guanli gongzuo yanjiu yu shijian.* Xuzhou: Zhongguo kuangye daxue chubanshe, 1997.

Wang Fan-hsi. *Memoirs of a Chinese Revolutionary.* Translated and with an introduction by Gregor Benton. New York: Columbia University Press, 1991.

Wang Jiliang. *Sinuo zhuanji.* Beijing: Huayi chubanshe, 1995.

Wang Ming. *Mao's Betrayal.* Moscow: Progress Publishers, 1979.

Wang Rihua, ed. *Shiyong shewai changshi shouce.* Beijing: Renmin Zhongguo chubanshe, 1993.

Wang Shengrong, and Zhang Feng, eds. *Waishi zhishi shouce.* Dalian: Dalian ligong daxue chubanshe, 1993.

Wang Shengsong, and Gu Guanjun, eds. *Shewai gonggong guanxi.* Qingdao: Qingdao chubanshe, 1996.

Wang Taiping, ed. *Deng Xiaoping waijiao sixiang yanjiu wenji.* Beijing: Shijie zhishi chubanshe, 1996.

Wang Xianyu, ed. *Chuguo renyuan bidu.* Jinan: Shandong renmin chubanshe, 1994.

Wang Xiaochun, ed. *Shewai gongguan yu liyi.* Taiyuan: Shanxi jingji chubanshe, 1995.

Wang Xing, ed. *China Remembers Edgar Snow.* Beijing: Beijing Review, 1982.

Wang Zhongnong, ed. *Duiwai jiaoliu shouce.* Wuhan: Hubei renmin chubanshe, 1995.

Wedemeyer, Andrew Hall. *The East Wind Subsides: Chinese Foreign Policy and the Origins of the Cultural Revolution.* Washington, D.C.: The Washington Institute Press, 1988.

Weng Jingsheng. *Shewai fandian shiwu shiyi.* Beijing: Zhongxin chubanshe, 1996.

Wenhuabu dangshi ziliao zhengji gongzuo weiyuanhui, Duiwai wenhua lianluoju dangshi ziliao zhengji gongzuo lingdao xiaozu, ed. *Dangdai Zhong wai wenhua jiaoliu shiliao.* Beijing: Duiwai wenhua lianluoju dangshi ziliao zhengji gongzuo lingdao xiaozu, 1990.

White, Theodore. *In Search of History: A Personal Adventure.* London: Cape, 1979.

Wilbur, C. Martin, and Julie Lien-ying How. *Missionaries of Revolution: Soviet Advisers and Nationalist China 1920-1927.* Cambridge, Mass.: Harvard University Press, 1989.

Winnington, Alan. *Breakfast with Mao: Memoirs of a Foreign Correspondent.* London: Lawrence and Wishart, 1986.

Witke, Roxane. *Comrade Chiang Ch'ing.* London: Wiedenfield and Nicolson, 1977.

Women de pengyou bian tianxia: fazhan tong ge guo renmin de youyi tongxun xuan. Beijing: Renmin chubanshe, 1972.

Wong, Jan. *Red China Blues: My Long March from Mao to Now.* Sydney: Anchor, 1997.

————. *Jan Wong's China: Reports from a Not-So Foreign Correspondent.* Sydney: Anchor, 1999.

Xian Xiubin. *Shewai yingyu xiezuo yu fanyi jiqiao.* Dongying: Shiyou daxue chubanshe, 1996.

Xibei gongye daxue geming weiyuanhui zhengyizu. *Mao Zhuxi shijie renmin re'ai nin.* Xibei gongye daxue, 1969.

Xie Muxi, and Zhang Wen, eds. *Shewai gongzuo shouce.* Chengdu: Chengdu keji daxue chubanshe, 1990.

Xie Yixian, et al. *Zhongguo waijiao shi 1949-1979.* Kaifeng: Henan renmin chubanshe, 1988.

Xin Can. *Xifang zhengjie yaoren tan heping yanbian.* Beijing: Xinhua chubanshe, 1991.

Xinan zhengfa xueyuan minfa jiaoyuanshi, ed. *Shewai hunying jicheng liuxue cankao ziliao,* 1982.

Yan Jiaqi, and Gao Gao. *Turbulent Decade: A History of the Cultural Revolution.* Translated and edited by D. W. Y. Kwok. Honolulu: University of Hawaii Press, 1996.

Yang Fajin. *Zhongguo shewai zhishi quanshu.* Beijing: Zhongguo shehui kexue chubanshe, 1993.

Yang Hua, ed. *Mao Zedong and International Friends: Selected Collections of the International Friendship Museum.* Beijing: Xiyuan chubanshe, 1994.

Yang, Mei-hui Mayfair. *Gifts, Favors, and Banquets: The Art of Social Relationships in China.* Ithaca and London: Cornell University Press, 1994.

Yang Quanbing. *Shewai mishu shiwu yu xiezuo.* Suzhou: Suzhou daxue chubanshe, 1994.

Yang Xianyi. *Autobiography.* Unpublished typescript, n.d.

Yu, Frederick T. C. *Mass Persuasion in Communist China.* London: Pall Mall Press, 1964.

Yu Jianhao, and Yu Danli, eds. *Shewai zhishi shouce.* Shanghai: Jiaotong daxue chubanshe, 1996.

Yu Maochun. *OSS in China: Prelude to Cold War.* New Haven: Yale University Press, 1996.

Yuan Wuzhen. "Guoji youren zai Yan'an." *Zhonggong dangshi ziliao* 46 (1993).

Yun Shui. *Chu shi qi guo jishi: jiangjun dashi Wang Youping.* Beijing: Shijie zhishi chubanshe, 1996.

Yunnan waishi. Kunming: Yunnan sheng zhengfu waishichu, 1997-1999.

Zhan Kaidi. *The Strategies of Politeness in the Chinese Language.* Berkeley: Institute of East Asian Studies, UCLA at Berkeley, 1992.

Zhan Yincai. *Shewai mishuxue.* Hangzhou: Hangzhou daxue chubanshe, 1993.

Zhang Jianshe. *Shewai shiyong shouce.* Beijing: *Beijing Ribao* chubanshe, 1988.

Zhang Shuguang. *Mao's Military Romanticism: China and the Korean War, 1950-1953.* Lawrence: University Press of Kansas, 1995.

Zhang Yan, and Han Yuhe, eds. *Shewai liyi.* Nanjing: Yilin chubanshe, 1993.

Zhang Yi, ed. *Shewai liyi.* Shanghai: Zhongguo fangzhi daxue, 1996.

Zhang Yonghua, ed. *Dazhong chuanboxue.* Shanghai: Shanghai waiyu jiaoyu chubanshe, 1992.

Zhang Yongjin. *China in International Society since 1949: Alienation and Beyond.* Hampshire, U.K.: Macmillan Press, 1998.

Zhao Dasheng, and Wang Lujie, eds. *Shewai gonggong guanxi yu tanpan jiaowang jiqiao.* Beijing: Kexue jishu wenxian chubanshe, 1989.

Zhao Pitao. *Waishi gaishuo.* Shanghai: Shanghai shehui kexue chubanshe, 1995.

Zhao Shaoling, ed. *Shewai hunying zai baozha.* Beijing: Zuojia chubanshe, 1989.

Zhejiang sheng waishi zhi. Beijing: Zhonghua shuju, 1996.

Zhonggong Guangzhou shiwei duiwai xuanchuan xiaozu bangongshi. *Shewai renyuan shouce.* Guangzhou: Xinhua shudian, 1985.

Zhonggong Zhejiang shengwei xuanchuanbu duiwai xuanchuanchu, Zhonggong Zhejiang shengwei xuanchuanbu duiwai xuanchuan xiaozu bangongshi. *Duiwai xuanchuan lunwen xuan.* Hangzhou: Zhejiang daxue chubanshe, 1989.

Zhonggong zhongyang tongyi zhanxian gongzuobu, Zhonggong zhongyang wenxian yanjiushi, ed. *Deng Xiaoping lun tongyi zhanxian.* Beijing: Zhongyang wenxian chubanshe, 1991.

Zhonggong zhongyang tongzhanbu yanjiushi. *Lici quanguo tongzhan gongzuo huiyi gaikuang he wenxian.* Beijing: Dang'an chubanshe, 1988.

Zhonggong zhongyang tongzhanbu yanjiushi. *Tongyi zhanxian gongzuo shouce.* Nanjing Daxue chubanshe: Nanjing, 1986.

Zhonggong zhongyang wenxian yanjiushi, ed. *Zhou Enlai shuxin xuanji.* Beijing: Zhongyang wenxian chubanshe, 1988.

Zhonggong zhongyang xuanchuanbu bangongting, Zhongyang dang'anguan bianyanbu, ed. *Zhongguo gongchandang xuanchuan gongzuo wenxian xuanbian 1915-1992.* 4 vols. Beijing: Xuexi chubanshe, 1996.

Zhongguo duiwai guanxishi jiaoyanshi. *Zhonghua renmin gongheguo duiwai guanxishi.* Beijing: Waijiao xueyuan, 1964.

Zhongguo gongchandang di jiu ci quan guo daibiao dahui wenjian huibian. Beijing: Renmin chubanshe, 1969.

Zhongguo gongchandang dijiu ci quan guo daibiao dahui wenjian huibian. Beijing: Renmin chubanshe, 1969.

Zhongguo renmin duiwai youhao xiehui. *Youyi de chuntian.* Changsha: Hunan renmin chubanshe, 1980.

Zhonghua renmin gongheguo gonganbu waishi ju, ed. *Libin gongzuo shouce.* Beijing: Jingguan jiaoyu chubanshe, 1997.

Zhonghua renmin gongheguo waijiaobu and Zhonggong zhongyang wenxian yanjiushi. *Zhou Enlai waijiao wenxuan.* Beijing: Zhongyang wenxian chubanshe, 1990.

Zhonghua renmin gongheguo waijiaobu and waijiaoshi bianjishi, ed. *Yanjiu Zhou Enlai—waijiao sixiang yu shijian.* Beijing: Shijie zhishi chubanshe, 1989.

Zhongyang dang'anguan, ed. *Zhonggong zhongyang wenjian xuanji.* 18 vols. Beijing: Zhonggong zhongyang dangxiao chubanshe, 1989-1992.

Zhongyang xuanchuanbu bangongting. *Dang de xuanchuan gongzuo wenjian pian 1949-1993.* 4 vols. Beijing: Zhonggong zhongyang dangxiao chubanshe, 1994.

Zhou Enlai. *Selected Works of Zhou Enlai.* 2 vols. Beijing: Foreign Languages Press, 1981 and 1989.

Zhou Enlai tongyi zhanxian wenxuan. Beijing: Renmin chubanshe, 1984.

Zhou Jikai, et al., ed. *Shewai hunying zhinan.* Guangzhou: Zhongshan daxue chubanshe, 1992.

Zhu Muzhi. *Zhu Muzhi lun duiwai xuanchuan.* Beijing: Wuzhou chuanbo chubanshe, 1995.

Zhu Yan, ed. *Waishi gongzuo changshi yu liyi.* Beijing: Zhongguo guoji guangbo chubanshe, 1997.

Ziliao xuanbian. Beijing, 1967.

Zui gao zhishi. Chinese/French edition, n.p. Beijing, 1969.

Index

238, 240-41, 249, 250, 252, 253-54
China Association for International Contact (Youlian), 200, 225
China Can Say No, 239-40
China Society for Human Rights Studies, 226
China's international AID, 127
Chinese Communist Party (CCP), 8, 25, 28, 36, 37, 38, 47, 49, 51, 54, 61, 188, 251; Central Committee Foreign Affairs Leading Small Group, 2, 187, 201; Central Committee International Activities Guiding Committee, 91; foreign policy, 56, 60, 61, 62, 63, 64, 66, 79, 80, 88, 104-5, 106, 120-21, 124-25, 127, 144-45, 146, 151, 154, 157, 160, 161, 164, 165, 167-68, 177, 179, 180, 181, 186, 199-200, 216, 218-19, 225, 236, 250, 251; historiography, 24-26, 249-50
Chinese People's Association for Cultural Exchanges, 90
Chinese People's Political Consultative Conference, 195
Chinese People's Institute of Foreign Affairs, 89
China Council for the Promotion of International Trade, 90
Chirac, Jacques, 224
Chinese Liberated Areas Relief Association (CLARA), 48, 62, 71n92
CLARA. *See* Chinese Liberated Areas Relief Association
Coe, Frank, 134-35, 194, 208
Cominform, 89
Comintern, 8, 9, 25, 36, 37, 38, 42, 47, 58, 69n47, 250
Confucianism and *waishi,* 8-9, 13-14, 190
Cradock, Percy, 195
Croft, Michael, 95-96
Crook, David, 87, 101, 129, 131, 164, 166, 168, 184, 186
Cultural Revolution, 136, 143-75, 184, 188, 191, 195

Dathier, Henri and Monique, 152
Da Shan (Mark Rowswell), 221, 222, 224
Dawson, Doris, 151, 152, 166-67
de Beauvoir, Simone, 94-95
de Segonzac, Adelbert, 83
Deane, Hugh, 197
Deng Xiaoping, 24, 91, 106, 180, 187, 188, 192, 196, 197, 199, 206-7, 222, 224, 225, 236, 238, 251, 252
dialogue, 226
Dixie Mission, 58-59, 60, 61, 196
Downey, John, 196
Dulles, John Foster, 216

English, Cecil (Ces), 98, 103-4
Engst, Sidney (Sid), 99, 101-2, 130-31, 148
Epstein, Israel, 90, 101, 103, 155, 156, 160, 165, 166, 185

Fairfax-Cholmeley, Elsie, 101, 118, 136, 165, 166, 185
famine years, 117-19
FEC. *See* Foreign Exchange Certificates
Foreign Exchange Certificates (FEC), 204, 230
Ford, Robert, 83
foreign affairs, xi, 168-69, 182, 190, 201 (*see also waishi*); offices, 3-4, 81, 91, 188, 202; system, xi, 2, 4, 13, 253
Foreign Culture Department, 91-92
foreign: enemies, 83-84, 53, 129, 160, 161-63, 165, 196; experts, 2-3, 6n9, 19, 67n78, 87-88, 91, 99-104, 106, 123, 131-36, 154, 156, 160, 162, 165, 167, 184, 185, 195, 204, 205, 229, 230-31; friends, xi, xii, 1, 2, 4-5, 7-8, 14-15, 18-19, 20, 21, 2, 23, 48, 53, 57, 62, 66, 89, 99, 101, 102, 103, 117-19, 123, 124, 131, 143, 179, 182, 184, 185, 186, 194, 169, 207, 218, 220-24, 251, 252; journalists, 19-20, 51-52, 53, 58-59, 61, 65, 82, 91, 98, 120, 162, 197, 203, 204-5, 217-18, 222, 232-

About the Author

Anne-Marie Brady is a lecturer in political science at the University of Canterbury in Christchurch, New Zealand. She is the author of *Friend of China: The Myth of Rewi Alley* (2002). Her current research focuses on Cold War history and the modernization of the propaganda system in China after 1989.